MEMOIR

OF

THEOPHILUS PARSONS,

CHIEF JUSTICE OF THE SUPREME JUDICIAL COURT
OF MASSACHUSETTS;

WITH

NOTICES OF SOME OF HIS CONTEMPORARIES.

BY HIS SON,

THEOPHILUS PARSONS.

BOSTON:
TICKNOR AND FIELDS.
M DCCC LXI.

UNIVERSITY PRESS, CAMBRIDGE:
ELECTROTYPED AND PRINTED BY WELCH, BIGELOW, & CO.

TO THE HONORABLE

LEMUEL SHAW,

CHIEF JUSTICE OF THE SUPREME JUDICIAL COURT
OF MASSACHUSETTS,

I DEDICATE

THIS SKETCH OF THE LIFE AND TIMES OF A PREDECESSOR IN THE PLACE HE HAS NOW HELD FOR MANY YEARS; AND DURING ALL OF THEM HAS SO DISCHARGED ITS GREAT DUTIES, AND SO LIVED, THAT, FOR MANY YEARS TO COME, THE JUDICIARY WILL BE STRONGER AND THE REPUBLIC THEREFORE SAFER, BY REASON OF THE PROTECTION AND SECURITY HIS HIGH OFFICE DERIVES FROM THE UNIVERSAL REVERENCE FELT FOR HIM AS A JUDGE AND AS A MAN.

THEOPHILUS PARSONS.

CAMBRIDGE, April, 1859.

CONTENTS.

CHAPTER I.

CHAPTER II.

OF THE ANCESTRY OF THEOPHILUS PARSONS, WITH A GENERAL SKETCH OF HIS LIFE.

CHAPTER III.

OF HIM AS A STATESMAN.

CHAPTER IV.

Of Him as a Lawyer.

CHAPTER V.

Of Him as a Judge.

CHAPTER VI.

Of Him as a Scholar.

CHAPTER VII.

Of Him in his Personal, Social, and Family Relations; and of his Death.

APPENDIX.

MEMOIR.

CHAPTER I.

THE MOTIVES AND THE MEANS OF THE AUTHOR FOR WRITING THIS MEMOIR.

My father died in 1813. If he were wholly forgotten, I should not seek to revive a recollection of him. But his official position, to which circumstances gave a peculiar importance, required of him to give some decisions which laid the foundations of important law. These must be remembered and sometimes referred to, at least by lawyers. They perhaps are almost the only men of this generation who know much about him. For nearly all others the veil of time has settled over him; and if his name be heard or read, it calls up no distinct image.

If this veil only obstructed or obscured the remembrance of him, or if it entirely prevented this remembrance, I should make no effort to remove it. But while he is remembered at all, he should be remembered aright.

He had no love of fame, contemporary or posthumous. It will probably appear to a reader of this Memoir, that it was one of his errors to despise public opinion exceedingly. He not only cared nothing whatever for fame, but was less desirous than he should have been to leave a just impression of himself. He had not many personal enemies; but no man can discharge the duties of the high office he held, without conflicting with some interests, and exciting some resentments, which perhaps have not yet died. And his political enemies, for reasons which will be more fully stated hereafter, were bitter. While he lived, they did not spare censure or reproach, as opportunity offered or could be made. But I believe he was never known to say or to authorize one word by way of answer, defence, or explanation, or to manifest anything but the most perfect indifference. He was, however, a just man, and loved the truth; and if his disposition to protect the truth was overcome by his unwillingness to defend himself, I know of no reason, and am conscious of no feeling, which should prevent my attempting at least to do him exact justice.

This is my object in preparing, at this late day, this Memoir; and, so far as I know my own purposes, it is my only object.

When he died, I was but sixteen years old; and had little knowledge, and now have but few trustworthy recollections, of him in his more public relations. What he was at home, what as husband, father, friend, I knew and remember better. In drawing his portrait in these relations, I shall trust, with some confidence, to my own impressions; but as to his public duties, and for what he was as a statesman, a lawyer, a judge, a scholar, I shall rely mainly upon documentary or other evidence. And if I have some confidence in family traditions, and some belief of facts or anecdotes, which cannot be proved but have been repeated until they can hardly be doubted, it will still be with the hope and the endeavor to give to the best evidence the greatest weight. I shall try to avoid all assertions of which it can be said only that they may be true.

Upon some points I have distinct impressions, due in part, I am certain, to my own recollections of his words and acts. But they are due also in part to the many conversations I have had, years and years ago, with his old friends, who loved to talk of him as much as I loved to hear them. I find myself unable to distinguish accurately, at this distance of time, between these two elements of belief. What seem to me only my own recollections may have been strengthened and filled out, and perhaps shaped or varied, by such conversations, without my being able to recognize this effect. They who knew him have, for a long time, been few in number ; and now they are very few. If now alive, he would be one hundred and nine years old; and of course all who could be called his contemporaries have passed away. There are still living, however, those who, although much younger than he, knew him intimately. Of late years it has been an infrequent pleasure to me to meet them. But I have called upon them to aid me in constructing this slight memorial, and they have rendered far more assistance than I had ventured to expect.

I propose, in the first place, to speak of his parentage and family. If I had no other reason for this, I should do it because it was one of his traits to be glad, and perhaps proud, of his descent from one man among our forefathers, whom he profoundly revered, — John Robinson of Leyden. I shall speak also of his childhood and youth, and of the few changes which occurred in his simple and uniform life. Then, in other chapters, I shall endeavor to present him to my readers as he was, as a statesman, a lawyer, a judge, a scholar, a religious man; and in his personal, social, and family relations.

Forty years ago I had an immense mass of his manuscripts. But then I did not think I should ever make use of them. Very many I have given away to those who wished for his autographs ; others, to those who desired them for other reasons. Some, or rather many, I have lost, I know not how. The residue — not the tenth part of what I once had — were saved, and now lie before me, because my friend, Mr. Charles Folsom, laid a hand of gentle compulsion upon them, some years since, and carried them off to the Boston Athenæum. It will be seen, however, that even this remnant is of much use to me. And I should be very glad if gentlemen having any letters or other manuscripts of my father's would send them, or copies of them, to me, or lend them to be copied; or would give me any information which I might use to correct errors in this book, or add to it interesting or illustrative facts. I should employ them for the public benefit, if this book comes to a second edition; or otherwise use them for my own.

In an Appendix I insert some of my father's productions; and reprint the Address of Chief Justice Parker (my father's successor) to the Grand Jury, in 1813, in which he gives a sketch of his life and character. This has never been published, excepting at the close of the tenth volume of the Massachusetts Reports. I add to this a brief Memoir, by Mr. Samuel L. Knapp, and one or two of the obituaries published at his death. These may be regarded as contemporary testimonials to his position, and to the extent and quality of his usefulness. They are annexed to this work, not to revive the recollection of my father, or extend or diffuse it, but that I may place on record those means of estimating him correctly, which — due allowance being made for my own filial bias, or for my leaning too far in my endeavor to resist this bias, and for the prejudices or predilections of other persons — may cause him to be, when not forgotten, not misjudged.

I will add a word on another topic. No one can be more aware than I am of the egotistic appearance imparted to this Memoir, and to this prefatory chapter, and to this very paragraph, by the circumstance that I write it in the first person, and speak of the subject of it as "my father." This appearance must needs be so offensive, that it would not be deliberately encountered but for what seem to be good reasons. One of these is, that, as matter of honesty, I wish my readers to remember that I am writing about my own father, that they may therefore make all due allowance.

Another is, that I wish to remember this myself, that I may therefore exercise due caution. Still another is, that I was obliged to choose between this way of treating and presenting my subject, and that other way which consists in an apparent withdrawal from all personal interest, and which is a little apt to withdraw from the book all interest whatever. We have eminent American works which repeat the capital "I" to the utter exhaustion of the printer's stock; and certainly this is a great fault. We have others which totally avoid the use of the first person singular, by an unwearied, but somewhat wearying, ringing of the changes upon all the phrases and indirections which go round and round this little word, and are always in sight of it, but do not touch it. This seems to me a great fault also; if for nothing else, because it compels the reader to remember that he who is perpetually laboring to avoid speaking of himself, can never, by any possibility, forget himself.

But these are small matters. No success in them would compensate for a failure in my principal purpose; nor will ill success in them inflict great pain, if I am permitted to believe that this Memoir presents a lifelike and true portraiture of my father and his friends.

CHAPTER II.

OF HIS ANCESTRY, WITH A GENERAL SKETCH OF HIS LIFE.

NEAR the close of the first half of the seventeenth century, perhaps about 1645, Jeffrey (or Geoffrey) Parsons sailed from England for the West Indies. He was then very young. He remained at Barbadoes, with an uncle, some years, and then came to Gloucester, on Cape Ann, about 1654. There he settled. On the 11th of November, 1657, he married Sarah Vinson. He passed the rest of his life in Gloucester, and died there on the 16th of August, 1689. He was a prominent citizen, having been chosen selectman for several years; and was a successful merchant, leaving at his death what was there and in those days regarded as a competent fortune.

So much, and but little more, is known with certainty of the origin of my father's family. An ancient letter or two, with a constant and consistent tradition, render probable a few additional particulars. They are, that Jeffrey (so the name appears to have been generally spelt) was a younger member of a family holding a respectable position among the gentry of Devonshire. He must have had means of his own, or been aided by his family, because, although a young man when he came to Gloucester, he carried considerable property there with him. It is at least certain that he bought a house and some lots of land, in 1655.

There are in the family various versions of a romantic story about his meeting Sarah Vinson — the beauty of the place — at a spring on her father's farm, which is still called Vinson's Spring; and sundry love passages ensuing, which ended, not without due tribulation, in their marriage. I would tell this more particularly; but, unfortunately, the traditions do not harmonize, and no one of them seems to me well authenticated or particularly probable.

The genealogy of the family, from Jeffrey down, has been well preserved. And the most noticeable thing about it is the extraordinary fertility of the marriages of those early days. This was true not only of our own immediate line, but of all those with whom our ancestors intermarried. And I have heard the same remark made of other families.

Moses Parsons, Jeffrey's grandson, being the youngest son of his youngest son, was my father's father. He was born in Gloucester, June 20th, 1716. He entered Harvard College in 1732, graduated in due course in 1736, and immediately applied himself to the study of theology, in further execution of that purpose of devoting himself to the ministry which had induced him to enter college.

For some years, however, he maintained himself by teaching a school in Gloucester. And there, on the 11th of January, 1743, he married Susan Davis, to whom he had been for some years betrothed.

She was the fifth in descent from John Robinson of Leyden; whose son Abraham had, in Gloucester, a son of the same name. This grandson of John had a son Andrew, whose daughter Anne married Abraham Davis; and their daughter Susan was my grandmother.*

---

* Some persons have even doubted whether any son of John Robinson came to America. But I have a document drawn up by my father about eighty years ago, and another which some years afterwards he gave a relative (from whom I have it), which agrees perfectly with the first, from which I gather the facts that I have stated in this paragraph. He was a careful genealogist, and loved to investigate questions of this kind; and in this particular question he felt a deep interest. And he had all the means of information which a

John Robinson of Leyden! How often have I heard my father utter that name, and always with every expression of admiration and reverence! I suppose he thought that this ancestor of his had done more to form the character of New England, by his direct influence, and by impressing his character upon those whom he sent forth to found a nation, than any other man. I cannot remember when I first became familiar with the beautiful address of Robinson to that portion of his church who were about to depart from him and seek a wilderness, which, in compensation for the enjoyments that civilization could give, offered them only freedom to worship God. After the tenderest words of farewell and the wisest words of counsel, he said:

"Brethren, we are now quickly to part from one another; and whether I may ever live to see your face on earth any more, the God of heaven only knows; but whether the Lord hath appointed that or not, I charge you before God and his blessed angels, that you follow me no further than you have seen me follow the Lord Jesus Christ. If God reveal anything to you by any other instrument of his, be as ready to receive it as ever you were to

---

wide acquaintance in Gloucester and its neighborhood could give him. From my boyhood I was accustomed to hear it said by him and others of my family, that we were descended from John Robinson. He never doubted it, and I did not know that any doubt existed, or could exist, on this subject, until many years after his death.

I am aware, also, that doubt has been cast upon Robinson's address. But there is no ground for this beyond the fact that Governor Winslow, from whom we have it, does not assert that he writes it out from a copy. He was, however, a careful, earnest, and honest man. And, to say nothing of the probability that the Pilgrims bore with them to their desert homes a copy, or more than one, of words which were clothed for them with all the interest which spoken words could have, Winslow was himself one of those to whom they were spoken; and he wrote his account of the address in the midst of those who heard it with him, and while their memory of it must have been fresh, if indeed they could ever have forgotten it.

receive any truth by my ministry. For I am verily persuaded, — I am very confident, — that the Lord hath more truth yet to break forth out of his Holy Word. For my part, I cannot sufficiently bewail the condition of the reformed churches, who are come to a period in religion, and will go at present no further than the instruments of their reformation. . . . . This is a misery much to be lamented; for though they were burning and shining lights in their own times, yet they penetrated not into the whole counsel of God."

On the 20th of June, 1744, my grandfather was ordained minister of Byfield, in Essex County, Massachusetts. There he lived a peaceful and useful life; and there he died, on Sunday, the 14th of December, 1783, at the age of sixty-seven.

In the following letter my father communicated the fact to my aunt, Mrs. Gray, then living at Epsom, in New Hampshire.

My dear Sister:

You must prepare yourself for most melancholy and distressing intelligence; but shall not the Judge of all the earth do right? Our dear father is no more. He left us to become a saint in heaven last evening, at forty minutes past seven. His disorder was originally a bad cold seated upon his lungs, and at last such a load of phlegm collected there that he could not expectorate. His strength failed him fast; but his piety and resignation were always uniform, and continued to the end what we have always known them. I first saw him on Saturday last, in the forenoon. He smiled upon me as usual, and professed his perfect readiness to go, saying that he was satisfied in his religion, and that his hopes were firm. Death had no terrors for him; and whether he stopped or died, seemed equally indifferent to him. William and Judith got in from Boston about an hour before the blessed man's translation. He squeezed their hands, and attempted to speak, but the phlegm interrupted that voice which delighted in expressions of kindness and love. Afterwards he had a little coughing spell, and I asked him to raise and throw off the phlegm, and Judith held a handkerchief to his mouth; but he replied that he had raised nothing, and that he should soon be gone. Then, turning himself on his right side, he fell into a sweet sleep, and, without a struggle, sigh, or groan, sunk into the everlasting arms of his Saviour. He lay without an alteration of feature, but with that same calm countenance which it was our delight to look upon. O, my dear sister, I have seen a Christian live, and now I have seen one die. To such a man death has no sting, no terrors; it is merely a kind passport to a blessed eternity. There are a thousand circumstances which we shall love to tell, and you will love to remember; but as the messenger is waiting, I must omit them. Compose yourself, my dear, and collect all your firmness to bear this stroke; and remember the hand from whom it came. And can we, shall we, now be unkind to our best of parents, by wishing him less happy than he is? Can we desire to recall him from heaven, and interrupt his happiness? Human nature has its weaknesses, however. But it is our duty not to indulge, but correct them. And may we mourn my father by living as he has taught us by his precepts, his life, and (O, too high the price of knowledge!) by his death.

We propose to inter the corpse of my father next Thursday, but we much doubt whether you can attend. Do not, my dear sister, expose your health, or that of your little ones. But if, without danger or distress, you can come to us, you will be exceeding dear to the afflicted society. My mother — poor woman! — supports herself much better than I expected.

I send by the bearer money for your use, that, if you determine to come, your journey may be made as convenient as possible.

We are all most affectionately yours.

THEOPH. PARSONS.

Monday Morning, 15 December, 1783.

Of my grandfather I believe I am authorized, by a large amount of concurrent testimony, to say, that he was an intelligent and thoroughly respectable man. His published sermons indicate that his mind was well cultivated; and all I have ever heard convinces me that he had an excellent judgment, and was a cautious and discreet person, who seldom thought or acted otherwise than right. That he was generally respected may be inferred from his being often called upon as referee or counsellor, sometimes from a considerable distance, to settle disputes or investigate matters of difficulty. It is something, too, that he was summoned from his obscure and distant country parish to preach the Election Sermon before the Legislature; for in those days this was a matter of considerable moment.

I had thought of giving some extracts from his printed sermons, and from those preached at his death, and other contemporary testimonials concerning him, because I was convinced, on what seems to me sufficient evidence, of their substantial truth. Instead of this, however, I give the following extract from Allen's American Biography. I know of no circumstance which should have prevented the author from forming or expressing a correct opinion. He evidently gives, in eulogistic language, the result of an investigation into all the testimonies accessible to him; and what he states may be considered (after a due allowance for the "*De mortuis nil nisi bonum*") as an approximation to the conclusion to which a fair consideration of the evidence would lead. He says:

"The Maker of the human frame gave him a most graceful and commanding presence, a quick conception, a fertile invention, an easy flow of thought and of expression, a correct judgment, a resolute temper, and a large share of the kind and tender sensibilities. These, expanded by a liberal education, polished by a large acquaintance with mankind, and sanctified by Divine grace, made him eminent as the gentleman and the Christian, the divine and the preacher. When he had once deliberately fixed his opinion or his purpose, no opposition could shake him. He always carried the dignity and decorum of the Christian minister into his most cheerful hours; and, though he often indulged his pleasant humor among his friends, he never degraded himself by the puerile jest, the boisterous laugh, or by vain, indelicate mirth. He usually mingled with his sprightly sallies some useful lesson of a moral nature. He knew how to be familiar without meanness, sociable without loquacity, cheerful without levity, grave without moroseness, pious without enthusiasm, superstition, or ostentation, — zealous against error and vice, without ill-natured littleness, — affable to all, without the least sacrifice of his ministerial dignity. There was a generous openness in his language and behavior ; and one could almost discern his heart in his frank, honest countenance. He was influenced by enlarged benevolence. He was a zealous advocate of the civil and religious interests of his beloved America. Eminent as a preacher, he yet greatly excelled in the gift of prayer. His last hours were brightened with the hopes of the Gospel. He anticipated the joy of dwelling in the presence of the Divine Saviour, whom he had served in his church below."

I will add a word more about my grandfather, which may illustrate, not his character only, but the times. He was invited to deliver the Election Sermon mentioned above, in 1772. It was preached before Governor Hutchinson and his Council, and the House of Representatives. The text was from Proverbs xxi. 1 : " The king's heart is in the hand of the Lord ; as the rivers of waters, he turneth it whithersoever he will." The character of the sermon may be inferred from the following extracts. Considering the time and occasion, and the audience, it may be thought even bolder than Dr. Osgood's famous " Bramble " sermon, which he preached from Judges ix. 14, when a Federalist Legislature of one year had appointed him for the next, and the change of parties gave him the opportunity of comparing a Democratic Governor with the bramble which the perverse and foolish trees had invited to rule over them.

" His present majesty ascended the throne of his royal ancestors amidst the joyful acclamations of his subjects. His way to the throne seemed to be paved with hearts, so great was the affection of his people for him. . . . . . How could we wish that bright day had continued clear and serene! . . . . . But the scene is changed. Grievances are complained of in Great Britain, in Ireland, in America, in this Province. The day has become gloomy and dark, and the waters are troubled. . . . . . The complaints heard among us are not only that the rivers are shifted into other channels, but that the waters have become bitter, yea, that the waters have become bloody! . . . . . I believe we have as much to plead in our favor as any part of the king's dominions, or as any people upon the face of the earth. . . . . . And we hope the time will soon come when it will appear that we . . . . . have acted the part of loyal and dutiful subjects; *though we cannot submit to shackles and chains, so long as we have a just right to the privileges of freemen.*"

My father's ancestors on his father's side were always respectable, and this is all that I claim for them. The genealogy, as was said before, has been well and minutely preserved. It discloses no crime, and no disgrace; but also no eminence. Perhaps something more than usual of a military spirit was indicated by a family which sent four of its members to war. One of Jeffrey's grandsons was a soldier in the expedition to Cape Breton, in 1745. Another joined in the expedition against the French at Crown Point, in 1756. A later descendant was a soldier in Captain Rowe's company, and was killed at Bunker Hill; and his brother was a soldier in the same company, but survived the battle, and was wrecked and lost in 1792. They were also perhaps unusually prosperous; displaying in all their generations much of the shrewdness and perseverance which insure reasonable success in life. But this was all. And if it should appear, from what I have to say of my father, that he exhibited more than usual force of intellect and character, I cannot but regard it as his inheritance from his mother. And it is at least a pleasing imagination, which he himself would not have repelled, that these qualities descended to her from that ancestor, the minister at Leyden, for whom she strengthened, if she did not inspire, my father's reverence.

The respect and admiration, not of her children only, but of all who knew her, — many of whom I knew, — testified to the remarkable qualities of my father's mother. She was, I believe, eminently distinguished for the vigor and clearness of her understanding, and the strength of her character. Within the parish which was her peculiar domain, she filled a position and exerted an influence that I do not venture to describe, only because they were most extraordinary, and I cannot transfer to these pages the evidence on which I believe them. But the uniform consent of all who knew her, and the traditions which lingered at Byfield until I was old enough to learn them, illustrated and confirmed as they were by many especial circumstances, do not permit me to withhold my conviction that she was a remarkable person.

My grandfather was settled over a rather small parish, composed wholly of farmers. No man in the place was wealthy, and no one engaged in any trade or any manufacturing business, other than the common handicraft occupations which exist everywhere. Of course he could not be largely paid. But, with a salary of two hundred and eighty dollars, he brought up a family of five sons and two daughters, educated three of his sons at Harvard College, and always maintained a comfortable and hospitable household. The impression left upon my mind by the innumerable anecdotes I heard when a boy was, that my grandfather's house — not a small one — was almost constantly filled with company. Much deduction must be made from this; but there will still be left enough to constitute a wide and liberal hospitality. I have often heard my father and my uncles speak of this; and after referring a part of it to the greater value of money in those days, and a part to the liberality of the parishioners in their gifts and general assistance, they always agreed that the apparent wonder was to be explained by my grandmother's systematic and admirable economy.

Attached to the parsonage was a large farm, which my grandfather cultivated so well, that he was regarded as quite a pattern farmer by the neighborhood. This was doubtless an important resource; and my father and uncles were fond of telling us stories illustrative of my grandmother's sagacity, order, and management, and of the way in which everything was made to yield the utmost advantage that could be derived from it.

It may surprise, or amuse, my readers, to be told that another important resource for my grandfather was his skill as a sportsman. Forty years ago, as I can testify, but little game was left in that neighborhood. But my uncles have told me that the geese, ducks, curlews, and plover from the neighboring river and marshes, and the pigeons and partridges from the uplands, which my grandfather brought home a hundred years ago, supplied his table with many a savory dish.

But to return to my grandmother, I would add, that however busy as a housewife, and as the ministress of the parish, — for I must coin this word for her, — she had an earnest and constant love of books and study, and was only preserved from indulging in this to excess by the absolute necessity of giving up the bulk of her time to her household and her parish duties. As it was, she employed in the most varied self-culture every moment which she could save from active occupations. This taste, or, as I may call it, this passion for books, my father inherited from her, in its full extent.

Another peculiarity may not seem to others so indicative of remarkable intelligence as it does to me. She was obliged to be much about the sick, and observed carefully various diseases and various modes of treatment. And she came deliberately to the conclusion, that medical science was no science at all, and that in many cases quite as much was to be feared as hoped from medical treatment; which, in that day, was what would now be called "heroic." In the summer following my grandfather's death (1784), she removed to Boston, and there lived until her death, in December, 1794, when she was seventy-five years old. While thus living with one of my uncles, in Boston, she had a violent and long-continued fever. Not one particle of medicine would she take from the beginning to the end. As her disease increased in violence, and she apprehended delirium, she called her sons together, and solemnly charged them, come what might, to give her no medicine whatever. And such was her hold upon them, that they obeyed her when she could not have known it had they disobeyed. She recovered, and lived some years in excellent health.

As an incident in my grandfather's household economy, and as a cause of a difficulty which gave him much trouble, I may mention that he owned, or had some interest in, three slaves,—two men and one woman. From 1770 to 1780, there was, in many quarters, a considerable agitation about slavery. In my grandfather's parish it rose, in one person at least, to fever-heat. One of his deacons became violently anti-slaveholding. He attacked sundry of the neighbors, and finally my grandfather himself, with what the deacon thought zeal, and they whom he assailed thought ferocity. There was no complaint of personal ill-treatment of the slaves, of any kind; but on the ground that he owned one slave at least,—Violet,—he was called a man-stealer, and told that his crime "ranked with the most enormous crimes that Scripture gives us any account of." And so on for some years. My grandfather invited his deacon to ascertain the wishes of the slave herself; and this he accordingly did; but the answer, although exceedingly emphatic, and well remembered in the family, was not precisely such as I should wish to record. Suffice it to say, the deacon never repeated his inquiries; but he did continue his assaults, until at length the church took the matter up, and suspended him from church-fellowship. He remained suspended until some time after my grandfather's death. Then, in 1785, after the excitement of controversy had passed away, the ex-deacon, who was, I believe, a very good man, but probably not quite so much better than his neighbors as he thought himself, made full and formal acknowledgment that, "in his treatment of the Reverend Moses Parsons, the late worthy pastor of the church, he had urged his arguments against the slavery of the Africans with excessive vehemence and asperity, without showing a due concern for his character and usefulness as an elder, or for the peace and edification of the church." And thereupon he was restored to full fellowship.

Of the two men whom my grandfather owned in some qualified way, — perhaps for a term of years, — I know little or nothing, and have forgotten even their names. Of the woman, "Violet," who was the main subject of this controversy, I know much more.

She was, to all appearance, of pure African descent. I think I never knew any person whose face was of a darker hue. She came into my grandfather's possession while she was very young, and when he was visiting at Gloucester, after his marriage. When it was generally believed that slavery was unlawful in Massachusetts, he summoned his slaves into his sitting-room, and there, in the presence of his children, declared to them that they were free. The men accepted the gift, or rather the declaration, for gift it was not. Not so Violet. "No, no, master," said she, "if you please, this must not be. You have had the best of me, and you and yours must have the worst. Where am I to go in sickness or old age? No, master; your slave I am, and always will be, and I will belong to your children, when you are gone; and by you and them I mean to be cared for." She was as good as her word. She lived in the family until she was nearly ninety. I remember her only as a pet, a perfectly privileged person. She lived with one or another of my grandfather's children, as her whims prompted; but during her last years my uncle William's house was her home. She was respectful, faithful, and affectionate to my father, and to my uncles and aunts, — always calling them, however, by their Christian names; but to others she could be, at least in extreme old age, somewhat cross and petulant. It was understood, however, that Violet was to liberate her mind upon any topic, and to any person, at her own pleasure, and with almost entire impunity, — for my uncles were very unwilling to rebuke her, and no one else dared to, — and on the whole, she used her privileges quite temperately. She had what money she chose to ask for, and spent it as she liked; and as she was fond of dress, few members of the family had more or richer garments. It was touching to see her, as I did more than once, groping her way, when her eyesight had become dim, through a large party in my uncle's drawing-room, to him, as he sat — younger, but almost as decrepit as she was — in his accustomed seat by the fireside. She passed among the guests, regardless of them, or gently moving them out of her way, and laid her hand on his shoulder, with "Billy, how do you find yourself to-night? Are you going to get a good sleep?" And he would answer, "Well, Violet, I am pretty comfortable to-night; and how is it with you?" And after a few more kind words, her errand was done, and off she went to bed.

She was extremely shrewd and observing, and the domestics did not like her; for, purblind as she was, no waste or negligence or misconduct could escape her vigilance or her tongue. It was not merely that she identified her interests with those of the family; but she believed that she was one of us. She remembered nothing of parents or relations of her own blood; she grew up with my grandfather's children, a child with them, — and somehow she had fallen into an indefinite sort of notion that she was of our kith and kin.

As she grew infirm, she had frequent and severe rheumatism, or what was called so, and troubled our family physician — good old Dr. Rand — very much. And let me say, as in a parenthesis, how few of my readers will be reminded, by this name, of one who was in his own day brilliant among the greater lights of his profession! The good Doctor, who had himself grown a little testy, said to her one day: "Violet, there is no use in calling on me so often; I can do nothing for you. Your pains are constitutional, and you must learn to bear them." "O dear!" said she, "I suppose I must. Master had the rheumatiz bad, and Suzy had it, and Theoph and Billy and Eben have it, though not so bad as I do; and I suppose it runs in the family." Master was the name she always gave my grandfather; the other names were those of my aunt, father, and uncles. And so Violet, the slave, the servant, the friend, lived among us and died. At her funeral President Kirkland officiated, and she was buried with every circumstance of expense or ceremony which could have taken place had she been a daughter of the house; and her remains now rest in the family tomb.

Even as I write these words, I am well aware that it may be only the garrulity of approaching age which makes me record such trifles. But I will let them stand; for, trifles as they are, they are among the recollections which I shall not lose.

My father was born in Byfield, on the 24th of February, 1750. He was my grandfather's third son and third child. He was educated at Dummer Academy, in Byfield, then under the charge of the Rev. Mr. Moody. Of this once celebrated and not yet forgotten man he was fond of speaking, and related many anecdotes about him. I will mention only that his favorite maxim, which he labored to impress on every one, and to which my father attributed much of his own success, and therefore perhaps inculcated it as strenuously as his old instructor, was this: "*Crede quod possis, et potes.*"

Of his infancy and childhood sundry traits and anecdotes have come down to us, but none worth telling, unless, perhaps, these two may be so. One, a very old lady told me, many years ago, when I asked her about my father's childhood. "I can't remember much," said she, "except that he was always playing harder or studying harder than any other boy; and which of these two he did the hardest, I do not know."

The other has seemed to me a good illustration of what are, or were, regarded by many as prophecies. When in his cradle, he was very ill with some infantile disease, and his immediate death was apprehended. An old crone of the neighborhood, who was thought to be a witch by many persons, but was rather a favorite *protégée* of my grandmother's, bent over him, and, after long and careful observation, lifted herself up and said: "You are all wrong. That boy can't die now. He has got to get well, and grow up, and live to be a judge, and ride in his own coach." When he became a lawyer, this was repeated by old people who remembered it, and repeated still oftener as his progress in his profession made the whole prediction probable. In 1806, when it was understood in the family that he was solicited to be Chief Justice, and there was some conflict of opinion among us on the subject, good old Violet said: "There is no use in making a fuss about it. A judge he has got to be, and most certainly will be; for it was foretold of him when he lay in his cradle." It was foretold of him, certainly, and probably of a hundred other sick babies in Byfield, being only an emphatic way of expressing the soothsayer's opinion that the child would get well; of which her experience and acute observation made her a good judge. And it was remembered only of him of whom alone it happened to become true.

He entered Harvard College in 1765, and graduated* in due course in 1769. My grandfather had, with some difficulty, sent his eldest son, Moses, to college, in 1761; and when my father was ready for admission, it became still more difficult to provide for his expenses. There was, however, a very strong desire that he should go, arising, as I have heard, from the universal conviction that his ability and industry promised great things. Something of this may have been true; but much of the assistance proffered and received must be attributed to the general desire to gratify his parents. Among other incidents, I may mention that a domestic of the name of Esther Day, whose wages were twelve pounds (lawful money, that is forty dollars) a year, proposed to relinquish her wages and let the amount go to his college expenses. This offer was refused; but many of the parishioners tendered provisions, clothing, and assistance in other forms, and these were received. And with similar aid, as I suppose, his younger brother, Theodore, also went through college.

Of the college life of my father I do not remember ever hearing him speak. I know, upon anything like authority, almost nothing of it beyond what was told by the late Judge William Tudor, who was of the same age with him, his classmate and chum, and his friend for forty-seven years. Judge Tudor is quoted by Chief Justice Parker as having said: "He was an insatiable student; and, after learning his lesson, would turn for his amusement to a mathematical problem, or a novel, with equal relish." I find in the eighth volume of the Massachusetts Historical Collections, Second Series, page 289, a sketch of his character, drawn

---

* I am perfectly aware that it is usually thought more correct to say "was graduated," and have generally yielded, although somewhat reluctantly, to what seemed to be the weight of authority. But having noticed that Walter Savage Landor, who certainly writes admirable English, and is a great purist in his use of words, says "graduated," I permit myself to say so.

by Tudor, in 1774, when they were both twenty-three years old. It seems to have been an amusement with them to describe characters "after the manner of Theophrastus"; and this is the way in which Tudor speaks of Parsons:

"Nature, when she made Chrysander, was unkind in point of externals. But though she left him defective in the trappings of person, that deficiency was amply compensated by the bestowment of ten thousand amiable and valuable qualities. To a vivacity of fancy and promptitude of invention, she joined a penetrating genius and a spirit of investigation that pervaded her deepest recesses. With an industry that difficulties invigorated, and a sagacity that nothing could elude, it is not to be thought strange that he soon became familiar with the whole circle of the sciences. Though mathematics, logic, and metaphysics gave employment to his abstruser hours, the happy turn of his mind led him to an acquaintance with, and the justness of his taste pointed out the beauties of, the belles-lettres. Thus, whilst he, one hour, laboriously traced the clew that conducted him to a demonstration of Euclid, abstractedly meditated with Locke, or trod the planetary rounds with Newton and Halley; he could the next feel, and, feeling, admire, the nervous diction, Attic wit, noble sentiments, and classic elegance that illume the immortal writings of a Bolingbroke, Pope, Hume, or Robertson.

"He is emulous of applause, yet superior to envy. His honesty is without severity, his benevolence without weakness, and his frankness without rusticity. As his friendships are built on these principles, they are few, but they are ardent and sincere.

"If great abilities, united to extensive erudition, are the steps to advancement and the road to fame; if the purest philanthropy can excite esteem and secure affection, — 't is impossible that Chrysander should continue obscure, or ever be friendless."

This is, of course, the language of friendship; and of friendship trying rather hard to write finely.

My father was always a writer, and a keeper of manuscripts; and among the mass which he left at his death, and even among the few which I now have, there are some which go back to his college days. These indicate most distinctly that he was a diligent but somewhat desultory student, especially fond of mathematics, and already exhibiting much of the extraordinary neatness and precision in the use of his pen and drawing-instruments which are the first things that strike one who looks at his manuscripts.

Soon after leaving college he began to teach a school at Falmouth, as the city of Portland was then called. His account-book, now lying before me, indicates that he began this school on the 25th of June, 1770, and kept it to the 8th of September, 1773; being a little more than three years. It seems to have been in some way a public school, because in his accounts he charges the town of Falmouth, for keeping it, £5 6*s*. 8*d*. a month; which, in lawful money, so called, (the currency then and now of Massachusetts and Maine, so far as pounds, shillings, and pence are used,) amounted to $17.79. But it would also seem not to have been a public school in our sense of the term; for he kept accounts with the parents and guardians of the pupils, charging for each one from two to six shillings (from thirty-three cents to a dollar) for each term. He credits the parents with the sums they paid him, but does not carry these sums to the credit of the town. He either had private pupils, or by his bargain with the town was paid so much from the town treasury, and as much more as the children should pay; and this I suppose was the case.

Among his papers are memoranda of his expenses in journeying from Byfield to Falmouth, and back. They sound strangely now. He rode on horseback, and slept one night on the road; and the whole expense, including "punch" at each dinner and at night, was twelve shillings and five pence, or $2.07. Thus, at "Littlefield's, Wells," the charge is, "Supper, punch, lodging, and horse-keeping," two shillings and threepence (or thirty-seven and a half cents); and at "Greenland, Clark's, oats, hay, dinner, and punch," one shilling and tenpence (or thirty-one cents).

During all this time he was studying law with Theophilus Bradbury, an eminent lawyer of Falmouth; and in July, 1774, he was admitted to practice. In the second volume of Willis's valuable History of Portland, (page 52,) it is said that "Those who remember him while engaged in this humble pursuit," (that of school-keeping), "speak of his close and unremitted application to study when not engaged in school." And in a foot-note to this passage Mr. Willis says: "Mr. Parsons boarded three years with Deacon Codman, and the remainder of the time with Dr. Deane. Mr. Codman's son, who went to school to him, told me that Mr. Parsons was constantly studying when out of school; that he was always in his chamber. It is well known that this great man, in addition to his vast attainments in the science of the law, was a profound classical scholar, and deeply skilled in mathematics." How far this praise was merited, my readers will be enabled to judge.

It must have been from Portland, and while he was a student, that he wrote the following letter to his brother Theodore.

Dear Brother:

The last letter I received from you was in French, dated some time last fall. Soon after the receipt of it, I wrote you one in that language, and sent it by Mr. S. Freeman, who left it at Cape Ann, with Eben, who told him he should see you soon, and would deliver it; whether he has or no, you have not been kind enough to inform me. I should suspect you had stolen off to some other climate, by your silence, if my father did not favor me with his correspondence. Through that channel, I learn that you spent the winter at Medford; that this spring you have visited Cape Ann. What can be the reason of your silence? I can't conjecture; do you tell me. The intelligence from Cape Ann gives me great anxiety; my only consolation is that the fears of Molly's friends have exaggerated her indisposition. Sister Susa, I am told, is there; and that my brother can't do without her. I am glad she is able to assist our sister; but I believe the collision of their tempers does sometimes produce fire. Though you care so little about me, I feel solicitous about your future destination; perhaps with as little reason as the snail regrets the tardiness of the hound. My father even now hints a word to me about preaching; but that I believe you hear oftener than I do. But never let a man think of being a minister, unless he can quietly deny himself the enjoyments of life, and expect his reward only above the stars. I am never more pleased with any metaphor, than when life is compared to a journey; and the sphere we move in resembles the steed which carries us on our way. A dull beast is disagreeable, and so is a situation in which we place ourselves with reluctance; and who is there that is not delighted with good entertainment and cheerful company through this gloomy vale? But when we dismount, horse, entertainment, and company vanish. If we were unfortunate in our choice, perhaps we may then relish the truth of the old proverb, that *acti labores jucundi sunt.* But philosophy is an empty name, if we mean to sweeten the bitter draughts of life with it; it is then no more efficacious than a ballad to chase away the headache. Hope is the grand catholicon for every evil but despair, and it is a remedy we are not easily deprived of.

Commencement is approaching, when you receive your manumission; but it is uncertain whether I shall be present. If I am not, I shall go to the westward soon after, when I suppose I shall see you. Those books of mine in your possession I should be obliged to have you return by the packet, as that is the most convenient way. Fuller on the Globes, and Martin's Grammar, I want; the rest are not of so much consequence.

I should take it as a favor if you would write me soon, before you leave Cambridge.

Your affectionate

THEOPH. PARSONS.

It may be inferred from this letter, that my father knew French, and was studying astronomy while in Falmouth. He compares his solicitude about Theodore to the regret of the snail for the tardiness of the hound. From my earliest childhood I was accustomed to hear my uncle Theodore spoken of as having been the star of the family. I am quite sure that as much was expected from him as from my father, if not more. He studied medicine, and was with the army in Rhode Island in 1778, and wrote many letters home, of which I publish in the Appendix all that remain. Immediately afterwards he went to sea as surgeon of a privateer, and after one letter (also in the Appendix), was never heard of more.

I have my father's docket-books through all his professional life; but they seem to be quite imperfect. At his first term, he made fifty-nine writs, of which thirteen were entered as issuable cases. I do not find an equal number again for some years; and the highest number I have seen was eighty writs, returnable at April term, Essex County, 1784. From the sudden burst of success with which it would thus appear that he entered upon his profession, I should infer that he had not only been a diligent student, but had acquired a good reputation as such. Perhaps he was much benefited by a circumstance which, for a time, seemed to threaten him with an important obstruction. The committee of the bar to whom his application for admission was referred, construed the rule then existing, which required three years' previous study of law, as meaning three years of exclusive study, and regarded him as not complying with it, because he had all the time taught a school, and could have given, as they said, only his leisure to the law. But he earnestly requested an examination; and, this being granted, he received a unanimous recommendation, in language of high praise.

This brilliant prospect was soon clouded. In October, 1775, Admiral Graves, then in command of the British squadron lying in Boston Bay, despatched thence some ships-of-war with orders to destroy Falmouth; and it was almost totally burned.

My father returned at once to Byfield, disappointed, saddened, and as nearly crushed by this calamity as it was possible for him to be. But it proved to be a most fortunate event; and he often referred to it as the true beginning and foundation of all his professional success; for in his father's house he found Judge Trowbridge.

This eminent and excellent man had resigned his seat on the bench in 1772, and now retreated to this quiet nook, ostensibly to escape from the small-pox, which then was, or threatened to be, epidemic in Boston and its vicinity. It was supposed, however, that the political convulsions of the day drove him from his home in Cambridge; for he was not free from suspicions of Toryism, although never molested. He remained in Byfield a considerable time; and when he found that my father was to be his companion and student, he ordered thither all his library; which was not only the best, but probably the only thoroughly good one, then in New England. He found in my father an intelligent student, of devoted industry, prepared by previous habits, as well as previous knowledge, to profit by this golden opportunity; and accepting as a gift of unspeakable value the instruction and assistance which the good judge was glad to render.

Edmund Trowbridge died in Cambridge, in 1793, at the age of ninety-four; and during half of this long life he was, by common consent, regarded as the most learned lawyer of New England. In the seventh volume of the Massachusetts Reports (page 20), my father speaks of his excellence as a common-law lawyer, and says: "The late Judge Trowbridge was an excellent common-law lawyer, of whose friendly assistance in my early professional studies I cherish the most grateful remembrance." And Chancellor Kent, in his Commentaries, calls him "the oracle of the common law in New England." And yet, so evanescent is professional fame, very few of my readers would know whom I meant by that name, unless they are, as lawyers, acquainted with his Treatise on Mortgages, which my father caused to be published in the eighth volume of the Massachusetts Reports.

Trowbridge was the adopted child and heir of his uncle, Colonel Edmund Goffe, who was with Phipps, in an expedition against Canada, in the days of Queen Anne; and he took the name of his uncle when quite young. Whether he was connected in any way with the family of the regicide judge, who was so long and so well concealed in New England, I do not know. He must have changed his name again about the time of the Revolution; for John Adams speaks of him in his Diary under both names, and indeed in one instance uses both in the same paragraph. It was said that he resumed his first name from some difficulty with his uncle; perhaps, also, he wished to forget his kinship, if any there were, to a king-killer, for he was very loyal. He was a Tory in heart, and to some extent in speech; but remained inactive, perhaps neutral, through the contest. He did not abstain from the conflict through cowardice or physical unfitness; for he had strong proclivities to war and combat, and was "a master of fence" and an excellent horseman. But he was a kind-hearted man, strongly influenced by social and family relations; and three persons, who were his nearest connections, were so strongly committed to the cause of independence, that they held him in check. These three were Richard Dana, Francis Dana, and William Ellery. Trowbridge had no brother, no children, and but one sister; and Richard Dana was her husband, and Francis Dana (afterwards Chief Justice) was their child, and his nephew and heir; and William Ellery had married the sister of Mrs. Trowbridge. I do not suppose Judge Trowbridge felt very strongly on the questions of the day, and at the beginning of the contest he certainly sympathized with those who resisted the usurpations of the royal ministers. These he could see to be illegal. But he was a thoroughly educated technical lawyer, and had been the king's Attorney-General, and was then a Judge by the king's commission, and he was accustomed to consider and decide all questions of right or of conduct, under the light of precedent, and perhaps was unable to regard them otherwise; and he could discern no ground that was tenable, according to his views and habits of mind, for pushing resistance to the king's authority quite to rebellion.

It has been always said, as I have intimated, that he retreated to Essex County from fear of the small-pox. But at the breaking out of the disturbances, Francis Dana, who was not only his nephew, but had married William Ellery's daughter, who was his wife's niece, had recently gone to England on a mission to Franklin and Quincy (though ostensibly to visit a brother who was a settled clergyman in England), leaving his wife and child with Judge Trowbridge, in Cambridge. The Committee of Public Safety then sat in that town; and General Warren, who was its most active member, made a call of friendship and courtesy on Mrs. Dana, and suggested to her that it might be more agreeable for her to withdraw for a while from the immediate neighborhood of Boston, and offered her a letter of safe-conduct. Such a document was then of much value; for the "Sons of Liberty" were always watchful, sometimes very troublesome, and did not always refrain from violence. She accepted it, and spoke of joining her father's family in Rhode Island. Judge Trowbridge was in the room; and General Warren, turning to him, very courteously made him the same offer. Possibly the Judge interpreted the offer as a hint that he had better seek quieter quarters. At all events, he accepted the proposition; and to escape the consequences of neutrality in so fierce a struggle that neutrality would have been deemed hostility, he departed with his safe-conduct to Byfield, and thus gave my father the opportunity of profiting by his invaluable instruction.

There was indeed an affinity between them in a tendency

which was common to both, and to my father's peace and comfort was most injurious; and this was a strong disposition towards hypochondria. I shall have more to say of this in connection with my father, in a subsequent chapter. He could hardly have caught it with his law from Judge Trowbridge; but in that great lawyer it was already well developed, although it did not break out into full perfection until years afterwards, when he had no work to do. Then it seemed to excite in him a terror of whatever disease was prevalent. Thus, when the measles were somewhat epidemic, his fears were concentrated into a dread of that disease. While it existed in Cambridge, he would not sit among the people on Sunday, but had a chair placed for him in the porch of the meeting-house; and while the disease continued in the neighborhood, he kept sand-bags at the doors of his house to exclude the mephitic air. When riding, he always sent his old and faithful servant, Sam Rylands, forward, to inquire at the house where he purposed to bait his horse, whether the measles were in it. He sometimes carried his precautions so far as to subject himself, and others also, to inconvenience. For example, when driving out in the neighborhood for purposes of business or recreation, if there were any passengers whom he would probably be obliged to meet or pass, — especially if the road were so narrow that he must come quite near to them, — it was one of Sam's strange duties to go to them and inquire whether they had the measles, or any other malady of which the Judge happened then to stand in especial fear, that some arrangement might be made in that case for his safety. The persons thus accosted were not always duly grateful for the Judge's solicitude about their health; but were sometimes greatly aggrieved, and manifested their displeasure by disagreeable answers.

In those days the Sons of Liberty made domiciliary visits, and sometimes with uncomfortable results. Trowbridge had in his parlor a full-length portrait of Governor

Hutchinson, in an elaborate frame. This he permitted, for a time, to be put into a dark closet under the eaves. Still, it might be found if the house should be visited by a mob, or even by a committee. So, one day, in the Judge's absence, some of the family, partly to protect him, and quite as much perhaps from their hostility to Hutchinson, cut the canvas from the frame, and burned it in a large fire, with closed shutters. In the frame they put a portrait of Richard Dana (father of the Chief Justice) by Copley; and this portrait, in this frame, now hangs in the parlor of Richard H. Dana, Esq., of Boston, grandson of Richard, and son of the Chief Justice.

Trowbridge's house stood in Cambridge next to the site now occupied by the Rev. Dr. Albro's meeting-house, and was some time since taken down. His office, which he occupied during his whole Cambridge life, and in which Chief Justice Dana, Rufus King, Royall Tyler, Christopher Gore, Harrison Gray Otis, and my father, with sundry others, studied law, was removed to Cambridgeport, and is now there, let as a domicile to an Irish family, or families.

After Judge Trowbridge's return to Cambridge, my father, although then in practice, continued to profit by his instructions. How much he valued, and how well he improved these opportunities, I shall show more fully when I speak of him as a lawyer. Now, I will only say that his assiduous study while the Judge was at Byfield prostrated his health; and at the age of twenty-seven he was emaciated and raised much blood, and was thought to be dying of consumption.

His mother believed the best remedy would be a course of life the very opposite of that which had brought on the disease. She bade him mount the old family horse and depart, and keep on horseback until he was well again. The first day, I have heard him say, he could ride only seven miles, at a walking pace. But he slept well that night, and the next day he rode farther, and soon was able to bear all the exercise the horse could give him. He was absent for a considerable time, wandering, I believe, to the western part of this State and to New Hampshire, riding as much as his horse could bear, and in the intervals walking in the open air as much as he himself could bear. He returned to his home with his health quite restored.

From his account-books it would seem that, during all the period of his residence at Byfield, he continued to do what business he could. He had some clients still in Falmouth; but his business there seems to have died out soon after he removed to Byfield, and for some time it was confined to Essex County. But there it increased very rapidly. At thirty years of age his position was established, his success certain and great. His office was in Newburyport. In that town, on the 13th day of January, 1780, he married my mother, Elizabeth Greenleaf, a daughter of Judge Greenleaf and granddaughter of Dr. Charles Chauncy of Boston, and the fifth in descent from Dr. Charles Chauncy, the second President of Harvard College.

Dr. Chauncy (my great-grandfather) married Miss Elizabeth Hirst, who was a sister of Lady Pepperell. When Mrs. Chauncy died, her daughter was a child, and went to live with Sir William, and there Judge Greenleaf became acquainted with her.

Since writing the above, a volume entitled "Chauncy Memorials" has reached me. It is compiled by the Rev. William Chauncy Fowler of Amherst, and gives the results of long and enthusiastic labors. It serves to illustrate a principle sometimes referred to elsewhere, but most distinctly stated and fully elucidated by my friend, Dr. Palfrey, in his able and learned work entitled "Relation between Judaism and Christianity." It is, that the increase in a geometrical ratio of the number of our ancestors as we ascend, proves that, after some generations, everybody is the descendant of everybody. If we say that there are twenty-eight generations in one thousand years, and every man has, on the average, two children, whoever lived one thousand years ago has now considerably more than a fourth part of the estimated population of the earth, if there have been no intermarriages, among his descendants. These of course there have been; but, as Dr. Palfrey says in a note: "You and I, reader, have had more than a thousand millions of progenitors since the time of the Saxon Heptarchy. Whoever you are, it is extremely probable that the blood of Egbert of England and of Egbert's meanest menial runs in the veins of both of us."

Thus, the Chauncy family, while entirely respectable, has never been, so far as I know, of any remarkable importance, at least not in modern times; but the genealogy of President Chauncy, the founder of the American branch, has been well preserved; and it goes back, certainly, to a Norman baron who "came over with the Conqueror," and had large estates in Normandy and in England; and by the marriages of his descendants with other baronial families, all who can trace back their lineage to the President can prove connection by blood with many of the highest families in English history; as, for example, the De Veres of Oxford, the Bigods of Norfolk, the Marshalls, Earls of Pembroke, Shakespeare's Siward of Northumberland, De Brito, the builder of Belvoir Castle and ancestor in a maternal line of the Duke of Rutland, the Earls of Bridgewater, and the family of De Roos, who are among the oldest of the nobility of England. If this seems strange, I suppose that the peculiarity consists only in the fact that the thing can be proved, because of the care with which all these genealogies have been preserved; for it would be easy to show that it is mathematically probable that a very large proportion of our New England families have — if we go back far enough — a parentage which extends its roots just as widely among, not the highest only, but the highest and the lowest, of the families of England. And so must it be inevitably, unless where the artifice of caste comes in to control the natural and wholesome law which compels this mingling of blood.

The Chauncys have labored strenuously to verify and preserve their pedigree; and about the beginning of this century, one of the family printed upon a sheet some three or four feet square the genealogy in all its details, from the baron whose name stands in the Battle Abbey roll as one of the Conqueror's knights. He brought a copy to my father, as he sat in his office, and apprehending from the manner of reception that it might not be carefully preserved, begged permission to nail it up over the fireplace. There it was spread out in all its beauty. But my father smoked nearly all the time he was in his office. Waste newspapers did not then abound; and scraps which could be written on were saved then as they are not now, and friction-matches were unknown. This sheet was sadly convenient; and he began with tearing a narrow strip from the white border; but he gradually extended his ravages, until, when I remember it, all our generations, as far back as the reign of Richard II., had fallen a sacrifice. What became of the fragment I do not know. I am happy to say that I inherited another copy of this map, a few years since, from an ancient maiden relative; and I take better care of it than my father did of his copy.

He built, soon after his marriage, a large house, which is now standing on Green Street in Newburyport, and lived there some twenty years.

My mother gave birth to twelve living children, of whom five died in infancy, seven grew to adult age, and three now survive.

Soon after his marriage, a portrait of him was painted, for his father, which I now have. It is a very poor painting, but was always said to have been a most excellent likeness. I confess, however, that I see in it but little resemblance to the man I knew. It represents him as thin, pale, somewhat sickly, and rather sad. But there is nothing like this in the head by Stuart, of which I place a copy at the beginning of this volume. This head was painted from memory, immediately after his death, and was never finished. I regard it as an admirable likeness. Stuart was earnestly requested by my uncle William to finish it; but he always refused to do so, saying that he had *seen* my father for an hour, and painted while the vision lasted, and if he saw him again he would finish it, and not otherwise. By all which he meant, that he had seized an hour of very vivid recollection to make this sketch, and that he could not recall it. I am glad he never attempted to finish this portrait. From it he made several, — one for my uncle and some for public bodies, — using this sketch as an original, and finishing up the copy as well as he could. But all of these portraits are, as I think, inferior to this sketch in force and in resemblance.

In 1800 he removed to Boston, and lived a year in an old house in Bromfield Lane, or Bromfield Street as it now is, on the site on which the Indian Queen Tavern afterwards stood, and the Bromfield House now stands.

In 1801 he bought a house with a large garden on the eastern side of Pearl Street, where now granite warehouses stand.

There, on Saturday, the 30th day of October, 1813, he died.

CHAPTER III.

OF HIM AS A STATESMAN.

It should not be difficult to understand what he was in this respect; for the key to his conduct and character as a politician, and to his influence upon the politics of the country, is easily found. He was eminently and thoroughly conservative. He was so by natural tendency, and by education and habit; and the longer he lived, the more conservative he became; either because experience and observation brought to him constantly new proofs of the correctness of his views, or because these opinions were so firmly fixed that he saw everything through them, and they gave to every object of thought their own aspect and color.

The two great principles of progress and of conservatism are as inevitable in all free countries as are the centripetal and centrifugal forces in the planetary system. By their conflicts, their compensations, and their influence upon each other, they preserve all things in an ever-shifting but never-failing equilibrium. They demand each other, produce each other, and confirm each other. A few, very few men may possibly stand so near the centre that they cannot be seen to incline to either side; but generally we may say of them something like that which an eminent moralist has said of the virtues of moderation and contentment: "Excellent things, no doubt, and always to be greatly respected; but for the most part closely allied to indifference and indolence."

Wherever there is freedom, there must be political agitation and party politics. Earnest men will engage in them earnestly; and, whatever may be the watchwords of these parties, the real, abiding, and essential distinction (so far as there is one of principle) will always be between the party of progress and the party of conservatism.

At all times, men capable of reflection must be aware that either of these may go too far. And while conservatism trusts to its anchor when it were far wiser to use the sail, and strives to employ the life and strength of the present in the vain endeavor to keep up the appearance of life in the dead things of a dead past, it is well that there are those who love progress better than obstruction and decay, and who insist that the garments which the age has outgrown shall not cling to its limbs and become its fetters. But when these lovers of progress threaten in their wild career to shatter the foundations of law and peace and well-being, all safety and all hope will depend upon the strong men who can arrest and curb the madness. And when the vulgar love of license is dignified with the name of the love of liberty, the plague can be stayed only by the minds that perceive and the lips that proclaim that order is the indispensable condition of liberty, and its only safeguard and its best friend.

If ever a man valued efficient government and law, precedent and order, my father did. If any one was ever conservative, he was so; but (perhaps because I sympathize with him) I cannot think that he was blindly so.

When he was a very young man, and the conflicts of the Revolution were beginning, he hoped, as long as hope was possible, that England would be wise enough to permit us to be free as a part of the British empire, equal in its rights to any other part. He could not be unaffected by the sentiments, perhaps the advice, of Trowbridge, for whom he always entertained sincere respect, as well as profound gratitude. He would not yield a particle of our liberties, for he was no "Tory"; but he wished to secure and preserve them with the least possible violence, because he was a conservative Whig. It was at this time that he wrote the following letter, which I owe to the kindness of the Hon. Charles S. Daveis of Portland, and to which I prefix, by way of preface, the letter which Mr. Daveis wrote to me, when he sent it.

Dear Sir:

Here you have the fulfilment of my promise, — a copy of the letter from your venerated father to John Waite, Esq., who was for a long time within my own remembrance Sheriff of the County of Cumberland, — until, I believe, his death, some way within the present century, — I think till about the period of the last war with England, and into the time when your father used to visit us as Chief Justice on the Eastern Circuit, when the Court used to dine together on the opening day. This was before my coming to the bar. Under what different circumstances they met from those which existed when this was written, and when I should judge their conservative sentiments harmonized pretty well!

Was not your father at that period pursuing his legal studies at Byfield under Judge Trowbridge, who, I believe, did not make much of a boast of his regicide descent? Colonel Waite, I think, had been a captain under Wolfe at Quebec, but was, I believe, native among us. His predecessor in the office of Sheriff was Colonel William Tyng of Gorham, who soon became a refugee, and returned here upon the peace.

Accept this tardy fulfilment, and believe me, dear sir,

Very faithfully yours,

C. S. Daveis.

To Professor Parsons.

Theophilus Parsons to John Waite, Esq.

Byfield, 12 March, 1776.

Sir:

I received yours by Harry, who is now at school and pursues his studies with great application. Mr. Moody informs me he finds him a very sensible, intelligent boy, who discovers not only a capacity, but a disposition, to improve his time well. He appears quite easy at the school, and tells me he has no inclination to return home. I shall be pleased with his being at the school, not only for his sake, but for my own, if I should thereby have an opportunity to oblige you by serving him. If I can promote either your interest or Harry's, I assure you I will do it with great cheerfulness.

To answer your inquiry, why you have not heard anything from me, — it was because there was nothing respecting myself worth writing; and as for public affairs, as everybody knew what I knew, I could tell you nothing. I am sorry for the present situation of Falmouth. Some designing men amongst you have overshot their mark, and are now receiving the reward of their own doings. I should be resigned to the dispensation, if the innocent did not suffer with the guilty. I can acquit you of being an author of the troubles of the town. I now please myself that the aspect of our public affairs is a little brighter. I believe we shall have commissioners to try to settle the dispute. Most of the people here are sick of it, and would gladly terminate it, if left to their own judgment. I am apprehensive some difficulties will arise about the mode of negotiation. But what prudent man would quarrel about forms and ceremonies, either in religion or politics, if he could but attain the end by securing his salvation, especially if he should by such quarrels finally miscarry? As the present plan seems to be not to treat with the Congress, the high Whigs say, Then we will not treat at all.

The moderate Whigs (whom I look upon to be the best patriots among us) are of a different opinion. They say, first, that a negotiation is absolutely necessary, for the Ministry have put some of our best friends in the commission, for two reasons; — one, to induce us to settle the matter; the other, that, if we will hear no terms, the mouth of opposition at home will be stopped, and the whole nation united in the Ministers' measures, and a vigorous prosecution of the war maintained. As to the mode of negotiation, they say the different Colonies need not proceed a step without the directions of the Congress.

It will be immaterial to the commissioners whose advice we take in forming the terms of accommodation, and though the several Provinces will be the ostensible parties in the negotiations, yet in fact the real party will be the Congress, and every end as effectually answered as it would be if the Congress were an ostensible party. They say further, that some of the Southern Colonies begin to cool. They look upon the Northern ones with a jealous eye. Their members have openly charged us with mercenary views in commencing and prosecuting the war; that we have raised the prices of everything, and exerted ourselves to make the support of the war as expensive as possible, that the money and wealth of the continent might centre with us; and that our real plan is independence, though we have not yet avowed it. These charges, though groundless, are alarming; for an ill-founded opinion will have the same influence on those who believe it that a well-founded one will. The consequence of this reasoning is, that there will be danger of the Southern Colonies securing good terms and deserting us. If that should be the case, the vindictive spirit of the Ministry will be gratified by making the Northern Provinces pay the reckoning.

I give you this reasoning without giving you my own opinion. Judge thou. I am fully persuaded that many of our present leaders will oppose any accommodation; and some would choose rather to support the war alone, than accept any. Mr. J. Adams declared his zeal for carrying on hostilities, if New York would adhere to us, without the assistance of the Southern Colonies. Many others, who have not half his abilities or honesty, are of the same opinion. There are so many mushrooms sprung up, got into place, and now have the rule over us, they would exert themselves to prolong their authority. Can you think that Major-General ——— would cheerfully be metamorphosed into Sam ———? or that the disinterested patriot, Samuel ———, Esq., member for Falmouth, Clerk of the House of Representatives, Register of Probate, Clerk of the Inferior Court, Clerk of the Sessions, and one of his Majesty's Justices of the Peace for the County of Cumberland, would willingly quit all his honors, all his importance, and all his profits, and again dwindle down to insignificance and potash? I could cover a sheet of paper with a long string of &c.'s. I do not mean to insinuate that all the gentlemen who have had appointments are of this stamp. Many of them are possessed of abilities and integrity, and may they long continue in their present offices. Never had a member of the House so great an opportunity of serving the Province as he will have next summer.

I wish to God the several towns in the Province would be

extremely cautious in their next elections, and return none but men capable and disposed to pursue the true interest of their constituents. Many new faces I hope to see, and some old ones. Every gentleman qualified for the trust ought to stand forward,— ought to speak and act his sentiments. Arduous will be the task, but great will be the reward, if the blessings of the country are a great reward. I have particular reference to you, sir. You ought to stand forward; to make interest to go yourself, instead of your present member. You have seen and felt enough to convince you of the impropriety of sending him again. I do not mean to flatter you. I suppose others are as capable as you are; but they have not interest sufficient to carry an election. You have.

If I was at Falmouth, I should exert myself to get you chosen. And if you refused to go on account of your private interest, I should think you ought to be given up to Satan or Sam ——— to be buffeted. Do tell Mr. E. Ilsley what I have said upon the subject. I rely upon it, I should have his opinion with me; and he and the other friends to the town could procure your election without your appearing in it.

If the present plan of accommodation shall miscarry, I shall tremble for my country. But if the present union shall continue indissoluble, I have great hopes we shall finally disappoint the malice of our enemies, and hand to posterity that blessing of liberty which our ancestors bequeathed to us. But if the same legacy can be transmitted without risking the prosecution of a civil war, who but villains will run the risk? I expect you will be at Byfield soon, to see Harry, and I should be very glad to wait on you at my father's, when you come this way. If you have anything curious at Falmouth, do hand it along.

Please to give my compliments to Mrs. Waite and to your family, especially to Mr. Bille.

Your humble servant,

THEOPH. PARSONS.

This letter shows his conservatism very plainly; and perhaps it indicates the influence of Trowbridge. At a later period, when it became certain that our liberties could be preserved only by establishing our independence, no one was more decided than he. My good grandfather, who dearly loved and carefully preserved the calm regularity of his retired and peaceful life, became thoroughly aroused at last, as the sermon from which we have already quoted indicates, and entered with enthusiasm into the great purposes and struggles of the day; and all his family were with him, and no one of them more decidedly than my father. The following letter of my grandfather gives some indication of this. It was written two years before, to my father at Cambridge, where, for a short time, he had a few pupils; which I neglected to mention in the preceding chapter.

Moses Parsons to Theophilus Parsons.

Byfield, June 17, 1774.

Mi fili:

Yours of the 6th instant lies before me; in answer I say, that according as you have stated your circumstances, your tarrying at or leaving of College the summer vacation will depend upon the fate of your pupils. If you are at liberty to come to Byfield, I should be very glad to see you here. Perhaps you may procure a horse at an easy rate at this present time, or may borrow one of your pupils' parents; or, if you can procure a conveyance here, you may have my horse, as occasion shall require. As to the Commencement, the College, or the governors of it, have acted prudently, considering how gloomy the day is. As to our public affairs, I have more to say than time or paper will allow. We are, be sure, severely, I may say barbarously and cruelly, dealt with. But if we were all united, I should not give all up as desperate. We can live without Great Britain as well as they can without us. I was in hopes the trial would not be made these thirty years, till we had doubled the number of inhabitants, and so could put a greater weight into the opposite scale. Our Southern Colonies are united to help us, and it is only keeping the storm from breaking on them. I say it again, a union among ourselves, (under God,) I make no doubt, would prove our strength, safety, and salvation. The measures of administration are alarming; they leave no room for repentance; and if they should go on as they have begun, we have no property or privilege, civil or religious, that we can call our own; for if there is no confidence in royal faith, we see there is no dependence on administration when the times are so corrupt. I should not have said anything about politics, for I could but begin to begin, and so must leave off, and perhaps may not have said anything that will afford satisfaction. May Infinite Wisdom direct, Divine Goodness support us, and Divine Power effect our salvation. The Lord reigneth, and his counsel shall stand.

They are well at Dummer School. Mrs. Moody has been very ill, but is better. Mr. Gray is with us as a tutor to your sisters. Polly is in her Accidence; Gorham in his Testament, and looking forward to his Bible. We depend upon seeing you, if your circumstances will allow it. Your grandmother is at Cape Ann. We are well, and the whole family salute you.

Your affectionate parent,

MOSES PARSONS.

It will be remembered by those of my readers who are acquainted with our Revolutionary history, that in the beginning of 1776 it was known that one or more commissioners would be sent from England, to propose terms of reconciliation; and it was quite generally hoped that these would be satisfactory. Lord Howe did indeed come, with authority as Commissioner from the king, and offered certain terms. But he did not arrive until after the Declaration of Independence, and his terms amounted to no more than submission on a promise of pardon, and they would not have been accepted at any time. It may seem strange, however, that, less than four months before the Declaration of Independence, my father should not only speak of the expected commission with much hope, but should regard "the charge" "that our real plan was independence" as groundless. But nothing is more certain than that the expectation, as well as the desire, of reconciliation with the mother country, upon principles which should preserve all our political rights, prevailed extensively throughout the country, almost to the last moment. It was indeed the measures and declarations of the British Ministry at this very time, which finally compelled the Colonies to choose at once between subjection and independence. On the 4th of

July, 1776, the choice was made, and the word "Colonies" was heard no more. But Washington, in a letter to his brother, written at Philadelphia so late as the 31st of May, 1776, more than two months after this letter of my father's and not six weeks before the Declaration of Independence, says: "Many members, in short the representation of whole Provinces, are still feeding themselves upon the dainty food of reconciliation."

This letter of my father to Mr. Waite seems to me not without its historical interest. Its testimony to the honesty and resolute courage of John Adams is something; and the reference to the South and the North, and their relations, is not without its significance. I have never seen elsewhere any distinct allusion to the possible falling away of the Southern States in 1776, and to the plan at that time existing in some minds, of the Northern States alone continuing the contest. But even then was that difference between the North and the South indicated, which has now reached far greater importance. Then, however, the "Free Soil" question did not divide between them, nor any hostility or mutual recrimination about slavery. Nor would this be sufficient now for all the alienation which separates them, if there were not a foundation for it, and perhaps for different opinions and institutions in respect to slavery itself, in an essential difference of character. The South and the North — speaking generally, and admitting all manner of individual exceptions and varieties — are but repeating and continuing that old distinction between the Cavalier and the Puritan, which the emigrants to this country brought with them from England. These accidental names may make us forget that it is almost as old and almost as wide as humanity, and has its origin in the depths of human nature. If this were the place, it would be very easy to show that the distinction is one which has often appeared in history. It is only that between those who, on the one hand, love labor and thrift, and individual strength and independence, and exactness if not severity of belief, profession, and life, and, with much kindness to others, habitually look out with skilful care and great success for *self,* — and those who, on the other hand, love to enjoy more than to win by toil the means of enjoyment, care more for power than for money, love class distinctions while they are uppermost, and are liberal and lax in word and thought to others, but very especially so to themselves. That the negro slave stands in antagonism to the Dollar, is one among the reasons why there are no slaves in the North; that he stands in subserviency to power, and feeds his master's sense of authority and command, is one among the reasons why there are slaves in the South. Wherever in history men of either of these classes are gathered together, the phenomenon puts on the special form or name or aspect which certain circumstances may impart; but it is an old thing, after all. It is much the same thing which now marks, not with hostility, but with observable difference, the South and the North of Europe. And it is the old difference between the Saxon race, of which the Puritan party was almost wholly composed, and the Normans, to whom most of the leading Cavaliers traced back their origin.

I venture also the remark, that this letter would hardly have been written by so young a man, for he was then but twenty-six years old, — I mean, that he would not, in his obscure retreat, have known so much of politics, and been so urgent and active in his advice and persuasion, — if he had not already acquired some position. It may be that this letter is not, of itself, sufficient to suggest this conclusion; but events soon occurred to prove it.

About the time of the Declaration of Independence, the formation of a Constitution became a matter of much moment in many of the Colonies, which had just become States. In Massachusetts the system of government went on with few alterations, although the Charter had lost all force. In June, 1776, it was proposed in the General

Court to prepare a form of government, or Constitution, to be presented to the people. It was thought better, however, to refer the subject somewhat more directly to the people; and the House of Representatives recommended to the towns to empower their delegates at the next election to frame a Constitution. Many towns, perhaps most, complied with this request. Early in 1778 a Constitution was agreed upon by the General Court, and offered to the people; and soon after rejected by them by a vote of about five to one.

The reasons for this decisive rejection were, first, that the draft was very imperfect, and evidently made without due care and consideration. Next, that the people preferred that it should be made, not by a legislature, but by a convention chosen for that express purpose. Then, that there was nothing prefixed in the nature of a Bill of Rights, defining and declaring the fundamental and inalienable rights of the citizens. And lastly, the proposed Constitution so carefully avoided a strong government, that the Executive was a mere cipher. The Governor and Lieutenant-Governor were both members of the Senate; and the twenty-second section contained an express provision that "the Governor shall have no negative as Governor in any matter pointed out by the Constitution to be done by the Governor and Senate, but shall have an equal voice with any Senator on any question before them."

It was this last objection which weighed most with many persons. And there are reasons for regarding the conflict on the forming and adoption of this Constitution as a very early manifestation that a new question was brought before the minds of men, and submitted to their decision, which threatened, or seemed to threaten, the disruption of civil society, and has continued to this day to divide, not politicians only, but the whole people; and will ever do so. This question is indeed that to which I have already alluded; it is, which shall prevail of the two great parties, into one or the other of which every man is forced, by nature, habit, taste, education, or circumstances. These are the parties of progress and of conservatism; of those who love the "largest liberty," with more regard to its quantity than its quality, and those who desire only the best liberty, and dread, as the greatest of evils, its corruption into license.

To all men of this last class, the Constitution offered to the people was wholly worthless; and to this large party my father belonged. His home was in Essex County; and there he was sustained by the warm sympathy of excellent men, and perhaps, young as he was, strengthened their love of order or their fear of anarchy.

A meeting of these men took place in Essex County, early in 1778. By whom it was called, or by whom attended, I have not been able to ascertain. It originated in Newburyport, and I have been repeatedly told that my father began it; but I have no evidence of this. A committee was appointed to prepare a report on the subjects which the convention proposed to consider, and then it adjourned to Ipswich; and there it met in the last week of April of that year, when a term of the Supreme Judicial Court was held there. A pamphlet was presented by the committee at this adjourned meeting, and approved and adopted by the convention, and by their order published. It contained eighteen distinct articles, in which were very fully stated the leading objections to the proposed Constitution. Its long title was: "The Result of the Convention of Delegates holden at Ipswich, in the County of Essex, who were deputed to take into Consideration the Constitution and Form of Government proposed by the Convention of the State of Massachusetts Bay." It is familiarly known in history as "The Essex Result." A large edition was printed, and it was widely circulated; and as it went very fully into the consideration of the objects and principles which should be regarded in the formation of a constitution, it not only made the rejection of the proposed Constitution far more decisive, but exerted an important influence on the structure of that Constitution which was soon afterwards framed by a State convention, and adopted by the people.

This pamphlet, which is now very rare, I reprint in the Appendix; because my father wrote it, and also because it seems to me to be worth reprinting for its own sake. As the Essex Result it had a wide celebrity in its day, and was one of the grounds — perhaps the chief one — for that nickname of "The Essex Junto," which Mr. Hancock afterwards fastened upon my father and his companions; a name of which he was as proud as it was in his nature to be of any political distinction; and he held on to it to the end of his life.

No doubt he obtained all the assistance, by advice and suggestion, which could be rendered to him in a matter of this importance, by the wise men with whom he acted. But he wrote every word of it; and this, I think, proves that the young man was already recognized by them, who were certainly among the ablest and most venerable men of the country, as one with whose work they were satisfied, and one whom they could trust to speak for them.

For proof that he wrote this pamphlet, I do not trust to family tradition and evidence, but might refer to the declarations of many who knew it. I need, however, only quote the direct assertion of Chief Justice Isaac Parker. He says, in his address to the Grand Jury, after my father's death: "The Report was undoubtedly his, though he was probably aided by others, at least with their advice. This elaborate Report is called 'The Essex Result.'"

I have, however, still further evidence. The original documents of the convention are now lying before me. That they were placed in my father's possession is an indication of his prominence in the body. But it seems that the movement (as has been said) not only began in Newburyport, but that my father was the first person named among the delegates from that town, although the youngest. The following paper is in his handwriting, and certified to be a copy of record; and from other memoranda I infer that the votes were of his drafting.

At a legal meeting of the freeholders and other inhabitants of the town of Newburyport, by law qualified to vote in town affairs, held March 27th, 1778:

Voted, This town are of opinion that the mode of representation contained in the Constitution lately proposed by the Convention of this State is unequal and unjust, as thereby all the inhabitants of this State are not equally represented, and that some other parts of the same Constitution are not founded on the true principles of government; and that a convention of the several towns of this county, by their delegates, will have a probable tendency to reform the same, agreeably to the natural rights of mankind and the true principles of government.

Voted, That the Selectmen be desired, on behalf and in the name of this town, to write circular letters to the several towns within this county, proposing a Convention of those towns by their delegates, to be held at such time and place as the Selectmen shall think proper to mention in said circular-letters; and that the Selectmen be directed in said circular-letters to propose to each of the towns aforesaid to send the like number of delegates to said Convention as the same towns have, by law, right to send Representatives to the General Court.

Voted, To choose five delegates for the Convention aforesaid, viz. Theophilus Parsons, Tristram Dalton, Jonathan Greenleaf, Jonathan Jackson, and Stephen Cross, Esquires.

A true copy from the minutes.

Attest: NIC. PIKE, *Town Clerk.*

I have also a draft of resolutions, apparently intended for consideration, and nearly the same as were adopted, of which nine are in my father's handwriting, and two in that of some other person.

The following document gives a list of the twenty-seven persons constituting the Convention at Ipswich:

Salem. — Mr. Richard Ward, Mr. Jona. Andrews, Mr. Benj. Goodhue, Jr., Capt. Saml. Flagg, Mr. Nathan Goodale, and Joseph Sprague, Esq.

Danvers. — Mr. Gideon Putnam and Capt. William Shillaber.
Ipswich. — Gen. Farley, Jona. Cogswell, Esq., and Danl. Noyes.
Newbury. —
Newburyport. — Theoph. Parsons, Tristram Dalton, Jona. Greenleaf, Jona. Jackson, and Stephen Cross, Esquires.
Marblehead. —
Lynn. — Mr. Samuel Burrill.
Andover. —
Beverly. —
Rowley. —
Salisbury. — Hon. Caleb Cushing, Esq.
Haverhill. —
Gloucester. — Peter Coffin, Esq., Saml. Whittemore, Esq., and Mr. James Porter.
Topsfield. — Dea. John Gould and Mr. Israel Clarke, Jr.
Amesbury. —
Bradford. —
Wenham. — Mr. Stephen Dodge.
Manchester. — Capt. William Tuck.
Methuen. — Mr. John Huse.
Boxford. — John Cushing, Esq., Mr. Benja. Perley.
Middleton. —

Then follows a document which purports to be a Record of the Convention; but only two half-sheets remain. These contain many "votes," of which three are in my father's handwriting; and the last of these (and the last but one which passed at that meeting) was:

"*Voted*, That the thirty-fourth article is exceptionable, because the rights of conscience are not therein defined and ascertained; and further, because the free exercise and enjoyment of religious profession and worship are there said to be *allowed* to all the Protestants in the State, when in fact that free exercise and enjoyment is the natural and incontrollable right of every member of the State."

I cannot persuade myself to deal severely with the fancy that the blood of Robinson of Leyden speaks in this last vote.

The Record closes thus:

"*Voted*, That Mr. Parsons, Mr. Goodale, and Mr. Putnam be a committee to attempt to ascertain the true principles of government; to state the non-conformity of the Constitution prepared by the Convention of this State to those principles; and to delineate the outlines of a Constitution conformable thereto; and report the same to this body."

Judge White of Salem, whose every word carries with it the weight of certain testimony, to all who know him, speaks to me, in a recent letter, of "the famous Essex Result, ... in which *your father* so admirably exposed the crude system first proposed in 1778, and explained the true principles of a republican government," &c. I would add, that the committee appointed to draft the Report, and from which it came, contained, besides my father, only two gentlemen, who were not writers, and could not have contributed to the Report more than advice. Indeed, it would naturally fall to my father, as chairman of the committee, to prepare this Report; and in doing it, a reader of the "Result" will see that he followed exactly the direction of the vote.

I may exaggerate the interest and the importance of this Essex Convention and Result; and shall undoubtedly be thought to do so by those who regard the whole matter as an old-world story. But it seems to me to have some claim to consideration, even in the present day.

Among the most distinguishing peculiarities of the actual institutions and government of this country is the singular blending of the progressive and conservative principles, in such a way that they do not so much neutralize each other, as promote each other's activity, while they compensate for each other. Indeed, I am persuaded that this will be regarded hereafter as a most remarkable instance of the far-sighted sagacity of our fathers. Coming generations may perhaps see in it the effect of that mysterious principle of compensation, always so powerful in the business of this world. The ages and the nations move in a vast procession; and to this movement every one contributes. Any man may influence, but no man can exclusively direct or control this movement; because, let him do or be what he may, some one or many will be doing or being that which will tend at least to restore the equilibrium with greater or less exactness. Since Franklin's day, it has been known that no particle of positive electricity can be excited, without instantly exciting an equal particle of negative electricity. This law may at least illustrate the analogous law which is putting in its claim to be considered by the student of human conduct and character. While our fathers were making history, there were some whose love for liberty had degenerated into a love of license, and whose idea of happiness it was to run riot through the fields of life; and they balanced and checked, and were balanced and checked by, the stern lovers of order, who appeared, in their extremity of opinion, to think that the first use of legs is to wear fetters, while walking is but a secondary and conditional purpose. Happily, there were wise men who were able to bring these extremes into compromise, and, by means of compromise, into union.

Nothing wiser can be done than to seek, in all the questions and exigencies of life, that middle point of rest in which extremes meet, and towards which extremes compel each other to tend. And the same law governs the well-being of a State. When our fathers were called upon to construct the Constitutions of this country, the necessity of discovering and establishing this equilibrium was felt by them. It came in a new form, and on a scale of unprecedented grandeur and importance. It was a work for which human experience had learned but little, and could teach but little. The problem was to reconcile and combine that absolute liberty, which for the first time a nation imperatively demanded, with those restraints and guards, without which freedom must perish as soon as it is born. The time had come when liberty and order, each helping the other, and each preserving the other, were to be combined and interfused into one, that the consummate flower of all history might open upon a rejoicing world. This work was given, in good part at least, for men to do. And I have been led, whether on sufficient evidence others must judge, to regard the Essex Result as a very early encounter with the great question then dawning upon this country and upon the world. It was an earnest endeavor to discover and declare how progress and conservatism, liberty and order, might be so adjusted in human institutions, that freedom should be secure, and peace and happiness be the children of freedom. I think I find in this document the leading principles by which all wise efforts to answer this question practically have been and are likely to be guided. It seems to me that a comparison of this document with history gives me evidence enough — aside from the testimony of individuals — that the principles herein stated exerted much influence in moulding the first Constitution of this State, and others also so far as they have copied this, and in making them the excellent instruments that they were for this great good. And it was a problem which could be solved only by a careful consideration of many facts and principles and probabilities, and by a far-penetrating insight into the laws of human character and action.

It is probable that this Essex Result will have but little interest to most readers now, for the reason that it will seem to them familiar and commonplace; so much so, indeed, that my commendation must seem extravagant. But if its reasoning or its conclusions have this aspect, it is only because of their general adoption as the true principles of republican government. It must be remembered that they are here stated fully, clearly, and systematically, without the aid of our experience. So far as I have been able to learn, the whole country had been so busy with the labor and the conflict which had won the possibility of republicanism, that few minds of sufficient capacity had been turned to the practical question, When this becomes possible, how shall the foundations be laid, how shall the structure be built? And that which gives to this pamphlet its value and interest in my estimation, is my belief that it was an answer to this question, remarkably complete and accurate, very generally accepted by the people of this State, and to a considerable extent beyond our boundaries, as the true answer; and therefore constantly reproduced in the constitutions which were afterwards formed. And these same principles are now so universally admitted, at least in theory, that they seem to be self-evident, and it is difficult to believe that there was a time when they were unknown.

To this there is one exception. The reader of this pamphlet will perceive that my father insists very strongly that power should be given, not to mere numbers alone, but that, for some purposes, property should so far be permitted to have its representation and its influence, that it might at least have some check upon measures which directly affected itself. The first Constitution of Massachusetts so far adopted this principle, that, while the Representatives were chosen on a basis of numbers alone, the Senators were chosen on a compound basis of numbers and amount of taxation. And in other of our early Constitutions some influence of the same principle may be discerned. All this has passed away, by amendments, or by changes which are called amendments. The unanimity with which this has been done, should perhaps be taken for proof of its propriety. Perhaps, however, time will show, not to us, but to some distant generation, that this principle was founded upon truth and essential justice; that, if it had not been wisely applied, an improvement on this point should have been sought; but that its entire abandonment took from the edifice of our legal liberty one of those foundations which were indispensable to its stability.

I do not pretend that this document was perfect, in its rhetoric, or its logic, or its political theories; but, such as it was, I draw from it the inference that my father, even then, in his youth, was thought by the wise and good of his day to be one of their number; and, while I write this because it seems to me to be true, no one can know better than I know, that the opinion I express may be but one more of the many examples which show that a son can never judge accurately of his father's character.

Although this Constitution proposed by the Legislature was thus opprobriously rejected, the need of one was universally acknowledged. A Convention was called, and met at Cambridge, in September, 1779, to frame a Constitution; and a committee was soon appointed to draft one. It consisted of twenty-six persons, who were selected from the counties, — from a few only one, from others two, from none more than three. In the enumeration of this committee, James Bowdoin (the President of the Convention), John Adams, and John Lowell, all of Suffolk County, are first named. Then follow Theophilus Parsons, Jonathan Jackson, and Samuel Phillips, Jr., from Essex; and then the members from the other counties. If the list of delegates is read, it will be thought, perhaps, of some significance, that on this the principal committee of the Convention, after the members from Suffolk County, (then as since entitled by usage to priority in the list,) my father was first named, being selected before the many older men of Essex who were already distinguished and influential persons; and, although then but twenty-eight years of age, he was thus placed at their head.

At a later period in the Convention, a committee of four, Samuel Adams, John Pickering, Caleb Strong, and William Cushing, none of whom was on the former committee, were directed to draw a Constitution and Bill of Rights. This was adopted by the Convention, after some discussion and amendment, and accepted by the people.

Whether my father had any particular share in the preparation of this Constitution, I do not know. It was drafted by John Adams, principally. In former years, some who have now gone have pointed to me this or that clause or provision, and said that it was due to my father. But I remember these references imperfectly, and doubt whether the statements were made to me on certain or sufficient knowledge. Perhaps the most direct authority on the point is Chief Justice Parker, who, in his Address, says: "Many of the most important articles of the Constitution were of his draft; and those provisions which were most essential, though least palatable, such as dignity and power to the Executive, independence to the Judiciary, and a separation of the branches of the Legislative departments, were supported by him with all the power of argument and eloquence."

For the next ten years I know nothing of my father's political life. He was busy in his profession, providing for the wants of an increasing family, and employing his leisure in the studies and recreations which he loved. But I am certain that he was doing all that could be done by the explicit declaration of his own opinions, whenever that was proper, to strengthen in the Commonwealth the love of legal liberty, rather than the love of liberty without restraint or order or security. And soon the time came for determining whether such views as he held, or their opposites, prevailed in the Commonwealth.

The Old Confederation of the United States was formed, November 15th, 1777, in the midst of war and danger and effort; and while these lasted, their pressure kept it together. But with the relaxation of peace, its debility and insufficiency became apparent. There was a general sense of its inadequacy to the wants of the country. None defended it, or were satisfied with it. And Shays's Rebellion in 1786, and other things of like kind, though differing in form or in degree, led to a general conclusion that a new Constitution was necessary.

A Convention of Delegates from the States assembled, for the purpose of framing a Federal Constitution, at Philadelphia, in May, 1787 ; and at once the new parties of the country, the Liberty party and the Government party, started into full life. The Convention had many difficulties; and that which sprung from the existence of slavery in some of the States and not in others, was an important one. But a reader of the debates, especially if he bring to this study any knowledge of contemporary history, cannot fail to see that the one great question, how much or how little power should be given to the government, and how far this power should be checked on the one hand, or on the other left untrammelled, underlay every other.

Hamilton perhaps, and soon, if not at first, led the party of strong government. It is asserted that at one period he openly avowed his want of faith in the worth or possible perpetuity of republicanism, but agreed that the circumstances of the day made any other form of government impossible, and therefore that must be tried; and he desired to give it all the strength he could, and proposed a plan which should have that effect.

It is possible that Hamilton made this profession and proposed his measures, not even with the desire of obtaining all he asked, but for the purpose of asking much that he might obtain something. It is certain that, when the Constitution was formed, it pleased those who desired an efficient government more than those who demanded the largest liberty ; although Hamilton declared himself dissatisfied with it, and signed it only as the best thing that could be had.

The two antagonist principles entered into immediate, constant, and energetic conflict; and the good sense and caution and love of peace, and the profound conviction that union would be improbable if not then consummated, and that without union there must be destruction, — all these were in perpetual requisition, and were only able to reconcile these hostile sentiments and principles so far as to produce the Constitution, which was throughout, and in almost every paragraph and every provision, a compromise.

After the Constitution was formed, the men who most loved peace and union labored strenuously to procure for it the signatures of all the delegates, that it might go to the people with the advantage of their unanimous assent. And all did sign it but three, — Randolph and Mason of Virginia, and Elbridge Gerry of Massachusetts, afterwards Governor of that State.

The Constitution contained a provision, that it should go into effect as soon as nine States should accept it. It was itself adopted by the Convention which framed it, on the 17th of September, 1787 ; then by Delaware, December 7th, 1787 ; by Pennsylvania, December 12th, 1787 ; by New Jersey, December 18th, 1787 ; by Georgia, January 2d, 1788 ; and by Connecticut, January 9th, 1788. Then came the question whether the Commonwealth of Massachusetts should accept it.

It had been generally expected that the five States above mentioned would ratify it without much difficulty. But it was feared that Massachusetts would be hostile, and that her example would operate with much power upon New York, Maryland, and Virginia, for good or for evil. On the 9th of January, 1788, a Convention of delegates from the various towns of Massachusetts (which then included the Province of Maine) assembled at Boston, to determine whether the Constitution should be adopted or rejected by that State. The Debates of this Convention were republished by the Legislature of Massachusetts, in 1856. The editorial care of the volume was intrusted to Messrs. Bradford K. Peirce and Charles Hale. These gentlemen performed their work with great skill and perfect success ; and

I shall have frequent occasion to quote from their interesting volume in the pages immediately following.

In their Preface these gentlemen say:

"The proceedings of the Convention were of great importance, and were so regarded throughout the country at the time. It is quite certain that, if Massachusetts had refused her assent to the Constitution of the United States, that well-devised scheme of government, the careful work of the patriots and statesmen of the last century, under which the nation has enjoyed so large a degree of prosperity, would have failed. There is ample evidence of this in the letters which are printed at the end of this volume."

And on the next page they say: "It is believed that, at the beginning of the session of the Convention, there was a majority against the Constitution."

It will be seen, from the documents presently quoted, that all who were engaged in Shays's Rebellion, — and some of his officers and soldiers sat in the Convention, — and all who sympathized with them, and most of the members from Maine, who feared that the separation of that State from Massachusetts would be retarded by it, and perhaps apprehended that their titles to their farms would be scrutinized too carefully, were opposed to the Constitution. With these were the great mass of the farmers of Massachusetts, still warm with the zeal which had led them through their war against oppressive authority. All these were hostile to the Constitution; and to them must be added the many, whether high or low in station, to whom it is reason enough for any course of conduct or opinion, that they are only the dry leaves of society, who always go as the wind goes; or, worse than that, self-seekers who ask subsistence from the mass, and pay for it by subserviency.

In favor of the Constitution were arrayed, some one said, the religion, the education, and the wealth of the community. But by this was only meant, that the clergy, the lawyers and physicians, and the merchants and the commercial towns, were very generally in its favor. The question, however, on which side was the majority in number, none could answer.

John Hancock and Samuel Adams were two of the most important members of the Convention. Both were doubtful; but it was generally supposed that, while they were not friendly to each other, they agreed in a decided leaning against the Constitution; and if both, or if either, had become professedly and actively hostile to it, its adoption would probably have been impossible.

How great was the importance of that crisis, how many of the wisest of the land were looking with anxiety for the decision of Massachusetts, may be inferred from the following extracts from letters and documents of the time, which are not a tithe of what might be presented. We make these extracts from Messrs. Pierce and Hale's edition of the Debates. They will exhibit the condition of things, and the hopes and fears of those most interested, better than any words of mine could do.

James Madison, writing from New York to George Washington, on the 20th of January, 1788, says:

"The intelligence from Massachusetts begins to be very ominous to the Constitution. The anti-Federal party is reinforced by the insurgents, and by the Province of Maine, which apprehends greater obstacles to her scheme of a separate government from the new system, than may be otherwise experienced. And according to the prospect at the date of the latest letters, there was very great reason to fear that the voice of that State would be in the negative. The operation of such an event on this State may easily be foreseen. . . . . . The decision of Massachusetts either way will involve the result in this State. The minority in Pennsylvania is very restless under their defeat. If they can get an Assembly to their wish, they will endeavor to undermine what has been done there. If backed by Massachusetts, they will probably be emboldened to make some more rash experiment."

On the 25th he writes to Washington again:

"The information from Boston by the mail, on the evening before last, has not removed our suspense. The following is an extract of a letter from Mr. King, dated on the 16th instant.

"'We may have three hundred and sixty members in our Convention. Not more than three hundred and thirty have yet taken their seats. Immediately after the settlement of elections, the Convention resolved that they would consider and freely deliberate on each paragraph, without taking a question on any of them individually; and that, on the question whether they would ratify, each member should be at liberty to discuss the plan at large. This resolution seems to preclude the idea of amendments, and hitherto the measure has not been suggested. I however do not, from this circumstance, conclude that it may not hereafter occur.

"'The opponents of the Constitution moved that Mr. Gerry should be requested to take a seat in the Convention, to answer such inquiries as the Convention should make concerning facts which happened in the passing of the Constitution. Although this seems to be a very irregular proposal, yet, considering the jealousies which prevail with those who made it, (who are certainly not the most enlightened part of the Convention,) and the doubt of the issue, had it been made a trial of strength, several friends of the Constitution united with the opponents, and the resolution was agreed to, and Mr. Gerry has taken his seat.'"

General Lincoln writes to Washington on the 27th, as follows:

"I have the pleasure of enclosing two newspapers, in which are the debates of the Convention to Saturday, the 19th. They are not forward enough to give your Excellency a just state of the business. I therefore am induced to observe that, yesterday, we were on the ninth section. The opposition seem now inclined to hurry over the business, and bring on, as soon as possible, the main question.

However, this they are not permitted to do. It is pretty well known what objections are on the minds of the people; it becomes, therefore, necessary to obviate them, if possible. We have, hitherto, done this with success. The opposition see it, and are alarmed, for there are a vast many people attending in the galleries, (we now assemble in one of our meeting-houses,) and most of the arguments are published in the papers. Both are of use."

Washington writes to General Lincoln from Mount Vernon, on the 31st of January, this letter:

"I am very sorry to find there is likely to be so powerful an opposition to the adoption of the proposed plan of government with you; and I am entirely of your opinion, that the business of the Convention should be conducted with moderation, candor, and fairness, which are not incompatible with firmness. Although, as you justly observe, the friends of the new system may bear down the opposition, yet they would never be able, by precipitate or violent measures, to soothe and reconcile their minds to the exercise of the government, which is a matter that ought as much as possible to be kept in view, and temper their proceedings.

"What will be the fate of the Constitution in this State is impossible to tell, at a period so far distant from the meeting of the Convention. My private opinion of the matter, however, is, that it will certainly be adopted. There is no doubt but the decision of other States will have great influence here, particularly of one so respectable as Massachusetts."

Madison writes to Washington on the 3d of February, saying that a letter, dated the 27th of January, from a member, gives the following picture:

"Never was there an assembly in this State in possession of greater ability and information than the present Convention; yet I am in doubt whether they will approve the Constitution. There are, unhappily, three parties opposed to it. First, all men who are in favor of paper money and tender laws. Those are more or less in every part of the State. Second, all the late insurgents and their abettors. In the three great western counties they are very numerous. We have in the Convention eighteen or twenty who were actually in Shays's army. Third, a great majority of the members from the Province of Maine. Many of them and their constituents are only squatters upon other people's land, and they are afraid of being brought to account. They also think, though erroneously, that their favorite plan of being a separate State will be defeated. Add to these, the honest, doubting people, and they make a powerful host. The leaders of this party are a Mr. Wedgery, Mr. Thompson, and Mr. Nasson, from the Province of Maine; a Dr. Taylor, from the county of Worcester, and Mr. Bishop, from the neighborhood of Rhode Island."

On the 5th of February, Washington writes to Madison:

"I am sorry to find, by yours and other accounts from Massachusetts, that the decision of its Convention, at the time of their respective dates, remained problematical. A rejection of the new form by that State would invigorate the opposition, not only in New York, but in all those which are to follow; at the same time, it would afford materials for the minority, in such as have actually agreed to it, to blow the trumpet of discord more loudly."

General Knox, after the Constitution was adopted, also writes to Washington, as follows:

"The opposition has not arisen from a consideration of the merits or demerits of the thing itself, as a political machine, but from a deadly principle levelled at the existence of all government whatever. The principle of insurgency expanded, deriving fresh strength and life from the impunity with which the rebellion of last year was suffered to escape. It is a singular circumstance, that, in Massachusetts, the property, the ability, and the virtue of the State are almost solely in favor of the Constitution. Opposed to it are the late insurgents, and all those who abetted their designs, constituting four fifths of the opposition. A few, very few indeed, well-meaning people are joined to them. The friends of the Constitution in that State, without overrating their own importance, conceived that the decision of Massachusetts would most probably settle the fate of the proposition. They therefore proceeded most cautiously and wisely, debated every objection with the most guarded good-nature and candor, but took no questions on the several paragraphs, and thereby prevented the establishment of parties. This conduct has been attended with the most beneficial consequences. It is now no secret, that, on the opening of the Convention, a majority were prejudiced against it."

Knox writes to Livingston in the same strain; and Washington writes to Madison, from Mount Vernon, on the 2d of March:

"The decision of Massachusetts, notwithstanding its concomitants, is a severe stroke to the opponents of the proposed Constitution in this State; and, with the favorable decision of those States which have gone before it, and such as are likely to follow, will have a powerful operation on the minds of men, who are not more influenced by passion, pique, and resentment, than they are by candor, moderation, and judgment."

Washington also writes to Knox, on the 3d of March:

"I pray you to accept my acknowledgments of your favors of the 10th and 14th ultimo, and congratulation on the acceptance of the new Constitution by the State of Massachusetts. . . . . . It will be very influential on the equivocal States."

All of these letters may be found in the recent edition of the Debates.

So much for the importance and the difficulty of the question. And now for the means by which Hancock and

Samuel Adams, on whom so much depended, who were hostile to each other, and were both opposed to the Constitution, were induced to agree in its support; and enough of the adverse majority brought over to save the Constitution, and with it, perhaps, the State and the nation.

The Convention met, as has been said, January 9th, 1788. From the first hour the prospect darkened with every day. The hopes of those who desired the acceptance of the Constitution grew continually more feeble, until, on the 31st of January, Hancock came in and took his place as President, having excused himself from previous attendance on the score of incapacitating illness.

After some members had spoken, my father moved "that this Convention do now assent to and ratify this Constitution." Two or three members spoke to the general question, and then "his Excellency the President rose, and observed, that he was conscious of the impropriety, situated as he was, of his entering into the deliberations of the Convention; that, unfortunately, through painful indisposition of body, he had been prevented from giving his attendance in his place; but, from the information he had received, and from the papers, there appeared to him to be a great dissimilarity of sentiments in the Convention. To remove the objections of some gentlemen, he felt himself induced, he said, to hazard a proposition for their consideration; which, with the permission of the Convention, he would offer in the afternoon."

The Convention then adjourned to the afternoon; and when it met, "his Excellency the President observed, that a motion had been made and seconded, that this Convention do assent to, and ratify, the Constitution which had been under consideration; and that he had in the former part of the day intimated his intention of submitting a proposition to the consideration of the Convention. My motive, says he, arises from my earnest desire to this Convention, my fellow-citizens, and the public at large, that this Convention may adopt such a form of government as may extend its good influences to every part of the United States, and advance the prosperity of the whole world. His situation, his Excellency said, had not permitted him to enter into the debates of this Convention; it however appeared to him necessary, from what had been advanced in them, to adopt the form of government proposed; but, observing a diversity of sentiment in the gentlemen of the Convention, he had frequently had conversation with them on the subject; and from this conversation he was induced to propose to them, whether the introduction of some general amendments would not be attended with the happiest consequences. For that purpose he should, with the leave of the honorable Convention, submit to their consideration a proposition, in order to remove the doubts and quiet the apprehensions of gentlemen; and if in any degree the object should be acquired, he should feel himself perfectly satisfied. He should, therefore, submit them; for he was, he said, unable to go more largely into the subject, if his abilities would permit him; relying on the candor of the Convention to bear him witness that his wishes for a good Constitution were sincere. (His Excellency then read his proposition.) This, Gentlemen, concluded his Excellency, is the proposition which I had to make; and I submit it to your consideration, with the sincere wish that it may have a tendency to promote a spirit of union."

The proposition was as follows:

COMMONWEALTH OF MASSACHUSETTS.

In Convention of the Delegates of the People of the Commonwealth of Massachusetts, 1788.

The Convention having impartially discussed and fully considered the Constitution for the United States of America, reported to Congress by the Convention of Delegates from the United States of America, and submitted to us by a Resolution of the General Court of the said Commonwealth, passed the twenty-fifth day of October last past; and acknowledging, with grateful hearts, the goodness of the Supreme Ruler of the Universe, in affording the people of the United States, in the course of his providence, an opportunity, deliberately and peaceably, without fraud or surprise, of entering into an explicit and solemn compact with each other, by assenting to and ratifying a new Constitution, in order to form a more perfect union, establish justice, insure domestic tranquillity, provide for the common defence, promote the general welfare, and secure the blessings of liberty to themselves and their posterity, — do, in the name and in behalf of the people of the Commonwealth of Massachusetts, *assent to* and *ratify* the said CONSTITUTION FOR THE UNITED STATES OF AMERICA.

And as it is the opinion of this Convention that certain amendments and alterations in the said Constitution would remove the fears and quiet the apprehensions of many of the good people of this Commonwealth, and more effectually guard against an undue administration of the federal government; the Convention do therefore recommend that the following alterations and provisions be introduced into the said Constitution:

First. That it be explicitly declared, that all powers not expressly delegated to Congress are reserved to the several States, to be by them exercised.

Secondly. That there shall be one representative to every thirty thousand persons, until the whole number of representatives amount to ——.

Thirdly. That Congress do not exercise the powers vested in them by the fourth section of the first article, but in cases where a State shall neglect or refuse to make adequate provision for an equal representation of the people, agreeably to this Constitution.

Fourthly. That Congress do not lay direct taxes, but when the moneys arising from the impost and excise are insufficient for the public exigencies.

Fifthly. That Congress erect no company of merchants with exclusive advantages of commerce.

Sixthly. That no person shall be tried for any crime, by which he may incur an infamous punishment, or loss of life, until he be first indicted by a grand jury, except in such cases as may arise in the government and regulation of the land and naval forces.

Seventhly. The Supreme Judicial Federal Court shall have no jurisdiction of causes between citizens of different States, unless the matter in dispute be of the value of ——— dollars, at the least.

Eighthly. In civil actions between citizens of different States, every issue of fact arising in actions at common law shall be tried by a jury, if the parties, or either of them, request it.

Ninthly. That the words, " without the consent of the Congress," in the last paragraph of the ninth section of the first article, be stricken out.

And the Convention do, in the name and in behalf of the people of this Commonwealth, enjoin it upon their Representatives in Congress, at all times, until the alterations and provisions aforesaid have been considered, agreeably to the fifth article of the said Constitution, to exert all their influence, and use all reasonable and legal methods, to obtain a ratification of the said alterations and provisions, in such manner as is provided in the said article.

And that the United States, in Congress assembled, may have due notice of the assent and ratification of the said Constitution, by this Convention, it is

Resolved, That the assent and ratification aforesaid be engrossed on parchment, together with the recommendation and injunction aforesaid, and with this Resolution; and that his Excellency John Hancock, Esquire, President, and the Honorable William Cushing, Esquire, Vice-President of this Convention, transmit the same, countersigned by the Secretary of the Convention, under their hands and seals, to the United States, in Congress assembled.

These amendments are often called, in the histories of the times, the " Conciliatory Resolutions," and they were eminently so. It was their purpose, and it was their effect, to reconcile conflicting opinions, and to procure the adoption of the Constitution. Samuel Adams at once arose, declared himself satisfied with the Constitution with these amendments, and seconded them. They were referred to a committee, and reported with little change; and after some discussion, in which one or two of the opponents of the Constitution spoke of the amendments as reconciling them to it,— as Mr. Turner of Scituate and Mr. Symmes of Andover,— the Constitution was adopted, by one hundred and eighty-seven yeas, against one hundred and sixty-eight nays; or by a majority of only nineteen out of three hundred and fifty-five votes. At once, however, many of its leading opponents hastened to declare that it had been fairly adopted, that they accepted it in good faith, and would go home and do their utmost to reconcile the people to it, and induce a general recognition of it as the law of the land. In Boston the rejoicing was universal. There was a great procession, with much burning of gunpowder, many dinners, speeches, songs, and other demonstrations of great joy.

I have said that these "Conciliatory Resolutions" saved the Constitution; and I say so, because everybody said so then, and nobody has since denied this, so far as I know. Some stanzas in a ballad made on the occasion, and sung to "Yankee Doodle," expressed the common opinion:

Then 'Squire Hancock, like a man
Who dearly loves the nation,
By a concil'atory plan,
Prevented much vexation.
Yankee doodle, keep it up!
Yankee doodle, dandy!
Mind the music and the step,
And with the girls be handy.

He made a woundy Fed'ral speech,
With sense and elocution;
And then the 'Vention did beseech
T' adopt the Constitution.
Yankee doodle, &c.

The question being outright put,
(Each voter independent,)
The Fed'ralists agreed t' adopt,
And then propose amendment.
Yankee doodle, &c.

The other party, seeing then
  The people were against 'em,
Agreed, like honest, faithful men,
  To mix in peace amongst 'em.
    Yankee doodle, &c.

I have dwelt on these amendments, because my father wrote them, and every word of them. It was also said, very commonly, that Hancock read them from the manuscript in my father's handwriting; but Mr. Quincy, in a letter to me, published a few pages farther on, does not think this probable.

I should not state so positively that my father was the author of these amendments, if my belief of it rested only on a family tradition, however clear and constant that might be; or even because I remember hearing of the following incident as long ago as I remember anything. He then lived in Newburyport, and when in Boston resided with his brother William, in Summer Street. On the Saturday after the amendments were offered by Hancock, my uncle made a "conciliatory" dinner. Some who had been hostile were there, as well as some of the faithful. My father was not present, having gone to Newburyport to pass his Sunday at home. A member who had been satisfied by these amendments, when the conversation fell upon them, took a copy from his pocket, and began to read it, with vast praise of Hancock as the saviour of his country. A young niece of my aunt was in the room. She was one of those bright, observing, and outspoken children — those *enfans terribles* — who do a good deal of mischief without intending it; but it is difficult for me to describe her in this way, for I knew her only as a feeble and sickly, and, as I then thought, aged woman. While the reading was going on, she plucked at my uncle's coat until he turned to her with, "Well, what is it, my dear?" "Why, Uncle, is not that the paper that Uncle Theoph was reading to Mr. Cabot last Wednesday night?" Those who were in the secret joined in making it out a jest or a blunder, and it passed by. But again and again in after years would my uncle laugh at his niece about her "letting the cat out of the bag."

Colonel Joseph May, the administrator of Mr. Hancock, found the original draft, in my father's handwriting, among Mr. Hancock's papers. "Laco," a writer in the newspapers of much celebrity in those days, was generally supposed to be Mr. Stephen Higginson, who was certainly as honest a man as ever lived, and one of my father's especial friends. After some account of the proceedings of the Convention, he goes on, in one of his essays, thus:

"The famous conciliatory proposition of Mr. Hancock, as it was called, was then prepared by the advocates [of the Constitution], and adopted by him; but the truth is, he never was consulted about it, nor knew its contents, before it was handed to him to bring forward in Convention. At the appointed time, Mr. Hancock, with all the parade of an arbiter of states, came out with the motion, not only in the words, but with the very original paper that was given to him; and with a confidence astonishing to all who were in the secret, he called it his own, and said it was the result of his own reflections on the subject in the short intervals of ease which he had enjoyed during a most painful disorder. In this pompous and farcical manner did he make that famous proposition, upon which he and his adherents have arrogated so much."

Mr. Higginson was hardly justified in the blame he cast on Mr. Hancock, unless he, or whoever else was Laco, was an eyewitness, and described what he saw. If the printed debates can be relied on, there was no "pomp," &c. in the manner in which he introduced the resolution; and there seems to be a careful and constant forbearance from all personal claim to their paternity. He speaks of them to the Convention as "your proposals," and "the amendments proposed," &c.; but avoids every expression which would seem to claim them as his own; speaking, as it appears to me, with an obvious, if not a studied ambiguity.

It has often been said to me, in reference to this matter, "Your father then saved the country"; and the same sentiment has been expressed in many ways. But my father was only one of many who co-operated to this good result. Washington, in a letter from which I have already quoted, in which he speaks with great joy of the adoption of the Constitution in this State, bears emphatic testimony to "the good sense, sound reasoning, moderation, and temper," without which "nothing else could have carried the question." In truth, the ablest men of the country labored together.

It was said then, and has been repeated again and again, that a bargain was made with Hancock that he should have and keep all the credit of preparing, as well as offering, these resolutions, and of saving the Constitution by them, and that the "Federalists" would join his friends in making him Governor, and giving him what further political distinction, in the State or the Union, he might desire. I have never seen any evidence of such a bargain, and believe it to have been wholly unnecessary. Hancock knew perfectly well that it was just as much the interest of the preparers of those resolutions as it was his own to keep the secret, for some years at least; and he knew, too, that if he took this position, and thus secured the adoption of the Constitution, it would not be possible to prevent his being chosen Governor, or from becoming the most popular man in the State. With his own party he was powerful, and they formed a strong, if not the strongest party; and the Federalists could not oppose him, if they would.

More than this: it should be said, I think, in justice to Hancock (of whom I am not an admirer), that it is certainly possible that, learning from day to day what was going on in the Convention, he might think some step of this kind would be wise and acceptable, and on his own account desire it. It was said that he delayed all interference until the friends of the Constitution succeeded in giving him the opinion that it *might* be adopted without his aid, and that he was thereby prevailed upon to take a position from which it would be inferred that it was carried only through his influence. I cannot say how this was.

The resolutions probably originated with the "Essex Junto." My father wrote these resolutions, or amendments, or propositions, — for they have been called, both then and since, by all these names. But it would be impossible now, and perhaps would have been difficult then, to apportion to each one of those who assisted, in one way or another, his exact share of advice or suggestion.

There is evidence enough that a plan of this kind was for some time in agitation. Madison, in a letter to Washington already quoted from, says, "With all this ability in support of the Constitution, I am pretty well satisfied we shall lose the question, *unless we can take off some of the opposition by amendments.*" By this time, probably, the plan was determined on; and it is so obvious an expedient, that it must have been in the minds of some from the beginning of the Convention, or even before it.

The resolutions were referred to a committee, as I have stated. It consisted of twenty-five members. My father was the third named on this committee. In this connection, the letter of General Knox to Robert R. Livingston is quite significant. He says, "As the propositions were the production of the Federalists, after mature deliberation, there cannot be a doubt that the committee will report in favor of the propositions as they are stated." This seems to me *conclusive* on three points: one, that they had been for some time under consideration; another, that neither Hancock nor any of his party wrote them; another, that, however carefully the secret was kept, the truth was known, in substance at least, to the leading Federalists of the day, and freely spoken of by them to each other. There is other evidence that the secret had leaked out a little. Mr. Stillman, in a speech delivered February 6, after much laudation of Mr. Hancock, says: "But what has been the consequence of your Excellency's conciliatory propositions? Jealousy! jealousy, sir, that there was a snake in the grass, a secret intention to deceive! I shudder at the ungenerous suggestion; nor will I dwell a moment longer on the distressing idea." General Thompson said, "As to the amendments, he could not say amen to them, but they might be voted for by some men,—he did not say Judases." And Dr. Jarvis said, soon after, "It has been insinuated, sir, that these amendments have been artfully introduced to lead to a decision which would not otherwise be had." But the secret was, on the whole, well kept. They had their expected influence; and the Constitution was saved. And if this were all their merit, it would be enough to win for them a place in history.

But this is not all. It is now quite certain that very few persons indeed, if any, were perfectly satisfied with the Constitution as originally adopted by the Convention at Philadelphia, and by them offered to the States. They who were most earnestly desirous that it should be accepted by the States were, perhaps, the most profoundly convinced that it had great defects. It would be an entire mistake to suppose that, because Cabot, Ames, Strong, and others, with my father, were ready to vote for it as it stood, and to do everything in their power to secure its adoption, they did not see its defects, or did not desire to supply them. The Constitution as offered was infinitely better than none; and rather than peril its adoption, they would have accepted it just as it was, and succeeded so far in exciting this feeling in the Massachusetts Convention, that a proposition to make the amendments a part of the Constitution as adopted by this State was voted down, and the Constitution was adopted as it was offered, leaving the amendments to be afterwards acted upon by the States. It must not be supposed, therefore, that my father merely reduced to writing what others desired, and he did not desire. On the contrary, no one was more solicitous than he was that some of them — I may name the first one especially — should be added to the Constitution. But his friends considered, at the time, that he had displayed the utmost skill in preparing amendments which should not only make the Constitution more acceptable to the Convention generally, and overcome the objections of opponents who were not agreed together in their opposition, and give to the Constitution a popular character which recommended it to the people and to those who sought the favor of the people, — but accomplish these objects by introducing provisions which he himself strongly desired, and which the best friends of the Constitution around him regarded as improving it very greatly. How far he deserved this praise, others can judge as well as I can, or better.

There could, at all events, be no greater mistake than that of supposing these amendments to be mere trivialities, with which a trick was played to preserve things of value. The fact is very far otherwise. The first of them has become, it is not too much to say, the very keystone of the national Constitution. It is that in which it is declared, that "all powers not expressly delegated by the aforesaid Constitution, are reserved to the several States." This provision now sets limits to all its other provisions, and is constantly invoked in the consideration of other important clauses. It was not in the original Constitution, but was written by my father, and placed at the head of those amendments which were put by him into Hancock's hands, and in this way made the means of saving the whole. Being adopted by Massachusetts, it was proposed by Congress to the other States (under the fifth article of the original Constitution); and its value and necessity being at once perceived, it was immediately accepted by the requisite number of States, and was so incorporated into the Constitution.

The eighth amendment, securing a trial of issues of fact in certain cases by a jury, and the sixth, that no one shall be tried for a capital or infamous crime except upon indictment by a grand jury, were also adopted, and are now in force as a part of the Constitution. Besides these, the principle and the intended effect of some of the others have been secured by legislation.

It may be thought strange, that, after all possibility of mischief from the disclosure had passed away, my father did not declare his authorship, and put the fact and the evidence of it on record. So it may seem strange that he never signed the "Essex Result," or caused or authorized his name to be published in any manner in connection with it. I can only say it was just so to the end of his life. It will be seen presently how much he not only did, but how much he wrote, and how much he gave to others to publish, and what masses of manuscript on various topics he left behind, some in a form ready for the press, and how sedulously and constantly he withheld his name. As far as I can find, he *never in his whole life* published anything under his own name and as his own production; unless the decisions of the Supreme Court may be so considered. In explanation of this I can only repeat what may seem incredible, that he had a positive dislike for, and disgust at, notoriety. I do not mean that he applied to the subject of fame the principle of Agar's prayer as to wealth,—"Give me neither poverty nor riches,"—and therefore desired only a simple respectability, as the condition most favorable for character and for happiness, for this I should have thought sound and wise. But I repeat what I have already intimated, that he indulged an extreme contempt for the "*vox populi*," which was developed at an early period of his life, and was strengthened with advancing years.

I insert here an interesting letter from President Quincy. It would be superfluous to say to any readers who or what Mr. Quincy was or is. I may remark, however, that his letter will be welcome evidence to those who love to believe, that unyielding tenacity of memory, and undimmed clearness of thought, may be preserved to a very advanced age.

JOSIAH QUINCY TO THEOPHILUS PARSONS.

SIR:

It would give me great pleasure to aid the design you communicated to me in your favor of the 21st instant, of writing the life of your father, deserving as he is of that tribute as much as was any of his contemporaries. But I can add little to the facts contained in the records of the time, and in the memory of many of his contemporaries who yet survive. I was far too young to appreciate his talents on his first appearance in public life. My first personal acquaintance was as a student at the bar, between 1790 and 1793, in which relation I had frequent opportunities to hear and be instructed by his learning and arguments. When he moved his family to Boston, he resided in the same street (Pearl Street) with me, and as a neighbor I had occasional, and sometimes professional intercourse with him; but he was not a man to encourage frequent and desultory intercourse. He had the aspect of one whose thoughts were concentrated on topics having little sympathy with the transient occurrences of daily life. Wherever he was, he was regarded somewhat as an oracle, particularly on legal questions, and in shaping the course of political measures. In his character as a mathematician and as a classical scholar, he stood quite as high, in the popular opinion, as in that of a lawyer. In visits to him in his office, when not engaged in professional pursuits, I have found him reading some Greek author in the original, apparently for amusement or relaxation.

My earliest remembrance of him was in the Convention for the adoption of the Federal Constitution in Massachusetts, where, though he spoke little, his influence in its measures was not second to that of any of its members. Concerning the conciliatory resolutions which Hancock offered to that Convention, you say, "They were written by my father, and Hancock read them from my father's manuscript." In the first statement you are right; in the last, unquestionably in an error. Hancock was too cunning for that. I had occasion, recently, to have my attention drawn to that point. Mr. T. C. Amory, the grandson of James Sullivan, addressed a letter to me, in February last, stating that he had found Hancock's conciliatory resolutions among the papers of his grandfather; and that it was from that paper he thought himself entitled to consider James Sullivan as the author of them.

An extract from my letter to Mr. Amory will explain my opinion on the point.

"I have no doubt, as you state, that James Sullivan, afterwards Governor of this State, *brought the amendments* Governor Hancock proposed to the Convention then in session, and which were, in fact, the conditions on which he gave his vote for the Constitution, and that those amendments were *in Sullivan's handwriting.* It is also true that Sullivan was the confidential adviser, at that time, of Governor Hancock. But the conclusion you draw from this fact, that Sullivan was the draftsman of those amendments, is repugnant to all the statements made in conversation at the time, and to all the relations which then existed among the parties which divided the Commonwealth. That *Laco* (a writer at that time supposed to be Stephen Higginson) did, as you state, assert that Theophilus Parsons drafted those amendments, I have no doubt. Such was the assertion at the time among the advocates of the Constitution, though of course not bruited about. The advocates of the Constitution were deeply sensible of the importance of giving Hancock entire credit for those amendments, to which any understanding between Hancock and those advocates would have been fatal. Their object was to secure the vote of Hancock on any terms. Although these amendments were confidentially stated to have been drafted by Parsons, yet it was well known that he had the aid and concurrence of other leading advocates of the Constitution, although his mind was probably predominating in the conception and the terms.

"The general facts were these: both Hancock and Samuel Adams were, from the first, in heart and soul opposed to the adoption of the Federal Constitution. They anticipated that it would quench the beams of State sovereignty, in which their pride and power were concentrated. They were both the most generally popular men in Massachusetts, and, united, they supposed their opinion would be all-influential, and at the outset, perhaps, they expected to defeat it. And their opposition was not yielded, until the development of public sentiment led them to apprehend that the Constitution might be carried in spite of their opposition. To Hancock, who of all men was the most sensitive to the popular pulse, the idea that the Constitution might be carried in opposition to his opinion was dreadful. The desire of having its success, if it must be carried, attributed to his influence, coincided with his predominating passions,—love of popularity, and ambition to be thought the pivot on which great public events turned. When his mind, either by its own action or the urgency of friends, had been brought to the conviction that the Constitution might be adopted notwithstanding his negative, and he came to the conclusion that it was his best course to join the advocates of the Constitution and cast the weight of his voice in its favor, he was naturally desirous of adopting such a course as would be satisfactory to them, and that, in some form, such an understanding should be effected as would meet their views, and yet provide a safe plank by which, without loss of reputation, he might pass over from a decided opposition to an open acquiescence in the Constitution. All this was well understood at the time. That Hancock's amendments had been deliberately weighed and prepared by leading advocates of the Constitution, of whom Parsons was one of the principal, and Judge Dana another (both in opposition politically to Governor Hancock), was circulated while these events were in progress among the friends of the Constitution, and believed unquestionably. By what means, or through what medium, the draft of those amendments had been transmitted, is unknown to me, but of the fact I can have no doubt. Their appearing in Sullivan's handwriting, and his bringing them to the meeting-house, is quite reconcilable with the above fact. Sullivan was the known confidential adviser of Hancock. It was essential to Hancock's reputation that every appearance of any understanding with the leaders of the advocates for the Constitution should be unknown, to which end their being in the handwriting of his known adviser, and transmitted by his agency, was not only important, but in a manner essential.

"Such were the views, at the time of those events, I was led to entertain, and, in the course of a long life, I have not heard or known anything to change them. James Sullivan was a man of uncommon intellectual powers, and his influence over the mind of Hancock was well understood. Party feeling, at that day, was very violent, and it is quite impossible that there should have been harmony of action between Parsons, Dana, and Sullivan in the concoction of those amendments. The current of public opinion must have been at the time wholly at fault, if Mr. Sullivan had any agency in drafting them."

I have copied the above parts of a letter to Mr. Amory, in reply to the same point, as the best mode of stating my opinions touching the subject to which yours alludes, which touches a vein of thoughts and of memories easy to open, but difficult to cicatrize. And like old divines, after they had finished the nineteenth head of their discourse, I close with, "This must suffice for the present."

I am, respectfully, your friend and servant,

JOSIAH QUINCY.

Boston, 23 April, 1857.

I insert also a letter which the Hon. James Savage was good enough to send me, in which he speaks of the same topics; and which all will be glad to read, who are interested in the history of that period, and who like to listen to indisputable evidence.

JAMES SAVAGE TO THEOPHILUS PARSONS.

Boston, May 4, 1857.

DEAR SIR:

Long before I had the pleasure of ever seeing your father, I had a sort of acquaintance with him from frequent conversations about him, with which I was favored by my uncle and guardian, the late Judge Tudor, who was his classmate. Opinions thus gradually formed were strengthened by notices derived from the late Chief Justice Parker, under whose instruction I began the study of the law at Portland, where he then lived, in 1803. Before your father was appointed successor of Chief Justice Dana, I had the same conviction with the rest of our community, that he was the fittest man for that exalted situation; and after coming to Boston, in 1805, to finish my preparation for the bar, I diligently watched his course, and benefited by his administration of justice at *nisi prius* and law terms.

That he was more instrumental in the formation of the Constitution of Massachusetts than any other citizen, was the opinion of every one who knew him as the author of the famous Essex Result, which exhibited the necessary elements of fundamental law for our republic, with as much completeness and precision as human sagacity could ever supply.

From the time of throwing off the royal government for its violation of the Charter of the Province of 1691 and its utter disregard of the foundation principles of English liberty, Massachusetts acted without any constitution; yet the authority of law was sustained, and a form of civil polity adhered to, by following the guidance of that Charter. More direct application of rules controlling the machinery of government than under that instrument was attainable, in our condition of revolution and of independence necessarily resulting, seemed urgent and indispensable. In February, 1778, our General Court, which by order or desire of its predecessor had been elected for this purpose, in part, sent out to the people a form of government for their consideration, which was very promptly by them rejected by a vote of nearly five to one of the voters. Very easy it is to account for such a result. In several parts of that document strange crudities appear; as, for a remarkable instance, when you recollect how well the body of our people had exercised their faculties in the controversy of 1774, as to the Judges of the Superior Court receiving salaries from the crown instead of the public treasury of the Province, as ever before had been the rule, and in the close of which, all those judges who accepted such compensation were impeached by the representatives of the people, — yet the provision as to tenure "during good behavior" — that must be always regarded as the *sine qua non* of judicial independence, without which there can exist no sincere republic or government of laws — was childishly extended to include *justices of the peace*, as if to incite contempt and provoke opposition. More puerile was the total inadequacy of constituting an Executive department especially for that state of foreign war when Massachusetts must assert equality of rights with other nations, and in the exercise of its belligerent privileges, through its navy, might be exposed to have controversy with every neutral maritime power. In that Constitution, commonly called Judge Paine's, one would suppose the seat of Governor had been artistically provided for the enjoyment of an individual, rather than the general good in support of every individual's right. As chairman of the Boston Board of Selectmen, John Hancock had, before the Revolution began, shown that his accomplishments were fully adequate to that station, in which dignity and grace like his were never surpassed; and something like the same exercise of talents and share of responsibleness would have attended the pageant of Executive head of the Commonwealth under the rejected form.

Early in the year 1778, a Convention of Delegates of the County of Essex was held. It is not in my power to give the names of the authors, or even to recollect the sequence of argument in The Result, as the issue of their deliberation was called. Of the modest pamphlet you may easily believe that my impression has been somewhat weakened in the four or five and thirty years since I saw a copy; but the seminal principles of our "government of laws, and not of men," that has so many years made my native State respected as having the best of any frames of polity, (as these concretions are termed,) at least on our side of the water, were fully exhibited and skilfully enforced in your father's writing of that tract. Pickering and Goodhue of Salem, Choate of Ipswich, Phillips of Andover, Cleaveland of Rowley, Chief Justice Sargent of Haverhill, Judge Holten of Danvers, above all, Cabot of Beverly, must have assisted with their wisdom or their sympathy, though which of them may have attended the Convention, if any, is unknown. Farther aid would come from his admirable townsmen, Jonathan Jackson and Nathaniel Tracy. All these were associated in that Convention, so soon after called by our General Court to assemble in September, 1779; and that Essex should not have all the superior minds of the republic to discuss the substance and model the form of the supreme law to be offered as the digest of wisdom, other parts furnished John Adams, James Bowdoin, Samuel Adams, Increase Sumner, Nathaniel Gorham, James Sullivan, Levi Lincoln, Caleb Strong, William Cushing, R. T. Paine, and Rev. Samuel West, to combine sagacity and experience in the product. You may judge, in some fair degree, how much is due to the sobriety of the members of that assembly, during the stormy period of our history, by the curious exhibit of members attending the sessions, as shown by the journal. At the end of October, before deliberation began on the Report of the Committee of Thirty, chosen early in September, to draw up the Declaration of Rights and Form of Government, which was offered on the 28th of October, the members were *three hundred and twelve.* The first question which was put to vote by a division of the house was on Saturday, November 6th; and it was on the cardinal point of independence of the judiciary, which was settled by seventy-eight against thirty-five, the whole number of votes cast being one hundred and thirteen. The next question brought in one hundred and nineteen. After the recess taken to permit the members to go home for consultation with their constituents, only fifty appear on the 26th of January, 1780, and sixty the following day; but from that time to the end of February, not more than eighty were counted at any day, except on the 4th of that month, when eighty-four were seen. Such was the confidence reposed in the integrity of that committee and the wisdom of their report.

Once more the mature skill of statesmen and the profound sagacity of observing students were called into operation to establish the glorious Union that could alone preserve the happiness of Masschusetts; and in which a dozen other States were to join for setting up a power to restrain each and benefit all. Our Federal Constitution owes to your father, for its wonderful simplicity and skill of organization, nothing beyond the wise discourses so few years before produced with reference only to that of this Commonwealth, or the deep sagacity often invoked in their perplexing politics by other members of the confederacy, termed in way of contempt the *United States*, who were rapidly moving, all without common principles of action, to the wildest consummation of anarchy. Severally, these thirteen members of the great family of civilized nations, in 1787, were an offence in the nostrils of each other; while, conjunctly, they were the laughing-stock of all the rest of the world.

Yet the projection of that immortal model of a government was to be lamented as an untimely birth, unless it should be accepted. Vain would be the dreadful experience of danger, deepening every hour in rebellions in Massachusetts, or the self-inflicted disgrace of violations of the treaty of peace in Virginia; vain the anxious labors of Washington, more wearisome in three years of civil anarchy than in the seven years of impoverished campaigns; vain the cautious explorations through quicksands, without the benefit of soundings or buoys, that guided Jay and Madison, Morris and Hamilton, in laying out that chart for the ship of state, — unless it were ratified by MASSACHUSETTS. Virginia, New York, and North Carolina would forthwith reject the benignant company of such a stranger; and even Rhode Island, that must derive more blessing than any other family, in proportion to its numbers, would suspiciously have forbidden his visit.

Fear that the majority of our Convention of 1788 was adverse to the proposed Federal compact, whose effect would, perhaps, be to elevate the body of people from being brawling mobs in a dwindling community to become citizens of a great nation; yet necessarily would reduce a few leaders of town-meetings to their proper level, was generally diffused among those who desired a better result. It was a wise apprehension lest the plan was too good to meet the acceptance of the agricultural part of our State, before the country should be subjected to a wider and even universal prostration. An indistinct dread of acknowledging any other sovereignty than that of Massachusetts withstood the experience of Dana, the judgment of King, the pure sentiment of Gore, and the liquid wisdom of Ames, *gurgitibus vastis exundans*. It might be silenced, but it could not be convinced. This childish dread was, therefore, to be overcome; and your father, late in the session, no doubt with the concurrence and advice of several of the prominent members in the Convention, submitted a draft of sundry amendments to Governor Hancock, the President of the assembly, chosen in his absence from that body, (in which he had never attended an hour before,) on the 9th of January, but in which he was expected to take his seat on the last day of the same month. All the parts of the Constitution had been discussed, and the Vice-President, a more able officer, William Cushing, (appointed one of the Justices of the Supreme Court of the United States on the organization of that tribunal,) had filled the chair up to that day. On that day, January 31st, your father made the motion "to assent to and ratify this Constitution." At the next meeting, in the afternoon of the *same* day, his Excellency, who had in the morning session mentioned his intention of "submitting a proposition to the consideration of the Convention," made the important motion for amendments, as written by your father. Well expressed, yet of the effect in no single provision to alter the force and principle of a solitary clause in that instrument, but only to supply deficiencies and explain the import of particular clauses in it, this proposition was received with the profoundest respect. Mr. Adams, who had very seldom taken any part in the discussions during the month, yet had expressed, seven days before, some "difficulties and doubts respecting parts of the proposed Constitution," but, as a member for Boston in this assembly, was by his constituents expected to sustain it, and who doubtless had been consulted by the writer of the amendments, — entitled also to great weight for his long experience in most of the Continental Congresses during the war, — was the *first* gentleman to propose that the amendments be considered before action on the motion made by the member from Newburyport. His plan was adopted, and the next day Governor Bowdoin, in a set speech, very well reported, approved the amendments, in which he was followed by Judge Dana, in the afternoon; and the next day by Mr. Strong, in a particular examination of each of the articles, nine in number, of the submitted proposition; which was then, by unanimous vote, referred on Saturday to a committee of twenty-five, Governor Bowdoin being chairman. Of course that committee was selected with great judgment. Your father, Dana, Strong, and Sedgwick, were on it; and the other side was fairly represented, as must be apparent, for, after all the wisdom and influence that could be exerted on such vital interests, nine of them voted for the rejection of the Constitution. The Report was presented on Monday, February 4th, and the diffusion of harmony was encouraged by Rev. Mr. Backus of Middleborough, followed, the next day, by Mr. Ames of Dedham and Mr. Barrell of York. This last gentleman had been of the committee, and seems to have become a convert from the opposition. On Wednesday, Mr. Adams introduced some amendments to be added to those in the committee's report; but they did not receive the approbation of those whom they were designed to conciliate, and after some debate he withdrew them. By the Rev. Mr. Stillman a very effective support was given in the forenoon, and Turner of Scituate and Symmes of Andover in the afternoon renounced their opposition, in direct terms; and the closing by Governor Hancock was succeeded by the vote of one hundred and eighty-seven against one hundred and sixty-eight, there being only nine members absent; which was a most honorable verdict from the body that could have counted fifty majority, as is believed, at its first meeting, adverse to the most important provisions of the Federal Constitution.

No doubt exists of the principal fact of the drawing of the amendments by your father, as I had it from the late Colonel Joseph May, who acted in the settlement of Governor Hancock's estate, from his death, in November, 1793, and was of course intimately acquainted with the relations between Parsons and Hancock, and paid occasionally the fees for professional services by your father, as shown in the administrator's accounts at various times. He had often seen and handled the original manuscript furnished by your father and produced by the President of the Convention, whose habitual self-indulgence would wish to be spared, even if in health, the labor of making a copy, though abundant apology existed, up to the very day preceding his first coming to the assembly, on which he brought forward the proposition, in his inveterate gout. Perhaps the precise expression implying the *identical* paper may be incorrect, for a fair copy may have been used by the Governor to lay upon the table; and I have heard that, by examination of the original papers in the office of the Secretary of the Commonwealth, it appears that the amendments are not in the handwriting of either your father or Governor Hancock.

Of that happy ratification the general effect is well observed throughout the civilized world; and I would gladly fasten attention of many (who in our times calculate the value of the Union) on the special benefits of the measure. From the hopeless state of debt, sunk so low that it was not matter even of exertion to pay the interest; from the universal public distraction between equal States owning no superior, and the private distrust, when no law could be invoked to compel justice to be done between man and man, the new creation sprang from our chaotic elements, to restore order, diffuse light, support equity, vindicate honor, establish individual happiness by national prosperity, take away our reproach as a by-word, and make us a name and a praise in the earth. Sun, moon, and all the host of heaven, exulted in the occasion of shedding their benignest aspects on the commerce, without which our country could do nothing for raising any other portion of our fellow-men, but with which in a single generation we might outvie the growth of any other nation for three centuries.

Excuse my reference, as a statist, to the circumstances of my native city. Its growth in population, for seventy years preceding this Convention, had not equalled thirty per cent; and in the seventy years following, nearly nine hundred per cent mark the increase. When I was a boy, as many houses fell down, or were torn down, in a year, as there were new ones erected.

When two houses were built in a season, it made a town's talk; and I suppose twice two hundred has been the addition for each year in the present generation.

With great regard, your obedient

JAMES SAVAGE.

At this distance of time, when we have forgotten the personal passions and interests which doubtless existed in that Convention, and often influenced their debates if they did not determine their conclusions, we are struck by the appearance at least — by the reality, as I believe — of intense earnestness which prevailed among all parties. Many were the interesting topics discussed. Slavery, now absorbing so much attention, was not forgotten then. From the debate on the paragraph which counts two freemen equal to five slaves, both for taxes and for representation, it is obvious that the gain on the "taxes" made the loss on the "representatives" quite endurable.

The third paragraph of the second section being read,

Mr. KING rose to explain it. There has, says he, been much misconception on this section. It is a principle of this Constitution, that representation and taxation should go hand in hand. This paragraph states that the number of free persons shall be determined by adding to the whole number of free persons, including those bound to service for a term of years and excluding Indians not taxed, three fifths of all other persons. These persons are the slaves. By this rule is representation and taxation to be apportioned. And it was adopted, because it was the language of all America. According to the present Confederation, ratified in 1781, the sums for the general welfare and defence should be apportioned according to the surveyed lands, and improvements thereon, in the several States. But it hath never been in the power of Congress to follow that rule; the returns from the several States being so very imperfect.

. . . . .

Mr. WEDGERY asked if a boy of six years of age was to be considered as a free person.

Mr. KING, in answer, said, all persons born free were to be considered as freemen; and, to make the idea of taxation by numbers more intelligible, said, that five negro children of South Carolina are to pay as much tax as the three Governors of New Hampshire, Massachusetts, and Connecticut.

Mr. GORHAM thought the proposed section much in favor of Massachusetts; and if it operated against any State, it was Pennsylvania, because they have more white persons *bound* than any other. . . . . . He concluded by saying, that the Constitution provides for an increase of members, as numbers increase, and that in fifty years there will be three hundred and sixty; in one hundred years, fourteen or fifteen hundred, *if the Constitution last so long.*

Judge DANA . . . . . drew a parallel between the Eastern and Southern States, and showed the injustice done the former by the present mode of apportioning taxes, according to surveyed land and improvements, and the consequent advantage therefrom to the latter, their property not lying in improvements, in buildings, &c. In reply to the remark of some gentleman, that the Southern States were favored in this mode of apportionment, by having five of their negroes set against three persons in the Eastern, the honorable Judge observed, that the negroes of the Southern States work no longer than when the eye of the driver is on them. Can, asked he, that land flourish like this, which is cultivated by the hands of freemen? And are not three of these independent freemen of more real advantage to a State than five of those poor slaves? As a friend to equal taxation, he rejoiced that an opportunity was presented in this Constitution to change this unjust mode of apportionment. Indeed, concluded he, from a survey of every part of the Constitution, I think it the best that the wisdom of man could suggest.

Mr. NASSON remarked on the statement of the Hon. Mr. King by saying that the honorable gentleman should have gone further, and shown us the other side of the question. It is a good rule that works both ways; and the gentleman should also have told us, that three of our infants in the cradle are to be rated as high as five of the working negroes of Virginia. Mr. Nasson adverted to a statement of Mr. King, who had said, that five negro children of South Carolina were equally ratable as three Governors of New England, and wished, he said, the honorable gentleman had considered the question upon the other side, as it would then appear that this State will pay as great a tax for three children in the cradle as any of the Southern States will for five hearty working negro men. He hoped, he said, while we were making a new government, we should make it better than the old one; for if we had made a bad bargain before, as had been hinted, it was a reason why we should make a better one now.

Mr. RANDAL begged leave to answer a remark of the Hon. Mr. Dana, which he thought reflected on the barrenness of the Southern States. He spoke from his own personal knowledge, he said, and he could say, that the land in general in those States was preferable to any he ever saw.

Judge DANA rose to set the gentleman right. He said it was not the *quality* of the lands, but the *manner* of tilling it, that he alluded to.

Friday, January 18, 1788.

The third paragraph of the second section of Article I. still under consideration.

Hon. Mr. DALTON opened the conversation with some remarks on Mr. Randal's positive assertions of the fertility of the Southern States. He said, from his own observation, and from accounts he had seen, which were better, he could say that the gentleman's remark was not perfectly accurate. The honorable gentleman showed why it was not so by stating the inconsiderable product of the land, which, though it might in part be owing to the faithlessness and ignorance of the slaves who cultivate it, he said, was in a greater measure owing to the want of heart in the soil.

Mr. RANDAL. Mr. President, I rise to make an observation on the suggestion of the honorable gentleman from Newbury. I have, sir, travelled in the Southern States, and should be glad to compare our knowledge on the subject together. In Carolina, Mr. President, if they do not get more than twenty or thirty bushels of corn from an acre, they think it a small crop. On the low lands they sometimes get forty. I hope, sir, these great men of eloquence and learning will not try to *make* arguments to make this Constitution go down, right or wrong. An old saying, sir, is, that *a good thing don't need praising;* but, sir, it takes the best men in the State to gloss this Constitution, which, they say, is the best that human wisdom can invent. In praise of it, we hear the reverend clergy, the judges of the Supreme Court, and the ablest lawyers, exerting their utmost abilities. Now, sir, suppose all this artillery turned the other way, and these great men would speak half as much against it, we might complete our business, and go home in forty-eight hours. Let us, sir, consider we are acting for the people, and for ages unborn; let us deal fairly and above-board. Every one comes here to discharge his duty to his constituents, and I hope none will be biased by the best orators; because we are not acting for ourselves. I think Congress ought to have power, such as is for the good of the nation; but what it is, let a more able man than I tell us.

Mr. Dawes said he was sorry to hear so many objections raised against the paragraph under consideration. He thought them wholly unfounded; that the black inhabitants of the Southern States must be considered either as slaves, and as so much property, or in the character of so many freemen; if the former, why should they not be wholly represented? Our own State laws and Constitution would lead us to consider those blacks as freemen, and so indeed would our own ideas of natural justice. If, then, they are freemen, they might form an equal basis for representation as though they were all white inhabitants. In either view, therefore, he could not see that the Northern States would suffer, but directly to the contrary. He thought, however, that gentlemen would do well to connect the passage in dispute with another article in the Constitution, that permits Congress, in the year 1808, wholly to prohibit the importation of slaves, and in the mean time to impose a duty of ten dollars a head on such blacks as should be imported before that period. Besides, by the new Constitution, every particular State is left to its own option totally to prohibit the introduction of slaves into its own territories. What could the Convention do more? The members of the Southern States, like ourselves, have *their* prejudices. It would not do to abolish slavery by an act of Congress in a moment, and so destroy what our Southern brethren consider as property. But we may say, that, although slavery is not smitten by an apoplexy, yet it has received a mortal wound, and will die of a consumption.

These extracts are taken from the edition of the Debates of the Convention before referred to. They were made generally, no doubt, by the editors or reporters of the newspapers from which they are taken, with more or less aid from the speakers themselves. My father kept for his own use brief and condensed notes of the debates, — such notes as a lawyer takes of a case in which he is interested. Many of the sheets containing these I found, a few years since, and placed in the Boston Athenæum, whence they were taken and printed in the same volume. It may be amusing to compare the somewhat stately report of the newspapers with the notes of my father. He says of this same debate:

Ordered to proceed to the next paragraph, viz.: "Representatives and direct taxes, &c., &c. — Georgia three."

Hon. Mr. KING. The principle on which this paragraph is founded is, that taxation and representation should go hand in hand. By the Confederation, the apportionment is upon surveyed land, the buildings and improvements. The rule could never be assessed. A new rule has been proposed by Congress, similar to the present rule, which has been adopted by eleven States, — all but New Hampshire and Rhode Island.

Mr. WEDGERY objects to the rule, as apprentices are not freemen, but blunders about it.

Mr. KING explains —

Mr. SHURTLEFF. His difficulty is, our negroes are free, but those of other States are not. But the number of representatives first chosen —

Gen. THOMPSON. The rule is unequal, as we have more children than the luxurious inhabitants of the Southern States. Congress will have no impost or excise, but lay the whole tax on polls. We live longer than they live. We live to one hundred; they, to forty.

. . . . .

Mr. WEDGERY wants to know whether all white infants are free persons. If they are, we are over-taxed.

Hon. Mr. KING. All persons born free are counted among free persons, to which three fifths of all persons born or imported slaves, make the census.

Mr. WEDGERY. If Mr. King is right, then we shall pay one quarter of the debt.

Mr. GORHAM. Mr. Wedgery is totally in the wrong. It will

lessen our old proportion nearly one seventh. As eleven States have agreed to this rule, among which is Massachusetts, it is a rule most likely to be adopted. As to representation mentioned —

Col. FULLER. The arguments against the representation are groundless. As the rule of proportion is by numbers, five slaves to three freemen is but equal, for slaves are but chattels.

Hon. Mr. DANA. If this government was a consolidation, and not a confederation, he should then think the number too small. But as it is federal, and we have our own governments to support, the expense would have been too great. We can send seven on the old plan, but have only sent four or five, which proves the sense of the people not to have a large representation. The Constitution provides for increasing the representatives. 'T is true Congress are not bound to increase representation as numbers increase, nor should they; for, from the rapidity of population, the representation would be enormous. We can instruct our representatives; they will not dare to disobey them. The old rule of apportionment by lands was against this State. Our lands are worth more by the acre. Lands cultivated by slaves are not worth as much as lands cultivated by freemen. Slaves are their masters' moneys, and at their risk; and it would be unjust to tax a slave as much as a freeman. If we think there should be a difference, the only question would be, what difference. The States have agreed in Convention on materials, which we have not. The Southern States have not half the value of buildings we have, arising from the climate and manner of living.

Hon. Mr. WHITE. If we are to be taxed by numbers, it will ruin all the poor people; but I do not understand the matter, and will wait to hear it explained.

Mr. SHURTLEFF wants to know whether five smart negro slaves are to be equal to three of our children?

Mr. NASSON thinks both sides should be stated. Mr. King says five of their infant slaves are equal to three of our Governors; but three of our infants are equal to five of their healthy, strong slaves. Besides, though our climates make us build houses, yet we have to work all summer for winter. Also, the representation is unequal between us and New Hampshire; also, our negroes are all free, and theirs are slaves.

Mr. RANDAL. Lands in the Southern States are as good as ours, if not better. It produces everything. Mr. Dana is mistaken; but as to the slaves, he is about right. The laboring part of the free men in the Southern States can live upon two days' work as easily as we can upon six. They can work all winter; we cannot.

January 18, 1788.

Mr. DALTON is in favor of the method of fixing the census; it is much in our favor.

Mr. COOLEY asks how the direct [tax] is to be apportioned among the inhabitants of any State.

Gen. BROOKS, of Lincoln. No rule is fixed in the Constitution; that is a legislative act, for Congress to determine.

Mr. RANDAL wants to know how far Mr. Dalton has travelled. Denies Mr. Dalton's facts.

Dr. HOLTON rises to give light; mentions the old rule of the census; found impracticable; compelled to have recourse to numbers, after long debate. As to the rule of representing a State's proportion, Congress must hereafter determine the matter, and make an internal tax, which is an *imperium in imperio;* it will bring on a war. I think the new rule is not in our favor, but am in favor of it, for it is all the rule we can get.

Dr. DAVIS wants to know of Dr. Holton, why our proportion has been lessened.

Dr. HOLTON does not recollect; but Massachusetts always insisted we stood too high; but the reduction was on no fixed principle.

SAM. THOMPSON. What States, in the debate, opposed the rule of numbers? Asks Dr. Holton.

Dr. HOLTON does not recollect. He was against the rule of numbers, because the Southern States had more land, and less numbers, than the Eastern.

Hon. Mr. DANA. Answers Dr. Davis's question, as it lies in his mind. The reason why our taxes were higher during the war than since, was because we were free from the public enemy, and money must be obtained where it could be had. Since the war, other States have been recovering.

Mr. DAWES observes that Dr. Holton likes this paragraph, if the Constitution prevails. Mr. Randal need no longer lament the want of abilities and eloquence on his side, since Dr. Holton has spoken. But to the question. Though slaves are reckoned five equal to three now, *yet in a few years slavery must be abolished*, and in the mean time slaves may be taxed on importation sixty shillings per head. *Slavery will not die of an apoplexy, but of a consumption.* As to direct taxation, Congress now have powers to make requisitions, but not to enforce them. Considers the revenue, as it relates to borrowing money abroad. Congress may never exercise direct taxes. Lands are not a proper rule of census; numbers are a better rule.

Mr. Randal. Sorry to hear it said that, after 1808, negroes would be free. If a Southern man heard it, he would call us pumpkins.

Mr. Wedgery objects to Mr. Dana's description of the Southern States. Their land is better than ours.

Mr. Dana says he never compared the value of the Eastern or Southern lands; he compared only the mode of cultivation.

Mr. Wedgery says, if this rule is for an equal poll-tax, he has no objection. But for a rule of apportionment it is unjust, Southern land being better than ours. In Virginia, one thousand acres has forty-eight polls; in Massachusetts, a family of six, to fifty acres, makes one hundred and twenty polls to the one thousand acres. In legislation, one Southern man with sixty slaves will have as much influence as thirty-seven freemen in the Eastern States.

Mr. Strong. This mode of census is not new. Our General Court have considered it, and the General Court have agreed. The Southern States have their inconveniences; none but negroes can work there; the buildings are worth nothing. When the delegates were apportioned, forty thousand was the number. Massachusetts had eight, and a fraction; New Hampshire two, and a large fraction. New Hampshire was allowed three, Georgia three, &c. Representation is large enough, because no private local interests are concerned. Very soon, as the country increases, it will be larger. He considered the increasing expense.

Mr. Wedgery asks whether the poverty of our lands was considered?

Mr. Sedgwick.

Mr. Randal talks a great deal, and says, as he sits down, that he has done better than he expected.

Col. PORTER.

Mr. RANDAL.

Col. PORTER.

Mr. ———, of Kittery, spoke against the slave-trade. We shall all suffer for joining with them, when they allow the slave-trade.

Mr. CABOT asks the gentleman from Sharon whether, in his five hundred miles' travel, he saw five thousand people who live as well as five thousand people of the lowest sort here. As to the slave-trade, the Southern States have the slave-trade, and are sovereign States. This Constitution is the best way to get rid of it.

Mr. RANDAL says he believes he has, but is not certain. If they do not, it is their own fault.

Mr. NASSON. Southern States are not poor.

Gen. THOMPSON. As to age — slavery — religion.

Adjourned to 3 o'clock.

The language used in debate, describing the reputation of our country abroad, forms an amusing contrast with the way of speaking on this topic which prevails at present. There are those who now think that we are not all of us always perfectly free from a slight tendency to vainglorious and boastful assertion of the great place we fill in the eyes of an admiring world. In this Convention, precisely such words as those of Captain Snow were not often used; but words of the same meaning frequently were, and seem to have startled nobody. This Captain Snow was a delegate from Harpswell in Cumberland County, Maine, and seems to have been an outspoken, common-sense kind of person. In arguing that the Constitution did not give Congress too much power, he says:

I, sir, since the war, have had commerce with six different nations of the globe, and I have inquired in what estimation America is held; and, if I may believe good, honest, credible men, *I find this country held in the same light by foreign nations as a well-behaved negro in a gentleman's family.* Suppose, Mr. President, I had a chance to make a good voyage, but I tiè my captain up to such strict orders that he can go to no other island to sell my vessel, although there is a certainty of his doing well. The consequence is, he returns, but makes a bad voyage, because he had not power enough to act his judgment (for honest men do right). Thus, sir, Congress cannot save us from destruction, because we tie their hands and give them no power ; (I think people have lost their privileges by not improving them ;) and I like this power being vested in Congress as well as any paragraph in the Constitution, — for as the man is accountable for his conduct, I think there is no danger. Now, Mr. President, to take all things into consideration, something more must be said to convince me to the contrary.

My father was not a frequent speaker, nor did he often speak at any length, if we may judge from the reported Debates. We extract the longest speech there ascribed to him, in part because it is probably as fair an exposition as can now be obtained of the views he was accustomed to express, and of his way of presenting them ; and in part because it states, in a very compact form, those opinions which seem to have prevailed among the friends of the Constitution. And there are remarks upon the working of this Constitution which might be not without their utility at the present day. The subject then before the Convention was the eighth section of the first article, which defines the powers of Congress. He said :

Mr. President : A great variety of supposed objections have been made against vesting Congress with some of the powers defined in the eighth section. Some of the objectors have considered the powers as unnecessary ; and others, that the people have not the proper security that these powers will not be abused. To most of these objections, answers, convincing, in my opinion, to a candid mind, have been given. But as some of the objections have not been noticed, I shall beg the indulgence of the Convention, while I very briefly consider them. And as it is my intention to avoid all repetition, my observations will necessarily be unconnected and desultory.

It has been said that the grant in this section includes all the possessions of the people, and divests them of everything; that such a grant is impolitic, for, as the poverty of an individual guards him against luxury and extravagance, so poverty in a ruler is a fence against tyranny and oppression. Sir, gentlemen do not distinguish between the government of an hereditary aristocracy, where the interest of the governors is very different from that of the subjects, and a government to be administered for the common good by the servants of the people, vested with delegated powers by popular elections at stated periods. The Federal Constitution establishes a government of the last description, and in this case the people divest themselves of nothing. The government and powers which the Congress can administer, are the mere result of a compact made by the people with each other for the common defence and general welfare. To talk, therefore, of keeping Congress poor, if it means anything, must mean a depriving the people themselves of their own resources. But if gentlemen will still insist that these powers are a grant from the people, and consequently improper, let it then be observed that it is now too late to impede the grant. It is already completed. The Congress under the Confederation are invested with it by solemn compact. They have powers to demand what moneys and forces they judge necessary for the common defence and general welfare; powers as extensive as those proposed in this Constitution. But it may be said, as the ways and means are reserved to the several States, they have a check upon Congress by refusing a compliance with the requisitions. Sir, is this the boasted check, — a check that can never be exercised but by perfidy and a breach of public faith, — by a violation of the most solemn stipulations? It is this check that has embarrassed us at home, *and made us contemptible abroad;* and will any honest man plume himself upon a check which an honest man would blush to exercise?

It has been objected, that the Constitution provides no religious test by oath, and we may have in power unprincipled men, atheists and pagans. No man can wish more ardently than I do, that all our public offices may be filled by men who fear God and hate wickedness; but it must remain with the electors to give the government this security. An oath will not do it. Will an unprincipled man be entangled by an oath? Will an atheist or a pagan dread the vengeance of the Christian's God, — a being, in his opinion, the creature of fancy and credulity? No man is so illiberal as to wish the confining of places of honor or profit to any one sect of Christians; but what security is it to government, that every public officer shall swear that he is a Christian? For what will then be called Christianity? One man will declare that the Christian religion is only an illumination of natural religion, and that he is a Christian; another Christian will assert that all men must be happy hereafter, in spite of themselves; a third Christian reverses this doctrine, and declares that, let a man do all he can, he will certainly be punished in another world; and a fourth will tell us, that, if a man use any force for the common defence, he violates every principle of Christianity. Sir, the only evidence we can have of the sincerity and excellency of a man's religion, is a good life; and I trust that such evidence will be required of every candidate by every elector. That man who acts an honest part to his neighbor, will most probably conduct honorably towards the public.

It has been objected, that we have not so good security against the abuse of power under the new Constitution, as the Confederation gives us. It is my deliberate opinion, that we have a better security. Under the Confederation, the whole power, executive and legislative, is vested in one body, in which the people have no representation, and where the States, the great and the small States, are equally represented; and all the checks the States have is a power to remove and disgrace an unfaithful servant, after the mischief is perpetrated. Under this Constitution, an equal representation, immediately from the people, is introduced, who by their negative, and the exclusive right of originating money-bills, have the power to control the Senate, where the sovereignty of the States is represented. But it has been objected, that in the old Confederation the States could at any time recall their delegates, and there was a rotation. No essential benefit could be derived to the people from these provisions, but great inconveniences would result from them. It has been observed by a gentleman who has argued against the Constitution, that a representative ought to have an intimate acquaintance with the circumstances of his constituents, and, after comparing them with the situation of every part of the Union, so conduct as to promote the common good. The sentiment is an excellent one, and ought to be engraved on the heart of every representative. But what is the effect of the power of recalling ? Your representative, with a threatening revocation over his head, will lose all ideas of the general good, and will dwindle to a servile agent, attempting to secure local and partial benefits by cabal and intrigue. There are great and insuperable objections to a rotation. It is an abridgment of the rights of the people, and it may deprive them, at critical seasons, of the services of the most important characters in the nation. It deprives a man of honorable ambition, whose highest glory is the applause of his fellow-citizens, of an efficient motive to great and patriotic exertions. The people individually have no method of testifying their esteem, but by a re-election ; and shall they be deprived of the honest satisfaction of wreathing for their friend and patriot a crown of laurel more durable than monarchy can bestow ?

It has been objected, that the Senate are made too independent upon the State Legislatures. No business under the Constitution of the Federal Convention could have been more embarrassing, than the constructing the Senate ; as that body must conduct our foreign negotiations, and establish and preserve a system of national politics, an uniform adherence to which can alone induce other nations to negotiate with and confide in us. It is certain, the change of the men who compose it should not be too frequent, and should be gradual. At the same time, suitable checks should be provided to prevent an abuse of power, and to continue their dependence on their constituents. I think the Convention have most happily extricated themselves from the embarrassment. Although the Senators are elected for six years, yet the Senate, as a body composed of the same men, can exist only for two years, without the consent of the States. If the States think proper, one third of that body may, at the end of every second year, be new men. When the Senate act as legislators, they are controllable at all times by the Representatives ; and in their executive capacity, in making treaties and conducting the national negotiations, the consent of two thirds is necessary, who must be united, to a man, (which is hardly possible,) or the new men biennially sent to the Senate, if the States choose it, can control them ; and at all times there will also be one third of the Senate, who, at the expiration of two years, must obtain a re-election, or return to the mass of the people. And yet the change of men in the Senate will be so gradual as not to destroy or disturb any national system of politics.

It is objected, that it is dangerous to allow the Senate a right of proposing alterations or amendments in money-bills; that the Senate may by this power increase the supplies, and establish profuse salaries; that for these reasons the Lords in the British Parliament have not this power, which is a great security to the liberties of Englishmen. I was much surprised at hearing this objection, and the grounds upon which it was supported. The reason why the Lords have not this power is founded on a principle in the English Constitution, that the Commons alone represent the whole property of the nation; and as a money-bill is a grant to the king, none can make the grant but those who represent the property of the nation; and the negative of the Lords is introduced to check the profusion of the Commons, and to guard their own property. The manner of passing a money-bill is conclusive evidence of these principles; for after the assent of the Lords, it does not remain with the clerk of the Parliament, but is returned to the Commons, who, by their Speaker, present it to the king, as the gift of the Commons. But every supposed control the Senate by this power may have over money-bills, they can have without it; for by private communications with the Representatives, they may as well insist upon an increase of the supplies, or salaries, as by official communications. But had not the Senate this power, the Representatives might tack any foreign matter to a money-bill, and compel the Senate to concur or lose the supplies. This might be done in critical seasons, when the Senate might give way to the encroachments of the Representatives, rather than sustain the odium of embarrassing the affairs of the nation. The balance between the two branches of the Legislature would in this way be endangered, if not destroyed, and the Constitution materially injured. This subject was fully considered by the Convention for forming the Constitution of Massachusetts, and the provision made by that body, after mature deliberation, is introduced into the Federal Constitution.

It was objected, that, by giving Congress a power of direct taxation, we give them power to destroy the State governments by prohibiting them from raising any moneys. But this objection is not founded in the Constitution. Congress have only a concurrent right with each State, in laying direct taxes, not an exclusive right; and the right of each State to direct taxation is equally extensive and perfect as the right of Congress. Any law, therefore, of the United States for securing to Congress more than a concurrent right with each State, is usurpation, and void.

It has been objected, that we have no bill of rights. If gentlemen who make this objection would consider what are the supposed inconveniences resulting from the want of a declaration of rights, I think they would soon satisfy themselves that the objection has no weight. Is there a single natural right we enjoy, uncontrolled by our own Legislature, that Congress can infringe? Not one. Is there a single political right secured to us by our Constitution, against the attempts of our own Legislature, which we are deprived of by this Constitution? Not one, that I can recollect. All the rights Congress can control, we have surrendered to our own Legislature; and the only question is, whether the people shall take from their own Legislatures a certain portion of the several sovereignties, and unite them in one head, for the more effectual securing of the national prosperity and happiness.

The honorable gentleman from Boston has stated at large most of the checks the people have against usurpation and the abuse of power under the proposed Constitution; but from the abundance of his matter he has, in my opinion, omitted two or three, which I shall mention. The oath the several legislative, executive, and judicial officers of the several States take to support the Federal Constitution, is as effectual a security against the usurpation of the general government, as it is against the encroachment of the State governments. For an increase of the powers by usurpation is as clearly a violation of the Federal Constitution, as a diminution of these powers by private encroachment; and that oath obliges the officers of the several States as vigorously to oppose the one as the other. But there is another check, founded in the nature of the Union, superior to all parchment checks that can be invented. If there should be a usurpation, it will not be upon the farmer and merchant, employed and attentive only to their several occupations; it will be upon thirteen Legislatures, completely organized, possessed of the confidence of the people, and having the means, as well as inclination, successfully to oppose it. Under these circumstances, none but madmen would attempt a usurpation. But, Sir, the people themselves have it in their power effectually to resist usurpation, without being driven to an appeal to arms. An act of usurpation is not obligatory, it is not law; and any man may be justified in his resistance. Let him be considered as a criminal by the general government, yet only his own fellow-citizens can convict him. They are his jury; and if they pronounce him innocent, not all the powers of Congress can hurt him. And innocent they certainly will pronounce him, if the supposed law he resisted was an act of usurpation.

My friend, Mr. John C. Gray, tells me that his father, the late Mr. William Gray, who was a member of the Convention, used to speak of my father as most zealous in his efforts to save the Constitution, and as leaving nothing undone which could help its adoption. He often related this, among other anecdotes of the time. At the close, when all were impatient for the vote, an aged gentleman, who had been a strenuous opponent, rose and asked permission to say a few words. But it seemed as if no one could be listened to any further, and he was stopped as by general consent. Then my father rose and begged for a hearing for him, and prevailed; and the gentleman avowed himself a friend of the Constitution, and determined to give it his support. And his few but emphatic words had much influence. It was afterwards found that my father had, in a long conversation of the preceding evening, finally overcome his objections, and he had promised to announce his conversion publicly if an opportunity were given him. Perhaps the following, (from the Centinel of March 8th, 1788,) on page 275 of the late edition of the Debates, may refer to this.

"On the day of the final decision on the question of ratifying the Federal Constitution by our Convention, when the Hon. Mr. Turner rose to make some observations on the subject, Dr. S., a delegate from a neighboring town, who voted in the minority, and who expected the honorable gentleman would do so too, whispered to a worthy member in the pew with him, 'Now, Sir, you will hear the truth.' When the honorable gentleman began to mention the dangers of rejecting the Constitution, the Doctor began to stare; but at the close of his speech, when he expressed his determination of voting in favor of it, the Doctor, rolling up his eyes and raising his hands, ejaculated, 'Help, Lord, for the righteous man faileth!'"

The anecdotes are indeed innumerable which have taught me how much my father had at heart the constitutional Union of the States, and how earnestly he labored for this end, in private and in public, and by all the means within his power. Yes, he was a Federalist, if ever there was one, and in the true and original sense of the word. With him and his co-workers, that phrase, The Federal Union, had a majestic meaning. In reviewing the history of those days, and reading the documents, public and private, in which that history was written, nothing strikes one more than the ardent zeal of the wise men of that day for a Union of the States; they earnestly desired a Union grounded upon the best principles, and protected by the best institutions they could get, but a Union at any rate. They believed that, if the Union were perpetuated, its own influence would gradually eliminate from it all evil, while it would confirm and develop all the elements of good. They were wiser than we, or they were more fortunate in seeing near enough for accurate measurement the tremendous mischiefs of non-union. To some of us, these mischiefs seem small matters; or rather, as I incline to think, they who, North, South, East, or West, talk with easy-flowing words about disunion, are able to do so for the very reason that in their inmost hearts they are not able to conceive of such a thing as disunion. The tritest of all possible figures is that which compares our Union to a tree, glorious in its strength and beauty; but it is trite because it is so true, that it suggests itself to the imagination at once. There it stands, with its deep roots grasping a hard but kindly soil, lifting its summit, year by year, nearer to the heaven from which come down the day and night, the summer and winter, the sunshine and storm, that in their very alternations nourish its might and its magnificence; towering into full sight of worn and wasted nations, who look to it with hope; spreading its great boughs wide enough to shelter all of mankind who may seek refuge under them, and giving in exuberant plenty food for all, — there it stands; but let the axe, the worm, or the tempest cast it down, and it becomes but a heap of broken branches.

Yet even this doom may be impending if the prosperity which this Union gives only hardens and corrupts the national heart. For then Providence will bring upon us, by taking the foundation of this prosperity away, the needed discipline of sorrow and humiliation.

The danger may not be so remote as is supposed. Hard words and hard thoughts, like other evil things, rapidly intensify themselves by indulgence; and threats, which in the beginning are idle, soon grow to be fearful. When so many of our people are saying, "Do this or do that, just at our own pleasure, or we will break up the Union," and so many are answering them, "We will do only what we think best, and you may leave us and dissolve the Union when you please," can a sober-minded man think that there is no danger? Can any man think of the thing less than disunion itself, that would be threatening, or should be alarming, if this be not? And yet how idle it is to utter even these feeble words of caution. When both parties are so far in the wrong as to justify the reproaches of opponents who are willing to see in their antagonists only what is wrong, and so far in the right as to excite the earnest sympathy of friends who can see in their own party only what is right, all human experience testifies that we have reached a point at which the very extremity of danger begins.

The great division between the lovers of liberty at any rate and of any kind, and those who thought that the best and most permanent liberty could only be secured by a wise and strong government, was as strongly marked in this Convention as in any assembly that ever sat; because this Convention adequately represented the State and the country. It is implied everywhere; and it comes out into open expression sometimes in an amusing way. Thus, Mr. Nasson, from Sanford, in York County, Maine, says:

> Great Britain, Sir, first attempted to enslave us, by declaring her laws supreme, and that she had a right to bind us in all cases whatever. What, Sir, roused the Americans to shake off the yoke preparing for them? It was this measure, the power to do which we are now about giving to Congress. And here, Sir, I beg the indulgence of this honorable body, to permit me to make a short apostrophe to liberty. O Liberty! thou greatest good, thou fairest property! With thee I wish to live, with thee I wish to die! Pardon me if I drop a tear on the peril to which she is exposed. I cannot, Sir, see this brightest of jewels tarnished, — a jewel worth ten thousand worlds! And shall we part with it so soon? O no! Gentlemen ask, Can it be supposed that a Constitution, so pregnant with danger, could come from the hands of those who framed it? Indeed, Sir, I am suspicious of my own judgment, when I contemplate this idea, when I see the list of illustrious names annexed to it; but, Sir, my duty to my constituents obliges me to oppose the measure they recommend, as obnoxious to their liberty and safety.
>
> When, Sir, we dissolved the political bands which connected us with Great Britain, we were in a state of nature. We then formed and adopted the Confederation, which must be considered as a sacred instrument; this confederates us under one head, as sovereign and independent States. Now, Sir, if we give Congress power to dissolve that Confederation, to what can we trust? If a nation consent thus to treat their most solemn compacts, who will ever trust them? Let us, Sir, begin with this Constitution, and see what it is. And first, "We, the people of

the United States, do," &c. If this, Sir, does not go to an annihilation of the State governments, and to a perfect consolidation of the whole Union, I do not know what does.

And Judge Sumner, from Roxbury, in reply, adverting to the pathetic apostrophe of Mr. Nasson, said:

I can with as much sincerity apostrophize: O Government! thou greatest good! thou best of blessings! With thee I wish to live; with thee I wish to die! Thou art as necessary to the support of the political body, as meat and bread are to the natural body. The learned Judge then turned his attention to the proposition submitted by the President, and said he sincerely hoped that it would meet the approbation of the Convention, as it appeared to him a remedy for all the difficulties which gentlemen in the course of the debates had mentioned.

This was precisely the question of that day, and of this day, as it will be of all coming days. I need not repeat, that my father stood firmly and consistently, in every word and act of his life, among them who desired a well and wisely balanced government, which should be strong enough to guard liberty from license and anarchy on the one hand, and from the iron hand of oppression on the other. His natural proclivity was certainly to the extreme of conservatism; and this he freely indulged in conversation, and perhaps in his common opinions; but when called upon to express or form a solemn determination, he seems to me to have labored, and not unsuccessfully, to find and stand upon the just medium.

The two parties were profoundly in earnest; and both rested, as they still do, on most real and substantial grounds. Each tended to an extreme, from which it was protected and saved by the influence of the other. And it was the misfortune of both, that each believed the other dishonest, and wilfully regardless of the true interests of the country. When Mr. Ames poured out his passionate and burning diatribes against revolutionary France, painting it — as he believed it to be, and on too good evidence — as a hell on earth, the Democrats of that day denounced his execrable ingratitude towards the country which had saved us from our tyrant, and verily believed he must desire a monarchy like that of England, where he might win nobility for himself. The wildest of his opponents uttered that outcry about "British gold," the inexpressible folly of which has not yet caused its entire suppression; and the milder among them thought that he and the whole party, with Washington at their head, in their fear of the British navy, and their desire of preserving from attack the infant prosperity of the country, truckled to the power which they had defeated, and ignominiously bought their peace by Jay's Treaty.

With Ames, Cabot, Strong, and others of that stamp, my father stood; and so convinced were they all, that in the example of England alone they could find anything in the world approaching the guarded liberty they loved, and in friendship with England the best protection against perils which then seemed to threaten us with ruin, — they could see in Jefferson and others, who loved a French alliance better, only an ill-concealed desire for the results of French republicanism, — for its rivers of blood, its defiance of God and man, its renunciation of all religion, and its destruction of all government.

In alluding to these opinions, I speak rather of a later phase of this controversy; of one not fully developed at the time of the Convention, but indicated then, and growing up into its full force in the years that immediately followed. Through all these years, my father did his share, no doubt, in abusing those whom he looked upon only as license-loving "Jacobins"; and he certainly had his full share of abuse as "an English aristocrat," whose pockets were full of English gold, and who would gladly have enslaved the people!

Quiet and temperate persons are sometimes shocked, and have reason to be, at the violence of party spirit in these days. But if we compare the present with the past, we may observe a great improvement, or certainly a great change, in this respect. If the pro-slavery and anti-slavery men, who are now the most fervent antagonists, sometimes exhibit anger and ferocity in their mutual objurgations, it is not true, as a general rule, that he who belongs to one of these parties is thereby entirely excluded from all social fellowship with members of the other party. They are not very forbearing or conciliatory towards each other, but they do sometimes meet within the same walls.

In my childhood, "Federalists" and "Jacobins" (as the Federalists called their opponents, intending to identify them with the revolutionary Jacobin Club of Paris) very seldom, I believe, met in society. I never saw one, to know him, until I was ten years old. Then, in 1807, a Mr. Cross, of Portland (who was called by us Uncle Cross, he having married my mother's sister), came to Boston on business; and my father, yielding I think to my mother's solicitations, invited him to dine. The fact was soon known in the family, and excited us all greatly; for Uncle Cross was a *Jacobin*, and that was the reason we had never seen him before. I waited for his coming with great interest. What I expected to see I do not remember; but it was something very uncommon; and very carefully I watched him. While the dinner was going on pleasantly, my father said, "Mr. Cross, take a glass of wine with me," and held the decanter to him; and in irrepressible surprise I uttered audibly, "Why, he is not a Jacobin, after all!" The remark caused some consternation. Uncle Cross, who was a very courteous gentleman, recovered at once from his share of it, and said, "No, my young friend, I am not a Jacobin; at least, I hope not. Did you think I was?" "Yes, sir," said I, "I have always heard so; but I see you are not, for I have heard father say, again and again, that nothing on earth would make him drink wine with a Jacobin." This explanation did not mend matters, and I was sent from the table;

and never again did I see Uncle Cross, although he lived many years after that first introduction.

My father-in-law, Nathaniel Chandler, was in the Legislature, about the year 1805, from Petersham, in Worcester County. He told me that a meeting of leading Federalists of the Legislature was held at the house of my father, who was not himself a member, to determine what should be done in a certain political crisis. The "Jacobins" seemed disposed to be quiet and conciliatory; and the question was, should the Federalists follow their example. Many thought they should; but my father scouted the idea. "Be sure," said he, "that, if you do not hear them at this moment, they have but retreated to their dens, there to concoct their venom into fiercer and more fatal virulence; and at the first moment they can catch you unawares, they will issue forth and strike." It seems to me that my father was a very kindly and good-natured sort of person, generally; but as a politician, I am afraid he was what Dr. Johnson delighted in, "a good hater." He certainly believed that in the "Jacobinism" of his day he saw principles and influences which, if not checked and suppressed, would end in the destruction of all liberty.

That was a day of violent language, and, I suppose, of violent feeling; but, with it all, there was some wisdom left. Then, as always, extremes produced extremes; and, in the excitement and exasperation of political antagonism, words were sometimes used which were more extreme than the speaker's thought. At a dinner party in New York, soon after the adoption of the Federal Constitution, the conversation turned upon the prospects of the country. One gentleman, whose name I never heard, was an earnest "friend of the people," and descanted with much enthusiasm upon the glorious future then opening upon this new-born nation, and predicted the perpetuity of our institutions, from the purity and intelligence of the people, their freedom from interest or prejudice, their enlightened love of liberty, &c., &c.

Alexander Hamilton was among the guests; and, his patience being somewhat exhausted, he replied with much emphasis, striking his hand upon the table, "Your people, sir, — your people is a great beast!" I have this anecdote from a friend, to whom it was related by one who was a guest at the table. After-dinner utterances have little value, unless, perhaps, their very levity makes them good indicators of the wind. We do not know the qualifying words which may have followed, or the tone and manner of that which was, perhaps, in part or in the whole, a jest. And it is fair to suppose that the remark, if it had any serious meaning, meant only that the people might be corrupted by prosperity and adulation, until they would lose all wisdom, and all principles of right, and all the guidance of reason. But after every possible allowance is made, the remark was a mistake; for the people is not a beast, but a MAN. It is no uncommon thing to hear it said of an individual, that he is a beast, or no better than a beast; and certainly nothing will so confirm in him the degrading propensities which brutalize him, as treating him like a beast. But, after all, he is a great deal more than a beast, even if a great deal worse; for he cannot cast off if he will the infinite possibilities and equal responsibilities which belong to him as a man.

So of the people. That foolish and wicked idolatry which panders to their self-conceit and nourishes that blinding vice, does all that can be done to degrade them, and make the pathway to a higher and better civilization long and difficult. But over us all there is Providence; and we may read His footsteps in the past, if we would know the direction towards which they point. History, which is but the biography of man, has much to say on this point; or, rather, when her instruction yields its utmost significance, says nothing else. We cannot observe how freedom has grown, from the despotism which has ever marked the Oriental World, through the lighter bondage of Greece, and the great municipal freedom which characterized the Roman Empire even under its despots, and the recognition of every man in his place and rights by the theory of the feudal system, — and so come to our own times, and see how woman, by a parallel progress, has advanced from the harem of the East to that position in our own day and land which gives her unprecedented power to assert and exercise her "woman's right" to make home happy, and co-operate fully with man in all that belongs to its peace, its hopes, and its unlimited influence for good, — we cannot observe these things, and doubt that it is the destiny of man to advance farther, and indefinitely farther. There must be with the whole, as with all masses and all individuals, discipline and whatever belongs to discipline. Therefore there must be lessons which will seem to be punishments; and the correction of grievous errors, even by grievous consequences; and fluctuations which make hope, for a time, difficult; and a freedom for self-culture which will sometimes be abused, and so lead to fearful mischiefs. But through it all there will be progress, because over it all there will be Providence; and how can this be denied by him who believes in the Infinite above us and beyond us.

There was a phrase in frequent use in my younger days, and not forgotten now, "*Vox populi, vox Dei,*" with which my father would have little patience. No one admitted more entirely that, in this country, and in each State, the people are sovereign, and have all the rights and incidents of sovereignty which in monarchical governments are vested in the king. All power, office, and authority come from them. Nor is the maxim of law, that "the king can do no wrong," inapplicable to the people in its just sense. All that this ever meant in law was, that there can be no higher power than the highest, and if there were a tribunal authorized to declare the sovereign wrong and pronounce sentence upon him, that tribunal, and not he, would be sovereign. So the assertion that the Pope is infallible was and is perfectly true in a similar sense, in the Roman Church, because he is the head of that Church, and there is no hierarchical authority higher than he (excepting, perhaps, an œcumenical council), who can declare him to be mistaken. The error is in supposing that these formulas mean that a king, personally, can do no wrong, or that a pope, personally, can make no mistake. Probably the great body of the subjects of a king understand the rule in this erroneous sense, and acknowledge the royal impeccability, or reject it, according to the strength of their loyalty; and so, undoubtedly, the great mass of Papists suppose that their Church recognizes its head as personally infallible. And precisely the same error is growing among us, and exists wherever persons believe that in the whole mass of the people corrective influences are powerful to compensate the intellectual or moral obliquities of individuals, and therefore that the decision of the mass is always right. It is undoubtedly an effect of this compensation, that the folly of the most foolish is corrected by the wisdom of those who are wiser; but it is just as certain, that their wisdom is also counteracted by the folly of their neighbors; because the common resultant of the whole must represent and exhibit the *average* good sense or silliness, purity or corruption, of all the individuals. In the illusion that the whole is or can be better than all its parts would make it, may perhaps be found our greatest danger. For this illusion must grow in strength and in mischief as long as they who have most to say to the people rest their claims to distinction or to subsistence upon a favor which they win by this adulation. And it is an illusion that tends strongly to make the people less able to see, or less disposed to obey, the truth, and less willing to believe their own need of improvement, because it hides from them the fact that a mass cannot be free from evil and error, while every individual of it has his own weakness and wickedness, and these are strengthened by mutual support and encouragement. Let this illusion, therefore, go much farther, and it must be permitted to cure itself in the only way in which it can be cured, and that is by its effects; and then the voice of the people will be seen and felt to be the voice of God, only as the tempest and the earthquake are his voice, and only as that is a voice of terror and destruction.

We are the only great nation in the world without a personal sovereign. We are the only great nation that possesses a constitution. The absolute dependence of these two facts upon each other should not be forgotten. Whatever may be thought of the possible utility of a constitution where there is a king, certain it is that the extremest need of one exists there where there is no king. For we who have no king, if we have no constitution, have nothing to reverence and obey; nothing to protect us from ourselves, from our own vagaries, our own follies, our own corruptions. Nor can a constitution, which is but supreme law, supply this want for a people that is not trained to love, respect, and obey the law. He that reverences and obeys nothing else, will be sure to obey himself, and the worst parts of himself, and will be the slave of a cruel master, who is made more cruel, more mad, and more destructive, by the unchecked exercise of his dominion; and this is as true of a nation as of a man. There are, however, principles of which the strong foundations were laid in the inmost depths of human nature, by Him who made man with the intent that he should associate with his brethren for his own happiness and theirs. Of these principles, those applicable to civil polity may, with their immediate and practical derivations, be constructed into a constitution, which is thereafter to bend, like the sky, over all, embracing all, and yet lifted far above the reach of any; there to rest, safe and giving safety; and unchangeable, until an unquestionable necessity teaches them whom it protects, how to make it wiser, stronger, and more protective. This is the theory. The practice is not quite so; and yet there is enough of it among us to justify the remark of a wise foreigner, that, with all our laxity and license, we are safe, because we alone among the nations do not look upon the law as our enemy. So may it be; for when it ceases so to be, we shall have passed across the line which separates political safety from political ruin.*

Let me say a word of the first of those whom I just now enumerated as the men with whom my father stood and labored. I never knew Fisher Ames personally. Born in 1758, he lived until 1808; but during his later years he was much confined to his home in Dedham, and I think, but am not sure, that I never saw him. Of nothing, however, am I more certain, than of the admiration and affection which my father felt for him, and often and warmly expressed. With what regard and confidence they were returned may appear, in some slight degree, from the letters of Mr. Ames which I insert in the Appendix. A slight incident occurred when I must have been a mere child; and why I remember it so perfectly I do not know. In my father's office a gentleman was urging him to do something, I forget what, but the answer I have never forgotten. "No, no. Go to Ames, and tell him to take hold at once, and he will; and give him a column of a newspaper, and he will do more than you and I and all of us can do by talking and writing for a month." I think I must have been struck with my father's earnestness, and that Mr. Ames's death, following soon after, impressed it upon my memory. I have said that

* It is, at the worst, but the waste of a small part of this page, if I quote here, from Hooker's Ecclesiastical Polity, a passage in which a great truth is clothed with adequate splendor of language. If any of my readers ask why I copy here what is so well known, I can only say, that the more it is known, the better, and none can know it too well.

"Of Law no less can be said, than that her seat is the bosom of God, her voice the harmony of the world. All things in heaven and earth do her homage; the very least as feeling her care, the greatest as not exempt from her power. Both angels and men, and all creatures of what condition soever, though each in different sort and manner, yet all with uniform consent, admiring her as the mother of their peace."

I did not know him personally; but I heard so much of him in the years immediately following his death, that there is no one of whose position and leading characteristics I have a more distinct impression.

No man in this community ever won so much public admiration, and, at the same time, the warm affection of so wide a circle of friends. His fame is now that of an eloquent man. It is deserved; for he was, perhaps, our most eloquent man. And his eloquence was also of a very noble character. It was not a gift, *per se*, consisting mainly of extraordinary power of speech; for it was formed by an harmonious union of the best and highest moral and intellectual qualities. As the very first among them, I name his perfect sincerity. It is an old rule, first uttered by a master of eloquence, If you wish to make others believe, you must yourself believe. His enthusiastic acceptance, without stay or doubt or hesitancy, of whatever he thought to be the truth, and his unreserved devotion to it, awoke in others a sympathetic faith. He was a strong man, and yet a child; and his strength was not weakened, but invigorated, by the tenderness, the playfulness, the simplicity, and the freshness, which seldom survive those early years which they make so attractive.

His logic was neither mechanical nor artistic. I would call it natural; for it seems to me precisely that. His own thoughts flowed on with an order so just, and led so directly to just conclusions, that other minds, if he could once win them to take one step with him, found no stopping-place until he and they had reached their journey's end; while his imagination presented everything to him so clearly, and so well arranged and defined, that he seemed always to be describing only what he looked upon. When we read, that after he had closed his great speech, in 1796, on Jay's Treaty, his opponents begged delay, that members might have an opportunity to recover their self-possession, we may wonder at this tribute to his power. But when we read the speech itself, we ask, What could delay do for them? what answer to his arguments could time suggest? what doubt could it throw upon his conclusions?

To return to my father: I think that, from the time of the Convention in 1788, he went very seldom into public life. And if he exerted any influence in politics, it was only by the depth of his convictions, by the strength of his reasons for them, and by the freedom and force of his expression of them.

He never shunned the subject of politics, whether in the shape of political principles, or measures, or men, or probabilities. Many and many were the animated conversations to which I listened, and heartily do I wish I could remember them more perfectly. The words or phrases, and nearly all of what may be called the particulars, have escaped me; but I think I cannot be mistaken in the substance.

If my readers remember that my only purpose in writing this memoir is to present my father *as he was*, they will excuse, or at least will understand, my strong desire to exhibit accurately his views and feelings in respect to the politics of the country. There is, however, this difficulty: while entirely certain of these *in general*, I am wholly unable to give them, either on authority or on definite recollection, *in particular*. After every effort which I can make to insure correctness, I venture to state what I believe to have been his views. His boldness, and his frequent use of unqualified language, led to the reproach in his own days (and it still survives), that he had no faith in the people, and no hope in the ultimate success of a democracy. This certainly was not true. Whatever were his fears, and whatever his disgust at the corruption and delusion which he saw or anticipated, there mingled with these a decided belief that curative, if not preventive elements, would be found in the very nature of democratic institutions.

I should say, then, that his principles and his opinions

would lead to the belief that there would be regular stages in the decline and decay of our actual system of government, and then in its restoration. At the beginning, the chief men of the country were placed, by the choice of the people, in the highest offices, and took them as a matter of course. He lived to see the day when such men were obliged to contend for prominence, and put forth their claims ; and to regard this as one sign that the people of this country had already begun to live upon the capital, both of political wisdom and political integrity, inherited from their fathers. In the next stage it would be necessary for great men who would have power, to descend to the same means of getting it which little men employed. Then would come a new period. On the one hand, strong and high men would be driven by disgust from the field of politics ; and on the other, the people would become unwilling to look up to their own creatures. Mediocrity would gain possession of nearly all power, by the free use of all the means of management.

The corruption of the constituent by the representative may then ascend, until it becomes the corruption of the representative by the constituent ; or by any who, at the doors of our legislative bodies, are begging for legislation that shall put money in their pockets. Plain bribery may ask, not always in whispers, for entrance to the halls, even the highest, from which our laws come forth ; and it may find not every heart inaccessible, and not every vote unpurchasable. They whose profession and business it is to live by office, may seek to mend their living by any means within their reach, with no check or limitation but those which are imposed by the necessity of caution in gathering such perilous gains. Vice may, therefore, continue to pay to Virtue the tribute of hypocrisy. But there may be explosions, from excess or incaution, and the secrets of the abyss may be, for a moment, revealed, by an exposure which will do as much harm as good ; for while the public turn away from it with a laugh of scorn, it will stimulate the greed of those who are longing to earn the same money, in the same, or in any way.

There may be some danger, when time shall confirm and consolidate these elements of evil, that the institutions and authorities of the country will, for all practical purposes, fall into the hands of an oligarchy as absolute as was that of the old republic of Venice; but it will be an oligarchy resting only on intrigue; or the worst form of government, standing on the basest foundation. It will be composed of professional politicians. This oligarchy, like that of Venice, will be somewhat hidden, but none the less powerful; and the chief magistrate himself, be he Doge or President, will be but its puppet. Like that, too, it will have the power of self-perpetuation, by absorbing into its ranks those who are fittest for its work. As a man shows himself skilful in intrigue and in the power of combination, and possessed of the proper audacity, and disposed to adopt office-seeking as a trade, he will be silently admitted into this oligarchy. There he will take rank according to his power and success in wielding the resources of corruption. If the country prospers and offers bread to honest industry, only the baser sort of people will accept subsistence from office; and then nearly all political and official power will be in the hands of those who stand low in intellectual rank, with little pretence to any higher talent than that of craft, and still lower in moral character. There will always be exceptions; for we cannot imagine a period when no man that is honest, and no man that is able, can hold high office in this country. But they will be only exceptions; and after a while they will be rare.

There is but one more downward possibility. Government and legislation cannot long go on under the prevailing control of self-seeking, of political corruption, and of mere cunning, without great practical mistakes, which will press heavily on the general prosperity. Then, it may be that the vast majority *on whom* power is exercised will no longer submit to the few who use it to their detriment. And then will come the great question, — and it will be indeed the question of life or death. I think my father sometimes feared that the general feeling would be, "We have tried liberty, and it means only misrule, and that means common disaster and distress." And the people will then consent, — at least by ineffectual resistance, — when a strong man comes to shatter the undermined fabric of constitutional liberty.

Hitherto, through all ages, the unvarying series has been regularly repeated, — freedom, corruption, anarchy, and despotism. If this fatal order is to be broken, — if a new result is to come in to vary the tale of history, it must be because new causes, of sufficient power, begin to operate. And this is so.

Generally my father, and they with whom he best agreed, were, I think, hopeful on this ground. Admitting that the downward path, to very near the bottom, would be by steps more or less similar to those above described, they still relied, with much hope, if not entire confidence, upon the fact that every man of the people of this country is in perfect liberty to say or to do what he thinks his interest or his duty requires, to preserve or improve the political institutions of the country, only keeping within the broad limits which exclude treason and rebellion. This is a new thing on the earth; a new thing in history; and it will be a new thing in its influence and effect. The decline in the political condition of the country will be arrested by it, when personal interest and prosperity are touched, and perhaps stricken down. For then will come the inquiry, What does this interest require us to do? and after a while the next question will occur, What does our duty require of us? and when duty is strengthened by interest, it has gained a great accession of power.

The first answer made to this inquiry of *interest* is, Look after the politics of the country; look after them as you look after your ships, your banks, your mills, your business, for it is of as much practical importance to you as any or all of these. And when duty asks also, the answer is, Begin at the beginning. Teach your children the true principles of politics, and how to keep a government free and prosperous; and impress upon them the duty, and exhibit to them the example, of vivid interest, and constant watchfulness, and careful discrimination as to the men to be placed in power; and teach all this as a thing which stands in positive rank and practical importance before Latin and Greek, or the calculus, whether integral or differential, or even book-keeping by single or double entry, however good in their place all these may be.

Then it may be hoped that the progress of things will be upward, instead of downward. Then, it may be hoped, with the advancing intelligence of the community, their understanding of their political duties will grow clearer; and with the improving morality of the community, their discharge of these duties will grow more complete and habitual; and it may even be hoped, that in that far distance Religion will find institutions which she may fill with her life, without casting upon them fetters, or finding her own purity tainted and diseased by their corruptions.

Even at the risk of a wearisome repetition, it must be said again, that I cannot name the place, or the hour, or the very words, at which or in which I know that my father expressed anything of this kind. If any reader choose to believe that I am wholly mistaken, and that I have no grounds for attributing these opinions to him, I can only say he may be right, but I think he is wrong. Impressions of this kind have lain on my mind from my boyhood, from the earliest day when I could have opinions on these subjects; and I have looked upon them as taught me by him; and as those which, if not in their full development, yet in their living germs, I was accustomed to hear from him and from those who were nearest to him in friendship and in sympathy. On this ground, and after earnest endeavors to make this statement *true*, I leave it to others to come to what conclusion, in respect to its accuracy, may seem to them reasonable.

I have already remarked, that my father was exceedingly unwilling to hold office. It has been often said, and sometimes in print, that the office of Attorney-General of the United States and a seat on the bench of the Supreme Court were offered him more than once. I happen to have some evidence that the place of Attorney-General of the United States was offered him; but I have my doubts whether a judgeship in the national court ever was. His determination not to hold office which would take him from home was early formed and expressed, and well known to his family and his personal friends. The following letter from the Hon. Timothy Pickering, and his answer, illustrate this determination of his. I infer from it that President Adams personally desired him to hold an office worth one thousand pounds sterling *per annum*, — in those days a large salary, — and added to the request what was, in fact, an assurance that, when this office ceased, he should receive any high professional appointment which should become vacant. It will be seen from his answer, that he declined the appointment, in terms and for reasons which would prevent a repetition of the offer.

Timothy Pickering to Theophilus Parsons.

Philadelphia, November 20, 1797.

Dear Sir:

I have now before me a letter from Colonel Innes of Virginia, one of our Commissioners for examining and deciding on the claims of British creditors of American citizens for debts contracted prior to the peace of 1783, by which it appears doubtful whether his health will be so far restored as to enable him again to join the board in this city. His colleague, Mr. Fitzsimons, has expressed a wish that we might think of a successor to Colonel Innes, in case he should not recover. The letter and this wish I have exhibited to the President of the United States, by whose direction I now communicate the information to you, for the purpose of ascertaining whether, in case of a vacancy, you would accept the office. The business, you are sensible, is of magnitude, and there will be some important law questions to be determined. None have yet been decided. The foundations of the board's proceedings are yet to be laid. Various causes have contributed to this delay.

Permit me to express an opinion, that you have long enough pursued the laborious practice of the law; and that your country is entitled to some portion of your life and eminent talents. These talents the President earnestly desires to bring into public action. In the strongest language he expressed these desires.

The business of the Commission will probably last two years; the salary of a Commissioner is one thousand pounds sterling *per annum*. When this employment ends, it is not improbable that you may be continued in the public service, if agreeable to you, in some other line, — if not immediately, yet with no long interval, — and in a station congenial to what has hitherto been the main business of your life.

The President is induced to ask, beforehand, whether, in case of vacancy, you would accept the office of Commissioner, that no time may be lost in supplying it, — seeing so great delays have thus far happened in this business.

You will oblige me by an early answer.

I am, with very great respect and esteem,

Dear Sir, your obedient servant,

TIMOTHY PICKERING.

THEOPHILUS PARSONS TO TIMOTHY PICKERING.

(No date on the copy.)

DEAR SIR:

I feel myself much obliged to the President and to you for the very friendly contents of your favor of the 20th ultimo. I have endeavored to prevail upon myself to meet the wishes of the President, and to believe that my present state of health is no objection. For about six weeks past I have been much oppressed by a vertiginous complaint, which at times deprives me of the power of reading. At the last terms of the courts, I was compelled to request some friend at the bar to read what the causes of my clients made necessary to be read. The disorder is in some degree removed, and I have delayed answering your letter, hoping that my health would soon be quite re-established. But I am disappointed, as I now have occasionally some slight returns of the original disorder. On this ground, my friends are opposed to my leaving home, and I confess that my opinion coincides with theirs, when I consider that the principles to be settled are new, of great national importance, and will require a close, critical, and probably a long attention. I am the more reconciled to the necessity of declining the appointment, as I have doubts whether the nomination of some other gentleman might not be more productive to the interests of the United States. The people certainly expect a rigid construction of the treaty, when perhaps it would not be difficult to convince me that provisions, whether introduced into a statute or treaty, for the purpose of redressing a *wrong* and of compensating an *injury*, ought to have a liberal construction.

I know it to be the duty of every man to support the government that protects him; and my vanity induces me to believe that, being in private life unconnected with the Administration by any honors or emoluments that are derived from it, I have been able from that situation the more effectually to contribute to its support among my fellow-citizens. Certainly the people of the County of Essex, from a union of political influence, have been kept, in the most critical seasons, firm and steady friends to the national government. In the political ship there must be common seamen as well as pilots; and a mutiny of the crew may as effectually destroy her as a division among the officers.

Believing, as I firmly do, that the political principles of the President are the only basis of an honest, effectual, and wise administration of the government, I wish him to be assured that he may command any assistance which he may think it in my power to furnish, and that a want of health or peculiar family considerations will alone prevent me from taking any ground he may think proper to assign me. I do not, my dear Sir, trouble you with these professions from any opinion that my services can be wanted in any place under government; for while the principal departments continue to be supplied with the characters of which they now boast, (not meaning to include the Vice-Presidency,) the people will rest assured that their sovereignty will be preserved, their honor protected, and their rights secured.

I am, with great respect and esteem, yours, &c.,

THEOPHILUS PARSONS.

It will be noticed that my father puts his refusal on the ground of ill health, and that he intimates that he might comply with the President's request at some other time. Soon after, he caused it to be understood that he could accept no office whatever.

After the adoption of the Constitution of the United States, he was never again active as a politician. In the very few instances in which he was in the Legislature, he was there rather as a lawyer, and he labored only in reference to certain reforms of the law.

To some of these I may refer in other chapters. To one of them, that relating to the rights and position of aliens in this country, which I mention here because it is in some measure a political topic, the following letter from Judge David Sewall drew my father's attention, or rather gave him especial occasion to consider it, for it was always a topic of much interest with him.

DAVID SEWALL TO THEOPHILUS PARSONS.

York, November 26th, 1781.

SIR:

My department in the revision of the laws, among other matters, includes *the inheritance, distribution, and partition of estates, conveyance of the same*, &c., the principal part of which I have done. The doctrine of alienage has attracted my attention for a day or two past, as an incidental matter, at least, to this part of my system. I have hammered out the enclosed bill, which I want your metaphysical head to scrutinize and polish. The general outline of the bill, I suppose, is the law of the land already, though, perhaps, not generally known. I conceive many nice distinctions may be made, in hearing a bill of this kind, between the Absentee Act, the Confiscation Bill, and the intention of the

Legislature in an act enabling the judge of probate to appoint agents to the estates of persons in Great Britain, and whether it can be thus heard without somehow interfering may be a question; and if it should cut off some of the excrescences of those statutes, — as perhaps they were originated on the spur of the occasion, — whether an act of this kind, even should that be the case, on general principles, would not be eligible. I have intentionally extended the disabilities, in some instances, beyond what some authorities seem to allow aliens; but I did not mean to injure the statute made in favor of the subjects of France, dying intestate, in personal estate, although I have neither of those acts before me. There is not, if my memory serves me, either in the Constitution or in any statute of this government, a precise definition of a *subject;* and it seemed to me expedient to approximate at least some degrees nearer the line of partition than has been done, and say who are not aliens. Your remarks on the bill, as well as the expediency of having one of the kind passed, to prevent inconveniences that may arise, will both oblige and gratify me.

Your humble servant,

David Sewall.

P. S. I wish you would draw an act for incorporating Dummer School into an academy, as that may put it beyond the power of a particular parish to frustrate the benevolent design of the donor. I should incline to have the master for the time being the incumbent, so that the estate might be brought completely within the usual phraseology of our tax acts, exempting grammar-school-masters, ministers, and their estates under their actual improvement, &c.; about seven trustees, of which the minister of Byfield for the time being should be one; the incumbent to be answerable for dilapidations; the trustees to take personal estate to a certain annual income, and, during the vacancy of a master, to bring trespass against any person who shall injure the realty, and take the profits until another master shall be appointed. There has been some talk in the Committee of Revision respecting a court merchant, or some speedy mode for foreigners that may trade hither to recover their demands; — perhaps a recognizance before some respectable person or persons in the seaports, and on a failure of paying the money at the day, execution to issue, in nature of a distress. But this is in Judge Sullivan's department.

Among his papers are some loose sheets, apparently forming part of an unfinished essay, or something of the kind, on the subject of aliens. There are many references to statutory provisions and to the principles of the common law, and various suggestions about them. But the beginning and the end are lost, and of what remains much is mere note or reference, unintelligible to any one but the writer; and I do not print it.

For many reasons I wish it had been more perfect, or that I could, from this or other authority, state with clearness and certainty his views in regard to aliens. I know very well what I believe them to have been; but I am not so sure of the grounds of my belief. I strive to recall his words, or those of his friends, but I cannot. But while my recollections on this subject are very dim, I have little or no doubt of their general accuracy.

I should say, then, that he was disposed to open to immigrants an entrance into this country without any reservation whatever, except against crime. It was his firm belief, that Providence was constructing here a refuge for the oppressed of every nation; and when they fled from suffering, or from rational fears of misgovernment, or to improve their condition by the facilities which our wide lands and unfettered industry offered them, he would meet them at our shores with sincere and earnest welcome, and would make all necessary provision for their entire security and their prosperity. But that this country might continue to be a refuge for those who were oppressed or threatened in other lands, it must be preserved from the mischiefs which have made the institutions and government of those other lands oppressive and destructive. It must be protected against the peril of importing with those who had fled from other countries the very evils and abuses from which they fled, or the illusions and corruptions which would lead inevitably to the same results. If in other countries guarded and legal liberty is impossible, it must be because the subjects of those countries are incapable of comprehending and preserving it; and let those subjects bring to this country the same unfitness and incapacity, and let them possess political power here, and the same impossibility of preserving constitutional liberty will exist here. If this country is to remain better than other countries, — better, that is, in all the advantages which our institutions permit or confer, — these institutions must be guarded equally from violent and from insidious assault. For the sake, not of ourselves merely, but of those very immigrants, they must be prevented from any interference with, or any influence over, our political institutions, until they have outgrown the ways of thinking or feeling or acting which belonged to the home they left. If they come here without the wish to become American in character as well as in nationality, assuredly they should not ask, or if they asked they should not be permitted, to possess the right of interference with the formation or the administration of our laws. And if they did wish to become American, and were rational and honest, their wish would be to become American not merely in their rights, but in their correlative duties, and in their fitness and capacity for the discharge of those duties.

In few words, my father's principle would be, that no foreigner should become a citizen of this country until all reasonable provisions and precautions were complied with, to promote his becoming so in heart and in intellect. He anticipated a rapid and extensive increase in the prosperity of this country, and a proportional increase in the attractions it holds out to those who hang loose upon the fringes of society elsewhere, and are easily shaken off. I am mistaken if he did not foretell, frequently and emphatically, that marvellous flood of immigration which fills our country with all the races, and all the habits, and nearly all the errors and abuses, which prevail anywhere in the world. And he hoped that this flood, with all its feculence and turbulence, might nevertheless enrich, and not overwhelm, our country, provided only the proper distinction was made. For he would have the coming immigrant welcomed to a full share in all our prosperity, but to no share whatever in the franchises which would affect the laws or institutions by which that prosperity was protected, until time, the great teacher, had taught him the true difference between all that he had left, and all that he had found. For it is too much to ask of any human beings, that they should comprehend at once things so totally novel as everything here must be to a European. And it is too much to ask of any human institutions, that, while young and yielding, and undefended by the protecting power of antiquity, they should successfully resist the unremitting blows of prejudice, passion, and ignorance; and therefore adequate provision must be made that those blows should not reach them.

But, now that I have written this, my recollection of it seems so indistinct, and my evidence so slight, that it seems to me little better than conjecture. But it may stand for whatever it is worth.

As an instance of the methods he sometimes adopted to make known his opinions upon interesting political or legal opinions, I may give here the following letter to Mr. Tracy, of which I find a copy among his papers. It has no date, but undoubtedly refers to Shays's rebellion.

Theophilus Parsons to Nathaniel Tracy.

Dear Sir:

I was informed, just as I left Boston, that it had been asserted in Mr. Paine's insurance office, in your presence, *as my opinion*, that the Governor had no authority to assemble the militia in martial array, and with them, by force of arms, to seize the insurgents, and to fire upon them if it should be necessary, in order to the defeating of their designs and the bringing of them to punishment, *inasmuch as the Legislature had not declared a rebellion to exist.* I was also informed that you contradicted the assertion, knowing my opinion to be very different. I feel myself much obliged to you for your friendly conduct; and I assure you that you were perfectly right. The authority of the Governor, at this day, is a matter of great consequence to the public, and I fear that doubts about the true extent of it have already produced measures which I think very unfortunate to the Commonwealth. As it is of so much importance that the public mind should be rightly settled upon this question, I wish gentlemen of influence and ability would take some pains to diffuse just apprehensions of the matter. Though, as a professional man, I have no influence, yet, to satisfy you and my friends that the opinion I have formed is not a hasty and premature one, I have devoted a leisure hour to send you the reasons that influenced me. But first let us settle the fact, before we reason upon the law. And I suppose it will be admitted that the insurgents have embodied themselves as an armed force under certain leaders; that they have acted in a warlike, hostile manner; that their declared intention is, the attacking of the administration of justice; that, in pursuance of this declaration, they have, in a warlike and hostile manner, prevented the sitting of the courts of common pleas in the counties of Berkshire, Hampshire, Worcester, Middlesex, and Bristol; that they have discovered the same hostile intention against the judges of the Supreme Judicial Court, and have collected, in a warlike, hostile manner, to support such intentions. If these facts are admitted, the perpetrators of them must be considered *as traitors, levying war against the Commonwealth; as persons who, in a hostile manner, are attempting and enterprising the destruction, detriment, and annoyance of the Commonwealth.*

Now, any private person may, by his own authority, arrest any felon or traitor; and, if he cannot do it without assistance, he may call others to his aid; and if the felon or traitor fly or resist, he may justify *killing* him, if he cannot otherwise be taken. This authority private persons have by force of the common law; and it would seem strange if the Commander-in-chief, and the citizens in martial array under him, should not have equal authority. But the authority of the Governor does not rest upon legal deductions, formed from the right an individual is, in this case, invested with by the common law, however conclusive such deductions may be esteemed.

The Constitution provides, among other things, that the Governor shall be the commander-in-chief of the militia; that he may, for the special defence and safety of the Commonwealth, assemble in martial array the inhabitants thereof; that he may lead and conduct them, and encounter *by force of arms*, and also *kill, slay, and destroy, if necessary*, all and every such person and persons as shall, *in a hostile manner, attempt or enterprise the destruction, invasion, detriment, or annoyance of the Commonwealth*, and that he may exercise over the militia *in actual service* the law martial, in time of war or invasion, and also in time of rebellion, *declared by the Legislature to exist.* Now if it is admitted that the insurgents are traitors, *levying war in a hostile manner against the Commonwealth*, they must be considered as attempting and enterprising the detriment and annoyance of it, and therefore come within the description of those persons pointed out in the Constitution; and the Governor must consequently have the authority contended for. The Constitution gives it to him. The safety of the Commonwealth requires it. Whatever doubts have been stated upon this question, they must, I conceive, have arisen from the clause giving the exercise of martial law. But I do not see how that clause can, upon consideration, affect the question. True it is, that martial law cannot be exercised over the militia in actual service during a rebellion, *but when such rebellion has been recognized by the Legislature;* but can this interfere with the Governor's right to use force to crush the rebellion, to bring the perpetrators to public justice, and to kill those actually in arms against the Commonwealth, and acting in a hostile manner, who cannot otherwise be taken? That traitors in arms against the Commonwealth, and acting in a hostile manner, are within the description of those persons whom the Governor may attack and kill, if necessary to support the government, there can be no doubt, for they come within the express words of the Constitution, — *and the Governor hath not any authority to use force to suppress any rebellion declared to exist by the Legislature, unless he derives it from the same words.* And further, the limitation he is under from exercising martial law is confined to the army, navy, or militia in actual service, and is not extended to include the rebels in arms.

It may then be asked, Of what import is this limitation? The answer is obvious. The militia are thereby protected from the effects of martial law; they must still be governed by the fixed and stated laws of the land, and subject only to the pains and penalties therein provided. The framers of the Constitution supposed, perhaps erroneously, that in ordinary cases of rebellion those pains and penalties would produce an adequate force for the public protection; that a sufficient number of brave, loyal, and determined citizens would always appear ready to support their government; that a majority of the people would be too wise and too well informed to permit the basis of their rights and privileges to be overturned by a needy, desperate banditti; that to support their Constitution, and to guard their liberties, motives superior to the sanctions of martial law would operate; that an attachment to the rights of mankind, a love to their country, and a regard to themselves and to their posterity, would produce a force superior to what the artifices of treason or the frenzy of rebellion could form; that the subjugation of traitors in arms would commonly be the work of a short period, during which every good citizen would cheerfully leave his ordinary occupation; and that, when a rebellion had acquired such strength as rendered a long time necessary to suppress it, and the militia must be kept some time in the field, then the Legislature might introduce the martial law, by declaring a rebellion to exist. If a case should ever arise when the militia should refuse to take the field in sufficient force to support the government, the Legislature must make such provision as the emergency shall require, by directing impresses, granting bounties, &c., &c.; but martial law, by the Constitution, is to be exercised only over the army, navy, or *militia in actual service.*

Such are the reasons which have induced me to form my opinion, and I sincerely wish that all our *rulers* had entertained the same, and given it its full operation. We should not then have been puzzled to distinguish between political wisdom and personal timidity, nor between lenient measures and a submission to the claims of rebels in arms. But, *nil desperandum de republica.* It is not yet too late; but if spirited measures are not adopted, *and executed,* before the next election, I fear the most alarming apprehensions will be justified.

Yours sincerely,

THEOPH. PARSONS.

To the close of his life he took an interest in the politics of the State, and exerted an influence upon them; but not, I am persuaded, so great an influence as was imputed to him by some persons.

It need not be said that he remained always a Federalist, for the Federal party was the party of conservatism; and therefore he was always, thoroughly and without reserve or qualification, a Federalist. He was of the school of Strong, Lowell, Cabot, Ames, Otis, Pickering, and Prescott; and was, I suppose, (Ames perhaps, not certainly, excepted,) the most determined, resolute, and uncompromising — his opponents said the most violent — of them all. Many of those whose names I have mentioned were, however, much more active than he was. I cannot, I think, be mistaken in supposing that he gave but little of his time or labor to politics. He was always at home when not called abroad professionally. His ways of life were perfectly well known to all his family, as his office was always in his dwelling-house, and he almost always in it. I doubt whether he ever attended a public meeting of any kind during the last twenty years of his life. I spent much of my time in his office. I can tell, and presently shall, of the many hours he spent with his books, his instruments, and his scientific friends; but I cannot recall any one gathering, great or small, in the office or elsewhere in the house, for political purposes. No doubt there were such meetings, but they were never frequent; and very few took place, I think, during the last ten years of his life.

In his day, most men of any prominence were accustomed to send communications to the newspapers, in support of whatever opinions they wished to enforce; generally under an assumed but recognized name. Some persons, as Ames, Sullivan, and the younger Lowell, did this very frequently. But I cannot exhibit or illustrate my father's opinions by writings of this kind, for I have not been able to ascertain that he ever published one such article.

Among those of my father's papers which I still have, are a few letters from eminent men of his day, relating, more or less directly, to political subjects. These I shall print in the Appendix.

CHAPTER IV.

OF HIM AS A LAWYER.

I HAVE not the slightest recollection of my father as a lawyer. When he went upon the bench I was nine years old. During the next seven years he was a judge, and as such I remember many things about him, but nothing of his professional position or conduct before that period.

The law was, however, not only his profession, but his only means of subsistence. If there be any foundation for what has been already said of him, it would be inferred that he would labor strenuously for success, and that he would succeed. And I suppose he did succeed, soon, completely, and permanently.

For this success it might be enough to refer to his general intelligence, his devotion to duty, and his earnest industry. By him, however, it was attributed in good part to a specific cause, to which I have already alluded; and that was, the opportunity he had of studying the law, under circumstances peculiarly favorable, with Judge Trowbridge. I have already anticipated upon this point what might have been deferred perhaps more appropriately to this chapter. I repeat, however, that this eminent jurist dearly loved the law as a science. He took with him to my grandfather's house the best law library then existing in America; for in those days law-books could only be had by importing them at great cost from England. There he found in my father a young man of intelligence, who possessed the power and habit of persistent industry, and who repaid the Judge's endeavor to teach by an enthusiastic desire to learn. There, by the compulsion of circumstances, which my father greatly regretted at the time, and which seemed to throw a blight over prospects that had opened brilliantly, they remained a considerable time; and, instead of pursuing the practice of his profession and earning a living as soon as he was ready to begin, my father was compelled to stay at home, doing only what little business came within his reach, and employed with all his might in a close and uninterrupted study of the principles and the authorities of the law.

The consequence of this was, that, when he entered more fully upon the practice of his profession, he had a decided advantage over every other man of his time; and the consequence of this, again, was the promptitude and entireness of his success. He first began business in Falmouth (now Portland), as has been said, and removed to Essex County when about twenty-five years old. When he was twenty-nine, Judge Greenleaf of Newburyport said to his daughter Elizabeth, who kept his house, that on such a day she must provide a dinner for a few friends, and among them he mentioned "Mr. Parsons," who at that time had never been in his house. "Do you mean Mr. Parsons whom everybody is talking about?" said Miss Betsey; "why, I shall not dare to utter a word." "Well," said the Judge, "you need not; he will talk for you and himself too, if you wish it." This story my mother used to tell; and, while very liberal allowances must be made for such an anecdote, so told, before it can have the value of an historical verity, there must have been some foundation for it, for we know that a year or two before this he had been the leading mind and voice of the "Essex Junto," which would hardly have happened unless he had won a decided position. At all events, he talked then and afterwards well enough to win a suit which he used to say was worth all the others he had ever gained in his life; for in less than a year after that dinner he married Miss Betsey.

Apart from family anecdotes and traditions, and the stories of old friends, which are much the same thing as family traditions, one circumstance indicates this early and decided success, perhaps conclusively. He was a prudent man, and lived within his means, from the first day in which he had means. At thirty, he married, and immediately hired a house in Newburyport, in which he resided until 1790, when he built, as I have already stated, a large house in Green Street, which he occupied while he remained in Newburyport. He kept servants and horses, and saw much company, and from his marriage lived in a way which would have been very extravagant, if he were not even then justified in relying both on the profitableness and the permanence of his business. His account-books, to which I have already alluded, prove that his business was large at the beginning, and, after it recovered from the check caused by the burning of Falmouth, never grew less, but constantly increased.

He remained in Newburyport until 1800, when, at the age of fifty, he removed to Boston. Before his removal he was in the habit of practising in all the New England States, as well as in all parts of Massachusetts; and sometimes, though very rarely, in New York, and before the Supreme Court of the United States.

When he left Newburyport for Boston, gentlemen in that town gave him a farewell dinner, of which I never heard anything but the enthusiastic toast of Robert Treat Paine, the poet, who had been my father's pupil, and continued to be, while he lived, his intimate friend: "Theophilus Parsons, the oracle of law, the pillar of politics, the bulwark of government." To which my father replied: "The Town of Newburyport, — may the blessing of Heaven rest upon it as long as its shores are washed by the Merrimac."

Let me in this connection mention another anecdote in which Paine is concerned, which was told me by one who was present. When Washington died, Paine was appointed to deliver a eulogy, and my father gave a large dinner on the occasion. The numerous guests were assembled, and the eulogy was praised emphatically and unanimously, with one important exception. The Rev. Mr. Cary had come, not to dine with the orator, but *to protest against the oration.* He was my father's minister, and one of the best of men. His trouble lay with this sentence of the eulogy: "Legate of Heaven, he has returned with the tidings of his mission; father of his people, he has ascended to plead their cause in the bosom of his God." My father did what he could to qualify or excuse these expressions; but it was in vain. "No, no, sir," said the faithful minister; "you cannot defend and you cannot explain that language; for you cannot prove to us that there can be more than one mediator between God and man."

Robert Treat Paine was the poet of his day, and in that day enthusiastically admired. I remember hearing what were thought the great sums of money paid him for his poems. He was then praised beyond his merits, and now his actual merit is forgotten. He was the son of Judge Paine, and was baptized with the name of Thomas. But when Tom Paine the infidel made that name infamous, he had his name changed, and took that of his father. Soon after, an old friend, forgetting the change, called him by his old name. "Don't call me Tom Paine any more," said he; "I have a Christian name now." He was a brilliant companion, but yielded to the seductions of society more than was consistent with a due devotion to his profession. He died in 1811, at the age of thirty-seven.

Of my father's almost intemperate study through the time spent with Judge Trowbridge, I have certain and abundant proof. After all the waste and dispersion of his papers, of which I have already spoken, I have still manuscripts enough to fill some volumes, which were written by him in that period. They fully confirm and illustrate what I have heard him say was his method of study. It was by writing. He took topic after topic, and after a thorough and exhaustive investigation of the decisions and dicta, he made an abstract of all the principles which belonged to it, and of all the authorities which bore upon them. These manuscripts indicate three things. One is, the very wide extent and thoroughness of his studies and investigations. Another is, the excellence and magnitude of the library he had at command. It seems to have contained all the valuable books on English law then in existence. And still another, which I might not have inferred from the manuscripts themselves, if I had not heard him say it; it is, that the fear lest he should be unable to gain access to such a library for many years, led him to make copious abstracts and quotations, which would answer his purpose in the absence of the books.

To this exact preparation on a variety of special subjects, my father owed, as I think, not only his early success, but much of the ease and comfort with which he practised or administered the law during his life. Chief Justice Isaac Parker, who was one of his most intimate friends, and for seven years his colleague, often told me that the manuscripts were continually used by him in forming his opinions; and that when away from home, and with neither them nor the books from which they were taken within his reach, his memory would recall any one as it was wanted; and some of his opinions, which embodied a series of important legal propositions, were drafted without looking into a book.

I have heard very many anecdotes of the advantages he gained from this method and completeness of study. I will mention but two. One I have heard from several sources, but most directly from Mr. William Wells, of Cambridge. He was a very young man, in Hartford, Connecticut, at the time my father went there, retained by the State of Connecticut to meet Alexander Hamilton in a case to be tried before Chief Justice Ellsworth. After the trial, he dined at

Mr. Wadsworth's, who had invited the leading members of the court and bar then in Hartford. At dinner, Hamilton said: "Mr. Parsons, pray let me ask you one thing. The point I made" (describing it) "was suggested to me only after much study of the case, and then almost by accident, but I thought it very strong. You were fully prepared for it, and gathered and exhibited the authorities at once, and prevailed, and I must submit; but I was a good deal surprised at it; and what I want to know is, whether you had anticipated that point?" "Not in the least," was the answer; "but, so long ago as when I was studying with Judge Trowbridge, the question was suggested to me, and I made a brief of the authorities, which I happened to have brought here with me, and I found the books in Judge Ellsworth's library."

The other anecdote my father was fond of telling, as an illustration of the assistance these notes had given him. He mentioned it to Mr. Webster, when he was a student in Boston; and by Mr. Webster it was often repeated. "While I was studying in Byfield, Judge Trowbridge said to me, that he thought the practice of the English common-law courts, in requiring proof of a will devising real estate whenever it was to be used in those courts in support of title, should not be held as applicable here, because, from the nature and practice of our courts of probate, and their relation to other courts, the original proof in probate ought to be sufficient and conclusive; and if the will were subsequently wanted as evidence in another court, a mere record of the judgment and decree of probate should be enough, and indeed all that could there be received, because those inquiries which precede probate belong here exclusively to a court of probate. Accordingly, I examined this question, and made my brief, and filed it away. Almost the first case I had in court presented this question. I was only junior counsel, and my senior was one of the leading lawyers of the day. We needed to use a will which had received probate; but the witnesses by whom we could prove it anew, in the

English fashion, were unexpectedly absent. I suggested to my senior that this new proof was unnecessary. 'Nonsense,' said he, 'I shall make no such point as that.' 'May I, then?' said I. 'Yes, but on your own responsibility.' I made the point. The court said the practice was uniformly against me, here as well as in England,— they had no doubt about it; but if I wished to be heard in support of my new views, they would hear me. Whereupon I argued from my brief, and just as well as if I had had a month of preparation. I satisfied the court, succeeded in my point, and gained a most undeserved reputation for marvellous readiness and universal knowledge. And I found the effects of this in the immediate increase of my business."

It was common, as some of the papers I print will show, to speak of his memory as wonderful, as never losing anything intrusted to it, and as keeping everything in readiness for instant use. But a distinction must be taken here. He had that memory for some things, but a very poor memory indeed for others. It has been said that memory is of two kinds, — the *arbitrary* and the *associative*. By the first, facts or words are retained and recalled, which stand in no necessary connection with anything else, and might as well have been any other things as what they are. The names of persons are words of this kind; and there are those who remember them easily and always. It is said to belong to the royal families of Europe seldom to forget the face and name of any one presented to them. If this be so, it may be but the inheritance of faculties invigorated by years of exercise through many generations. Ludicrous stories are told of Napoleon the First, who tried to manifest this attribute of royalty, and made amusing blunders in so doing. This memory is called arbitrary, because the words remembered are arbitrary. Mr. John Smith might as well have been named Thomas Brown, or *vice versa;* and therefore it is not easy to see any theory or proposition or truth which derives illustration from the fact that this individual rather than another has this rather than any other name.

On the other hand, facts or principles from which inferences may be drawn, and which lead to or from conclusions, and to this end connect themselves indissolubly with other facts or principles, — these are not isolated or arbitrary. Change them, and you change the whole structure of which they are a part. They are fastened to the mind by their antecedents or consequences or associates; and the memory which retains and recalls them has been called the associative memory.

I have stated this to illustrate a peculiarity of my father's mind. His *associative memory* was, I believe, very remarkable. So I have always heard, and multitudinous are the anecdotes which help to prove it. I have a strong impression, but nothing more, that I have heard him say that he never lost his hold upon a fact, a statement, or a principle, of which he could make any use. I think I have heard him say such things when speaking of his very feeble memory of mere names. About this I remember only that it was a matter of jesting occasionally in the family, and that he often laughed about his inability to recollect such words. It led to a habit which sometimes amused us. He was apt to classify persons, and apply to all of each kind some name fixed in his mind as belonging to them. Thus, soon after his marriage, he used to deal with a Mr. Patch, of Essex County, — I think of the town of Ipswich, — for horses, and always afterwards he called everybody he dealt with about horses by that name. When I was a boy, he bought horses of a Mr. Trask, in Boston; and I have often heard him call him "Patch"; and when my elder brother, who was a little scandalized by this would tell him, more than once, "Father, this is Mr. Trask, not Mr. Patch," the answer was, "No matter, my son; Patch does just as well"; and, well or ill, it continued to do service for Trask.

I attribute to this peculiarity of memory also, at least in part, the fact that, in his opinions as judge, he cites fewer cases than any judge reported in our language, with the possible exception of Chief Justice Marshall. Judge Parker used to say of him, half in jest, that he knew everything that was in every case in the Reports except the name. He used the reports freely, and studied them with great care; and, from what I have heard, I should say he could find his cases with unusual facility and rapidity. But after he had found a case, and read it, and made of it all the use of which it was capable, he seemed to let the name and place pass from his memory.

My colleague, Chief Justice Joel Parker, relates to me a circumstance that occurred in Hillsborough County, New Hampshire, some seventy years ago, which illustrates the strength of his memory for facts and principles. He had argued a case there, and got a verdict. The losing party claimed a review, and the case was tried again the next year. My father was retained to argue it again; but some delay occurred, and he came into court only after the evidence was in, and the arguments were closed, all but his own, and the counsel with him was preparing to speak for him. He said to my father at once, that he must argue the case. "But how can that be? I know nothing of the evidence, or of the points or questions raised." He was then told that they were substantially the same as they were the year before; and upon this statement, and trusting to his memory only, he argued the case again, and again obtained a verdict.

His early success was promoted by his making himself master of the law of prize and admiralty, of which few lawyers then knew anything. I think he did this from an intimation from Judge Trowbridge, that this branch of business would probably be made profitable by the events of war. In fact, he had almost the monopoly of it; and it was very profitable. I infer, from all I can learn about it, that the late Governor Sullivan, Judge Lowell, and my father were the only practising lawyers who had much knowledge of this interesting department of the law. They, certainly, were masters of it. My mother used to speak of the "prize times," which lasted but a year or two after her marriage, as the most profitable, in her view, which she had ever known. The clients got their money easily, and spent it as easily. She used to show me, in my boyhood, a chest or box, such, I suppose, as used to be called a "strong-box," which served in my day only as a tea-chest. But it had a lock of peculiar strength, and I think was intended to hold valuables. At all events, she said my father kept it in her closet, and put therein bullion or coin when he received it, and she had seen it nearly full. We have now in the family a dozen heavy, silver-gilt spoons, that a master of a privateer, after paying my father's bill, threw into her lap as she sat in his office, — which was always in his house, and occasionally resorted to by all the members of his family, — "because," said the sailor, "I don't think the squire has charged me half enough." In the letters I put in the Appendix, there are indications that our privateers were busy and successful. My father used to speak of one of his clients (a merchant in Newburyport), who often said, "I have prayed to the Lord to make me rich, and I believe I have prayed too hard, for I think he means *to drown me out*." The same man said, at my father's table, "If I threw a shingle in the water as the tide turned out, and laid a dollar on it, I believe the next flood tide would bring it back with ten more." He was then thought to be exceedingly rich; but, not many years afterwards, he died a bankrupt.

I never saw my father in court, as a lawyer, but have heard so much of him, that I have a well-defined idea of his manner. It was said to have been easy and familiar to the last degree. There was no studied beginning nor ending, nothing of the manner, or the tricks, or the graces of the orator, and no approach to them. His business was to persuade those twelve men of the truth of certain propositions; and he did his work in the most direct, the plainest, and the simplest way. His strength undoubtedly lay in his reasoning. But there was an actual, and I rather think a studied, absence of all appearance of eloquence, and even of technical logic.

Chief Justice Isaac Parker often spoke of the first case in which he ever saw him, and heartily would he laugh about it. Parker was living in Maine, and either a student, or very young in his profession. My father, then also a young man, had been sent for in some important case. He was quite unknown to all persons outside the bar, and not well known even to the lawyers. Parker had only heard of him as a rising man. When his turn came to argue the case he put one foot in his chair, and, with an elbow on his knee, leaned over, and began to talk about the case as a man might talk to his neighbor by his fireside. "Pretty soon," said Parker, "I thought I understood him. He was winding that jury round his fingers. He made no show; he treated the case as if it were a simple affair, of which the conclusion was obvious and inevitable; and he did not talk long. He got a verdict at once; and after the jury were dismissed, one of them, whom I happened to know, came to me and said, 'Who is this Mr. Parsons? He is not much of a lawyer, and don't talk or look as if he would ever be one; *but he seems to be a real good sort of a man.*'"

Judge Parker, in the Address to the Jury, to which I have often referred, and must refer again, says: "At that early period of his life, his most formidable rival and most frequent competitor was the late Judge Lowell, whose memory is still cherished with affection by the wise and virtuous of our State." This gentleman died in 1802, at the age of fifty-eight. I could not have known him personally; and before I was old enough to remember much of what I heard, he had ceased to be spoken of frequently. I have learned — principally from books — that he was a Federalist, and an active and influential member of the Convention of Massachusetts which formed the Constitution of that State; and that he led the bar of the State for many years. In 1789, he was appointed Judge of the District Court of the United States, and held that office until 1801, when he was appointed Chief Justice of the First Circuit, and this office he held until the act creating the court was repealed, in 1802. So evanescent is professional reputation, that the eminence of this gentleman is now known to few persons who are not connected with his family, or unusually well acquainted with the early history of the State.

He left three sons. The second, Francis C. Lowell, was a distinguished merchant and manufacturer. The third, the Rev. Charles Lowell, now lives in Cambridge, one of the most venerated clergymen of the Commonwealth, for his excellence and his usefulness.

The eldest, John Lowell, I knew well, for many years; and he was certainly among the most remarkable men whom I have ever known. Born in 1770, he was twenty years younger than my father, but was one of his most valued friends. In 1804, at the age of thirty-four, he left his profession, and never resumed it. Under the pressure of a very extensive business, his health broke down. He told me that on the day when he determined, in obedience to medical advice, or rather command, to give up all attention to business, at once and entirely, he had ninety-three cases on his docket, marked for trial. He went abroad, and there his health improved; and he confirmed it, after his return to this country, by regular labor on his farm in Roxbury. He suffered little more from ill-health; but perhaps felt that his nervous system had been too much weakened to permit him to engage again with safety either in his profession or in official duty, and the residue of his life was passed in retirement.

He was a retiring man, and never thrust himself into employment or public notice, but accepted cheerfully the opportunities of usefulness which were not so much offered as forced upon him; for he had no avarice, and his ambition was satisfied. But it was impossible that his extraordinary abilities could be idle, or his enthusiastic energy wholly suppressed. He wrote often for the newspapers, and was regarded as taking Ames's place in that duty. He published, at different times, from twenty-five to thirty pamphlets, on various topics. As an ardent Federalist, he exerted great influence upon the politics of his State. A series of papers which he wrote, under the name of "A Boston Rebel," were celebrated then, and are remembered now by many. In Harvard College his interest was vivid and constant, and he was a Fellow of the Corporation for twelve years. He was among the founders of the Massachusetts General Hospital, of the great Insurance Company connected with it, of the Boston Athenæum, and of the first Savings Bank of Boston. He was also one of the Trustees of the Agricultural Society, and a most skilful practical farmer. He introduced a system of observation and careful recording of facts in relation to agriculture, which has been followed by others, (although not with his exact accuracy,) and has proved of the utmost utility. His various papers on this class of subjects, under his favorite signature of "A Roxbury Farmer," exerted much influence in his own day, and are frequently quoted now in magazines and papers on the culture of fields and gardens. I could do more than assert his kindness and generosity, if I were at liberty to illustrate his warm heart and open hand by relating instances in which they were manifested.

But I return to my father. His arguments were always very brief. I have heard it said, that he *never* exceeded an hour; but this, I think, cannot be literally true. Usually he was much less than an hour; and I have heard from good authority, that he was less than half an hour oftener than he was more.

I have recently been told an anecdote illustrative of this point, on the authority of the late Mr. Hoar of Concord; and higher authority, for any word he chose to say, there could not be. My father went to Concord to argue a very important and difficult will case. Other lawyers spoke, and at length, and my father closed on his side. He spoke but thirty minutes; but his argument was conclusive, and prevailed.

It has often been said, too, that he never used a brief, trusting only to his memory. But that he took notes of the evidence and points I am certain, for some such papers I have now; and to these, of course, he could refer as he wished. I suppose, however, that he seldom prepared in writing full notes for an argument.

I should have said he was not eloquent, and could not be; but Chief Justice Parker says: "Instances may be recollected when, in causes which required it, he has assailed the hearts of his hearers with as powerful appeals as were ever exhibited in the cause of misfortune or humanity." Still, I do not believe that he could be called an eloquent man.

He was exceedingly fluent, had much power of rich and varied expression; could feel, and could express with great force, all strong emotions, from the *sacra indignatio*, which a great orator has called a chief weapon of eloquence, to the softer feelings, which move but do not pain; and moreover, he had a vivid imagination, and in conversation made much use of figure and illustration. Why was he no orator? With all these qualities, perhaps he lacked some others, and could not have been an orator. But I think he had a theory on this subject, which, if it grew in part from his incapacity for eloquence, certainly prevented him from cultivating what capacity he may have had. It was, as I believe, his opinion that eloquence is a great hinderance to a lawyer, and of no great value anywhere.

One reason for this opinion was probably his want of that love of admiration and applause which those who philosophize about these things consider a principal source and stimulus of eloquence. These were never desired by him;

and indeed he sometimes avoided them and manifested his disgust for them in a rude and peremptory way. He never came before the public at any time, or in any manner, but from necessity; and, I verily believe, went through all his duty of that kind merely as duty, looking for enjoyment only to home and close retirement. I think he never delivered an oration, or an address, or made a speech, in his life, excepting in court or in a legislative body. Whether his taste formed his opinions, and then he made reasons for them, I cannot say; but I have good ground for believing that he thought, that, if an eloquent lawyer was sometimes eminently successful, — which certainly none can dispute, — it was by other means than his eloquence; and that he who had no other means could not succeed. He would admit, that, in one action in a hundred, mere eloquence was the thing that was wanted; in a few more, it was very well; but in the vast majority of cases, it was only in the way. He who has a fame for eloquence, or who shows that he trusts to it, rouses every jury at once against him. It cannot be a favorable thing for counsel, when a juryman says to himself, as the advocate begins, "That man is famous for making fools of people, and he means to make a fool of me too, but I think he won't." And my father's students were often advised, that no young lawyer could make a more fatal mistake than to rely with so much confidence upon the mere power of speech, as to cultivate it at the expense of the learning, industry, and habits of prompt and accurate perception, which any man of good intelligence may attain, and which make success certain. That there was much foundation for these views, I have no doubt; but that he carried them to an extreme, must be probable, for his tastes and habits, and the whole character of his mind, would lead him to do so. Indeed, he was altogether a despiser of eloquence, and made a mistake on this point. It may be true, that, from the days of Moses and Aaron to our own, all the world over, the men who do not talk govern the world, and make use of the men who do. But it is true, notwithstanding, that eloquence is a great power. I may mention, as perhaps falling in with his notion, that silent and retired men are often most influential and useful; — that, of all the great men of Rome, my father most admired Atticus, the quiet, withdrawn, almost unknown friend of Cicero and Hortensius, Cæsar, Pompey, and Brutus, Anthony and Octavius. I have heard him give reasons, derived from a thorough investigation of all that is said of Atticus, for believing that he exerted, from his distant home in Athens, or his retirement in Rome, a powerful influence; and have some impression that he once threw these reasons on paper. But I have not seen such a paper for many years, if ever, and remember nothing of its details, nor even its general character, with any distinctness.

Mr. Webster wrote a notice of my father, in his journal written in 1804, when he was a student of law in Boston; and his description is as follows:

Theophilus Parsons is now about fifty-five years old; of rather large stature, and inclining a little to corpulency. His hair is brown, and his complexion not light. His face is not marked by any striking feature, if we except his eyes. His forehead is low, and his eyebrows prominent. He wears a blue coat and breeches, worsted hose, a brown wig, with a cocked hat. He has a penetrating eye, of an indescribable color. When, couched under a jutting eyebrow, it directs its beams into the face of a witness, he feels as if it looked into the inmost recesses of his soul.

When Parsons intends to make a learned observation, his eyebrow sinks; when a smart one, — for he is, and wishes to be thought, a wit, — it rises. The characteristic endowments of his mind are strength and shrewdness. Strength, which enables him to support his cause; shrewdness, by which he is always ready to retort the sallies of his adversary. His manner is steady, forcible, and perfectly perspicuous. He does not address the jury as a mechanical body to be put in motion by mechanical means. He appeals to them as men, and as having minds capable of receiving the ideas in his own. Of course, he never harangues. He is never stinted to say just so much on a point, and no more. He knows by the juror's countenance, when he is convinced; and therefore never disgusts him by arguing that of which he is already sensible, and which he knows it is impossible more fully to impress. A mind thus strong, direct, prompt, and vigorous, is cultivated by habits of the most intense application. A great scholar in everything, in his profession he is peculiarly great. He is not content with shining on occasions; he will shine everywhere. As no cause is too great, none is too small for him. He knows the great benefit of understanding small circumstances. It is not enough for him that he has learned the leading points in a cause; he will know everything. His argument is, therefore, always consistent with itself; and its course so luminous, that you are ready to wonder why any one should hesitate to follow him. Facts which are uncertain, he with so much art connects with others well proved, that you cannot get rid of the former without disregarding the latter. He has no fondness for public life, and is satisfied with standing where he is, at the head of his profession.

There are some mistakes in this description. His hair was never brown; but in early life it was dark, and when Mr. Webster knew him, what he had was gray. But he wore a brown wig. The portrait I have of him, which was painted when he was thirty years old, and wore no wig, but was already quite bald, shows that his forehead was remarkably high. But his wig came down near to his eyes, and gave the impression that his forehead was low.

Mr. Webster says: "He was, and liked to be thought, a wit." I suppose this is altogether true. But what I remember of my father is not his *wit*, but his *fun*. If ever any man loved fun and frolic, he did. He laughed easily and heartily, although often with his mouth shut and silently; he loved to laugh and to make others laugh, and knew how to do it. He was not, I believe, disposed to be sarcastic or bitter. Some stories indicating the capacity to sting I have heard, but I have no personal recollection of anything of the kind. Nothing, however, do I remember better than the hours of chat and laughter, — the very many such hours, — the gay dinners, the simple but festive suppers, which, as they come now before my recollection, seem to me full of unrestrained frolic. The fashion in that day was more tolerant of anecdote and fun of all kinds, in conversation and at all times, than it is now. Innumerable are the stories which have come to me of my father's sayings and doings in the way of jest, in all the periods of his life. Many of them are now stock stories, which run through the papers periodically, and are sometimes applied to him, and sometimes to others.

It would do no good to try to tell these stories; they could only be understood or appreciated with their accessories, and these I cannot always give. They were but bubbles of the moment, but they helped to make the moment cheerful. I think his gayety of temper was of vast advantage to him. It was of some little value as a weapon of offence or defence. He could turn into a laugh what might have become a quarrel, and his ready answer, witty or only funny, as the case might be, sometimes subdued an opponent and sometimes suppressed his opposition. The bar and the court were on a different footing in some respects from that which now prevails. There was as much, and perhaps more, reverence and respect for official or personal rights; but it was then felt to be safer to permit freedoms, than now. I could fill many pages with stories illustrative of this ease, not to say license, of manner. One I tell, partly because it happens to occur to me as I write, and partly because I had it from the best authority. James Sullivan, afterwards Governor of this State, was opposed to my father in a case, and there was some little war of words, in which my father for that time got the better; which, by the way, did not always happen, for Sullivan was an able man, and very ready. Soon after, as my father was arguing to the jury, Mr. Sullivan espied a bit of chalk lying on the table, and took up his opponent's broad-brimmed black hat and wrote upon it, "This is the hat of a damned rascal," and laid it down again, after showing it to the bar. There was some smiling, — perhaps audible smiling, — for my father turned round, and as his eye fell on the hat, he read the words. He instantly stopped in his argument, and turning to the court, and exhibiting the hat, said: "May it please your honor, I crave the protection of the court. Brother Sullivan has been stealing my hat and writing his own name on it."

Another anecdote, illustrative of the convenience to my father of his ready wit, has been told to me a hundred times; and I have sometimes seen it attributed to others, and told with some diversity of form. I tell it substantially as it was written for me by the Hon. Charles P. Phelps of Hadley.

"Your father had been at Hartford on business, towards the end of winter. He got through on Saturday night; and as there were signs that winter was breaking up, and he was in a close carriage on runners, there was danger in delay, and he prepared to leave on Sunday. The innkeeper told him he would certainly be arrested; but a storm had set in, and he concluded to take his chance, and began the journey. After going a few miles, the 'tithingman,' as the officer charged with this duty was called, came up and ordered him to stop. Your father asked his authority, &c., and, being satisfied on those points, said he should certainly obey the law, and stop; and directed his driver to draw up to one side of the road, fasten the reins where he could reach them from within, and come inside. The tithingman inquired what all this meant. 'It means,' said he, 'that the law authorizes you to stop me, and you have stopped me, and here I intend to stop.' 'But I want you to turn back with me.' 'Perhaps so; but I prefer to do what the law requires. You say that you have authority to stop me. Very well, you have stopped me, and I submit;

and now I shall stop where I am as long as I see fit.' After a little further controversy, the officer concluded to return, muttering, 'I might have known I should never catch you,' and thus satisfying your father of what he had suspected, — that the man had been sent out purposely to 'catch him,' as a signal application of the law. After a certain time, your father rode on, and soon passed beyond the bounds of Connecticut."

A part of my father's universal readiness, and of his great facility and abundant resources in *technical* cases, arose from the extent and variety of his knowledge, and a part from his careful preparation of his cases. He had also a great deal of mechanical talent; or, rather, he had that love for practical mechanics from which one is apt to infer talent.

While writing this sheet, a friend sent to me this paragraph, cut from a newspaper.

"The late Chief Justice Parsons, when on a circuit, met with an accident to his carriage, and stopped at a blacksmith's to have some iron-work repaired, and then went to a carriage-maker's and conversed with him as to the necessary wood-work, and then to a painter's, and directed him how to prepare his paints so that they should dry at once. After he went on, those mechanics conferred together. Said the first, 'That man rides in his carriage now, but I am sure he was a blacksmith once.' 'No,' said the carriage-maker, 'but he has been a worker in wood.' 'I think not,' said the painter, 'for I am sure he has learnt my trade.'"

It need not be said that this story is impossible. Such anecdotes, indeed, are common enough about all distinguished men. In my father's case, it may have had so much foundation as that one or another person engaged in some mechanical employment may have expressed his surprise at my father's acquaintance with his own specialty, but I think nothing more.

He always had a variety of tools, and always kept them in excellent order, and was ready to use them for the amusement of his children at any time. My bows and arrows, and skilfully contrived rabbit-hutches, were the envy of my playmates; and he seemed to take just as much interest in them as I did. I have now the remains of a set of models made by him, of mahogany, to illustrate the problems of conic sections. Beside this taste for mechanics, his universal and insatiable thirst for knowledge made him desire to understand everything he saw, and to learn from every one in whose company he found himself whatever could be learned from him. One remark on this subject I have heard him make so often, that it is most distinctly impressed upon my memory. It was in substance this: that many persons wondered at his studying all sorts of things, and supposed this diversity of pursuits must interfere with his profession; the contrary, however, was true; for there was scarcely anything which he had learned, particularly if it were of a scientific character, which he did not find, at some time, or in some way, useful to him as a lawyer or as a judge. The following extract from a letter to me from the Hon. C. P. Phelps, to whom I have already referred, may have some interest. He says: "A striking peculiarity in your father, as an advocate, was the wonderful knowledge he exhibited of the details and minutiæ of whatever art or science was especially involved in the causes which he managed, and his perfect familiarity with all the technical phraseology belonging to the subject. His hearers could hardly avoid the conclusion, that he must have been at some time a practical mechanic or operator in the art or science the principles of which he was so aptly and skilfully describing and explaining. Thus, when arguing a cause involving the principles of naval architecture, or of practical navigation or seamanship, the jury would have felt satisfied that he had not only had the experience of a master shipwright, but that he must have been at sea, and acted there as a sailor. At any rate, he never failed to convince both judge and jury that he was a perfect master of the subject in hand. In this peculiarity I never saw his equal at the bar."

Let me add, that Mr. Phelps was my near connection by marriage, studied law with my father, and always maintained the most intimate relations with him. Soon after writing me these letters, he closed, with peace and hope, a long life of unsullied purity and worth.

In his ordinary practice, my father did not greatly interest himself in his cases. I mean, that he did not identify himself with his clients, and feel as if he were personally concerned in the case. In his time, it was usual for eminent lawyers to traverse the State, including the then Province of Maine, and to go with the Supreme Court wherever its terms were held. He therefore saw his clients and his cases in the country, for the most part, only just before trial, and after all preparation had been made. And he was so much and so often absent from Boston, that the same thing was true to a considerable extent there also. Indeed, the practice of our profession was, even in my own early recollection, more as it is in England, where attorneys prepare all the cases for trial, and have all or nearly all the personal intercourse with the client, and barristers argue their cases from the briefs which the attorneys furnish them. Formerly the distinction between these grades of the profession was quite distinctly recognized. After three years' study, a student was admitted as attorney at law; after two years more, as counsellor; and after two years more, as barrister; and only those who had attained this elevation argued cases in the Supreme Court. The barrister wore a black gown of some woollen stuff, and a bag-wig; and though my father, who first put his on about 1778, soon after discontinued the use of them, I remember them perfectly, as they were carefully preserved by my mother, and occasionally exhibited to the children.

The effect of the personal intercourse between client and

counsel, which is now much more common, at least in New England, makes the practice of the profession more burdensome, and its labors more continuous and harassing. But it tends strongly to identify the client and his lawyer. I have no doubt he argued his cases with as much zeal as any one; and I have heard many things which would lead to the belief that he was sometimes, though not generally, very earnest and impetuous. But when, after he was on the bench, some one, complimenting him on his success as an advocate, uttered the absurdity, "I have heard it said, Sir, that you never lost a case. Can that be literally true?" "It is, Sir," said he; "I assure you that it is literally and precisely true. I never lost a case in my life; and the reason I suppose is, I never had one. *My clients have lost a great many; but their cases were not mine.*" Sir Walter Scott says, that no lawyer ever lost his dinner or his sleep from anxiety about his client's case. This may be true in England or Scotland, but is certainly not true with us. The late William Prescott often said to me, while I was studying law with him, that it was seldom that the anxiety of preparing the case, or even of trying it, destroyed his sleep; but it sometimes happened that the next night after the case was finished was passed without a moment's sleep. "I have always found," said he, "that the waves run highest after the wind has ceased to blow."

I should be glad to say something of the position conceded to my father by the lawyers of his day; but I find it difficult to do this. It would be easy to state that he was older than most of the distinguished men with whom he practised, and had devoted much more time and systematic labor to the study of the law, and very steadily refused to permit politics or office to draw him away; and that it would follow, almost necessarily, that they would recognize in him a certain measure of superiority. But it would be just as easy, and altogether reasonable, to reply to me, that I am the worst possible judge of this matter; not only because my own feelings must influence my opinion, but because my relation to him necessarily shuts out from me nearly all unfavorable or disqualifying facts or opinions. If they get into print, I can read them, like anybody else; but who will tell them to me? That I have never heard anything of the kind, goes for nothing; and that I have not seen it in print, is worth little more. I might quote strong language on this point. Thus Story, in a lecture to the Cambridge Law School, which I give in the Appendix, speaks of his "wonderful wisdom and vigor of mind," and says "he had no equal," and was "a head and shoulders taller than any other man in the whole State." And Chief Justice Parker says: "Twenty-six years ago, when I with others of my age were pupils in the profession of the law, we saw our masters call this man into their councils, and yield implicit confidence to his opinions. Among men eminent themselves, and by many years his seniors, we saw him by common consent take the lead. . . . . . I do not disparage others by placing him at their head. They were great men; *he* was a wonderful man. . . . . . His enemies designated him by an appellation which, from its appropriateness, became a just compliment, — *the Giant of the Law*. . . . . . He was regarded by those lawyers with whom I have been conversant, *as the living oracle of the law*. His transmitted opinions carried with them authority sufficient to settle controversies and terminate litigation." After all due allowance for eulogistic language, such words from such men must still have some significance.

Every child is apt to think his father rather a remarkable man, — for he is so to him, — and must greatly exaggerate any remarkableness which may exist. I would avoid this almost inevitable mistake as far as I can, and will let the following letter speak on this topic for me. It is one of the many ordinary business letters I have; but it comes from no ordinary man, and the fact may have some little value, at least to lawyers, that such a man as Samuel Dexter, in the fulness of his strength, for himself and for his client, insists that my father must begin and give direction to a case, because he could not.

Charlestown, 1st April, 1797.

DEAR SIR:

I once mentioned to you that Clark and Nightingale, of Providence, were desirous of engaging you in an action to be brought by them against Samuel W. Pomeroy and others. The action has not yet been instituted, but Mr. Clark called on me yesterday, and requested that it might be brought for Suffolk Common Pleas, and that I would again mention it to you. It is not probable that I shall attend the trial, though he would not release me on telling him so, and therefore I wish you to shape the declaration. I wish it for another reason: I am utterly at a loss how to try it. The facts are these: Pomeroy *et al.*, by their agent, William Allen, exchanged with Clark *et al.* certain North and South Carolina State notes for Loan-Office certificates; and under a schedule of the State notes Allen wrote: "Providence, July 31st, 1790. This certifies that I, the subscriber, exchanged the above certificates with Clark and Nightingale, and warranted them all true and good, and promise to exchange any of them if they prove counterfeit." His principals approved of this expressly. Some of the State notes were *fraudulently* issued by the commissioners, though really signed by persons having authority to issue notes for *bona fide* debts, and the Legislature of the State has declared them void, and refuses payment. I shall leave the matter with W. B. Adams, who is with me in the office, and he will wait until he receives a form of a declaration from you. I think you had better file the writ and take the sole care of the action; but Clark seems to want me not to be off, though it is not at all probable I shall be here.

I am, Sir, with great esteem,

Your obedient friend,

SAMUEL DEXTER, JR.

Charlestown, 22d April, 1797.

DEAR SIR:

I am provoked that we had not the intended conversation at Concord. The letter which I handed you there from myself contains a statement of the demand of Clark and Nightingale. Pray write me how you think the action should be brought, *for I never will bring it without your opinion.* Moreover, it is their wish that you should direct as to the mode of declaring. 2d. Pray write me what you can do for Jos. Stacey Read, and on what terms I can engage you to go through with the business for him. 3d. Capt. Swain is here from Nantucket, and says a general engagement is expected at Barnstable Supreme Court; that the directors of the bank have written to you, but that I must write you lest that should fail. I beseech you to send me an answer on the above three subjects.

Yours truly,

SAMUEL DEXTER, JR.

My father was generally unwilling to engage in criminal cases. He once successfully defended some persons accused of piracy, through a long and difficult trial, and its effect upon him made him avoid such things ever afterwards.

Of any special cases which he engaged in, I have very little to say. Perhaps the following, to which I have already alluded, interested him as much as any, though not for the case itself, but for one incident of it. The State of Connecticut had granted to Halsey and others certain lands lying on the borders of that State and New York, in consideration of their agreement to finish the State-House in Hartford. A suit was soon after brought to determine the title to these lands, and it was tried before Chief Justice Ellsworth, in September, 1797. The actual parties were New York and Connecticut. New York had for counsel, Hosmer, Hoffman, and Aaron Burr; Connecticut had retained an equal number; and then New York added Hamilton, and Connecticut added my father. The case was not reached upon its merits, but after much argument went off upon a collateral question. I have already alluded to one anecdote connected with this case, as told to me by Mr. Wells, for its illustration of my father's method of study.

Judge Thomas S. Williams, now living in venerated old age in Hartford, was then a student at law in Litchfield, and was a part of the time present in court. In a letter addressed to a valued friend, who at my request wrote to him for an account of this case, he states the facts I have above narrated, saying, however, that he has "but a very general knowledge of what occurred." He adds: "Now the lips of all engaged in the trial are sealed in death, and I doubt whether there remains alive one intelligent man who was present throughout the trial. I am confident that no professional man survives." In another part of this letter he says: "The first I recollect hearing of Mr. Parsons, who was then a practising lawyer, was after the return of Chief Justice Ellsworth from Massachusetts, where I suppose he had held a Circuit Court. I was told that he said he found Mr. Parsons a complete magazine of learning."

On the trial, Judge Ellsworth treated my father somewhat as he himself was charged with treating others after he was on the bench. Upon some objections being offered to the jurisdiction of the court, Judge Ellsworth stopped him with, "This court, Sir, will take care of its own jurisdiction." An answer whereof my father complained, in somewhat the same way as we shall see in the next chapter that others afterwards complained of him.

The Hon. Zachariah Eddy, now of East Middleborough, was good enough to reply to a similar letter. He also was a student at Litchfield in 1800, and it seems that the case was then freshly remembered. He says: "I heard the lawyers speak of a case in which Parsons met Hamilton and the New York lawyers, (I think before Judge Ellsworth,) in which he astonished Hamilton by his legal knowledge, and especially by his skill in special pleading. I cannot state any occurrence with exactness, but he was then considered by the lawyers there as the very first of the profession in New England."

I remember hearing of a retort of Hamilton's in the argument before the court, which passed into a sort of proverb. In replying to some nice distinctions my father was trying to make, he said: "May it please your Honor,

I have known gentlemen to split a hair, and I may have tried to do it myself. But I never before saw any one decimate a hair and count the pieces before the court."

Hamilton and my father always had a great regard for each other. They then were together as much of the time as they could so spend, and afterwards corresponded. However conservative Hamilton may have been, he found my father almost, if not quite, as much so.

I find it difficult to select particular cases from the multitude in which he was engaged, and exhibit them as the most interesting. I could name very many, which were lions in their day; but they seem to me all the same thing now, and no great thing either. Perhaps among those which were most interesting in their time, and which involved points that would be equally interesting now, had they not ceased to be questions, is one in which he was retained in defence of the parish in Gloucester, or the minister of that parish, against the Rev. Mr. Murray, who more than any other person introduced the doctrines of Universalism into this country. In 1782, he had gathered a small society in Gloucester, formed in great part of the most respectable citizens of the town. They declined paying their taxes to the established minister of the place; and an action was brought to determine whether they were under any obligation to do so. Many counsel were engaged at different times, and there were many trials. But the principal counsel for Mr. Murray were Sullivan and Tudor, and for the defendants, Bradbury and my father. In 1785, a trial before a jury took place. The defendants relied upon certain clauses in the Declaration of Rights, which forms a part of our State Constitution. The third article provides that the Legislature may "require the several towns, parishes, precincts, and other bodies politic, or religious societies, to make suitable provision, at their own expense, for the public worship of God, and for the support and maintenance of public Protestant teachers of piety, religion, and morality. . . . . . Provided, however, that the several towns, parishes, precincts, and other bodies politic, or religious societies, shall at all times have the exclusive right of electing their public teachers, and of contracting with them for their support and maintenance. . . . . . And all moneys paid by the subject for the support of public worship and of the public teachers aforesaid, shall, if he require it, be uniformly applied to the support of the public teacher or teachers of his own religious sect or denomination, provided there be any on whose instructions he attends. Otherwise, it may be paid towards the support of the teacher or teachers of the parish or precinct in which the said moneys are raised."

The plaintiffs denied that Mr. Murray's society was a religious society within the meaning of the Constitution, and also asserted that Mr. Murray could not be considered as "a teacher of piety, religion, and morality." This last question seems to have been that which was submitted to the jury; and they rendered a verdict in Mr. Murray's favor, against the undisguised opinion of the court, which consisted of Dana, Sewall, and Sumner. A review was granted, and the case was tried the next year; and tradition says that Sullivan made an extraordinary and most successful effort, — so successful as to have changed the opinion of the court, and especially of Judge Dana. He charged the jury that the clauses in the Declaration of Rights were liberal in their purpose, and should be liberal in their effect, and that their influence was not to be impaired or obstructed by a narrow construction; that Mr. Murray's society was organized and formed as they thought fit, and this was enough; that it existed for a religious purpose, and that the previous verdict of the jury had determined the character of Mr. Murray. Strange to say, while the court had come to this conclusion, the jury were tending to the old position which the court had left. After being out a long time, they returned and said they could not possibly agree. But Judge Dana, replied with much sternness, that they *must* agree, and bade them take up their papers and return to their room. After remaining there many hours longer, they came into court with a verdict affirming the former verdict. And thus this case was settled as undoubtedly it should have been.

In a previous chapter some allusion was made to my father's services as a member of the Legislature. To me, the most interesting of these, by far, occurred in 1790. In that year, Mr. John Gardiner, an able man and lawyer, proposed in the Legislature, and maintained with great zeal and force, sundry reforms — as he deemed them — of great importance. My father was his principal opponent. And on one point especially, — that of special pleading, which Mr. Gardiner sought to abolish, and which has since been not only abolished, but forbidden by law, — my father at that time defeated him. Of this subject of special pleading I shall have much to say in the next chapter. Here I will only extract from Willis's History of Portland the best account I have ever met with of this affair.

The excitement which existed against lawyers and the courts to an alarming extent in Massachusetts, in 1785, and some years after, was not much felt here: the Shays Rebellion had no advocates in this part of the country. A prejudice, however, did prevail against the profession, which was concentrated and carried into the Legislature in 1790, by John Gardiner of Pownalborough, a barrister at law. He introduced a resolution in January of that year, that the House would resolve itself into a committee of the whole to take into consideration "the present state of the law and its professors in the Commonwealth." He prefaced his resolution by some able and spirited remarks, which he subsequently enforced and illustrated, against lawyers and what he termed abuses of the law, some of which were merely imaginary. He objected to the association of members of the bar, and the formation of bar rules, the modes of taxing cost, and other practices, which he termed illegal and unwarrantable usurpations. He thought the law ought to be simplified; that many customs had crept in from the English law which should be eradicated. His desire was to thrust in the knife and remove entirely all those customs which he and others considered grievances. While the subject was before the Legislature, Mr. Gardiner, in the heat of debate and in a highly excited state of feelings, cast many aspersions upon lawyers, which had a tendency to bring the whole class into disrepute and encourage the unfounded prejudice which existed against them out of doors. He had not, however, many supporters in the House. The bills which he introduced were rejected by large majorities. The one to annihilate special pleading was debated with great earnestness, and the late Chief Justice Parsons opposed it with a power that could not be resisted.

To this passage there is the following foot-note:

At this time Judge Parsons drew from Mr. Gardiner the following eulogium: "This erroneous opinion of the gentlemen of the profession here was taken from a mere *dictum* of the late Mr. Gridley, who, though a mighty pompous man, was a man of considerable learning and abilities, — in learning and genius, however, almost infinitely inferior to that great giant of learning and genius, the law member from Newburyport." Mr. Parsons was then but forty years old.

Perhaps the most important act that he drew was the Statute of Distributions, which, almost as it came from his pen, regulates the distribution of the personal property of an intestate, to this day. I cannot but think the following letter worth preserving, for the lawyer at least, as throwing light on some of the questions which this subject then presented, and on the principles which were adopted in reference to those questions. It is without date, and is addressed only to "Chief Justice," but must have been written about 1805, and addressed to Chief Justice Dana.

DEAR SIR:

Agreeably to my promise, I enclose you a draft of a new Statute of Distributions. After you have weighed the principles and the language of the bill, I wish we could have some conversation on the subject. If some Saturday morning you could call upon me, and stay and take your fish with me, I should feel much obliged to you. I make the following remarks on the bill, with the desire that you would pay attention to the paragraphs to which they refer.

2. This provision is agreeably to the old law, except the *jus primogenituræ*. But on the second paragraph one question has occurred to me in my practice. One of the daughters died under age and unmarried, but twenty years old, possessing a large personal estate which she received from her father as her distributive share. She bequeathed it by last will. Could she do it, or would the surviving brothers and sisters take it to the exclusion of the legatee? Another question may arise. Suppose the mother of the intestate's children had issue living by a former husband, and a child of the intestate dies under age and unmarried, will the half-blood be considered as one of *the surviving brothers and sisters?*

3. Can the general provision in this paragraph affect by construction the second paragraph?

4. A question has been made, whether, if the intestate leaves father *and mother*, shall the mother have a moiety? The practice has been conformably to the paragraph, but Judge D. Sewall has, I am informed, given a different opinion.

5. If the intestate leaves only nephews and nieces, they are excluded in favor of the mother; but if he leaves a brother or sister, then the nephews and nieces may take with the mother by representation.

6. This paragraph settles the question agreeably to the decision in Nurse's case.

7. On this paragraph a question has arisen, but was compromised. The widow had a provision in lieu of dower, but she claimed dower in lands after purchased. Can she have it? and shall she have one third or one half, as the case may be, of the undevised personal estate after debts, &c. are paid?

8. This paragraph prefers the nephew to the uncle, the child of a nephew to the child of an uncle, &c.; but it does not extend to kindred when some are lineal and some collateral. Thus the grandfather will share with the brother, the great-grandfather with the nephew and the uncle, &c. In which last case the uncle will take with the nephew, which he will not do if the great-grandfather be dead.

9. This exclusion of remote collateral representation extends to all cases, as sections two, three, and five.

10. This settles a question among lineal descendants. The intestate leaves only grandchildren, children of several sons and daughters deceased. Shall the grandchildren take *per capita* or *per stirpes?*

12. This paragraph settles the prerogative of the Commonwealth, as it relates to personal as well as real estate. Ought not the widow, if there be one, to have all the personal estate?

14. Great frauds have been practised, for want of some provision of this nature, by an executor not interested in the residue. After the will has been made, moneys intended for the residuary legatee have been vested in after-purchased lands, which the executor would not sell, but applied all the estate given the residuary legatee to the payment of debts and legacies, and then divided the after-purchased lands among the heirs.

I am, with great respect, your very friendly

THEOPH. PARSONS.

December 8th.

I append to this chapter the letters which have been sent to me in reply to my request for assistance. I know it will be said to me, for certainly I say it to myself, that these gentlemen could not write to a son about his father otherwise than kindly; and that distance of time, operating like distance of space, has clothed the subject with hues that were not its own. But let all due allowance be made on these grounds, and it seems to me that something remains which may be worth reading.

The first is from the venerable Ezekiel Whitman, now residing in East Bridgewater. I have not the pleasure of his acquaintance, but in reply to my request, he sent me, promptly and kindly, the following:

East Bridgewater, April 3d, 1857.

DEAR SIR:

Your favor of the 31st ultimo came duly to hand. It would afford me great pleasure to be able to render any essential aid in the preparation of a biography of Chief Justice Parsons. But I was not personally acquainted with him till he made his appearance at Portland as Chief Justice of the Supreme Judicial Court, in 1807. I had, however, heard of him, from an early period of my life, as the "giant of the law" in Massachusetts. He was at the head of his profession, I believe, quite soon after he became a member of it, and so continued until the day of his decease. I know but little of him, except as Chief Justice, presiding at the law terms in the County of Cumberland. I think he never held a *nisi prius* term there. As Chief Justice he was perfectly at his ease, for he was not unconscious of his superior acquirements, nor of the deference every one was ready to pay to them. He was uniformly pleasant, and often seemed to be playfully facetious.

I have heard many anecdotes of him, illustrative of his wit, which I presume are yet current and well remembered, and therefore need not be repeated by me.

With much esteem, I am, Sir,

Your obedient, humble servant,

EZEKIEL WHITMAN.

The next is from the Hon. William Baylies, of West Bridgewater, with whom I practised for some years at the Taunton bar, at the head of which he stood, *longo intervallo.* Many years have passed away since that time; and even then he was declining business, although no one but himself suspected that his years demanded rest. Long may he continue in his present enjoyment of all the blessings which crown his loved and honored age.

West Bridgewater, August 10, 1857.

MY DEAR SIR:

It was, I think, in the year 1803 or 1804, that I had the pleasure, or honor I may say, — for so I consider it, — to become acquainted with your father. He was, at the time I refer to, at Plymouth, attending the Supreme Court, then sitting in that town, in the practice of his profession. I called upon him, in the course of the term, at his lodgings, upon a matter of business. He received me with much kindness, and the business matter being soon disposed of, he proceeded to converse upon other subjects. The topics were various and somewhat diverse. Among them were *Special Pleading*, — which, you know, among the old lawyers of my time, was considered as the "sinews of the common law," — the *Law of Real Actions*, *Booth's Treatise*, the *Essex Bar*, anecdotes of individual members of it, &c., &c.

I listened attentively to his remarks, and was not only entertained, but instructed, by them; and left him delighted with my interview, and fully convinced that a great and profound lawyer, with a texture of brain as strong as that of Newton, could be, at the same time, notwithstanding these impediments, an amiable and agreeable man in social and private life, and a gentleman, using that word in its best sense.

I heard him several times, at Plymouth, address a jury; but of his manner and style of argument I cannot speak so distinctly and particularly as I could wish; for, after the lapse of more than half a century, the vivid impression made upon me at the time of hearing him has partially faded from my mind. It appeared to me, however, as far as I can now recollect, that his style and manner were well suited to the solid, philosophical, and logical character of his mind. They were plain, natural, and without a particle of affectation. There was no attempt at display, no parade, no note of preparation, — nothing of the theatrical or the rhetorical. In one word, there was no bluster. Cool, collected, and self-possessed, never surprised or embarrassed, he proceeded at once to lay before the jury the great and leading points of the case, and paid little or no attention to the minor points. He spoke with facility, but not with that rapidity of utterance which sometimes confuses not only the hearer, but the speaker himself. His language was clear, simple, and perfectly adapted to the subject of which he was treating, and easily understood by any person of ordinary intelligence. Though he omitted nothing important to the strength of his argument, he never was redundant, and might properly be called a concise speaker. He had the power of condensation, which, as the late Colonel Pickering once remarked to me, was a rare and great talent, and further said, that among the few that he had ever known to possess it was Theophilus Parsons. His manner, though not vehement, was earnest and energetic. He used but little gesture; and his voice, though not loud, was pleasant and persuasive. He spoke like one anxious to get at the truth; and if the power of convincing by strong and forcible argument may with propriety be denominated eloquence, he possessed as much of that faculty as any one I ever heard. He never was oppressed by the magnitude of the case in which he appeared; however difficult, or perplexed, or complicated it might be, he would, whether addressing the court or the jury, "the Gordian knot of it unloose familiar as his garter."

It is not for me to assign his rank at the bar, or to designate the niche in the Temple of Fame which his bust shall occupy. But I know this, — that he stood pre-eminent at the Massachusetts bar, at the head of his profession in the opinion of all the lawyers with whom I have been conversant; and it must be recollected that, even at that time, there were *some* giants in the land.

To show the high estimation in which he was held by his contemporaries, I will particularly refer to the just and beautiful sketch of his character by the late Chief Justice Parker, in his Address to the Grand Jury of the County of Suffolk, 10 Mass. Reports, 521; and also to the Life of Judge J. Smith, page 428.

His appointment to the office of Chief Justice of the Supreme Court gave great and general satisfaction, not only to the bar, but to the public. It was thought that so learned a lawyer and powerful an advocate as he was could hardly fail of making a good judge; and this reasonable expectation was not in the least disappointed. From his first appearance in court as a judge, it was evident that he was admirably fitted and qualified for the high and important office to which he had been promoted, and that he was as familiar with its duties as though he had been seated on the bench a dozen years.

It is not necessary to go into particulars. It is enough to say, in general terms, that he displayed on the bench the same great talents, the same powers of mind, the same strength of argument, and the same professional knowledge, which he had exhibited at the bar.

But a great and learned judge may have defects of temper and manners that impair his usefulness, and in some measure disqualify him for the proper discharge of the duties of his office; and I have understood that Judge Parsons was, in some quarters, charged with being harsh and overbearing in his treatment of the members of the bar, and of encroaching upon their rights. *My* opportunities for observation in this respect were, as you know, very limited. I am not certain that I ever saw him acting as a judge, except at Plymouth and at Taunton. But at these places, Plymouth and Taunton, I attended several terms of the Supreme Court when he sat as judge, or presided; and, speaking from personal observation and my best recollection, I say, with confidence and without hesitation, that I saw nothing and heard nothing that in my judgment would justify the imputation that he was harsh and overbearing in his treatment of the bar. On the contrary, his usual deportment towards the bar appeared to me mild, friendly, and familiar.

It is true, however, that I have heard him on a few occasions reprehend members of the bar for their negligence or carelessness, by which their client's case was lost, or the trial delayed. These reproofs, however, were rare, and did not appear to arise from an irascible temper, but to proceed from a desire to elevate the character of the bar by impressing upon the minds of its members the importance of the relation they held to the court, and of their duty to their clients.

That Judge Parsons had a kindly nature while at the bar, I personally know; and it can hardly be conceived that that kindly nature could be changed in passing to the bench.

I will conclude by saying, that Chief Justice Parsons was, in my opinion, an honor to his profession and to the State of Massachusetts; and that, if he was not a wise and great man, I know not where we shall look to find one.

I am, very respectfully, your friend,

WM. BAYLIES.

THEOPHILUS PARSONS, ESQ.

The next is from the Hon. Zachariah Eddy, who has long since retired from the labors of a profession in which he held a high rank. Not having the pleasure of knowing this gentleman personally, I requested my friend and colleague, Professor Washburn, to ask of him the assistance I needed. He received at once the following reply.

MR. WASHBURN:

Such reminiscences as I have of the late Chief Justice Parsons must be given *calamo currente*. My first acquaintance with him was on my admission as a counsellor in the Supreme Judicial

Court, which I think was in 1809, when he enjoined us thus: "Young gentlemen, read your books, read your books." The title to Marshfield Beach was on trial, Dr. Isaac Winslow being demandant. The charge called up all the doctrine of seizin and disseizin, and indeed almost all the law of real property, and the charge to the jury was the most thorough and learned of all the opinions I have known him pronounce, and filled me with astonishment.

I had before heard him argue a case, when he was counsel with George Blake (the case is in 1 Mass. Rep.), which called up the *nullum tempus* act. I remember Mr. Blake addressed the judges full half a dozen times, and that Mr. Parsons, every time, told the judges he did not agree with his colleague (as to the law) in what he said. The judges made two or three circuits before any of the lawyers in the Old Colony ventured to make a law argument before him; but submitted their cases unreservedly to the court. Judge Parker told me that the course was the same in the Eastern circuit. Such was the veneration of the bar for him as a lawyer, that they exhibited an unusual awe in his presence.

There was great neglect in preparing the papers for the court, and it was several years before it was properly attended to; and I have seen him nonsuit our oldest counsellors for that cause very often, in order to induce future attention to the rule requiring the furnishing of the papers in the case. Sometimes, when he found the cases were important, and a speedy decision very desirable, he would (out of court) advise them to move "that the nonsuit be taken off."

He had not much patience to hear an unsound argument, nor to hear counsel advance an untenable point; and the lawyers were so poorly versed in legal lore, that they were not only willing, but desirous, that he should take the disposal of the whole case into his own hands. I have known him, many times, do this with great reluctance.

My first case before him was a demurrer to a special plea, which I had drawn with much care and attention. He asked me if I relied upon it. I said I did, and the opposite counsel said the same of his demurrer. I felt much gratified with his full approval of the plea, and overruling the demurrer. I found he intended to put a stop to pleading with a reservation, and I made special pleading a special study from the time of his coming upon the bench. I was young, and during his administration was not a companion of the Chief Justice, but a hearer and a learner, and scarcely saw him more than once a year, once or twice at *nisi prius*, and always at the law term for the Old Colony.

Yours truly,

Z. Eddy.

East Middleborough, April 1, 1857.

P. S. I remember one or two things at table. When the conversation became interesting, the sheriff would sometimes say, "It is three o'clock; shall I order the bell?" His answer was, "It is not three o'clock till the court *say* it is three o'clock."

To Mr. Judson, the father of the missionary, he said, "You have a son who is going on a mission?" "Yes." "Well, if I had a son who could work miracles, I would send him on a mission."

On one occasion he said: "Fisher brought me forty notes of hand to collect, and ordered them all to be sued, and said he had taken the administration from his brother's hands, because he would not do it. Nothing was recovered; and when Fisher called for his costs, he paid the bills and said, 'I have learned the meaning of administration *de bonis non;* it means *where there is nothing to be got.*'"

In preparing the course of debate on the adoption of the Federal Constitution, Governor Strong said of one article, "Parsons, that regards the law; and you are the one to expound and enforce it." To which the Judge replied, "Strong, you can do more with that honest face of yours than I can with all my legal knowledge." Judge Thomas was present, and told me this.

He said Fisher Ames used to call the court bell "the birch stick" (in allusion to the court being kept in order like a school); and on one occasion, when the court had ruled all the points in a case entirely in his favor, and his opposing counsel still went on arguing them, Ames said, "The gentleman puts me in mind of an old hen which persists in setting after her eggs are taken away."

In recurring to what I have written, I find I have said nothing as to the new course of trying cases which Judge Parsons introduced. The dockets were very full in all the counties, and the cases had accumulated by reason of the loose and desultory manner of trial, caused, I think, also by the imperfect state of legal knowledge, which was quite limited, not only among the bar, but with many of the judges. There were no American reports, and few had any from England.

Judge Parsons was very provident of time. He would not permit it to be uselessly spent. He had not much patience with counsel or client who had not his case prepared; nor would he hear impertinent or irrelevant testimony, or groundless argument. He said the multitude of cases called for promptness, as did also the finances of the county. When a term ended, he would enjoin counsel to be better prepared in their cases in time to come (and sometimes, to *read their books*), that the time and money of the county might not be wasted.

All of these letters speak as much, and perhaps more, of my father as a judge, than as a practising lawyer, and for that reason might perhaps have been appropriately placed at the close of the next chapter. But what they say of him as a lawyer is better here, and what they say applicable to him only as a judge will serve as well to introduce that subject as to close it.

I indulge myself with adding a letter, which is not from an old man, but from one who must live very many years before anything of decrepitude or decay can make him an old man. I refer to Dr. Oliver Wendell Holmes of Boston. I wrote to him in the hope that he might have papers of the late Judge Jackson (his father-in-law, and one of my father's very best friends), which would be of use to me. With the letter I sent him a lithograph of Stuart's sketch. Here the relation which exists between me and some of the correspondents whose letters I give, is reversed. I am withdrawn from public observation, while he lives in its fullest light, and is known far more widely than I am. It may be but one more instance how Yankees turn everything to account, that he, the wittiest of the race, has discovered, and is teaching others, that the true function of wit is to be the vehicle of wisdom. Many a true thought has he thus sent to the hearts of his readers, which, as a moral formula or a logical abstraction, would not have penetrated their understandings. His armed rockets are impelled and driven home by the flame which makes them sparkle as they fly.

Boston, March 4th.

MY DEAR SIR:

Many thanks for your kind gift of your father's portrait. It is full of interest for me, his name having been so long associated in my mind with all that my imagination can picture of sagacity and wisdom, acuteness and breadth of mind, united with the qualities that commanded the respect and conciliated the love of those around him.

My father-in-law, Judge Jackson, was less in the habit of repeating his reminiscences of the past, and living over *better times*, in narration, than many men of advanced age. There was a reserve and modesty in his character that would have prevented him from *glorying*, as some old men harmlessly do, in the name and fame of an early friend or revered instructor. But whenever he mentioned the name of "Mr. Parsons," it was as one speaks of the wisest man whom he has known, and not only the wisest, but the most honored and trusted. I have rarely heard him *praise* "Mr. Parsons," except when a question called up the mention of some of his high qualities; but he always seemed to assume that, in his own experience of life, this was the one great man whom he had met with and known, and whose memory and thoughts were the best inheritance that his professional life had bequeathed him.

I do not know that I shall be able to add anything from my vague recollections to your Memoir; but I am rejoiced that you have undertaken to write one, wondering only that it has not been done before this, by other hands, if not your own. I shall talk over the Judge's recollections with "the Doctor"; and if I can glean anything, be assured it will give me the greatest pleasure to communicate it to you.

Yours very respectfully,

O. W. HOLMES.

"The Doctor" whom he speaks of is his uncle, Dr. James Jackson, of whom I need say but little, for few men are better known in this community. And if I said more, I should have to choose between a most inadequate expression of my respect and regard, or a testimony to his worth which would seem extravagant to them who do not know that, in his old age, — of which the peace seems to be even the more profound, because his usefulness has not abated, — he lives in the fullest enjoyment of all

> "That should accompany old age,
> As honor, love, obedience, troops of friends." *

In a recent interview, he related to me a conversation to which he listened when quite young, between my father, John Jay of New York, and his own father, — "Treasurer Jackson," as I used to hear him called, — in his father's home. He could not give me the words; but it was substantially this: Mr. Jay had expressed his regret, and almost his surprise, that Providence permitted the benefits of experience to descend to others only in so imperfect a degree; and he remarked how much wiser the world would be if, when the father died, he could give to the son all those lessons which he had himself learned in the hard school of personal experience. And my father replied, that this would defeat the chief purpose for which we live; for that is the culture and moral improvement of each individual *by his own efforts.* Hence it seems to be provided, that experi-

* A year or so ago, while conversing with Dr. Jackson, I happened to remark that, at my age, I felt as if one's days must be few, and the capacity of usefulness well-nigh exhausted. "You mistake there," said he. "At sixty, a man in fair health may enter upon a series of years equal in usefulness and happiness to those of any period, provided proper precautions are taken and proper habits formed." And upon further inquiry into these essentials or conditions, I found he summed them up in "employment without labor; exercise without weariness; temperance without abstinence." These rules have no bearing on my father's life, unless by way of contrast, for he labored to his last sickness without one jot of abatement, and took little exercise, and was free and careless in his diet. But I give them here because they seem to contain as much sound sense and wise advice as could easily be compacted into the same number of words.

ence may so far be transmitted, and its lessons accumulate, as, on the whole, to make the world wiser, and to assist each person in the work of building up his own character, but not so far as to permit the father to do this work, or any part of it, in the stead of the son, because the whole work, and all that belongs to it, must be done by each individual, in his own freedom, and upon his own responsibility.

I must be permitted to say a word more of one who was among my father's most valued friends. Jonathan Jackson was born in Newburyport in 1743. His father was a merchant. He graduated in 1761, and was, at different times, a member of the Provincial Congress, United States Marshal for the District of Massachusetts, an inspector of excise, and Treasurer of the Commonwealth, and also Treasurer of Harvard College. From boyhood I was accustomed to hear my father speak of him in terms which placed him before me as the embodiment of sound sense and absolute integrity. His family exhibit a remarkable instance of a father's imparting to his children, by blood or education, or both, his own elements of excellence; each of those whom I have known having in his own walk attained a distinction which might well have satisfied more ambition than the father or the sons possessed. Of Dr. Jackson I have already spoken. His younger brother, Patrick, was a merchant, and, after a life of eminent usefulness, died in the year 1847, at the age of sixty-seven, leaving behind him no member of the community to whom more of its respect was given. Charles Jackson, the eldest brother, was a lawyer, and a thoroughly good lawyer in every possible sense of the word; one to whom duty was the only rule of life that he could even think of; and to whom departure from the exactest line of right was simply an impossible thing. In 1813, he left as great a business as one man could have, and accepted a seat on the Supreme Bench. He held it for ten years, and then was compelled by feeble health to resign it. No man ever took that high office with a more unanimous acknowledgment of his fitness; no one ever exercised its functions with a more universal acceptance, or left it with a more universal regret. Upon the commission to revise the statutes of the Commonwealth which reported in 1835, his services were, as I can testify, invaluable.*

I close these letters with the following from the Hon. C. P. Phelps.

MY DEAR SIR:

I have prepared at some intervals the following desultory statements, in answer to your request that I would furnish you with such incidents in the early life of your father as may have come to my knowledge.

My acquaintance with him commenced after he was forty years of age. I then knew nothing of his previous history, and the little knowledge of it that I subsequently acquired was mostly derived from irresponsible hearsay.

I entered his office as a law student in January, 1792, and remained there till April, 1795, — about three years. But his professional business called him away from home during the greater part of the year; I should think at least three fourths of the time. His practice in the courts in the State of New Hampshire, in the counties of Suffolk, Middlesex, Essex, and Norfolk in Massachusetts, and occasionally in Rhode Island, occupied a large portion of his time. Except when attending the Supreme Judicial Court in Boston, he usually returned at the close of the

---

* In the 75th volume of the Probate Records of Boston, folio 36, there is a deed of manumission of "Pomp" by his master and owner. It is dated one fortnight before the Declaration of Independence, and begins thus: "I, Jonathan Jackson, of Newburyport, in consideration of the impropriety I feel, and long have felt, in holding any person in constant bondage, more especially at the time when my country is so warmly contending for the liberty every man ought to enjoy," and also in consideration of promises, &c. to "my negro man Pomp"; and then goes on formally to liberate and manumit him. "Pomp Jackson," as he is called in the records, served as a freeman, and a fifer, in the army of the Revolution, settled in Andover in this State, and gave his name to "Pomp's Pond" in that town, and died there in 1822, being almost a century old.

week, and passed the Sunday at home. He seldom spent many consecutive weeks with his family, except in midsummer.

His habits outside of his profession were very domestic. His attachment to his wife and children was sincere and marked, and his attentions to the younger members of his family were particularly endearing and affectionate.

He was a great reader, as well as a great and original thinker. About the time of his commencing practice, I have understood that his midnight studies and intense application to business prostrated his health to such a degree that his friends became seriously alarmed, and for some time were doubtful of his recovery. I have seen a portrait of him taken about that period of his life, which seemed to warrant all their fears.

No one that knew him at the beginning of the nineteenth century needs to be told that he was well versed in astronomy, a fine belles-lettres scholar, and a profound mathematician, who made it his pastime and amusement to solve questions and problems, which would occupy days of calculation, and fill sheets of paper in their solution. And all who knew him, knew also that he was a thoroughly read lawyer in all the departments of that science, an able and astute special pleader, an unflinching, powerful, and successful advocate.

His conversational talent was very attractive, when he felt inclined to exert it, which he was sometimes provokingly unwilling to do, much to the regret of his friends. He was an admirable story-teller, and his repartees were pungent and effective, and his general information upon all subjects was very remarkable. I had the pleasure of introducing to him, not long after his removal to Boston, Judge Gould of Litchfield, Connecticut, a man of rare powers of mind. They were both much gratified with the meeting, and Judge Gould spoke of him as a wonderful man; not only as great in his profession, but brilliant and fascinating in his social powers. But Mr. Parsons was not in the habit of mingling much in mixed society. He seldom appeared at dinner-parties, or gatherings on public occasions, and I have no recollection that he ever attended any great political meeting. I much doubt if he ever made an evening visit to a family in Newburyport, during the three years of my residence there, except among his family connections, or to the houses of his physician (Doctor Sawyer) and his ministers (Messrs. Carey and Andrews).

As he was subjected through life to occasional attacks of nervous disease, it frequently happened, that, when released from his active professional services during the summer vacation, the want of out-door exercise brought on physical complaints, which produced hypochondria, and often confined him to his house for weeks, when he was rarely seen by any, except his particular friends. But when the court term came on, he always rallied, and was seen in his place at the bar.

As to the preparatory professional studies of Mr. Parsons, I have heard very little. My impression is, that he read law a year or more in the office of Theophilus Bradbury in Portland, (who was afterwards a Judge of the Supreme Judicial Court of Massachusetts,) and at the same time taught the Grammar School in that place, and, I believe, first opened an office there. This was probably near the commencement of the Revolution. But about the time Portland was burned, he removed to Byfield, and was a member of his father's family some time; and while a resident there, Judge Trowbridge of Cambridge, a distinguished jurist of that day, who was driven from his home by the dread of the small-pox, then raging in Boston, sought refuge in Byfield, and became a boarder at the parsonage. And Mr. Parsons has often said, that he acquired during that period, from his intercourse with Judge Trowbridge, more knowledge of law as a science, than he had done in all his previous study.

After that, he practised law in Newburyport some time. I know not exactly how long before his marriage, which took place, I think, in January, 1780.

Not long after the death of Judge Greenleaf (Mrs. Parsons's father), he removed to Boston, in the year 1800.

In 1806, I believe, near the close of the first term of Governor Strong's administration, he was appointed Chief Justice on the bench of the Supreme Judicial Court of Massachusetts. From that time his life and services were devoted to the Commonwealth, until his death, which took place in October, 1813. Since that period, his name and character have become, in this country, coextensive with the knowledge of English and American jurisprudence.

As a statesman and politician he occupied a high and commanding position, and was an acknowledged, though not openly self-avowed leader. He was a member of the powerful "Essex

Junto," a political club in bad repute with the radicals and Anti-Federalists of the last century, and feared, not less than hated, by the disorganizers and insurgents of that and a later day. But the political influence of Mr. Parsons was not obtrusive; it was always more felt than seen. Among the leading men of the times were James Bowdoin, John Lowell the elder, Timothy Pickering, George Cabot, Stephen Higginson, and others.

His elevation to the bench was hailed by the citizens of Massachusetts with great and very general satisfaction. Many of the bar highly approved it, as most fit in itself; a few, because it would open to them a wider field of practice; and some were dissatisfied from various motives, not necessary to specify. In the discharge of his judicial duties, he gave almost universal satisfaction, except with the bar. The business had so accumulated upon the county dockets, that few cases could come to a trial in less than three years. Judge Parsons at once resolved that the dockets should be cleared, if possible. No delays were to be allowed, unless for *real* and sufficient reasons. The rule was established, that the cases were to be tried each in its regular turn, and the parties and their counsel were made to understand that they must be prepared for trial when called.

A new face of things was soon visible in the courts, and all but the lawyers were satisfied. The litigants who gained, were of course delighted; and even those who lost their causes were glad to find themselves at last clear of a lawsuit of which they began to despair of ever reaching the end.

But the lawyers, many of them, said he was overbearing and arbitrary. The Chief Justice seized, undoubtedly with wonderful facility, the great points of a case, and kept the counsel close to them. He never allowed an advocate to *make a speech*, and *talk against time*, merely for the purpose of displaying his rhetorical powers, or to satisfy his clients that he had earned his fee; and there were, doubtless, instances where, in his opinion, the justice of the case was so transparent, that he would not waste the time of the public in listening to a needless argument in support of an obviously just claim. But I do not believe that he ever refused a reasonable and patient hearing to any party who maintained a doubtful, or even a manifestly bad cause.

I am not indeed a very competent judge to decide the question, but I have always supposed that, in the trial of *nisi prius* cases, he sat on the Massachusetts bench unrivalled. Many members of the bar, however, were unquestionably, at that period, dissatisfied.

I have heard him relate an incident which affected himself professionally, and which occurred in his early practice, as showing the effect that a change of location and surrounding objects might produce in the mental powers and in the physical sensations.

On the trial of a capital case in Boston, Mr. Parsons had been assigned by the court as counsel for the prisoner. As the case had awakened considerable interest in the town, it was found, soon after the trial began, that more space than the court-room afforded would be necessary to accommodate the assemblage. The court was accordingly adjourned, I think to Faneuil Hall. The trial proceeded, and when Mr. Parsons rose to address the jury in defence of the prisoner, the total disarrangement of judges, lawyers, and jury, the disruption of all local associations, and the entire novelty and strangeness of the whole scene, so disconcerted him, that it required several moments of painful effort to recover his lost self-possession. Many years afterwards, I heard the late Judge Jackson mention a somewhat similar occurrence, illustrating the operation of the same principle, in a case of his own professional experience. But I am rather inclined to the opinion, that neither of them ever *had the disease a second time.*

His high professional character gave him great celebrity as an instructor, and during the greater part of his residence in Newburyport his office was usually crowded with pupils; indeed, so much so, that, as I have been told, the jealousy of the bar became awakened, and a rule was adopted, that no lawyer should have under his tuition more than three pupils at any one time, with a special view to his particular case. Of course, many have entered the profession through the doors of his office; among them, a few of most distinguished eminence. Rufus King and John Q. Adams are names prominent on the page of history; Samuel Putnam, Charles Jackson, and Benjamin Gorham have done honor to their master, and also to Massachusetts; and a few others, whose names I do not at this moment call to mind. The greatest distinction which is likely ever to be attached to one of his pupils is, that he is believed to be the sole survivor of all those who have shared the teachings of that great master, — a distinction of which neither time nor circumstance can deprive him. Of that large number, all but the writer have passed away, and in a short time his exit will have closed the procession.

I have thus, my dear Sir, tried to gather up a few scattered fragments that remain of my fast-fading recollections of your venerated father. In the lapse of sixty-five years since I first saw him, and of forty-three since his lamented decease, I have forgotten most things that I ever knew; but among those recollections that will be the last to forsake me, are the scenes and pleasures so intimately associated with that large portion of my life spent in an uninterrupted and harmonious intercourse with his family, and which was so often brightened by the sunshine of his own superintending presence.

I suppose that few of the foregoing incidents or opinions can be deemed of any great importance to your undertaking; and those which are so, I doubt not, are already familiar to you. They are all that my memory can furnish, and are at your disposal, to be used or destroyed.

Yours, with sincere regard,

CHARLES P. PHELPS.

Hadley, April 2d, 1857.

I should not do justice to my father, if I did not mention one trait, or practice, in which I am happy to say he did not stand alone in our profession. He made it an imperative rule, from which he never swerved during his whole professional career, never to make any charge against, or accept any fee from, *a widow*, or *a minister of the Gospel.*

Of my father's contemporaries at the bar, I suppose that the four most eminent were Sullivan, Dexter, Otis, and Prescott.

Governor Sullivan was older than my father. He died in 1808, and I never knew him.

Samuel Dexter was eleven years younger. He died in 1816, aged fifty-four. I cannot say that I ever knew him personally. I have seen him, however; and a year or two before his death I heard him make a speech in Faneuil Hall, in which he gave his reasons for not supporting the measures of the Federal party, of which, to that hour, he had been a leader. If this was not *his* greatest speech, it was one of the greatest ever delivered in that hall, or, as I think, anywhere. Few events of my early years do I remember so perfectly. I cannot recall the line of argument, but the tone and manner, and the effect, I well remember. There was nothing in it of apology, nothing of entreaty, little indeed of self-defence; but such an explanation of his conduct, and such a statement of his principles, as a man might make to his fellow-citizens, while he respected them, and was determined that they should respect him. As I recall him, it does not seem to me that he had much elegance, or even eloquence, of language or of delivery; but that the whole speech, in tone, words, thoughts, and effect, was characterized by *power*. He did not seem to persuade men to believe with him, but to compel them to see that as truth which he thought to be true. I suppose he was not a scientific lawyer, — not one, I mean, acquainted with the whole system of the law, and seeing every part in the light of all the rest. But he was a very great lawyer *in rem;* for he brought to the examination of a case extraordinary ability, learning enough to guide his study, and thorough devotion to his work. As an advocate in cases which demand a close investigation of complicated facts and rules, and a clear perception and a strong hold of the guiding principle that is to solve the problem finally, and then the power to carry the court and jury with him through the long research or argument, I am confident that he was never surpassed in New England, if in our country.

From Mr. Dexter, Mr. Otis differed about as much as a man could. As a book-lawyer, I suppose he stood on a par with him. Without undertaking to say which of the two was the greater advocate, it is enough that no common standard could be applied to them, unless it were that of success; and measured by this, they were perhaps equal, for they stood together in the foremost rank of the profession.

Harrison Gray Otis lived until 1848, then dying at the age of eighty-three. I knew him long and well, due allowance being made for the difference in our ages. I had the good fortune to hear him argue his last case. Some twenty-five or thirty years ago, long after he had retired from general practice, he had an important action of his own, and argued it himself; and I listened eagerly to every word he said. It was something unlike in kind to anything else I ever heard. The winning music of his voice made the hearer reluctant to lose a word; the flow of his language, which was as charmingly constructed and cadenced as if it had all been carefully written by a practised writer; and the persuasive logic, which led you along almost unconsciously until you stood in the very position in which he would place you, — in each and all of these he was unrivalled. And to all these was added their strongest charm, perhaps, in the apparent spontaneity of it all. There was no effort, no appearance of saying or doing anything in any way which did not come of itself. And I believed then, and I believe now, that this was not apparent only, but real. He had, if ever man had, the *gift* of eloquence. And all, — grace of delivery, sweetness of tone, beauty of illustration, perfect taste in words, and rapidity and clearness of thought, — all blended into one, flowed on like a river, and the hearer was borne along upon the rapid stream, not conscious of its power, and not resisting it.

This may seem, and may be, the extravagant picture of a *laudator temporis acti*. Let me state, however, that by my side there sat a gentleman who had not reached his own foremost place in our profession without knowing as well as any one what were the elements of successful speech, — I hope I do not offend against social courtesies when I name Judge Fletcher, — and he turned to me, as Mr. Otis closed, with the whispered remark: "There is nothing like this now."

From these two men William Prescott differed as much as they differed from each other. He confined himself to his profession far more than either Dexter or Otis, and for many years stood, by universal consent, at its head. Some six years ago, I published a Treatise on the Law of Contracts; and in a dedication to my friend, W. H. Prescott, I indulged myself with saying a very little of what I gladly would have said of his revered father. I said it then, because it was my first opportunity to discharge this duty. And I repeat it now, because none outside of my profession have ever seen it, and, in a memoir of my father, I feel justified in saying of one of his most valued friends what I am sure he would wish me to say.

To William H. Prescott, Esq., the Historian of Spain, Mexico, and Peru.

I might, perhaps, find some excuse for dedicating this work to you, in the natural desire of connecting my own labors with those which have won for you and for our country so much renown; and even more in the friendship which began so long ago we cannot remember its beginning; and in the long years that, through childhood, youth, and manhood, have brought us upon the confines of age, if not beyond them, has never for a moment been broken.

But neither of these is my principal motive. That I must confess to be a strong and irrepressible desire to speak of your father; to express, however imperfectly, my gratitude to him; and to execute, even in this slight degree, the purpose I have long had, of putting on record my testimony to the excellence of one who stood for many years at the head of his profession, who was my master during my apprenticeship to the law, and ever after my revered instructor and invaluable friend.

It was in 1815 that I entered his office as a student. I had been accustomed all my life to see him often, and hear him often spoken of, for our families were intimate, and he was among my father's most valued friends; and I had always heard him mentioned with a kind and degree of respect that seemed to be paid to him alone. I knew that he had held the highest place in his profession for some years; but the regard and reverence generally accorded to him were more than any mere professional success could win. When I entered his office, he had already given up a large part of his business. He did not go often into court; but I heard him in some important cases, and was a constant observer of the relations between him and his numerous clients. It was not long before I learned the grounds of his high social and professional position.

In the first place, let me speak of his judgment and sagacity. I cannot conceive of any person possessing, in greater perfection, that admirable thing we call *good sense.* I doubt whether, in his long and active life, he ever made any one mistake of importance. Whoever employed him in any business, soon saw that the wisest thing that could be done in his case, and at every step of it, was always the very thing that was done. Hence a confidence without limit was reposed in his opinions; and his advice was accepted and followed by all who received it, as if it made farther inquiry or consideration wholly unnecessary.

The next quality I would mention was a kindred and connected one; I mean his perfect truthfulness. It seemed as if he could not deceive; and if he had the faculty originally, he must have lost it by *non-user.* It made no difference on which side of a question the party propounding it to him stood; for his answer was to the question, and not to the man. Whether he dealt with a client, an adverse party, a witness, the jury, or the court, he dealt with them all honestly. He had what I am sorry to call the rare quality of loving truth so well, that his view of it was not to be distorted or obstructed by any interest or any feeling either of his own or of those whom he represented, or by any disturbing influences of circumstances or position.

I speak last of his learning, although this was perhaps more frequently remarked upon than his moral qualities, however deeply these were felt. He had passed many years in laborious and well-directed study; for he was led to this, both by his sense of duty to his clients, and by his sagacity, which told him that here he must find the means of sound judgment and usefulness and success; and also by the love of his profession and of the law as a science. For many years after he had withdrawn from the profession, both as advocate and chamber counsel, he still continued his legal studies; and often when I have called upon him and stated some difficult question which had occurred in my practice, he would — not for a fee, but in his kindness to me, and his love of the law — enter upon the investigation with the zeal of earlier days, and give me the whole benefit of his vast knowledge and his unerring sagacity.

To these qualities I must add that of universal kindness and unfailing courtesy. And certainly I have given good reasons why he held so long the headship of a profession in which it is not easy to climb to the high places, and very difficult to hold them; and also why, outside of his profession and by society at large, he was venerated during his long life as few men among us have ever been. Let me add, that, while he manifested, wherever in the conduct of his affairs it was needed, the firmness and fearlessness that he inherited from a father who stood like a tower of strength in command of the American forces at Bunker Hill, he was ever, and remarkably, unassuming, retiring, and modest. It is difficult to believe that he could not measure his own success, or that he did not know his high position; but no one ever heard a word or a tone from him which indicated such knowledge.

He was not eloquent, and never, to my knowledge, attempted to be; and yet he was a most successful advocate. It was his purpose and endeavor to do for every client, and in every case, all that could be done by learning, sense, industry, and honesty; this he knew he could do, and did. And more than this he had no desire to do.

Such was William Prescott. When he died, in 1844, at the age of eighty-two, I had known him intimately for twenty-nine years, and had known of him many more. And I never yet heard a word spoken, and I never heard *of* a word spoken, to his disparagement or dispraise, during his long life or since its close, by any person whomsoever; not even have I heard the "but" or "if" with which many indulge themselves in qualifying and clouding the commendation they cannot but render. He has left behind him no brilliant speeches to be remembered and quoted; no books in which the fruits of his learning and wisdom were gathered and preserved; and they who knew him are passing away, and already his reputation is becoming traditional. And very glad shall I be, if, by this slight memorial, I may for a single moment arrest the waves of time, in their advancing flow over the sands in which are written his name, and the names of many others of our best and greatest.

THEOPHILUS PARSONS.

I must close this chapter in a sadder strain. While these pages were passing through the press, William Hickling Prescott, on Friday, the 28th of January, 1859, was suddenly stricken with apoplexy, and, after a few hours of unconsciousness, he died.

As I speak in this volume of his father, by reprinting what I wrote of him for another purpose, so I now venture to repeat here what I said of Prescott at a meeting of the American Academy, on the evening of the 8th of February, 1859. The newspapers which contained the proceedings of that meeting, gave to them a far wider circulation than these pages will have. But I cannot deny myself the solace of placing, permanently, in my own book, this feeble, but most sincere, tribute to one whose death took from me what nothing in this world can replace.

"When you intimated to me, Mr. President, your wish that I should say a few words on the topic which will occupy us this evening, it was difficult to assent, but impossible to refuse. I know not in what words to speak of Prescott. He was my oldest friend, — the last friend of my boyhood. Our fathers were intimate friends, and their intimacy fell to us as an inheritance. His genial face, and that cordial manner, which was but the transparent vesture of his constant kindness, I shall meet no more. But this is not the place in which to speak of my personal relations with him. Nor need I add my testimony to the universal recognition of the ability, the industry, the accurate learning, the admirable judgment, and the perfect taste, which have placed him at the head of our literature, and made him our pride.

"There was, however, one peculiarity in his character, which I have studied carefully, and have not as yet seen fully noticed by any one of the many who have spoken of him; and I should be glad to say a few words in relation to it. I refer to the blending in him of qualities which are usually regarded, not only as opposites, but as antagonists, and as mutually destructive.

"On the one hand, he was by nature tender, sensitive, and impressible. I never knew a person who had so much capacity for enjoyment; and I never knew one who had a greater love for it. And this was universal. It seemed as if he were alive to all the emotions, and possessed all the sensibilities, which are divided among other men, and in their division constitute the means of happiness for each. And I will add, that he was naturally as susceptible as any one could be, of every curled rose-leaf that threatened to mar his enjoyment.

"But, on the other hand, this man had an iron will; before his invincible energy, obstacles which to others would have seemed, and would have been, insurmountable, melted away. By his strength of purpose, obstructions were converted into helps. He had a resolute and unflinching self-control and self-restraint, and an unfailing power of self-government, upon which he knew that he could depend, and on which he did depend, always advancing, never losing a step that he had gained, and never doubting that he should gain the next, until at length he stood upon the eminence which from the beginning had been his goal, and upon which death found him.

"It has seemed to me that these qualities concealed each other, even from many who knew him. They who were most assured that he had won his high position by a stern devotion to his own lofty aims, and by unexampled force of character, sometimes imagined that such a man could not be sincere in his ready sympathy with all, in his full enjoyment of common pleasures, in the cordiality with which he came forward to meet all who approached him, in the smile which made all who saw it believe that he was happiest when he could make others happy; and it seemed to them as if this must be only a thin varnish, a mask of courtesy, which his knowledge of the world taught him to wear.

"Nothing, nothing, could be more untrue. Believe me, Mr. President, when I say that an experience of more than fifty years justifies my assertion, that it was out of the abundance of his full and overflowing heart, that his mouth spake his many words of kindness. And they who were certain of this, — who saw him day after day, entering with as ready gladness into all social pleasures as if he were the merest idler, and giving himself up to the enjoyment of the hour as if he had no other use for his time but to give it wings, — they found it difficult to believe that there was not something of unreality in his world-wide fame; or that something of accident had not helped him in his extraordinary career; or that his unconquerable will had fairly paid for his great success the full price of severe labor, of effort, and of sacrifice. As difficult as it might be for one who looks on a mountain clothed with beauty and fruitfulness from its foot to its summit, — its flowers breathing fragrance, and its foliage bending to the summer wind, — to remember while he looks, that its framework and substance are of the everlasting granite that bids defiance to accident and to the assault of the tempest.

"Prescott will ever give a valuable lesson to all who knew him, and to all who, without knowing him, form a just idea of him, — and they must be many, for surely History will long love to speak of him, — and this lesson will be, that all of a man's nature may be cultivated and exercised and indulged and enjoyed, if only all its faculties and tendencies are duly arranged and subordinated. These two elements of character of which I have spoken did not merely coexist in him, but co-operated. If either had been absent, or either had been less, he never would have done all that he has done. Every one admits, that, without his unyielding energy and his invincible endurance, he could not have accomplished his great works, in defiance of the great obstacles which cumbered his path. I am quite as sure, that even this energy and this endurance would have failed and fainted, if they had not been constantly invigorated, and refreshed, and filled with new life, by his exquisite sensibility to all innocent enjoyment.

"Let no one who would pluck a leaf of laurel from the topmost bough, imagine that he must nurse his strength for this achievement by the sacrifice and suppression of whatever in him is sympathetic and sensitive and responsive to others. Let Prescott tell him how all the gifts of a rich nature may be kept in full life, and may invigorate each other. Let Prescott remind him, that there was a laborious student, whose hours of toil nothing was permitted to interrupt, and whose determined industry nothing was permitted to abate, and yet whose companionship was sought as no other man's was; because, when the hour for labor had passed, he went forth among his friends like sunshine, and filled them with sympathetic gladness from his own joyous nature.

"We sometimes hear it said that a man has succeeded in some great effort because he put his whole soul into it. This would be true of Prescott in its ordinary meaning, which is only that he succeeded by enthusiastic labor. But it is true of him in a more definite, and, as I think, in a higher sense. If I were asked to give in the fewest words the explanation of his career, I should say that he did great things in despite of great difficulties, because he was richly endowed with many and various qualities and faculties, and in all his work the whole man worked together, with a harmony which gave to every faculty the support and the strength of all the rest."

Further I did not go, and could not go, that evening; but now I will advert to still other instances of apparent incongruity. His facility of utterance, and perfect openness of face and words and demeanor, concealed from others, not only his inner thoughts and feelings, but even the fact that he had them. Those who met him familiarly in society did not know, that, with all his seeming carelessness of speech, there was a reticence and reserve about him, which covered with an impenetrable veil that part of his nature which he chose should remain inaccessible. Thus, to those who judged only from appearances, he seemed to be a worldly man, — for who ever laid a stronger grasp upon the world, or upon whom did it ever lay a stronger grasp! And yet within this seeming worldliness there lived a profound, constant, and operative religious sentiment. Many, even of his nearest friends, who knew his general habit of self-examination, may still be surprised to learn, that this favorite of society, who loved it as well as it loved him, for more than thirty years had one invariable rule, in obedience to which, every Sunday, as the day came round, he had his hour of seclusion and privacy, and employed it in a careful examination of the whole preceding week, from its first to its last hour. He sought, by this investigation, to know where he had been wrong or weak; what purpose needed to be strengthened, or what new resolution to be formed, that the past might throw a guiding light upon the future. I regard this as one of the causes of his continued improvement, of his unfaltering progress, in all his relations, as a scholar, or to his family, to his friends, and to society; or, in simpler words, — for I would not be mistaken here, — I think this one of the causes, that, on the one hand, his last volume was his best, as by common consent it is; and, on the other, that with every succeeding year he became *a better man.*

They who know my relations with him will understand my desire to present this portraiture of my friend; and they who do not, will, I hope, pardon it, for the sake of the instruction and the influence of such an example.

CHAPTER V.

OF HIM AS A JUDGE.

In 1806, Chief Justice Dana, upon whom the infirmities of advancing age had begun to press heavily, resigned the office which he had filled most honorably and usefully for fourteen years.

A generation had passed away since the Commonwealth had become independent; and during all that time, its judicial affairs had been in a somewhat confused and troubled condition. The royal authority was lost. Its power and pressure were taken away, and had not been adequately replaced. The turmoil and strife of the Revolution had injuriously affected the bar. There were a few able and well-instructed men; but the great majority were not so. The seniors got through their business somehow, and the juniors saw little in their example to incite them to more diligent study; and out of the largest towns this was scarcely possible, for want of the necessary books. A system of costs, founded on mere delay, had grown up, which made delay profitable. The prevailing party was allowed for his attendance upon the court thirty-three cents a day. This was moderate in amount, and just in principle while confined to actual attendance. But in practice every party was considered as attending every day, because his attorney was or might be there. Hence a lawyer in large practice, although his business might be merely that of collecting debts, made a large income. If he had fifty cases in court, he was receiving $16.60 every day while the court sat. Some made this number of entries at every term; and as the cases were kept as long in court as could easily be done, they would have a very large number continually running up their costs. Here was an obvious inducement, not only to make the terms as long as possible, but also to keep the cases in court as long as possible. This injurious system remained in force until a few years since. In this way, and from other causes also, the courts found it very difficult to accelerate their business, and impracticable to bring the lawyers to any great accuracy of procedure; and the right and prevailing habit of appeal, which caused most cases of any interest to be tried two or three times, added to the mischief. A lax, irresponsible, and dilatory course of procedure had become established, which crowded the dockets so that no business could be done that was not old and stale. But it gave to a few leaders of the bar almost despotic power, and at the same time furnished sufficient profits to the lawyers who aimed at nothing more than to collect debts and get bills of costs. It pressed, however, severely on the business of the community; and the people *felt*, although they might not distinctly *see*, the abuses under which they suffered; nor did they discern any effectual remedy.

When Chief Justice Dana resigned, the remaining judges, ranking in order of seniority, were Theodore Sedgwick, Samuel Sewall, George Thatcher, and Isaac Parker. Judge Sedgwick, according to the ordinary procedure, had some right to expect promotion to the Chief-Justiceship; and this right was strengthened by the acknowledged fact that he was an eminent jurist, had been Speaker of the House of Representatives in Congress, and was generally and rightly regarded as among the ablest men of the State. Judge Parker was appointed in December, 1805. From his knowledge of the practice at the bar in Maine, confirmed by a year's experience as a judge, he was profoundly convinced that errors, not to say abuses, existed, which imperatively demanded reform, and which an *entirely new man* would find it easier to reform. He was holding court (at Ipswich I think, in Essex County I am sure), when he first learned that Chief Justice Dana intended to resign. He that evening rode over to Marblehead, and conferred with Judge Sewall, who lived there, and who thought as he did on this subject. It was determined that Sewall should go the next day to Boston, and represent to Governor Strong, that, if my father could be appointed at once, without consulting him, every exertion would be made to persuade him to accept the office, even if he took it for a short time only. And the appointment was made at once.

Before going further, let me say that Judge Sedgwick, although at first hurt and disappointed, became convinced that no disrespect was intended him, that his personal merit was fully acknowledged, and that there was a general and strong desire that he should retain his place upon the bench; and he consented to do so. Although I think he was never so well satisfied with my father's proceedings as a judge as were the other members of the court, the relations between them were always entirely friendly.

From the tenor of some remarks in the newspapers of the day, and from all that I have heard, I believe there was much surprise felt when my father accepted the office. He had a large family, was not rich, and was then in full practice, earning in the year before he left practice about ten thousand dollars, which, for those days, was a larger sum in its indications, and perhaps in its value, than twice the amount would be now. He had always shown an aversion to office, and a love for home and privacy, which seemed to grow with his years. But it is not difficult to see some of the reasons which induced him to comply with the earnest solicitations that came to him from many quarters.

In the first place, I incline to believe that he already contemplated leaving court practice, and confining himself to giving chamber counsel, and to the decision of questions referred to him. He had reason to suppose that this practice would be sufficiently remunerative. Among the papers I still have, are letters showing that his opinion and advice were called for frequently from distant regions of the country, as well as from all parts of New England. I believe he thought it might be easier to break off from court practice at once, by going on the bench; as he could leave office when he chose to do so, and place himself in a position for whatever chamber practice might come.

I add, that his personal friends urged him to take the office, doubting whether he would break off from bar business in any other way, and believing that the change of employment, the travelling, and the diminished labor would be beneficial to his health, which threatened to fail.

But by far the strongest motives with him, as I have abundant evidence, arose from his clear perception of that need of some reform in the courts to which I have already alluded, — his belief that he could effect this reform, and his desire to do it. Nor can I exhibit the full strength of these motives without stating at some length what I suppose were his views on this subject.

My father's attention had been very much drawn to the theory of the Constitution. We have already seen how prominent he had been in the discussions and conflicts which took place in reference to the state and national constitutions; and, with his tendencies and habits of mind, we may be certain that he had exerted whatever strength he had, to comprehend the whole truth in reference to this great subject, even to its foundations. I have reason to believe that he formed an opinion in relation to the judicial department of government, which might now be thought extreme, and certainly would not be popular. But it was accepted in his own day, and if in this generation we have learned to think otherwise, it may be that coming events will prove to us, or to our children, the greater wisdom of our fathers.

It was, as I suppose, (and on this point I might refer, to some extent, to documentary evidence,) his belief, that the success of the great political experiment to be tried here would depend very much upon the degree in which the three great elements of government were kept each within its proper sphere, and within that sphere were respected and supported. The Constitution was a prior fact, on which, as on a prepared foundation, the whole government rested. It was law, but law made by the whole people. It was intended to be sovereign over all other law, and to secure at once perfection of form and fulness of life to the body politic, and wise guidance and well defined and guarded limitations to all the powers of the government. While, of these powers it was the proper function to bear that life forward, and promote its healthy flow, even to the remotest and most recondite corners of the social fabric.

Hence, legislatures were to meet often, and adapt existing and practical law to all the wants and capacities of society, as far as possible, but always in exact conformity with the requirements and restraints of the fundamental law.

Then the executive, beginning with the governor and ending with the constable, was to enforce and carry into full effect all the laws which the legislature should make; but always with the same controlling power to set limits to its action.

And then came the judicial power, originating nothing, executing nothing, unless so far as it must do either of these things indirectly by the mere process of judging, but exhausting its whole capacity and fulfilling all its mission in two forms. In one, with reference to individuals, it declares aright what the law requires, and what it forbids; in the other, in reference to those other elements of political power which, together with itself, constitute all government, its great duty is to guard them from excess or error, to keep them in the right path, and prevent, as far as possible, all mischief from their wanderings, by declaring null, and making null, whatever either of them should do outside of the scope and field provided for it by the Constitution.

Thus far I have said little more than everybody says; and to say that my father thought thus, is only to say that he thought as everybody thought. But I add, — and it seems to me a great addition, — he thought and believed these things honestly and earnestly. He was profoundly penetrated with their truth, and lost no opportunity of declaring and illustrating it.

Few persons, as it seems to me, appreciate the vital importance of the judicial functions in a republic. Let the constitution be as perfect as any work of man can be, it will have no power of self-protection; and the executive and the legislature will constantly require to be kept within its limits by some controlling power.

Even if the laws are all they should be, they must be clothed in human language, and therefore must often need wise interpretation. And the inexhaustible and ever-shifting complications of human life continually demand that these laws should be adjusted anew, that they may respond to new questions and adapt themselves to new conditions, and bring the new forms and arrangements, which are constantly taking place among the commercial and the social relations of men, into harmony with existing law.

Then, too, after all this is done, there remains the incessant duty of so visiting the crimes, so ending the quarrels, and so determining the rights and enforcing the obligations of all persons, that the community may repose under the conviction that wrong is reduced within its least limits, and that the prevalence of right secures the peace and prosperity of the Commonwealth.

To all this it must be added, that the love of precedent and stability, which comes to us by inheritance from our Anglo-Saxon ancestors, gives to judicial decisions an authority almost like that of law itself; and thus compels the judiciary to discharge important functions, which closely resemble, to say the least, those of a legislative body.

This faint portraiture of the work which the judiciary

must do, — which will not be done unless they do it, and will be done well or ill *as* they may do it, — faint and imperfect as it is, may show that a state should provide with the utmost solicitude all those means which will place upon the seats of justice those persons who are best qualified to fill them ; and regard their independence and their purity as the safeguards of the state, and protect them equally from assault and from temptation ; and give to their hands all the strength their high functions demand, because this will be only the strength of the state, used for its own defence and security. And, finally, that no care and no wisdom are more than should be given to the great purpose of securing to the state its best possible judiciary, and that no necessary cost can be more than an adequate price for this inestimable good.

When a republic, as free from all external control as our own, has passed its meridian, and begins to decline, the first and the surest signs of this descent will be that the judiciary will lose the respect and confidence of the people, and will in some way deserve to lose it. The people themselves may undervalue the worth and magnitude of judicial duty, and the absolute necessity of preserving the independence of those upon whom this duty rests.

It is most true that the judiciary should be personally responsible to the people. But the people, seeing this, may become willing that its independence should be sacrificed to the fallacy of an immediate and frequently recurring responsibility; and for this purpose may change the tenure of judicial office to a term of years, instead of "during good behavior" ; and even make the office of judge elective. Or they, or an influential portion of them, while moved by some strong impulse, may desire that the judiciary should feel this impulse also, and place itself on the one side or the other of conflicting parties. When this is done, even the partisans who rejoice, cannot approve, or at least can no longer respect that judiciary which has become their own. They, and then the whole people, will lose all just idea of what the judiciary should be, and how it should be regarded; and then a step has been taken, a large step, of steep descent, from which it will be difficult, and perhaps impossible, to recover and re-ascend.

I believe there was nothing which my father more desired than that the people should cultivate in themselves a kind and respectful, but watchful jealousy of the judicial department; and should feel a deep and sincere, and yet a rational respect for it, founded upon a just understanding of the vast importance of its functions. And that the people might so feel, the very first and most essential cause must be, that the judicial department should *deserve* to be so regarded. He wished that the people should see and know, clearly and certainly, the utility of the judiciary *to them;* and that they should see and know as clearly the means by which their utility might be secured and preserved.

In this department he included, not the judges only, but all who were officers of the courts; and among them he placed all who practised at the bar. And I believe that he was earnest and constant in his endeavors to impress upon his students, and upon others who came within his reach, that it was the duty of every lawyer to feel that upon himself rested some portion of the responsibility, and of the power for good or for evil, with which the institutions of a constitutional republic invest its judicial department.

No suspicion of political or personal corruption ever attached itself to the judiciary of Massachusetts. In these respects there was nothing to desire. But during the transition period from the condition of a royal colony to that of a self-governing republic, no human sagacity could foresee all the changes and all the means by which the judiciary must be re-adjusted to the new exigencies of a new political condition; nor could they be discovered, excepting as the necessity for reform should reveal them.

I have, however, stated this at much greater length than

I otherwise should, in part because I believe that his views on this subject operated to induce him to accept the office of Chief Justice. No one knew better than he the actual condition of the courts of law, and the mischiefs arising from it; and he knew, too, the force and ability and learning of some who then adorned, and of some who had adorned, that bench. But he sympathized with those who thought that it would be far easier for a new man to make the necessary reforms, than for one who had been a judge during the period in which these abuses had insensibly, and perhaps inevitably, grown up.

But a much stronger reason for stating these views of my father is, that they will help us to understand his conduct as a judge.

I think he took that office mainly to reform what he thought needed reform, and with the desire to do this as speedily as was consistent with doing it effectually; and then it was his purpose to leave the office.

In 1804, what are called *nisi prius* terms of the Supreme Judicial Court were established. To those of my readers who are not lawyers, it may be well to explain, that by this arrangement terms of the court were held by one judge in almost every county of the Commonwealth, for the trial of jury cases. These were called *nisi prius* terms; and questions of law arising from these trials, or otherwise, were heard before the whole court (or three judges), at certain terms held for this purpose, and known as *law* terms. Before this change was made, all the judges sat together to hear jury trials. This new arrangement was an excellent one; and as it permitted a far more frequent trial of cases before a jury than the old system, it promised to do much towards preventing that costly delay of justice which had become such a burden. The judges approved it, and so, I believe, did all the best lawyers of the State; but by the bar generally it was much disliked, and very much obstructed. My father thought the change an important one. He had been so active in support of it, that by some persons he was — I think incorrectly — considered as the author of it. At all events, a desire to insure this system fair play, and to exhibit the working and effect of it, was one motive for his acceptance of the office of Chief Justice.

He took the opportunity offered him by the duty of charging the grand jury of each county, to state very distinctly his views upon some of the most important principles of our Constitution. This charge he delivered at nine places in the course of 1806. A good deal was said about it at the time; and I now publish the close of it:

The last class of misdemeanors, Gentlemen, to which I shall call your attention, are those which relate to the laws providing for the instruction of youth, and the diffusion of religious knowledge through the State.

Without public schools, the children of many citizens will grow up in ignorance, without a knowledge of their rights or duties, and will become a burden on that government which it should be their duty to support. The laws, therefore, enjoin us to teach the rising generation to be good citizens, and to provide, as nearly as possible, equal advantages for all who are to possess equal rights.

The diffusion of religious knowledge is also essential to the well-being of the State. And it cannot be effected but by the settlement and support of teachers in towns, parishes, and societies incorporated for religious purposes.

Some persons have professed dissatisfaction with our Constitution, and the laws made in obedience to it, for its interference (as they supposed) with religion; and they have considered the people as assuming a power which the founder of it reserved to himself. A short review of the subject may, perhaps, satisfy us, that the people not only had a right, but that it was their duty, to provide by law for religious instruction.

Every well-regulated government, established for the people, ought to contain within itself the principles and powers necessary to promote and secure their happiness. This happiness must result from the practice of a correct system of moral duties, founded in the nature of man as a reasonable and social being.

The knowledge of such a system the civil magistrate is therefore bound to spread among the people, and to exhibit the most rational and effectual motives for its practice. But the practice of a part of this system cannot be enforced by temporal penalties. The moral duties of imperfect obligation, as charity, liberality, hospitality, gratitude, parental affection, filial attachment, and all the benevolent acts which constitute good neighborhood, cannot be the object of human legislation. To compel by law the practice of these virtues would destroy their nature.

Further, human laws can punish offences only of which there is evidence. Crimes committed in secret are, therefore, out of the reach of the civil magistrate. Thus our lives and our property lie at the mercy of every man who can assail them without witnesses, and who has no restraint on his actions but the dread of temporal punishment. What then could the people do to provide a remedy for these defects necessary in a government merely civil? Like all wise legislatures, they called to their aid the unceasing operations of religion.

In Christianity they found a pure and perfect system of morals, embracing all ranks, stations, and conditions of men, and exhibiting the strongest motive to the practice of duty by declaring the existence of a future state of rewards and punishments. Here every citizen could learn all his civil and social duties; and here the man meditating mischief would be informed, that, though wrapped in darkness, he was not unseen, but was in the presence of a Judge whose wisdom he could not deceive, and whose justice he could not escape. The people, therefore, as a wise and indispensable means of civil and social security and enjoyment, established the religion of Protestant Christians; not any one sect, but all sects indiscriminately, without subordination, and giving to each equal protection and equal privileges.

To diffuse the knowledge of this excellent system, that civil society might enjoy its salutary influences, there must be teachers. And the laws have accordingly enjoined it on all towns, parishes, and other societies incorporated for religious purposes, to elect and support public Protestant teachers of piety, religion, and morality, leaving it in the absolute power of these corporations whom to choose, and the nature of their support. By adhering to this liberal and equal establishment, as we prevent all possibility of vesting in any one sect peculiar privileges or prerogatives over the others, so we obtain for ourselves that civil and temporal safety which is unattainable but by the sanctions of religion. And, Gentlemen, while we are instructed how to be good citizens, good neighbors, good in every relation of this life, if we should also be taught that there is another and a better country, and should learn the way to gain an inheritance in it, surely we should not complain because patriotism may be exalted to piety.

Of these offences you will diligently inquire and true presentment make, without either envy, hatred, or malice, and without love, fear, favor, affection, or hope of reward. When the result of your inquiries shall lead to accusation, the Solicitor-General will assist you in reducing your proceedings to the forms necessary for legal animadversion.

The importance of executing the duties of your office with honest attention cannot be explained more clearly than by describing its nature and design. Government being instituted for the support and protection of rational liberty, laws must be enacted to restrain the passions and appetites of individuals from violating the just rights of others. The laws, to be effectual, must annex penalties to the breach of them, and make provision for the prosecution of offenders. For this purpose it is necessary that there be a public accuser. Were this office permanently vested in any one man or body of men, our liberties would be unsafe. The exclusive right of accusing would attach to itself an influence and power that would be irresistible. It would be able to dispense with the laws; to deny protection to innocence, and to shield guilt from punishment. To avoid these evils, our laws, in designating the men who are to discharge the duties of an office necessary to the Commonwealth, have applied the principle of election. The several towns choose a number of their fellow-citizens competent to this office; and from this number, you, Gentlemen, are selected by lot. When impanelled and sworn, you are to execute the functions of public accuser; and, having discharged this painful office for a short time, you are again blended with the mass of our fellow-citizens. To guard against the escape of criminals, and to secure to yourselves freedom and independence in your inquiries, the Commonwealth's counsel and your own you will keep secret. Thus constituted, liberty is without danger, innocence will have protection, and only guilt will have cause to fear.

This principle of election is further inseparably connected with our courts of judicature. To preserve the judicial department from the control of the other departments of government, and to enable the judges to acquire the knowledge and experience necessary for the proper discharge of their duties, they hold their offices during good behavior; but it is a general rule that they cannot pass upon the life, liberty, reputation, or property of any man, without the consent of his fellow-citizens, expressed by a jury elected and sworn for that purpose, if he choose to put himself on his country.

As we survey the other parts of our government, we shall find this principle of election pervading every department. Indeed, it is the animating principle, the soul of our Constitution. The people, from their numbers and dispersed situation, being incompetent to exercise the legislative or executive powers, hold, as the foundation of those powers, the right of election. Our Constitution is, therefore, founded on principles of real freedom, having for its great objects public liberty and private safety. And, as we value these blessings, so should we sincerely adhere to the means of procuring them.

If further motives should be required, they will result from the consideration that an elective constitution is the only politically free one the people of Massachusetts can have. Whenever the executive and legislative powers are united, a subjection of the judicial will follow, and there can be no political liberty. An hereditary executive, not deriving his authority from the people, nor accountable for its exercise, will, either by force, corruption, or fraud, render a popular legislature dependent on him, — or the popular legislature will annihilate the authority of the monarch. In either event, the balance of the several powers of government being destroyed, public liberty could have no security for its existence. Let it therefore be repeated as an axiom in politics, that our Constitution, to be politically free, must be founded on elections by the people. For my own part, possessing some means of information, I know of no diversity of sentiments on this subject. The opinion is as general as it is correct.

Having such a constitution, it must depend on the people to cause it to be administered with wisdom and fidelity, upon its true principles. It is, therefore, our interest, and a duty we owe to posterity, to elect to public offices our wisest and most virtuous citizens; and so long as they behave well in office, to give them our sincere and unbiased approbation, which is the highest reward an honorable ambition will covet. As public offices are created, not for the emoluments of those who may fill them, but for the public interest, frequency of elections is a privilege very important for the people. By the exercise of this privilege they may, by wise substitutions, remove from power and trust unsuitable men; and by their continued confidence excite and reward the labors of good men. As it is not to be presumed that the people enjoying these fundamental rights and privileges will voluntarily abandon the Constitution, if it should ever be destroyed from internal causes, these causes must arise from the improper use of their powers. And the ambition of a few men, availing themselves of the passions, or the mistakes, or the careless indifference of their fellow-citizens, will aim the first blow. If these principles be correct, our political rights and privileges assume the character of most important moral duties, upon the upright and intelligent discharge of which depends the felicity of the present and of future generations. For no longer than we act wisely and virtuously, no longer than we exercise the rights of election with care, prudence, and discretion, can we reasonably expect that our free government will escape the calamities under which other republics, ancient and modern, have fallen, to rise no more.

These very general observations, which at all times deserve the attention of citizens enjoying the blessings of an elective constitution, I submit to your candid examination, assuring you, that, whatever may be their merits or defects, they flow from a heart devoted to the best interests of our country.

President Dwight of Yale College published in 1821 his "Travels in New England and New York." In the second volume, page 13, he says, under date of the 12th of October, 1807:

"The next day we rode to Plymouth before dinner. Here we had the satisfaction of being present while a luminous and impressive charge was delivered to the grand jury of the county by the Hon. Theophilus Parsons, Chief Justice of Massachusetts. I know not that I have ever heard a moral discourse which was conducted with more skill. The scheme of thought was in the highest degree clear and correct; and the style eminently distinguished for its perspicuity, precision, and strength. The definitions were obvious and complete; the arguments conclusive, and the discussions introduced exactly where they were necessary, and were extended no further than they were necessary. The whole was so concise, that from almost any writer it would have been obscure; yet it was managed so as to become more intelligible from its succinctness. It was received by a numerous audience with a solemn, profound, and eager attention. After the charge was ended, we dined with the court, and were not a little gratified with the conversation at the table."

He entered upon the duties of his office with great vigor, and, as some thought, with more vigor than discretion. I have heard so much of his conduct as a judge, and from so many different quarters, that I have formed a very distinct idea of it; and hold this with the more confidence, because, although there was a difference of opinion as to the propriety of what he did, there was very little as to the facts.

He began by directing the sheriffs and clerks, in some of the counties where *nisi prius* terms were about to be held, to summon jurymen enough for three juries, instead of two. Before his time, and ever since, our court-rooms have permanent seats for one jury on one side of the court, and another jury on the other side; and when one jury is employed in hearing a case, it is usual to indulge the other jury with a recess, if it is not supposed that they will be wanted immediately. The requirement for three juries was some indication of what was to be done; and he followed it up by shortening the trials very much. Now, all judges wish and endeavor to shorten trials as much as may be, and for this purpose exhort the counsel to brevity, and keep out what extraneous matter they can. This my father did; but he did much more. He generally required the counsel to state to him his points before he began. If they were in his judgment wholly untenable or insufficient, he permitted no argument, and allowed the case to go no further than was requisite to present to the whole court the question of law, if there was one, by which it might be decided whether the nonsuit or default he ordered should be taken off.

He was probably more impatient with diffuseness and verbosity, because no one quality was more characteristic of all his own productions than that of compactness and condensation. In giving the opinion of the court in the case of Deblois *v.* The Ocean Insurance Co., 16 Pick. 310, Judge Putnam said, "As light and spongy articles are reduced to portable size by hydraulic pressure, so the verbose readings of the law were, by the force of his great mind, reduced to clear, practical rules."

If the case proceeded to trial, the examination of witnesses was made as brief as possible; and when it was over, if it seemed clear to him that the weight of testimony was strongly and decidedly on one side or the other, he would not permit an argument in favor of a position which was, as he thought, unsupported by evidence. The effect of all this was, that the business of the courts was done with a rapidity never before witnessed, or even attempted. Of course, no such mode of doing business as this could be carried out without great resistance, and he met with this from many quarters. To it he opposed an invincible firmness, a frequent reference to the necessities of the times, and an imperturbable good-humor. If he said or did the harshest things, it was always with suavity of manner, and if this did not mitigate the sting, it at least prevented all unnecessary laceration of the wound.

The anecdotes which were told of him in this respect are innumerable. Let me select a few which I suppose to be perfectly authenticated, and sufficient to illustrate the way in which things went on. Mr. Dexter was more disturbed by my father's course than, perhaps, any other lawyer; not because he was diffuse or tedious, for his style of speaking was compactness itself; but because he was more employed than any other man in difficult cases, or in that large class of cases which call on the advocate to make up by his own power for some little want on their part of law or evidence. One day, when my father stopped him in an argument, on the ground that he was trying to persuade the jury of that for which there was no evidence, he replied, "Your Honor did not argue your own cases in the way you require us to." "Certainly not," was the reply; "but that was the judge's fault, not mine."

He was on terms of great intimacy with Mr. Otis, then certainly among the foremost in his profession In the trial of a cause in Boston, Mr. Otis had offered some testimony which my father ruled out. Mr. Otis submitted, but in his argument was beginning some allusion to it, when my father said, "Brother Otis, that will not do; you know that evidence was ruled out." But it was very important, and perhaps Mr. Otis thought he ought to have had the benefit of it; at all events, he pretty soon referred to it again. Then my father said, "Mr. Otis, please understand and remember that fact is not in the case, and not to be brought in thus indirectly." Mr. Otis again submitted and apologized; but, before long, again ventured upon an allusion to it. "Sit down, Mr. Otis, sit down, Sir," was the somewhat stern command; and without permitting him to say anything more, my father arose and charged the jury. This anecdote his friend, Mr. William Bond, used to repeat, as having passed under his own eye.

At Worcester, the first term that he held there was after the bar had some intimation of the course likely to be pursued; and the leaders determined to resist. Frank Blake, as everybody called him, perhaps the leading lawyer of the county, and one of my father's most intimate friends, arose to argue a case. "Stop a moment, Brother Blake," said my father, "what points do you propose to present to the jury on this evidence?" "I will, if your Honor pleases, state them to the jury." "No, you must state them to the court first." "I decline doing so, may it please your Honor; and

I insist on my right to address the jury in my own way." "Certainly, if you address them at all, you may address them in your own way,—and there can be no better; but I must first know whether you have any case to speak about. I do not now see one; but perhaps you may point one out." "I will endeavor to do so to the jury." "No, you must do so first to me." "This I positively decline." "Very well, with any view of the case I can now take, you will waste the time of the jury, the court, and the county, by any argument." Mr. Blake then arose, and, turning to the jury, began, "Gentlemen of the Jury," — when my father instantly said, "Mr. Sheriff, commit Mr. Blake to close jail," and quietly arose, and began charging the jury. The sheriff approached Mr. Blake, who rose to follow him, and my father, interrupting his charge, said to the sheriff, "Stop, Sir, a few moments"; and went on and gave the case to the jury. He then turned to the bar, and said, "Brother Blake, will you go to the jail now, or wait until you have got through some of your cases?" "I think," said Blake, "if it is all one to your Honor, I will wait a little." "Do just as you like." One of the gentlemen who narrated to me this incident said he was the same evening at a supper party at Mr. Blake's own house, at which my father was present. They both laughed over the affair, which did not seem in the least to diminish the cordiality, or, to use the phrase he used to me,—he was speaking of fifty years ago,—the "jollity" of the party. In 1821, eight years after my father's death, I was travelling in Worcester County, and a member of the bar assured me that he had seen a caricature of the scene, representing Mr. Blake as in the act of addressing the jury, but petrified with the command to the sheriff to commit him. He thought it was still in existence, and said he would endeavor to procure it for me; but he was unable to do so.

In Taunton, Mr. Burgess, of Rhode Island, entered into the combat. He came, dressed with the elegance and nicety of a gentleman of the old school, in silk stockings, and with lace ruffles and powdered hair. He, too, was an old personal friend of my father; and had been sent for to do what could be done to gain a cause which required all the strength which could be given it, to supply the want of any strength of its own. The trial went on as usual, until Burgess rose to argue to the jury. Then much such a conversation ensued as in Blake's case. By this time it was ascertained that, if the points were asked for, they *must* be given. Mr. Burgess so far yielded, therefore, as to state one. "That is no point at all, Brother Burgess; have you another?" "Yes, your Honor," and stated it. "You have not a particle of evidence for that point, as you very well know, Brother Burgess; what other?" And so the thing went on, until my father flatly refused to let him speak. "May it please your Honor," said Mr. Burgess, "I think I have a good case, an excellent case, and believe I can satisfy the jury of it, and I demand, as matter of right, permission to try." "A very good case you have, no doubt, Brother Burgess; but, unluckily, no evidence, and therefore nothing to go to a jury on." Mr. Burgess at once gathered up his papers, and marched indignantly out of court, while my father proceeded to charge the jury. All this occurred near the close of a forenoon's session. My father noticed that the crowd began to leave the court-room, and there appeared to be something going on outside. When the court adjourned for dinner, he came out and saw what it was. The Taunton Court-House of that day was a large wooden building, of which the lower story was appropriated to offices, and a flight of long and broad stairs led from a platform in front of the court-room doors down to the level of the street. Half-way down the stairs stood Mr. Burgess, haranguing the crowd about the Chief Justice's insupportable tyranny, and urging upon them to rise and stop the courts, if they would not lose the protection of law and all their liberties. My father stopped and listened with much amusement; and this amused the crowd in front; and Mr. Burgess soon observed that they were looking beyond him and laughing, and, turning round, he saw the new-comer and stopped. My father at once came to him and said, "Brother Burgess, if you get through in season, I wish you would come in and dine with me." And Brother Burgess paused a moment, and then, exclaiming, "I give it up, I give it all up," took my father's arm, and they had a very pleasant dinner together. I have heard this story from many persons; but no one used to enjoy the telling of it quite so much as good old General Cobb, of Taunton.

It must not be supposed that this was his ordinary course of proceeding. It will be seen from some of the letters I insert in the former chapter or in this, that the lawyers frequently desired him to take the whole case into his hands and dispose of it; and that when it seemed fairly open for argument, he was very unwilling that the case should go to a jury without one. Only when he felt certain that an argument could have no effect (unless that were a bad one), and that nothing could be attempted but to supply the want of evidence by deceiving a jury, would he insist thus peremptorily that no argument should be made.

It is not to be denied that he gave very great offence in this way. In Boston particularly, some of the lawyers were very angry, and declared, unreservedly, that such conduct could not be tolerated, and amounted to a subversion of all justice.

Among the few letters I have which were written home by my mother while with my father on his circuits, is one in which she says:

"Wednesday Morning. [Place and day omitted.]

"DEAR MARY:

"The mail is just going, and I have but little time. The court business goes on rapidly. Your father sent out, yesterday, for the third jury. The bar make themselves very merry now about it, and say he drives them tandem. There was a great deal of business to be done at first, but it sinks fast under your father's hands."

Perhaps all she knew was, that they were *merry;* but they, or some of them, may have been angry, too.

It is not to be denied that my father sometimes made mistakes in this mode of doing business. The late Judge Jackson had a case before him, and being told that he had nothing to stand on, and must not argue it, he insisted that he had, and finally persuaded my father that there was at least room for argument. Argue he did, and so successfully, that the jury gave him a verdict. When the opposite counsel prepared to move to set the verdict aside as against evidence, my father advised him to do no such thing, as the verdict would not, he thought, be disturbed; and it was not.

In another case, a lawyer in Worcester County, a very estimable man, but not distinguished for knowledge or intellect, found himself cut down by a ruling of my father, and expostulated quite vehemently. He succeeded in exciting some doubt as to the course to be pursued; the proceedings were stayed, and an hour assigned for a hearing on the point; and after the hearing, my father reversed his former decision. "Well," said the lawyer, "I am sure I am much obliged to your Honor. I felt sure that I could make you take my view of the case, *if you would only let me talk long enough to get it all out.*"

So, too, a gentleman now living tells me, my father once decided a point in a case of some importance against him, and the next day, on coming into court, stated that he had made a mistake in doing so, and corrected it. Nor were the juries always submissive. Chief Justice Isaac Parker used to speak, with some glee, of a case which was tried when he and my father were both sitting, and my father hurried it through as a very plain one, and charged the jury strongly on one side; and lo! the jury brought in a verdict for the other side. "I was delighted," said Parker, "and told him the jury had served him just right; first, because he ought not to have charged them so one-sidedly; and secondly, because he was wrong; — to which I got no other answer than '*Humanum est errare,* Brother Parker; it won't do to be right always.'"

One reason why my father was able to carry such a system thoroughly out, to its full extent, was that characteristic pleasantry of manner to which I have already alluded. It was not possible for any human being, or for any contingency, to make him manifest, in word, tone, or look, the emotion of anger. As he used to say himself, only an angry man makes other men *very* angry. Where there is no anger on the one side, and nothing but a perfect amenity of expression, it is difficult for the other to feel or express much personal hostility. Impertinence was very seldom attempted; and when it was, he would generally contrive to meet it without open war, and usually he gave the offender a lesson which prevented a repetition of the experiment.

In an interesting sketch of Mr. Dexter's life, recently published in pamphlet form from articles in the Boston Evening Transcript, the writer speaks of Mr. Dexter's contemporaries, and among them mentions my father. He represents him as arbitrary and oppressive as a judge, and, by way of illustration, says that Fisher Ames was so much irritated by my father's treatment, that he declared "he would never go into court again, unless he could carry a bludgeon in one hand and a speaking-trumpet in the other." This anecdote is entirely true, excepting that Fisher Ames said it of Judge Paine, and not of my father. It has long been one of the anecdotes of our profession, and one which the late Judge Wilde often related, as equally illustrative of Ames and of Judge Paine. For the one was sensitive, and his own delicacy and refinement made rude treatment insupportable; and the other was not only sometimes harsh in manner, but for many years he was quite deaf, — an infirmity no one ever charged upon my father. There are few works of greater value or interest, to the student of the history of our country, or to him who loves to contemplate intellect and character in their highest manifestations, than the Memoir of Fisher Ames, recently republished, with interesting additions, by his son, Seth Ames, — whom I am permitted to rank among my valued friends. On page 255 of the first volume, Mr. Ames gives a letter of his father to Christopher Gore, in which he says: "The next day I went into court, to enjoy the soothing civilities of Judge *Ursa Major*, R. T. Paine." And Mr. Seth Ames appends to this passage the following note: "Judge Paine was somewhat deaf, and not at all distinguished for suavity of manners. After an uncomfortable scene in his court, Mr. Ames said, no man could get on there unless he came with a club in one hand and a speaking-trumpet in the other."

Among the stories of that day is this: My father, some years before he went on the bench, was arguing before Judge Paine, and did not speak so loud or so distinctly as the Judge's infirmity required, or perhaps as he should have done; and the Judge cried out suddenly, "Mr. Parsons, Mr. Parsons, I tell you once for all, *take that glove off your tongue*." "Certainly, Sir," was the answer; "and may I beg your Honor to take the wool out of your ears." This anecdote does not present a very pleasing picture of the relations between court and counsel in those days, but I think it is a just one.

My father was by nature very irritable. It is one of our family stories, that, soon after his marriage, he frightened my mother exceedingly by an explosion of anger against a person who attempted to impose upon her; and that he then resolved that no person should ever again hear him speak an angry word. And I believe he kept his resolution firmly, to the letter, under all circumstances. I have seen him — very rarely, however — when it was obvious enough that he was angry; but then he was either perfectly silent until the mood passed away, or, if he must speak, suppressed the feeling so that it found no utterance in words.

I never heard him allude to the circumstance above mentioned as causing any especial effort or resolution against ill-temper; but I know that he deemed it politic and profitable, or I would rather say important, to the last degree, that a lawyer, and a judge, should be the absolute master of his temper. He often tried to impress upon his students, that the man who cannot be excited, and cannot be made to lose his self-command, has an immense advantage, in the simple fact that he is at all times fully possessed of all his own powers, and ready to take full advantage of every opportunity.

As a judge, I believe he found this imperturbability eminently useful. Again and again have I heard it said, that one among the important means by which he — to use the phrase that has been often used by those who spoke of him — "always had his own way," was his perfectly unfailing courtesy of demeanor, and frequent pleasantry; although these sometimes clothed, and perhaps disguised, peremptory, if not despotic treatment.

It was said of Lord Kenyon, that he would sometimes get excessively angry while holding court, and make a sad exhibition of himself. One day, old George the Third said to him at court, "My Lord, I am told you lost your temper yesterday. I was very glad to hear it; and I hope you will be able to find a better one."

My father was perhaps too much disposed to be jocose. I have heard it intimated that, while the entire absence of irritation was a great help to him, he made too much fun, and sometimes resorted to pleasantry when it was out of place.

Another reason of his success was his perfect impartiality; or, rather, his way of treating great men rather worse than little ones. No better illustration of this can be given than the anecdote mentioned a few pages back, of his silencing Mr. Otis. I believe I am justified in saying that he was never cruel; the young and timid and unresisting he would help all he could; and as the majority are not great men, they sided with him. If a young man, in whom he thought some ignorance or inadvertence might be pardoned, made a mistake, he would in the gentlest way correct the error or supply a want, which would have brought down a sharp rebuke upon an older and abler man.

One of the letters I have given quotes a phrase which I believe he often used. It was common with him, when taking leave of the bar at the close of a term, to urge the lawyers to prepare their cases better, *and read their books*, that they might take better care of their clients' interests, and embarrass the courts less. This was not very pleasing or complimentary advice, however necessary it might seem or be. But it is to be remembered that the bar of that day was, *generally*, deficient in the knowledge which every lawyer should possess; and it was one of his most earnest desires to raise the standard of professional education. He always had many students, and loved to have as many as he could possibly accommodate; and from my own imperfect recollection, aided by the testimony I have received from very many of his students, I know that the most delightful relations existed between him and them.

It will be seen by a reference to the letter of Mr. Phelps, inserted in the preceding chapter, that the bar did not like his monopoly of students, and made a rule that no barrister should have more than three at any one time. And even then there seems to have been some suspicion that his students had more than their share of favor from the court and the bar. Mr. John Gardiner, of whom I have spoken before, in a speech in favor of law reform, delivered by him in the Legislature, in January, 1790, and reported in the Herald of Freedom, a newspaper published in Boston, said:

"The great Giant of the Law at Newburyport (if my information be true) had a young gentleman lately studying with him, whom the Essex *Bar-call* not long since agreed should accept the place of a tutor in our University for one year, there receive the emoluments of his tutorship, and yet be considered, all the time, as studying in the office of Mr. Parsons, at Newburyport."

I know nothing about this particular circumstance; but if my father could obtain this favor for a deserving student, I dare say he did it without any especial reference to the bar rules.

I have heard some anecdotes indicating that some of the seniors were a little, or not a little, jealous of his kindness to young men. One, which comes to me very directly, is this. Mr. Elijah H. Mills, afterwards an eminent lawyer and statesman of Northampton, was admitted to practice as counsellor in the Supreme Court about the same time that my father became Chief Justice. An old lawyer in Hampshire County was prevented by illness from attending the court at Northampton, and gave young Mills his papers, with advice to employ some older counsel to help him through his business; and he also gave Mills a letter of introduction to my father. Mills waited upon him, and they had some chat, in the course of which my father inquired particularly about his studies, and probably saw what kind of man he was. Presently Mills stated that he proposed to employ senior counsel, and asked some advice about it. "I think, on the whole," said my father, "you had better employ no one. You and I can do the business about as well as anybody." Mills had no unwillingness to try; and everything went on well, with the help of a little hint here and a suggestion there, and the term was ended. Mills called on my father, the last evening, to thank him, and say good-by; and while there, a prominent senior counsel came in on the same errand. Possibly he was one who would have been, or thought he should have been, retained by Mills, if my father had not interfered. However this may be, when he rose to go, my father bade him farewell until the next term, expressing the hope to see him then. "I am not sure about that, Judge," was the answer; "I think some of sending my office-boy with my papers. *You and he together will do the business full as well as I can.*"

On one particular point much ignorance existed, which he thought peculiarly harmful; nor can I explain myself, without treating, at some length, of a topic which only professional readers can be supposed to understand, and which not many of them will care for. This subject is special pleading; and as I must say something about it, I will try to say this intelligibly.

By *pleading* is commonly understood *arguing* a case; but, with lawyers, something very different is meant by this word. For in its legal meaning, pleading is now never oral. It includes the written allegations and replies of the parties before the case is argued or tried, and nothing else. The common law of England, which is ours by inheritance, has been called "the consummation of experimental wisdom." I verily believe it to be so; and I further believe that no one of its principles is more certainly wise than that which required the parties to a suit to determine, and state before the trial of the case, the precise question to be tried. And this is all that is meant, or ever was meant, by special pleading. That is to say: First, the plaintiff must set forth in his declaration the cause or causes of action on which he intends to rely. Then in his plea the defendant must set forth with equal precision the defence or defences on which he intends to rely. Then the plaintiff may answer, and the defendant answer again; and so on indefinitely, until the end is attained, and the parties, the court, and the jury know precisely what question is before them.

The old Joe Miller story, which has amused many generations, may, after all, serve as well as anything to illustrate the common notion of pleading. A plaintiff brings an action against a neighbor for borrowing and breaking the iron pot in which he cooked his dinner. The defendant says he never borrowed any pot; and that he used it carefully and returned it whole; also, that the pot was broken and useless when he borrowed it; also, that he borrowed the pot of somebody not the plaintiff; also, that the pot in question was the defendant's own pot; also, that the plaintiff never owned any pot, iron or other; also, that the defendant never had any pot whatever. This pleasant and instructive anecdote is repeated occasionally at this day, in some newspapers, almanacs, &c., to show how lawyers conduct their business. Even if it were true, it might be answered that it would be well for the plaintiff to have a list of all the defences which could be attempted; because, at all events, the law would not permit the defendant to go outside of his list, and nothing beyond it was to be feared; and of these defences the plaintiff would know which the defendant could offer testimony upon, and upon these, and only these, he need prepare his case.

But a better answer may be given by supposing such a case as might occur. For example, A sues B on his promissory note for a thousand dollars. There are a great many defences possible against a note; as that defendant never signed it, or that it has been materially altered in date or sum, or that it was obtained fraudulently, or without consideration, or that the defendant was a minor, or that the note was due more than six years ago, in which case the statutes of limitation do not permit its recovery, or that it was usurious, &c., &c. If there be no special pleading, the defendant may simply say he does not owe the plaintiff, and then come into court with any one or all of these defences, or of many others; and the plaintiff can only be safe by preparing his evidence beforehand to meet every possible defence. But special pleading says this must not be. The defendant must say what he relies on. If, then, we suppose that his real defence is the statute of limitations, he pleads that the note has been due (or, in the language of the law, that the cause of action has accrued) more than six years. The plaintiff may meet this in many ways; but he too must select and state his case; and we will suppose him to rejoin that the defendant gave him an acknowledgment of this debt in writing, within six years; for, by law, this restores the obligation. Now the defendant must again specify his answer to this; and it may be, for example, that this writing was obtained from him by force, in which case it has no validity. This we will suppose the plaintiff simply denies, and now, in legal phrase, *an issue is joined*, or, in plain English, a precise question is raised, and court, jury, counsel, and parties all know what it is, and no evidence or argument can be heard beyond it. The defendant virtually admits that he signed the note, that it was given for a good consideration, and was valid; the plaintiff admits that it has been due more than six years; the defendant admits that he has given a written acknowledgment within six years; and the only possible question to be considered is, whether or no this last writing was obtained by force.

It may be that one party or the other has more than one allegation or one defence; and then as many issues may be raised, that is, as many specific questions presented, as actually belong to the case. But still the rule holds, that no other question than that or those distinctly presented by the pleading can be heard or tried.

It is undoubtedly true, that, in part from the difficulty of presenting some questions fully and clearly, but with a rigorous exclusion of all extraneous matter, and in part from the natural tendency of rules and precedents to accumulate and become intricate, this business of special pleading became very difficult, and was encumbered with abuses. In England, a considerable class of lawyers, known as "special pleaders," devote themselves exclusively to this work; and without ever speaking in court, or even going into court, are constantly employed in preparing "the pleadings" for other lawyers. In this country we have no such class; nor were the rules of special pleading ever so strict or technical as in England. But, from the nature of the case, and the absolute necessity that the court and the parties should know what questions a case presented, there were rules and principles of special pleading which constituted a system; and this could only be learned by a proper amount of diligent and intelligent study.

In my father's time, there was a very general ignorance on this subject. Only a few of the leading lawyers pretended to be good pleaders; and the inaccuracy or insufficiency of the pleading was one of the causes of the disorder and confusion which prevailed in the courts. He was himself a very good pleader, having devoted much time to the science. When he had students, every one was expected to write out, in a book prepared for that purpose, declarations, pleas, and forms, which my father had prepared or adopted. I have some of these books now; and the volumes of precedents, afterwards published for the use of the profession, by Anthon, Story, Oliver, and others, were compiled in a good degree from these books.*

On this point my father was very urgent. He insisted on good pleading. It will be remembered that, in 1790, he successfully resisted the strenuous efforts of an able lawyer to procure the prohibition of special pleading. When he became a judge, and it was found that he would not try a case where the pleading was incurably defective, strenuous were the efforts, and strange the results, in many of the counties. I have heard innumerable anecdotes about this; but they were all in substance like one my friend, Mr. Charles S. Daveis, of Portland, tells me. There was a libel case before the court. It was one of especial interest, and a great array of counsel and witnesses were in attendance. The plaintiff, in his anxiety to make a declaration that would stand criticism, filed thirteen "counts," as they are called, which are in substance so many different and dis-

---

* The first of these, by John Anthon, was called, "American Precedents of Declarations, collected chiefly from the Manuscripts of Chief Justice Parsons."

tinct ways of stating the case. The defendant had filed a still larger number of special pleas. But when the case was opened and the papers read, my father simply remarked that *all* the counts and *all* the pleas were bad, that a trial would be of no use, and advised the plaintiff to withdraw his suit, and the defendant to take no costs, — which was done.

While speaking of Mr. Daveis, let me add, that I am indebted to him for another anecdote, for which he does not *vouch*, but he gives it to me as *probable;* and I am afraid it is so. Judge Mellen, while at the bar, arose to argue the law questions of the case of Beckford *v.* Page (2 Mass. R. 455). Being a tall man, he looked over the bench and saw a folded paper there, marked with the name of the case, and the ominous label thereon, "Opinion of the Court." I have heard, also, that Judge Ezekiel Whitman, whose letter I insert in the preceding chapter, being called upon in another action, with the encouraging and complimentary words, "Brother Whitman, the court expect from you a thorough and lucid argument on this case," rose as if reluctantly, and in a low tone, not *addressed* to the court, but audible to all the bar, said, "It's a mere farce; the old fellow has got his opinion in his pocket at this moment, and will never change a word of it." It will be seen, however, in Beckford *v.* Page, that Mellen was "stopped" by the court, which was an avowal that they had made up their mind in his favor, and did not need to hear him.

To return to special pleading, let it not be supposed that, in all cases of deficient pleading, my father was harsh or severe. On the contrary, I have abundant testimony that it was his constant habit to assist the lawyers, especially the young ones, in making their pleas. It was no uncommon thing for him, when on a circuit, to take the papers to his rooms, and call the young counsel there, point out the defects in the pleadings, show how they might be amended, and illustrate, as fully as he could, the *principles* involved. More than one of those who long survived him, but have now passed away, have gratefully acknowledged to me this valuable instruction.

In the neighboring State of New Hampshire, there was even less of accuracy in pleading and in practice than in Massachusetts. The Rev. Dr. Morison, in his charming Life of Chief Justice Smith, shows the vast reform made by that eminent judge in this respect, and the need there was of that reform. In a letter written by him in 1803, he says: "Some evil genius has been for years stirring me up to look into the science of pleading; and I have yielded, and am now enveloped in counts, bars, replications, estoppels, traverses, &c. You will say, and justly, what has a New Hampshire lawyer to do with special pleadings? If he acquires any knowledge, standing alone, he will have nothing for his pains but mortification. He must be disgusted with every record he reads." On the next page (173), Dr. Morison quotes from Chief Justice Joel Parker's account of Chief Justice Smith: "With him there arose a new order of things. Those members of the bar who were diligent and attentive to their business were commended and encouraged; and those who were negligent were lectured and reprimanded." If I do not mistake, similar words might be used in describing the changes then going on in Massachusetts.

I have very recently heard of a droll story told by my father at the table of Governor Wentworth, in Portsmouth, at a dinner made for the court then in session, and the bar in attendance. To make it intelligible to my unprofessional readers, I must premise that "demurrer" is a technical term of special pleading, which means that the party who resorts to it demurs, or rests, upon his law; that is, admits all the facts of his opponent, but denies that these facts are sufficient in law for his opponent's case or defence. As the lower courts have the right to try and determine questions of fact, but only the highest courts can *finally* determine questions of law, — because these determinations must be uniform for the whole State, — a kind of factitious demurrer was made use of, to take a case from a lower court to an upper court. That is, a party would "demur" to his opponent's case or defence; and as this raised a question of law, the case necessarily went up to the court that could determine the law; and there the demurrer was waived by agreement, and the whole case, as to its facts as well as its law, was opened anew. This process — very common in Massachusetts and New Hampshire, and, for what I know, elsewhere — was called "taking a case up by demurrer."

My father, who then practised extensively in New Hampshire, was laughing at the lawyers assembled at the table, about the utter ignorance of pleading which prevailed in that State. Some one said, "But you make matters worse than they really are; some of us do know something about pleading." "Yes," was the answer, "something; but I have just passed four days at court in Stratford County, and I will tell you all I heard there in the way of pleading. The crier, Mr. ——, whom some of you know, was something of a lawyer once, but fell into dissipation and broke down; and his friends procured for him the office he now holds. The morning after I was there, I went to court rather early, and saw Mr. Crier on the floor, very drunk indeed, and so drunk that he could not move a step up the stairs. Two or three friends were about him, consulting how they should get him up without compelling the judge to notice his condition; for they thought, if they could once get him into his seat, he could go through his accustomed routine pretty much as usual. One and another suggested this way and that; and at last Mr. Crier, who had sense enough left to see the strait he was in, cried out, 'Take me up by demurrer; for Heaven's sake, take me up by demurrer. *Judge —— don't know enough of pleading to see through that.*'"

I would add, that the reform which Judge Smith began was effectually carried out; and the pleading in New Hampshire, as long as any pleading was left, was probably as accurate and skilful as in any State in the Union.

Perhaps it was his early intercourse with my father which led Judge Smith to set this value on accurate pleading. The Judge cordially acknowledges my father's readiness to assist all whom he could, in the following passage about him: "He was highly favored in a most able instructor, and at his death was certainly better skilled in the New England law than any other man on either side of the Atlantic. It is much to be regretted that he left behind him so little of the great stores of the law peculiar to New England, which his diligent and discriminating mind had been collating and digesting for more than half a century. It was my good fortune to become acquainted with this truly great man and learned lawyer at the time I commenced my law studies; I cannot suffer this occasion to pass without expressing my heart-felt acknowledgments of his kindness. He was ever ready to assist such as manifested a desire for instruction. This part of his character, I believe, has not had that justice done to it which in an eminent degree it deserved. I will not say that Theophilus Parsons was the greatest lawyer that ever lived; but I risk nothing in saying, that he knew more of the New England law, which existed while we were yet British Colonies, than any other man that has lived, or perhaps that shall ever live." (Morison's Life of Smith, p. 428.)

In another place, Dr. Morison quotes from Judge Smith's "Advice" to the young lawyer. "Have you more acuteness, genius, mind, knowledge, than Parsons? Yet who was more indefatigable in his profession, and in his pursuit of knowledge?" (p. 182.)

After my father's time, the pleading in Massachusetts became very much better. When I began practice, no young man was thought to be at all fit for his business if he could not make a special declaration, or a special plea, whenever wanted. Many lawyers in the country counties had the reputation of being skilful and accomplished pleaders. But still, upon the profession generally, special pleading was a burden; and in the year 1836 it was abolished by law. The need, however, of accomplishing in some way the object of it is obvious, and denied by none. The courts, here and in other States, endeavor to do this by a system of "specification" of the case and the defence, under certain rules which are gradually acquiring shape, regularity, and system. Just so far, these rules are forming a new system of special pleading, or becoming one. And whether it was wiser to endeavor to reach this result in this way, or by a careful and skilful removal of the abuses which had encumbered the ancient system, is a question on which there may be a difference of opinion.*

---

* In a letter to a friend, Lord Tenterden, then Chief Justice of the King's Bench of England, says: "The preservation of forms, however unpopular, is of the essence of all establishments, — of the judicial in particular, — for if judges disregard them, they become authors, not expounders, of the law. If a judge does not understand them, he will violate the law in some instances by breaking them; and if of a cautious temper, do injustice in many by a mistaken adherence to their supposed effect. The less a judge knows of special pleading, the more nonsuits take place under his direction." I take this from the third volume of Lord Campbell's Lives of the Chief Justices of England (page 297).

Let me add from the Life of Lord Ellenborough, in the same volume, the following passage on this subject. Ellenborough was an admirable special pleader; and it is in reference to this fact that Campbell says, — with perfect truth in my judgment, — "In the exquisite logic of special pleading, rightly understood, there is much to gratify an acute and vigorous understanding. The methods by which it separates the [question of] law from the [question of] facts, and, having ascertained the real question in controversy between the parties, refers the decision of it either to the judges or to the jury, favorably distinguish our procedure from that of any other civilized country, and have enabled us to boast of a highly satisfactory administration of justice, without a scientific legal code."

In the Life of Tenterden, — who also began his professional career as a "special pleader, ... citing, as one of his reasons for so doing, Mr. Law's [Lord Ellenborough's] splendid success from following the same course," an amusing anecdote is quoted from an account of him in the Edinburgh Review, which at least illustrates the common notion that this science is merely ridiculous, although its only legitimate object

I cannot withhold the remark, that my father could not have been very oppressive to the bar without some injury to their clients, that is, to the people. And our sharp-sighted fathers would have found this out. Nor can I reconcile with any such fact his exceeding popularity as a judge. I do not see how I can be mistaken about this. The evidence of it was plenary; it came from all quarters and in all forms; it completely overrode even the bitterness of party feeling, and manifested itself in every way in which it could be exhibited. Being his son, it was not probable that reproaches of him would reach me directly, and it was probable that one and another might take opportunities to praise him. But, after due allowance for this, the earnest, constant, and overflowing approbation of him as a judge, which for many years met me wherever I turned, and not unfrequently comes to me even now, justifies, I think, my belief that it had some real foundation. It is not enough to say, that the people liked to see him snub the great lawyers; nor that a bold, strong man, who goes along in his own way with irresistible force and energy, generally carries the multitude with him. These and similar things may be said. But I should not be honest, if I did not confess my belief that the true ground of my father's general and permanent popularity as a judge, was the conviction among the people that his whole object was to do justice, according to law, promptly, accurately, and effectually; and that, upon the whole, he attained this object.

---

is to secure exactness and accuracy in allegation, answer, or question. The writer, by way of showing that a "special pleader" must be technical and absurd, says: "He had contracted so strict and inveterate a habit of keeping himself and everybody else to the precise matter in hand, that once, during a circuit dinner, having asked a county magistrate if he would take venison, and receiving what he deemed the evasive reply, 'Thank you, my Lord, I am going to take boiled chicken,' his Lordship sharply retorted, 'That, Sir, is no answer to my question. I ask you again if you will take venison, and I will trouble you to say *yes* or *no*, without further prevarication.'"

When my father took the office of Chief Justice, the salary was but twelve hundred and thirty-three dollars. Not unfrequently grants were made to the judges; but this practice he thought illegal and unconstitutional. It was understood that this salary would be enlarged; and he went on the bench, intending, as I think, to hold the office only about two years. In his letter of acceptance to Governor Strong, he touches upon this point, and intimates that he took the office *not* with the expectation of holding it permanently.

Boston, June 5, 1806.

May it please your Excellency:

I have lately, by your Excellency's order, received a commission of Chief Justice of the Supreme Judicial Court of this Commonwealth, with very grateful emotions for the confidence thus reposed in my integrity, and ability to discharge the duties of that honorable and important office.

I am sensible that those duties must at all times require great labor and application; but in the present state of the Commonwealth, the discouragements from attempting to give satisfaction to our country are increased by the immense mass of business which has accumulated in that court, and by the little time allowed to the judges for deliberation before decision.

The salary annexed at present to the office being so very inadequate to the decent support of it, must further increase the embarrassments of a judge, by compelling him to appropriate to the maintenance of his family a portion of that time the whole of which might be usefully employed in fulfilling the various duties connected with the office.

So far as regards the salary of a judge, my difficulties are peculiar. In all questions of expediency, I have never declined to conform to the opinions of others, when necessary to promote harmony or union; but in questions of principle, I must necessarily be governed by my own opinion, although, in the judgment of others, it may be incorrect. It is my opinion, that, by the Constitution of this Commonwealth, a permanent and honorable salary ought to be annexed to the office of a judge of the Supreme Judicial Court, and that all grants in part of this salary made by the Legislature, which are not permanent, are against the provisions of the Constitution, and are appropriations by the General Court of the public property not authorized by the people. Of this principle, so wise and reasonable, intended to secure an impartial administration of justice among all classes of citizens, and to guard the judges against the influence, not only of powerful individuals, but of every other department of government, I am perfectly satisfied. Nor am I able to persuade myself that I can lawfully take what I believe the General Court cannot constitutionally grant. The only salary, therefore, which I can receive, is that established by the statute of the 27th of February, 1790, unless the General Court, who alone can lawfully provide salaries for the judges, should think it reasonable to make an alteration in the establishment, by some permanent provision.

I mean not to imply the most distant reflection upon gentlemen, whose talents and integrity none can question; but in the consideration of any subject involving a moral principle, however erroneous may be the result of my own reasoning, yet by that result must I be conscientiously governed.

That unreasonable jealousies and suspicions may be entertained of the conduct and opinions of judges, is sometimes to be expected. When they exist, the situation of the State is extremely unfortunate. For a due administration of the laws is the only security of our social and civil rights, and it is a source of consolation, if our political rights should ever be abused. The only shield of the judges is a consciousness of having done their duty with fidelity, and with as much ability as their talents, and the system of judicial proceedings established by law, would admit.

For my own part, I trust that your Excellency will not deem it vanity in me, when I profess a confidence in my intentions of acting with the strictest impartiality, and of sincerely endeavoring to know nothing of any cause but its merits. "Tros, Rutulusve fuat, nullo discrimine habebo."

I have taken the liberty thus to state to your Excellency my views of the duties, difficulties, and embarrassments of the station to which you have been pleased to call me. I should not have so long hesitated to accept the appointment, and exert all the little talents I possess to justify your Excellency in making it, had I not feared the inconveniences my family must suffer by my retiring from a profession the profits of which enabled me to give them a decent support. At the same time, I have been sensible that our country has claims upon the services of its citizens, which should not lightly be rejected. I have, therefore, concluded to accept the office of Chief Justice of the Supreme Judicial Court of the Commonwealth; and, relying on the aid of that Being who is the fountain of justice, I will endeavor to discharge the duties thus imposed on me, with integrity and impartiality, so long as the irresistible claims of my family for support will allow.

From my experience of the equity of my fellow-citizens, I am persuaded that, when, from the inadequacy of the salary annexed to the office, those claims shall press upon me, my leaving the office and returning to a private station, for the support of a numerous and dependent family, will not be considered as the desertion of a public trust.

I am, with great respect, your Excellency's
Most obedient and humble servant,
THEOPHILUS PARSONS.

TO HIS EXCELLENCY, GOVERNOR STRONG.

The salary was raised from twelve hundred and thirty-three dollars to twenty-five hundred dollars. The office suited him; he enjoyed much of its labor, which was less a labor to him than it would have been to most others. He was earnestly solicited and urged to remain, and, in 1809, he concluded to do so, if the salary were again increased, but not otherwise; and he addressed to Governor Gore the following letter on this subject:

Boston, June, 1809.

MAY IT PLEASE YOUR EXCELLENCY:

When, three years since, I entered on the arduous duties of a Chief Justice of the Supreme Judicial Court, I was not insensible that I was about to abandon the means of a decent support, for a salary very inadequate to that object; but I was prevailed on to accept the office, in the expectation that the Legislature might establish a permanent salary, sufficient to defray the very great expense I must necessarily incur, and also to provide for my family.

To your Excellency I need not mention that my family is large; that the expense of supporting it in Boston is unavoidably very great, without adding to it house-rent, or the price of a dwelling-house, if the owner is the occupant; that this expense is very little diminished by my absence from home; that the expenses on the circuits are known, to all who travel them, much to exceed the charges arising on ordinary journeys; and that by using a close carriage for the preservation of my health, in guarding against the inclemency of the weather, which I am often obliged to encounter, my own particular expenses are much increased.

Since I have holden the office, I have annually been obliged to expend my whole salary, all the interest of the capital I had previously acquired, and also a portion of that capital, which will be my whole dependence for maintaining my family, when, through age or infirmity, I can no longer hold my present office, nor be able to make any other provision for their support.

Could my capital have remained entire, as a fund for future pecuniary demands, I acknowledge to your Excellency, that I would have longer submitted to the inadequacy of my salary; but when that fund is annually failing me, I cannot anticipate my future situation without anxiety. To avoid this situation, I think it my duty to resign my office, that, by availing myself of some less expensive employment, I may retain some means of support at a time when I can no longer make any provision for myself.

I trust in the candor and justice of my fellow-citizens to believe that I am willing to make any reasonable sacrifice to our common interest; and that I do not leave the office because it is not lucrative, or on account of the fatigues and responsibility of it; but because, by longer holding it, I must involve myself and my family in inconveniences too great to be reasonably required from any individual citizen.

The second quarter of the year will terminate the last day of the present month, till when I will continue to execute, as well as I am able, the duties of the office; and at the end of the quarter, I request your Excellency to accept my resignation. I have given notice thus early of my intention, that your Excellency, having the Council now in session, may make the necessary preparations for filling the office, that no inconvenience may result to the public from a short vacancy.

It is not necessary to assure your Excellency of my affectionate attachment, nor to express my warmest wishes that your elevated station may contribute as much to your personal happiness as it will to the public utility.

I am, very respectfully, your Excellency's

Obedient and humble servant,

THEOPHILUS PARSONS.

To GOVERNOR GORE.

Thereupon the Governor sent to the Legislature a recommendation to enlarge the salaries of the judges of the Supreme Court. At that time, an increase of the salaries of the judges to three thousand dollars for each side judge, and thirty-five hundred for the Chief Justice, was no small affair. If we compare the value of money, the difficulty of procuring it, the habits of the people, and the resources of the Commonwealth at that day with the same things at the present day, it was equal to an attempt to give the judges now six or eight thousand dollars a year. And it is certainly to the credit of the Commonwealth, that the change was made by a large majority, and with little more difficulty than that of making the legislators understand the true merits of the question. Prominent as my father had been in the political conflicts of the time, the angry hostility to him as "a Federalist" did not show itself here. Judge Story, then a practising lawyer and a leader among the Democrats of the most uncompromising enthusiasm, was a member of the Legislature, both when the salary was first increased and when it was enlarged the second time; and he entered into the question with his usual energy, and with entire success.

In the interesting Life of Judge Story, by his son, a letter from the Judge to Mr. Everett is published, in which he describes his own doings in reference to the first increase of the salaries, in 1806. He speaks frankly, and it might seem boastingly; but I believe he does justice, and only justice, to his motives, his conduct, and his influence. The subject was referred, in the House of Representatives, to a committee, of which Judge Story was chairman; and he made a report on the subject, which his son publishes at full length. It is an able comment upon the clause in the Constitution requiring that "permanent and honorable salaries shall be established by law for the justices of the Supreme Judicial Court."

If this second increase had not been made, my father certainly would not have remained on the bench. Nor did he seem to take much interest in the question. The reasons for and against his retaining the office were so nearly balanced, that I suppose it was a matter of indifference to him.

The salary was increased to thirty-five hundred dollars, and he remained Chief Justice of that court until his death. After the first two or three years, the dockets were relieved, the necessity for pressing forward trials abated, and habits of less dilatoriness and more accuracy began to be established among the lawyers; and I have reason to believe, that his method of conducting the business of the courts became essentially modified, or, perhaps it might be said, moderated. He was still impatient under anything which wasted the time of the court, or manifested culpable ignorance or negligence; and was still vigilant lest the abuses which he had labored to correct should again gather strength by sufferance; and he was still, sometimes, very positive and peremptory. But I have observed that all the stories I have heard of his "putting down" the lawyers, and driving along at a pace which it tasked the strongest to keep up with, refer to the first year or two of his judgeship.

To sum up all that I think can be said on this subject, and as the best result to which I can come, I would say, that he was habitually peremptory and decided, and that he sometimes erred in demanding of all men a promptitude, rapidity, and precision, a fulness of preparation and of learning, and an economy of words and of time, which, taking men as they are, cannot reasonably be expected from the mass; but that there were reasons and necessities in the circumstances of the day, which, in fact, in the opinion of most of the best men at the bar, and in the judgment of the people, if they did not wholly justify all his requirements and all his conduct, were a good excuse for them.

The raising of the salaries of the judges after a two years' experience of his administration, and when it was known that, if they were raised, he stayed, and if not, he went, may perhaps be regarded as expressing the opinion of the Legislature.

That in so short a time he swept away the accumulations of years, does not, of itself, prove too great haste or pressure. In his letter to Governor Strong, he speaks of "the immense amount of business which has accumulated in that court," as of a thing which everybody knew. While correcting this paragraph, I have received a note from the highest living authority on this subject. After remarking, that one cause why the dockets of the Supreme Court were so crowded, was the right that every losing party in the Common Pleas Court had to appeal any civil action from that court to the Supreme Court for a new trial of the facts, and that every losing party in the Supreme Court might, on a review, have a new jury trial, unless there had been two verdicts against him, or he had waived the right at some previous stage, he adds: "The Supreme Court had also a large criminal jurisdiction, partly original and partly appellant. These causes combined to crowd the court with a great number of cases, many of which were of very little importance, either in amount or in the legal principles involved in them. To reach such cases was almost equivalent to disposing of them." Chief Justice Parker says: "His profound learning, long and uninterrupted employment in the country and in the capital, and especially his accurate knowledge of forms and practice, peculiarly fitted him to take the lead in the new and improved order of things. How fully public expectation has been satisfied, I need not declare. The reformed state of the dockets throughout the Commonwealth, the promptness of decisions, the regularity of trials, attest the beneficial effects of a system, which he has done so much to render popular and permanent."

I once possessed a document addressed to the Legislature, giving the most unqualified and emphatic commendation of his course. It was signed by nearly (not quite) all the leading members of the bar. I remember the names of Otis, Prescott, Amory, Davis, Lowell, and some others. It was sent to him, to be sent by him to the Governor, or to the Legislature, when the question of raising the salaries of the judges was before them. But he made no use of it. It was in my possession within a few years, and I suppose that some collector of autographs has it now.

As yet I have said nothing of his administration of the law, and his influence upon the jurisprudence of the State. For lawyers, this topic might have great interest; but they alone could understand it, and for them all that he did stands permanently recorded in the Reports of Massachusetts. From near the beginning of the second volume to near the end of the tenth, it will be found that his opinions fill the bulk of the volumes. A few years after his death, a volume was published in New York, entitled, "Commentaries on the Law of the United States, by Theophilus Parsons, late Chief Justice of Massachusetts." It consists only of the principal decisions rendered by him, without change or addition of any kind; and being in very small and very close print, it contains an amount of matter equal to two or three ordinary law volumes.

It may be interesting to some readers to be reminded, or informed, of the question that arose in 1812, the decision of which adversely to the wishes of the national government, not only caused much commotion at the time, but has deprived Massachusetts of a very large sum due for the services of her militia. Governor Strong laid before the justices of the Supreme Judicial Court the following questions:

"1. Whether the commanders-in-chief of the militia of the several States have a right to determine whether any of the exigencies contemplated by the Constitution of the United States exist, so as to require them to place the militia, or any part of it, in the service of the United States, at the request of the President, to be commanded by him, pursuant to acts of Congress.

"2. Whether, when either of the exigencies exist, authorizing the employing of the militia in the service of the United States, the militia thus employed can be lawfully commanded by any officers but of the militia, except by the President of the United States."

The answer of the Supreme Court (with the exception of Sedgwick and Thatcher, who were not within reach, and could not be consulted) was, that the Governors of the States could alone determine whether the exigencies alluded to existed; and if they did so determine, the President could command them only through the State militia officers. Because, if the President and Congress had the exclusive right to determine when exigencies existed which authorized the calling out of the militia, and the exclusive command of them when called out, there was at once a military consolidation of the States, without any constitutional remedy. Any reader wishing to understand the principles and arguments upon which these conclusions rested, will find them very briefly, but I think clearly, stated in the answer of the court, page 548 of the eighth volume of the Massachusetts Reports.

His labors in the law were not trifling even in amount and quantity; of their quality I am hardly the person to speak. One or two words, however, I may say. From the concurrent testimony of all who have spoken or written on this subject during the many years which have passed since his death, I should say that he was particularly useful on three subjects; — one, pleading; another, the law of shipping and insurance; the third, the law of real estate.

What he did in reference to pleading has, perhaps, passed away. Of insurance, he has been said to have laid the foundations of our law; but they were laid before his time, by Lord Mansfield. I think my father's highest claim in this respect is, that he had the good sense to follow Mansfield's example, and learn of merchants what were their usages; and then he made out the principles embodied in those usages, and gave them consistency with established rules and forms, so that the whole fabric might cohere; and he recognized these principles as rules of law. His long and very large commercial practice made him as well acquainted as, perhaps, any lawyer ever was with the facts, the customs, and usages of trade; and upon these he brought to bear whatever learning the books could give him.

His knowledge of the law of title and of real actions was, I suppose, very considerable. For this belief I have an especial reason. The late Judge Jackson, who was himself regarded by common consent as one of the most learned lawyers in this very branch of the law whom we ever had, told me he had begged my father to put his vast learning of this law into a form which should preserve it; and had pressed it with so much importunity, that my father consented to join with him in making a book. Each party began his work; and I have now quite a mass of papers and memoranda prepared by my father with a view to it. But he never finished his share, nor any part so completely that it could be used. Judge Jackson went on, and, in the leisure which followed his retirement from office, he prepared that work on "Real Actions," which, although the change in the law and practice on this subject has rendered it of less immediate and practical value, will ever remain a monument of his learning and sagacity.

I will add, that William Pinkney, of Baltimore, who was very generally placed near, and by many *at*, the head of the bar of the United States, said to me, forty years ago, "Do you know one point in which your father surpassed all the lawyers of our country? It was in his thorough study and comprehension of Coke Littleton. I have read that book more, perhaps, than any one among us now, and I know what it can do for a lawyer."

Perhaps nothing strikes even a cursory reader of his opinions more than the apparent endeavor to give to Massachusetts a system of law founded upon her own usages, her own circumstances and exigencies. And the more they are studied, the more this impression will be confirmed. In looking, just now, at the Reports, for the purpose of getting the exact dates of his earliest and latest decisions, I noticed that most of the early cases turned upon our local law; and in one of them (2 Mass. Rep. 115) he declares that "the law is well settled, that parents are under obligations to support their children, and are entitled to their earnings." This declaration, perhaps, settled the law for Massachusetts, and from this State it has spread widely through the country; but it was not a settled and recognized principle of the common law of England until of late, if it be indeed now. Nor is there any statute settling this law in that country or in this; and my father's authority must have been his personal knowledge of the usage and law of the State.

I had prepared a large number of extracts, to show how frequently he declared important rules, sometimes only on the authority of his personal knowledge or recollection, and sometimes not resting them even on this ground, but simply declaring that this rule or that was the law. His infrequent citation of authorities has often been remarked upon. Some of the rules thus laid down have been overthrown; but upon the whole, so far as I have been able to learn, the great body of his law stands unquestioned.

Any lawyer who examines the earliest volumes of the

Reports of Massachusetts, must observe the almost chaotic condition of the law which they indicate. The court appear to take the opportunity which each case afforded, not only of deciding that case, but of establishing rules of very general application. And in doing this, truths and principles are often enunciated, so very simple and elementary in their character, as to show that it was deemed necessary to lay the foundations of the law, as well as to enlarge or repair the superstructure.

I feel that I ought to exhibit, if I can, some adequate specimen of the manner and method of my father's decisions. In them are embodied everything which he himself saw fit to give to the public. It would, however, be impossible, without too copious quotations, to cite instances of the various ways in which he disposed of the various questions which came before him. As these differed, so the tone and character of his opinions, or rather of the form in which he clothed them, must have differed, if they were to be appropriate. I select one case, however, because, while it affords a fair specimen of his general juridical style, it has, if I mistake not, a peculiar interest. It is one in which the question occurs, what constitutes a valid marriage. One would suppose that there is no topic concerning which the law would be more certain than this; for all possible reasons for this certainty coexist in it. It is the most ancient of contracts, and the most universal. No nation and no age can be pointed out in which, in some form, it has not been recognized. In its importance, viewed as a civil contract only, it surpasses all others. And whatever feeling or belief invests it with a spiritual or religious character, augments this importance almost infinitely. Nor has it been neglected; for everywhere, and especially in England and in every State of this country where we must look for our own rules of law, there are legal provisions concerning marriage.

It is nevertheless true, that there is no certainty respecting the essentials of a valid marriage. It is easily ascertained that a marriage celebrated in a certain way is unquestionably valid; but when it is asked whether the absence of this or that ceremony or form or act invalidates the marriage, it may be impossible to answer. I think a reference to the last authoritative cases in England and in this country will show that the highest tribunals in both countries are unable to state the law concerning marriage. Indeed, it is not too much to say, that this question is at once the most important that the relations of human society can offer for adjudication, and the most difficult and uncertain which can be presented to a court or to a lawyer.

The Roman civil law declared that "Sufficit nudus consensus ad constituenda sponsalia," or "consent alone suffices to constitute marriage"; and elsewhere, "Nuptias, non concubitus, sed consensus facit," or "consent, not cohabitation, makes marriage." Chancellor Kent, in his excellent Commentaries on American Law (published in 1826, and previously delivered as law lectures in Columbia College), apparently founds his opinion on the law of marriage upon these rules of the Roman law. He says: "No peculiar ceremonies are requisite by the common law to the valid celebration of the marriage. The consent of the parties is all that is required; and as marriage is said to be a contract *jure gentium*, that consent is all that is required by natural or public law. The Roman lawyers strongly inculcated the doctrine, that the very foundation and essence of the contract consisted in consent freely given, by parties competent to contract. 'Nihil proderit signasse tabulas, si mentem matrimonii non fuisse constabit. Nuptias, non concubitus, sed consensus facit.' This is the language equally of the common and canon law and of common reason. If the contract be made *per verba de præsenti*, and remains without cohabitation, or if made *per verba de futuro*, and be followed by consummation, it amounts to a valid marriage, which the parties, being competent as to age and consent, cannot dissolve, and it is equally binding as if made *in facie ecclesiæ.*" Kent then goes on to enforce and illustrate these remarks. But after the case of Jewell's Lessee *v.* Jewell, before the Supreme Court of the United States, in 1843, he, in subsequent editions of his work, after the phrase "it amounts to a valid marriage," interpolated the words, "in the absence of all civil regulations to the contrary." By this alteration, however, Kent leaves the actual question wholly unanswered. This question is *nòt* whether, in a state which has no civil regulations to the contrary, people may marry in any way they please; for no one ever doubted that. The exact question *is*, Are the civil regulations about marriage, in England and in all our States, "to the contrary"? That is, do they provide not only *a* way in which persons may marry, but *the only way* in which a valid marriage can be contracted; or, on the other hand, are these regulations only directions, telling how marriage may be contracted, if the parties like that way of doing it?

This case of Jewell's Lessee *v.* Jewell first came, in 1842, before the Circuit Court of the United States for the District of South Carolina, and in this case the precise question was raised, whether these words of Kent, in his first edition, — in which he certainly seems to hold that these regulations provided only one way, but not the *only* way, of contracting a valid marriage, — stated the law of marriage accurately. The court were much embarrassed by the question, and finally fell back upon Kent's high authority, and, citing his exact words, declared that they did state the law accurately. This case was appealed to the Supreme Court of the United States, and there argued in January, 1843. Chief Justice Taney delivered the opinion of the court; and, after disposing of the rest of the case, he comes to the precise question whether Kent's words do state the law accurately. And his language is as follows: "Upon the point thus decided (by the Circuit Court), *this court is equally divided; and no opinion can therefore be given.*"

By a singular coincidence, the same question came about the same time before the highest courts of Ireland and of England. A man entered into a contract of marriage in Ireland, *but not according to the law of Great Britain and Ireland*, and afterwards married in England. In 1842, he was indicted in Ireland for bigamy, and the question arose, whether the first marriage was valid; this question being substantially the same that was raised in the American case, namely, whether the first marriage was valid by force of the contract and engagement of the parties, although not solemnized according to the requirements of law. There were four justices of that court, *and they were equally divided, and could give no decision.* But, for the mere purpose of entering a decree on record from which an appeal could be made to the House of Lords, the Chief Justice of Ireland, though thinking the marriage invalid, nominally agreed with the two who thought it valid, and a judgment against the defendant was entered accordingly, and from this he appealed. When the question came before the House of Lords, in London, they called upon the judges of England to give their opinions. The judges differed in their views; but on the whole, their answer, given through Lord Chief Justice Tindal, was to the effect that a marriage contracted like the first marriage was in itself invalid, but gave to either party (by the peculiar English law on this subject) the power of calling on the ecclesiastical courts to compel a legal solemnization of the marriage. The case was then most ably argued before the House of Lords, by the best counsel in England. My unprofessional readers may not know that, when a question of law is argued before, and decided by, the House of Lords, this means in fact only those peers who are, or have at some time been judges, and who are familiarly called the Law Lords. At that time there were six of these,— Brougham, Denman, Campbell, Lyndhurst, Cottenham, and Abinger. They all gave opinions at great length; the whole case filling nearly half of a large octavo volume.

The result was, that *they also were equally divided;* the three lords first named considering the marriage valid, and the three last named considering it of no force or effect.

I have stated this history at some length, in part because both the importance of the question and the strange condition of the law, as thus exhibited, may be thought interesting; but more for another reason. It may be asked, if all these courts confess themselves unable to decide this question, is there no answer which can be given to it on authority? There were cases in England, and some in this country, which have considered the question, whether mere cohabitation for any length of time, without other evidence of an intention and agreement of marriage, can be considered as equivalent to, or as constituting, a regular and valid marriage. The answer is always in the negative.* The question, whether, *with* such intention and agreement, a marriage is valid, although there be no compliance with the statutory regulations on this subject, remained open. But there is a decision to be found in the Reports of Massachusetts,† which goes so much farther as to decide this precise question. The Supreme Judicial Court of this State, speaking through my father, is the only tribunal which has distinctly met and answered the question, whether a marriage is valid which rests upon no other foundation than the mutual agreement of the parties, followed by cohabitation as husband and wife. The decision was in the negative. I should premise, that the parties in this case came to a tavern in the town where they lived, when a justice of the peace happened to be there, and, producing a certificate that their intentions of marriage had been published, they requested him to marry them; but it was distinctly proved that *he refused to marry them.* They however went through the usual forms, in the presence of the justice and of others,

* The case of The State *v.* Samuel, in 2 Dev. & Bat. 177, amounts, I think, to nothing more than this.

† Milford *v.* Worcester, 7 Mass. R. 48.

and afterwards lived as husband and wife. In giving the opinion of the court, my father, after saying that the legality (or validity) of the marriage was the only question in the case, goes on as follows:

Marriage is unquestionably a civil contract, founded in the social nature of man, and intended to regulate, chasten, and refine the intercourse between the sexes, and to multiply, preserve, and improve the species. It is an engagement by which a single man and a single woman of sufficient discretion take each other for husband and wife. From the nature of the contract, it exists during the lives of the two parties, unless dissolved for causes which defeat the object of marriage, or from relations imposing duties repugnant to matrimonial rights and obligations.

Marriage being essential to the peace and harmony, and to the virtues and improvements of civil society, it has been, in all well-regulated governments, among the first attentions of the civil magistrate to regulate marriages; by defining the characters and relations of parties who may marry, so as to prevent a conflict of duties, and to preserve the purity of families; by describing the solemnities by which the contract shall be executed, so as to guard against fraud, surprise, and seduction; by annexing civil rights to the parties and their issue, to encourage marriage, and to discountenance wanton and lascivious cohabitation, which, if not checked, is followed by prostration of morals, and a dissolution of manners; and by declaring the causes and the judicature for rescinding the contract, when the conduct of either party and the interest of the state authorize a dissolution. A marriage contracted by parties authorized by law to contract, and solemnized in the manner prescribed by law, is a lawful marriage; and to no other marriage are incident the rights and privileges secured to husband and wife, and to the issue of the marriage.

The inquiry, therefore, in this case is, whether the mutual engagement of Stephen Temple and Rhoda Essling, made at the tavern in Upton, under the circumstances there existing, was a lawful marriage. Let us now examine the law.

When our ancestors left England, and ever since, it is well known that a lawful marriage there must be celebrated before a clergyman in orders, and that all questions of marriage, divorce, and alimony regularly belong to the ordinary. When our ancestors first settled here, smarting under the arbitrary censures of the ecclesiastical courts, they were not disposed to invest their own clergy with any civil powers whatever; but to leave them wholly to the exercise of their pastoral functions. With this impression, in 1646, by an ordinance passed for the due solemnization of marriages, no person is authorized to join together in marriage any persons, but a magistrate, or some other person to be appointed in such places where no magistrate was near. And all persons were forbidden to join themselves in marriage, but before some magistrate or other person authorized as aforesaid. Neither was the magistrate authorized to permit the parties to contract marriage in his presence, unless the intention of marriage had been previously published.

Thus stood the law until the repeal of the first Charter. Under the Provincial Charter, new and different regulations for the solemnizing of marriages were made, which were in force in 1784, and by which the case before us must be governed.

By the Provincial statute of 4 Will. & Mar. c. 10, every justice of the peace within his county, and every settled minister in any town, are authorized to solemnize marriages between persons who may lawfully intermarry, and who have the consent of those under whose immediate government they are, producing a certificate of the publication of the intention of marriage. This statute containing no negative words, it was afterwards enacted by the statute of 7 Will. 3, c. 6, that no person other than a justice of the peace, and that within his county only, or ordained minister, and that only in the town where he was settled, should join any persons in marriage; nor any, unless one or both of the parties were inhabitants or residents in such county or town respectively; nor without certificate of publishment; nor without evident signification that the parents or guardians were knowing of and consenting to such marriage, on the penalty of forfeiting *fifty pounds* to the county. The authority of an ordained minister to solemnize marriages was afterwards, by the statute of 3 Geo. 3, c. 4, and 13 Geo. 3, c. 6, enlarged in some special cases, which it is not necessary now to mention. These statutes remained in force until January, 1787, when the statute of 1786, c. 3, came into operation.

No form of words is established for the solemnization of a marriage. The usage is for the justice or minister to require of the parties respectively an assent to a mutual agreement to take each other for husband and wife; after which, he pronounces them to be husband and wife. But the statute would be substantially conformed to, if the parties were to make the mutual engagement in the presence of the justice or minister, with his assent, he undertaking to act on that occasion in his official character. But without such assent and undertaking of the justice or minister, notwithstanding their personal presence, the marriage, I am well satisfied, will not be solemnized pursuant to, nor be a lawful marriage within, the statute.

When a justice or minister shall solemnize a marriage between parties who may lawfully marry, although without publication of the banns of marriage, and without the consent of the parents or guardians, such marriage would unquestionably be lawful, although the officer would incur the penalty of fifty pounds for a breach of his duty. If, therefore, a mutual engagement of marriage made by the parties in the presence of a justice or minister, he not assenting to act in his official character on that occasion, would be a solemnization of the marriage by him, it would be equally so whether the intention of marriage had or had not been published; and if it had not, he might incur the penalty of fifty pounds where he had been guilty of no breach of official duty. This consequence is not to be admitted; and the necessary inference is, that such marriage engagement, so made by the parties in the presence of a justice or minister, not consenting to act officially on the occasion, is not a lawful marriage pursuant to the statute.

But it has been argued, that this marriage, although not solemnized pursuant to the statute, is yet a lawful marriage, had between parties competent to contract marriage, and not declared void by any statute.

This ground for supporting the marriage deserves consideration, as, if it be tenable, the consequences are very extensive. Where the laws of any state have prescribed no regulations for the celebration of marriages, a mutual engagement to intermarry, by parties competent to make such contract, would in a moral view be a good marriage, and would impugn no law of the state. But when civil government has established regulations for the due celebration of marriages, it is the duty, as well as the interest, of all the citizens to conform to such regulations. A deviation from them may tend to introduce fraud and surprise in the contract; or, by a celebration without witnesses, the vilest seduction may be practised under the pretext of matrimony. When, therefore, the statute enacts that no person but a justice or a minister shall solemnize a marriage, and that only in certain cases, the parties are themselves prohibited from solemnizing their own marriages by any form of engagement, or in the presence of any witnesses whatever.

If this be not a reasonable inference, fruitless are all the precautions of the Legislature. In vain do the laws require a previous publication of the banns, or the assent of the parents or guardians of young minors, or prohibit a justice or minister from solemnizing the marriage without these prerequisites. A young and inconsiderate couple may, at a tavern or elsewhere, with or without the presence of witnesses, rush into matrimony, distress their friends, and destroy their own future prospects in life.

As the notoriety of marriages is of importance to the people in furnishing an easy method of proving descents, the statute of 1786, c. 3, requires a certificate of a justice or minister of every marriage by him solemnized, to be entered on a public record, which cannot be impeached unless by evidence of fraud. Marriages otherwise solemnized cannot therefore be recorded, and cannot be presumed to be marriages recognized by law.

It has been truly observed by the counsel for the plaintiffs, that a marriage engagement of this kind is not declared void by any statute. But we cannot thence conclude that it is recognized as valid, unless we render in a great measure nugatory all the statute regulations on this subject.

It may be objected to these principles, that, if they are correct, a marriage among Quakers, agreeably to the rules of their society, is void. I know not that the conclusion would not be just. I know that such was the opinion of lawyers before the Revolution; and so general was this impression, that, to guard those people from consequences so mischievous, in the eighth section of the revising statute of 1786, c. 3, all such marriages before had were confirmed, and such marriages authorized in future.

Marriages may be considered as void or valid, with respect either to civil rights incident to marriages, or to penal consequences to the parties, where marriages are questioned. Whatever foundation for the distinction there may be, when the parties might have lawfully intermarried, there can be none where the parties are prohibited from marrying. This last case comprehends by our laws incestuous marriages, marriages within the age of consent, marriages when either of the parties has a husband or wife living, and marriages between a white person and an Indian, negro, or mulatto.*

Marriages between parties who might lawfully have intermarried, deserve a further consideration. No person can lawfully solemnize such marriages but a justice of the peace or an ordained minister. And a record of a marriage so solemnized by either of those officers, founded on a certificate duly made, is legal evidence of the marriage, and no inquiry is further made as to the publication of banns, the assent of parents or guardians, or the inhabitancy of the parties. When, therefore, the marriage appears to have been celebrated by a competent officer, as a justice or a minister, the marriage is deemed lawful, although the officer, for his irregularity, may have incurred the penalty of fifty pounds. But a marriage, merely the effect of a mutual engagement between the parties, or solemnized by any one not a justice of the peace or an ordained minister, is not a legal marriage, entitled to the incidents of a marriage duly solemnized. The woman, when a widow, cannot claim dower, nor the issue seizin by descent.

Whether cohabitation, after such a pretended marriage, will subject either of the parties to punishment as guilty of fornication, may depend on circumstances. If either of the parties were circumvented, and verily supposed the marriage legal, perhaps such party would be protected from punishment; on the general principle, that, to constitute guilt, the mind must appear to be guilty. But every young woman of honor ought to insist on a marriage solemnized by a legal officer, and to shun the man who prates about marriage condemned by human laws as good in the sight of Heaven. This cant, she may be assured, is a pretext for seduction; and if not contemned, will lead to dishonor and misery.

Upon the whole, it is the opinion of the court, that the mutual engagement of the parties in this case, to take each other for husband and wife, in the room where a justice was present, he

* This last provision is now repealed.

not assenting, but refusing to solemnize the marriage, is not a lawful marriage.

In another work, in which a full consideration of a legal question is more appropriate, I have stated my belief that this is the true doctrine of the law, and have given some additional reasons for this opinion. Here I have only to say, that, *if this be the law*, those persons whom we often read of in the newspapers, who undertake to marry merely by mutual consent, before witnesses, on such terms as they choose to agree on, but without any of the formalities required or directed by law, may, if the question ever comes before a court of justice, find themselves in the unfortunate predicament of those who have lived in unlawful intercourse. Questions of dower, of inheritance, of wills, or other disposition of property may come up, and the self-called wife find herself no wife; and what would be far worse, the children born from such a connection would be branded by the law as illegitimate, and as possessing no rights of inheritance. I should however add, that in some of our States there seems to be a strong disposition, both in legislatures and in courts, to make any contract of marriage legal, whatever be its form or want of form, whenever the parties, or one of the parties, believed the marriage to be legal and effectual when they entered into it.

Perhaps the most interesting trial which took place while my father was a judge, was that of Thomas Oliver Selfridge for killing Charles Austin. Fifty-two years have elapsed since that event; and to readers of this generation the facts of the case should be stated.

Mr. Benjamin Austin was a leader of the Democratic party, and a political writer of great force; and had said something about a suit at law brought by Mr. Selfridge, which, in that gentleman's opinion, was untrue and scandalous. Thereupon he applied to Mr. Austin for a retraction; and Mr. Austin appeared to be satisfied that he had been in some error, and made some concessions, but not enough to satisfy Mr. Selfridge, who put into a newspaper an advertisement calling him a liar, scoundrel, and coward. In the forenoon of the day in which this advertisement appeared, Charles Austin, a son of Benjamin Austin, went down State Street, advanced towards Mr. Selfridge with an uplifted cane, and, according to some witnesses, struck him; and Mr. Selfridge, before a blow, according to some of the witnesses, but, according to other witnesses, after being struck a heavy blow on the head, and another being threatened, and after retreating from near the middle of the street towards the side as far as the sidewalk, fired a pistol at Austin, and the ball went through his lungs, and he died almost instantly.

The case involved difficult questions of fact, which were presented to the jury. But besides these, it involved questions of law, which cannot be considered as definitely settled, and perhaps, from their own nature, can never be expressed in exact formulas. These questions relate to the law of self-defence; they ask, what kind or measure of threat or danger justifies the imperilled party in taking the life of his assailant, and how far he who is thus endangered must endeavor to retreat from the assault, or otherwise escape from it without doing harm, before he resorts to the ultimate right of killing in self-defence.

The case took, from the outset, a political character. Selfridge and Benjamin Austin were prominent in their respective parties, and very hostile to each other; and the original cause of the difficulty had a political aspect. But even among those who most strongly favored Mr. Selfridge, there could not but be much sympathy with the son, who was then in college, but eighteen years old, and of great promise, and who died in the defence of his father's good name. Nor could the worst political enemies of Mr. Austin — I do not know that he had any other — withhold their deepest commiseration for the father so suddenly and so painfully deprived of one upon whom so much of his affection and his hope rested.

The papers of the day, and the full report of the trial, show the excitement which prevailed, and show too how largely political hostility mingled with this excitement; indeed, at the trial, the presiding judge deemed it necessary to urge the jury, emphatically and eloquently, to guard against any such influence.

It was my father's duty to charge the grand jury; and this he did in the following words:

Observing in the list of prisoners returned by the jail-keeper, that two persons are in custody charged with felonious homicide, it may be useful to you, in your inquiries, to mention some principles of law relating to this subject.

In every charge of murder, the fact of killing being first proved against the party charged, to reduce the offence below that crime, by any circumstances of accident, necessity, or human infirmity, he must satisfactorily prove these circumstances, unless they arise out of the evidence produced against him.

When the act which occasions the death is unlawful, yet if malice, either express or implied, be wanting, the killing is not murder, but manslaughter, the act being imputed to the infirmity of human nature.

Neither words of reproach, however grievous, nor contemptuous or insulting gestures, without an assault on the person, are sufficient to free the party killing, with a dangerous weapon, from the guilt of murder.

An assault is any attempt or offer, with force and violence, to do a corporal hurt to another, as by striking at him, or even by holding up the fist at him in a threatening or insulting manner, or with such other circumstances as denote an intention and ability, at the time, of using actual violence against his person. And when the injury, however small, as spitting in a man's face, or unlawfully touching him in anger, is inflicted, it amounts to a battery, which includes an assault.

Any assault made, not lightly, but with violence, or with circumstances of indignity, upon a man's person, if it be resented immediately, and in the heat of blood, by killing the party with a deadly weapon, is a *provocation*, *which will* reduce the crime to manslaughter; unless the assault was sought for by the party killing, and induced by his own act, to afford him a pretence for wreaking his malice. To illustrate this exception, a case is stated of the falling out of A and B. A says he will not strike, but will give B a pot of ale to touch him; on which B strikes A, who thereupon kills B. This is murder in A, notwithstanding the provocation received by the blow from B, because A sought that provocation.

A man may repel force by force, in defence of his person, against any one who manifestly intends, or endeavors by violence, or surprise, feloniously to kill him. And he is not obliged to retreat, but may pursue his adversary, until he has secured himself from all danger; and if he kill him in so doing, it is *justifiable self-defence*. But a bare fear, however well grounded, unaccompanied by any open act indicative of such an intention, will not warrant him in killing. There must be an actual danger at the time; and (in the language of Lord Chief Justice Hale) it must plainly appear by the circumstances of the case, as the manner of the assault, the weapon, &c., that his life was in imminent danger; otherwise the killing of the assailant will not be *justifiable homicide*.

But if the party killing had reasonable grounds for believing that the person slain had a felonious design against him, and under that supposition kill him, although it should afterwards appear that there was no such design, it will not be murder, but it will be either manslaughter or *excusable homicide*, according to the degree of caution used, and the probable grounds of such belief.

These principles have been recognized by the wisest and most humane writers on criminal law.

After a due and impartial inquiry into the several cases that may require your attention, you will ascertain the facts, and afterwards apply the principles of law, to obtain a just and legal result.

The coroner's jury rendered a verdict against Selfridge for murder; but the grand jury brought in an indictment for manslaughter only; and it excited no little remark among the friends of Austin, that his slayer was not to be tried for murder. As manslaughter is not a capital offence, one judge could try it; and the terms of court having been divided among the judges before the affair took place, and the holding of the next term in Boston having fallen to Judge Parker, no change was made; the case was tried before him alone; and some fault was found with the court on this ground also. After the evidence and arguments were in, Judge Parker charged the jury as to the law, in these words:

First. A man who, in the lawful pursuit of his business, is attacked by another, under circumstances which denote an intention to take away his life, or do him some enormous bodily harm, may lawfully kill the assailant, provided he use all the means in his power, otherwise, to save his own life or prevent the intended harm, — such as retreating as far as he can, or disabling his adversary without killing him, if it be in his power.

Secondly. When the attack upon him is so sudden, fierce, and violent, that a retreat would not diminish, but increase his danger, he may instantly kill his adversary without retreating at all.

Thirdly. When, from the nature of the attack, there is reasonable ground to believe that there is a design to destroy his life, or commit any felony upon his person, the killing the assailant will be excusable homicide, although it should afterwards appear that no felony was intended.

Of these three propositions, the last is the only one which will be contested anywhere; and this will not be doubted by any who are conversant in the principles of criminal law. Indeed, if this last proposition be not true, the preceding ones, however true and universally admitted, would in most cases be entirely inefficacious. And when it is considered that the jury who try the cause are to decide upon the grounds of apprehension, no danger can flow from the example. To illustrate this principle, take the following case. A, in the peaceable pursuit of his affairs, sees B rushing rapidly towards him, with an outstretched arm and a pistol in his hand, and using violent menaces against his life as he advances. Having approached near enough, in the same attitude, A, who has a club in his hand, strikes B over the head, before or at the instant the pistol is discharged, and of the wound B dies. It turns out that the pistol was loaded with *powder only*, and that the real design of B was only to *terrify* A. Will any reasonable man say that A is more criminal than he would have been if there had been a bullet in the pistol? Those who hold such doctrine must require that a man so attacked must, before he strike the assailant, stop and ascertain how the pistol is loaded; a doctrine which would entirely take away the essential right of self-defence. And when it is considered that the jury who try the cause, and not the party killing, are to judge of the reasonable grounds of his apprehension, no danger can be supposed to flow from this principle.

The jury rendered a verdict of not guilty, to the disappointment of many persons, and to the extreme anger of some. None could deny that there was much evidence in Selfridge's favor, and still less could it be doubted that the very great ability and eloquence of the eminent counsel who defended him, Dexter and Gore, aided most materially in his acquittal. But it was often said at the time, and has been sometimes intimated since, that my father assisted his escape, by stating the law so as to favor him in his charge to the grand jury, which prevented an indictment for murder; and that he then had much influence in determining the course pursued by Judge Parker.

I suppose these accusations to be wholly groundless. They rested mainly on the statement in the charge, that "if the party killing had reasonable grounds for believing that the person slain had a felonious design against him, and under that supposition kill him, although it should afterwards appear that there was no such design, it will not be murder, but it will be either manslaughter or excusable homicide, according to the degree of caution used, and the probable grounds of such belief." There can be no question whatever, that this was a careful and perfectly accurate statement of a principle which rests upon the most uniform and indisputable authority.

Mr. Austin, senior, made a memorial on the subject to the Legislature, by whom it was referred to a committee. The Governor, the Senate, the House of Representatives, and the committee were Democratic. A report was made, intimating that the charge did not go sufficiently into detail; and there was some reference to cases and principles not mentioned in the charge, which the committee thought might illustrate or qualify the law of self-defence; but no censure was cast upon the court. The report was read and adopted, and nothing more was done.

Some fault was also found, although not much, with another clause in his charge. It was that in which he uses these words: "And he is not obliged to retreat, but may pursue his adversary, until he has secured himself from all danger; and if he kill him in so doing, it is justifiable homicide." No one disputes that there is high and distinct authority in the adjudicated cases for this doctrine. But it was said that the weight and current of the authority, and the reason and principles of the rule, required that it should be stated with important qualifications, which were wholly omitted; as, that the party is not obliged to retreat, if retreating be itself dangerous or useless. And in the charge of Judge Parker to the traverse (or trial) jury, after saying that the party assaulted should retreat as far as he could, he adds: "Secondly, when the attack upon him is so sudden, fierce, and violent that a retreat would not diminish, but increase his danger, he may instantly kill his adversary without retreating at all." It is doubtless true, that my father stated the rule more briefly and succinctly, because all he had to do was to give such general directions to the grand jury as were necessary for their purpose, leaving to the judge who should try the case the duty of presenting the law with the special qualifications or illustrations which the facts might seem to require.

I do not suppose, however, that he intended to say, nor have I any evidence that he was understood by any one to say, that any man who is feloniously attacked is under no obligation to avoid putting his assailant to death, if he can avoid this by safe and easy retreat, or by any other mode of escape; or that a party thus attacked is by the attack itself authorized to kill the assailant at once. Two or three years since, I read in a newspaper the report of a trial in one of our Southwestern States, — I think Arkansas, but took no memorandum of the paper, not then intending to write this work, — in which the judge instructed the jury, that, as no man had a right to attack another, so he who was attacked, in any manner threatening death or grievous bodily harm, was under no obligation to seek or use any means of escape, but might at once exercise the right of self-defence, and put his assailant to death; and my father's charge to the grand jury in Selfridge's case was cited for this rule. But neither is the whole case open to this conclusion; nor can it be inferred from the ruling of the court. Besides what has already been cited, Judge Parker, at a later period of his charge, said:

But whether the firing of the pistol was before or after a blow struck by the deceased, there is another point of more importance for you to settle, and about which you must make up your minds, from all the circumstances proved in the case; such as the rapidity and violence of the attack, the nature of the weapon with which it was made, the place where the catastrophe happened, the muscular debility or vigor of the defendant, and his power to resist or to fly. The point I mean is, whether he could probably have saved himself from death or enormous bodily harm by retreating to the wall, or throwing himself into the arms of friends who would protect him. This is the *real stress* of the case. If you believe, under all the circumstances, the defendant could have escaped his adversary's vengeance, at the time of the attack, without killing him, the defence set up has failed, and the defendant must be convicted.

If you believe his only resort for safety was to take the life of his antagonist, he must be acquitted, unless his conduct has been such prior to the attack on him as will deprive him of the privilege of setting up a defence of this nature. It has, however, been suggested by the defendant's counsel, that even if his life had not been in danger, or no great bodily harm, but only disgrace was intended by the deceased, there are certain principles of honor and natural right by which the killing may be justified. These are principles which you as jurors, and I as a judge, cannot recognize. The laws which we are sworn to administer are not founded upon *them*. Let those who choose such principles for their guidance erect a court for the trial of points and principles of honor; but let the courts of law adhere to those principles which are laid down in the books, and whose wisdom ages of experience have sanctioned. I therefore declare it to you as the law of the land, that unless the defendant has satisfactorily proved to you that no means of saving his life, or his person from the great bodily harm which was apparently intended by the deceased against him, except killing his adversary, were in his power, he has been guilty of manslaughter; notwithstanding you may believe with the grand jury who found the bill, that the case does not present the least evidence of malice or premeditated design in the defendant to kill the deceased or any other person.

This I believe to be the law; and although I am sure that Judge Parker stood upon his own ground, and expressed his own sentiments, yet in a trial of such magnitude and interest, and involving principles of so much importance, he would undoubtedly confer with his colleagues so far as he had opportunity; and especially with the Chief Justice of his own court, between whom and himself there had always been the utmost intimacy and confidence. I should infer from this, if it were necessary to resort to it, that his instructions must be regarded as not opposed to the brief statement of the law in my father's charge; and that he did not differ at all from my father in his view of the law.

Chief Justice Parker says of my father, in his charge delivered after his death: "In the administration of criminal law, however, he was strict, and almost punctilious, in adhering to forms. He required of the public prosecutors the most scrupulous exactness, believing it to be the right, even of the guilty, to be tried according to known and practised rules; and that it was a less evil for a criminal to escape, than that the barriers established for the security of innocence should be overthrown. He was a humane judge, and adopted, in its fullest extent, the maxim of Lord Chief Justice Hale, that doubts should always be placed in the scale of mercy." In a capital case lately tried in Boston, eminent counsel are reported to have said: "Judge Parsons declared that a man had a right to quibble for his life." My colleague, Chief Justice Parker, informs me that he heard this from Chief Justice Richardson, a long time ago.

Among his law papers were many opinions which he had given; and some of these were published, some years since, in "The American Jurist." He also left many essays,—if I may call them so,—more or less complete. That which I thought most valuable was upon the Constitutionality of the Embargo. It covered many sheets, and, as far as I remember, was entirely finished. He believed the embargo unconstitutional. This paper was lent by me to Chief Justice Isaac Parker, and I never knew what became of it afterwards. Many persons read it in the years immediately following my father's death, and it was much spoken of. I remember that he went into a full consideration of the question, how far the right to regulate commerce could be extended by construction into a right to restrain and suppress it. I cannot recall the line of argument; but he must have invoked his favorite clause of the Constitution,—that which reserves to the several States all powers not expressly delegated to Congress;—a clause for which he may well have had the affection of paternity. Whether he valued this provision too highly, time will show. I cannot but think, as I believe he thought, that it is to this principle our country—if it is to remain one country—must look for political salvation, or look for it in vain.

I had prepared quite a large number of extracts from leading cases decided while he was on the bench, with comments, intended to illustrate their effect and their value. But I have concluded to withhold them. Lawyers will understand them far better in the Reports, in which they now stand in full; and to readers who are not lawyers I could hardly hope to make them intelligible or interesting in any way. But my strongest reason is my distrust of the accuracy of my judgment in regard to these things, and my conviction that I ought to distrust it. They are the fruits of my father's life. It would be wrong for me not to reverence them; but it would also be wrong for me not to remember that this very feeling cannot but obscure, and perhaps distort, my perception of their merits and their defects. And, instead of endeavoring to form and express an opinion of my own in reference to my father's influence upon the law of this Commonwealth, I refer to the printed Reports, and also to the documents in the Appendix.

NOTE. — Since these pages were electrotyped, I have received from the Rev. Dr. Sanger a letter giving me two anecdotes, which seem to illustrate some parts of this chapter, and I will try to compress them into what is left of this page. In 1806, he, then a collegian, went into the court-house while the Supreme Court was sitting in Cambridge, and heard Mr. Sullivan argue a case, apparently of much importance, at great length and very earnestly. My father rose to reply, and said, very slowly and quietly: "This case presents three points. The first is this; the second is this; and the third is this"; — stating each with perfect clearness, but occupying less than five minutes with the whole. "The statement and argument seemed as clear to me," said Mr. Sanger, "as any demonstration in Euclid. The jury gave your father a verdict without leaving their seats." The next time Mr. S. saw him, he was holding court in Cambridge. Mr. Timothy Bigelow (the leading counsel of the county) arose to a case with many papers before him, and, after a word or two about its great interest, went on. "Very soon, your father said: 'Brother Bigelow, don't waste your time on that point; there is nothing in it.' And so he said of the next; and so, too, of the third. Mr. Bigelow stopped, and with some irritation said: 'I regret that I find myself unable to please the court this morning.' 'Brother Bigelow,' said your father, with a pleasant smile, 'you always please the court *when you are right*.' And the case was disposed of."

CHAPTER VI.

OF HIM AS A SCHOLAR.

No trait or quality more distinctly and emphatically characterized his mind, than a universal and ardent desire for knowledge. This was the ruling love of his whole life; and the indulgence of it constituted nearly all his enjoyment. I have called it universal, because it not only embraced every topic, but every means of acquiring information. Whenever, by business or accident, he was thrown into the company of any person who had any special and peculiar information, he never rested until he had learned all there was to get; and his quickness, extent of knowledge, and habits of inquiry enabled him to obtain this information promptly and thoroughly. Whether he annoyed people by thus exhausting them, I do not know. I never heard that he did; and in the instances in which I saw him converse thus, his pleasantry, vivacity, and interest, and his facility in giving as well as receiving, to all appearance, prevented annoyance.

Whenever any mechanics were employed about the house, I perfectly remember how he watched and studied them, and seemed to understand their doings and their tools, and the whole *rationale* of their business, better than they did, as I have heard them say. I believe there was no manufacture or mechanical business established within his reach, that he did not examine and study thoroughly. I can recollect his having a fireplace constructed with a system of tubes, to receive air from without, and give it forth when heated. It was made of soapstone, from his drawings (which I now have), in his office, after he went on the bench. I well remember how he busied himself with an array of thermometers, making a long course of experiments, of which I understood nothing, but that he was trying to ascertain what was the saving in the heat.

So, too, learning from some of his foreign books, and from some partial importations or imitations of it, the success and utility of Count Rumford's apparatus for cooking, he imported a complete set of it, and had it placed in what we called the "upper kitchen," — and very proud he was of this apparatus. The difficulties springing from the novelty of it and the ignorance of our cook, he overcame by the most patient instruction, until at last everything went well. This was in or about 1807; and I shall never forget it, for it gave rise to the most ludicrous of all his blunders about words, — so ludicrous as to seem incredible; and I confess that I did not dare to write until I had conferred with my sisters, and found that they too remembered it perfectly, and just as I remember it myself.

I have already said, in speaking of the peculiarity of his memory, that his hold on mere names seemed to be as weak as his grasp of everything else was strong; and sometimes, in moments of inadvertence, he would miscall them strangely. We had a large dinner-party, for which the new cooking-apparatus proved entirely adequate. Judge and Mrs. Seaver, from Kingston, dined with us; excellent persons, and most highly valued, but very decidedly of the old school. Her brocade dress seemed to me as stiff as tin, and her manners were as precise and exact as they were elegant. My father had held court all the forenoon, and was trying an interesting insurance case about a schooner. As soon as he came home he was apprised of some difficulty about the aqueduct, — then another recent and favorite improvement, — which he hastened to remedy. Very soon after, dinner was announced, and Mrs. Seaver took her place at the right hand of my mother, with my father at the opposite end of a long table. Grace was said; the company sat down; he took up his carving-knife, and as he began to use it, cried out to Mrs. Seaver, with great distinctness, "Mrs. Schooner, all the food on this table was cooked in the aqueduct." As I recall the scene at this moment, it is as vivid as when it passed before me fifty years ago. Delightfully did my mother's consternation contrast with my father's glee. She said, — dropping the broad fish-knife from her hand, — and almost screamed, "Lord's sake, Mr. Parsons, what *do* you mean?" But she got no other answer than a long and hearty, not to say uproarious laugh, in which all the company joined. Other mistakes of this kind have I known him make; and sometimes my mother would say, "I do believe you say such things that you may laugh about them." And he would answer, "By no means, my dear; I would speak as accurately as you do, if I could." I must, however, say, that any other thing like the "Mrs. Schooner" mistake I never heard from him, nor from anybody else.

My father sought for knowledge of every kind, eagerly, insatiably, and in every way; but books were his great means of information. I should say, that he had a perfect passion for reading. I have heard it denied that there is any such thing as a love of reading for its own sake, and without reference to its results. I should as soon think of doubting whether there was any such thing as a love of eating without reference to its utility or necessity. Undoubtedly he read to learn; and first loved to read because he loved to learn. Perhaps that process which Tucker, in his "Light of Nature Revealed," calls "Translation," took place in his mind. In that charming, but rather prolix book, there is a most entertaining, not to say instructive chapter, on the tendency of the human mind to transfer the pleasure it finds in the effect, to the means by which that effect is produced. Thus, one who takes a nauseous medicine, and gradually finds it giving him relief or health, will as gradually be reconciled to it, and soon learn to love it. Tucker has a great deal of curious philosophy about this tendency, which is very amusing, at all events. Whether my father's love for reading grew up only thus, I cannot say. But, from his early childhood, a book was the thing he loved best. If ever the old phrase, "helluo librorum," was applicable to any one, it was so to him. I do not remember, if I ever knew, whether this phrase originally meant one who loved to accumulate books, or one whose passion it was to read them; but I use the phrase in this latter sense, although it would have some application in both.

His library, for that day, was a very large one. I believe it contained, altogether, between five and six thousand volumes, of which by far the greater part were imported. No book was ordered or bought, except for a specific reason, and with the purpose of making some use of it. They were all nicely bound and well cared for; and when, at his death, the library was sold by auction, it brought more than its original cost with interest. Such a sale was then without precedent, and has not occurred since that I know of. It was ascribed in part to the number of those who wished to possess memorials of him, and in part to the recommendation which a book derived from having been owned by him. But I think neither of these causes could have operated largely; and I look upon the sale as evidence of the care and skill with which the books were selected.

His use ot his books was that of one who loved them. When brought down from the library, each was covered; and few things vexed him more than carelessness about a book. He read with marvellous rapidity. There seem to be three ways of reading. One, to spell the words as the reader goes on, recognizing each letter by itself; this is the way of beginners. Another, to take into the eye whole words at once; and this is the way in which most persons read. The third way is, to take in whole phrases and sentences at once, without distinguishing the words or the letters; and this is the way in which those read who have read most, and have learned to read fastest. This was the way in which he read what might be called light reading; by which I mean books which do not require the reader to pause and meditate upon what he reads.

How much he read, that is, how many hours, I cannot say. But I suppose it to be literally true, that for fifty years he was always reading or writing, when not obliged to be doing something else. He had, fortunately for himself, many interruptions; but he avoided them as far as he could; and there were weeks and I believe consecutive months, when he passed nearly two thirds of his day with books and papers.

One who applies a quick and retentive mind to various study during so long a period, must necessarily acquire a great amount of varied knowledge. To his contemporaries, this amount seemed almost marvellous. Often have I been told that his knowledge was universal, and in every department complete. For example, the late Mr. John Lowell, himself one of the ablest and most eminent men of his day, frequently said, that, while my father knew more law than any other man, he knew more of everything else than of law. And Chief Justice Isaac Parker has said to me, that he thought the law was the only thing my father seemed to study only because he must. He never went to it for amusement; but when he had done with the law whatever needed then to be done, he turned for refreshment to anything else, and seemed equally at home everywhere else.

Very much of this opinion was mistake and exaggeration; and often, as it came back to my father, he would laugh at it himself; for he was no such impossible prodigy, and knew the limits of his own knowledge better than any one else could know them.

Among the many things which fell within his cognizance, there were three of which he knew most, and which he loved best to study. These were Greek, the physical sciences, and mathematics.

I have some impression that he had always paid much attention to the Greek language; but his early papers are full of science and mathematics; nor do I find evidence there of any diligent or critical study of Greek, until after he was thirty years old. The family tradition is, that he undertook to make himself master of that language, when he began to think that he should wish to assist his eldest son in his study of it. However begun, he kept up his interest in this study until his death. Whether he ever became what Johnson would have called "a man of much Greek," I do not know. He had the best editions of "the authors," — to use the pet phrase of our good Doctor Popkin, the late Greek Professor at Cambridge, — and a most ample apparatus for the study of them, containing all the best dictionaries and grammars; and of these he made great use.

Until near the close of the last century, all our grammars of the Greek language were written in the Latin language; and of these the Westminster Grammar was in common use in England and in this country. My father thought that our own grammars for all languages should be in our own language. In reference to Greek, however, he thought there was an especial reason for this; and this he found in his favorite theory, that Greek should be taught first, and Latin afterwards. This theory he always maintained, sometimes very strenuously; and at one time he thought somewhat seriously of urging the introduction of this system upon the government of Harvard College. I believe I know the reasons for this theory, for, before he died, I was old enough to be interested in them.

They were generally stated thus. Greek is not *much* more difficult than Latin; and so far as it is more difficult, it is so because Greek is the *larger* language, being not only more copious in words, but superior in grammatical precision and resources; the Latin being, in substance, *composed of little else than the coarser parts of the Greek.* For the science and philosophy of grammar, or what may be called the essential principles of universal grammar, the Greek stands so far beyond any other language, that there is almost nothing in the grammar of any other European language which a thorough knowledge of Greek would not help one to understand.

In the next place, as the Greek was first in excellence, so it was first in time. It borrows nothing, — certainly nothing from Latin,— but lends to everything else; the Latin is very much composed of what it has borrowed from the Greek; and all this it is better to learn as it is *in situ,* so to speak, before its true nature and meaning become disfigured or disguised. Latin helps one comparatively little in learning Greek; whereas the Greek almost contains and implies the Latin.

Finally, the Greek language contains the most admirable literature of almost every kind that the world has ever seen; and the very best things in Latin are but "Greek and water."

That Greek might be learned by those who knew only English, the first requisite was a Greek Grammar in English; and this my father undertook to prepare, when about forty years old. He gave to it most of his leisure for a considerable time, and had it nearly completed and ready for the press, when the Gloucester Greek Grammar, which had been published in England a short time previously, was reprinted here, about 1794, at his earnest recommendation, as I have been told; and then he laid his manuscript aside. After his death I found it, or the greater part of it, (for it was in sundry parcels,) and kept a good deal of it — all that was not "conveyed" away by one person or another — until some fifteen years ago, when a friend from Worcester took it from my office in Boston, with the leave not asked but taken, which antiquarian collectors sometimes use, and gave it to the American Antiquarian Society at Worcester. Their very civil acknowledgment was the first intimation I had that it had left my possession. I felt no disposition to recall it from such excellent hands; and there it has been safely preserved, which probably would not have been the case if it had remained with me.

It will be seen by a note to Chief Justice Parker's Charge, that Professor Luzac of Leyden spoke of my father as "a giant in Greek literature." How the correspondence between my father and Luzac grew up, I do not know. I had once, as well as I can remember, interesting letters from the Professor to him; and here, as on every other subject connected with my father, I have to regret that I have yielded so easily to the voracity of collectors of autographs and manuscripts, for I have but this left, which I now publish; saying, by way of preface, that Luzac was Professor of Greek in the University of Leyden, and one of the most eminent of the Greek scholars of his day. I remember, but very dimly, my father's grief, when the news came, in 1807, that a vessel laden with gunpowder lay in a canal at Leyden, and by some accident the powder exploded and destroyed many buildings and lives, and that Luzac was amongst the killed.

Leyden, July 17th, 1801.

HONORABLE SIR:

I have successively been employed by my friend, Mr. Cremer of Rotterdam, with whom I have been intimately acquainted many years, to execute your commissions of books, by getting them from one or two of our principal booksellers. These commissions were the more agreeable to me, as I have from my youth cultivated those letters of which I see, dear Sir, you are not less fond than myself. After having practised at the bar, both in our courts of justice at the Hague and at Leyden, during a period of sixteen years, (in which time I became acquainted with your worthy late President, John Adams,) I was, during eleven years, Professor of Greek Literature and of the History of our Country in the University at Leyden. After that time, six years ago, I, who had always been a friend of true republicanism, was obliged by our modern patrons of liberty to resign my public station, if I did not choose to submit to their arbitrary and unjust dictates. You will see my principles and sentiments by the Discourse, of which I have the honor to present you a copy. I pronounced it at the very time of the French invasion, when I had the misfortune of being, in a most dangerous and troublesome time, at the head of the University, a few months before my resignation. You will see, Sir, that my boldness was not of a nature to please our Democratical Gallomanes; but I hope those principles and sentiments shall not be judged by you unworthy of a member of your Bostonian Society.*

You ask, Sir, the opinion of a literary friend about the merits of the Deux-Ponts Editions of the Classics. It will be difficult to give it about them all, of which you will find the list here enclosed. I do know by perusal but a few of them, viz.: the Plato, which is a very good edition, taken from that of Stephanus or Serranus, with critical remarks on other lessons [readings] taken from the manuscripts. There is also a Thucydides of Deux-Ponts; but there the war obliged the Bipontine Society of Editors not only to stop publishing any more Greek classics, but (as Deux-Ponts was frequently taken, retaken, and plundered out) the flames destroyed the typographical magazines, by which accident those editions of Plato and Thucydides have become more difficult to be procured than before. As for the Latin classics, they are beautiful, neat editions, on good paper, and generally correct, with a judicious recension of former editions, the lifes of the writers, short critical annotations and collations with the manuscripts, but not all of them are of the same stamp and exactness.

If I can be of any service to you, Sir, I will employ myself with great readiness; and you, Sir, — you will excuse the bad English language of a foreigner, who nevertheless, so bad as it may be, does assure you by it of the purity and sincerity of his esteem and sentiments, having the honor to be, honorable Sir,

Your obedient, humble servant,

JOHN LUZAC.

---

* He means by this the American Academy of Arts and Sciences, of which he had recently been made a member, at the instance of my father.

In 1810, my father induced Mr. Elisha Clap to leave a school which he was then teaching in Sandwich with great success, and to come to Boston, where twenty-five scholars were obtained for him at one hundred dollars a year for each. This was then thought a great price. My father interested himself very much in this school. He caused an abridged edition of the "Greek Primitives" to be published, which was used in it;* and, either at his suggestion or with his approval, a method of learning Greek was adopted there, which I have never known to be carried out to such extent elsewhere. First, the Greek grammar was divided into four nearly equal parts; and the scholar was required to commit all the large type matter to memory, so perfectly that he could repeat the whole grammar with but four verbal mistakes in each quarter. That is, the boy began to recite at the beginning of the grammar, and went on until he had made his four mistakes in the first quarter of the book; then he stopped, and began, the next day, a little before the place of his last mistake, went through that quarter, and began it again; and so on, until he could go from beginning to end with only his four errors. Then

* This work was first published in Paris, in 1657, under the name of "Le Jardin des Racines Grecques," and it was one of the many learned and excellent productions of the Port Royal writers. Dr. Nugent published a translation of it in English, in 1748, in a large octavo volume. This my father imported, and liked so much, that he induced Mr. William Wells, whose thorough scholarship fitted him for the task, to prepare an abridgment of it, with some additions from Buttmann's Grammar, in 1811. I believe the book was never generally used in our schools. My friend, Mr. Charles Folsom, tells me that he has a copy of the original French work, which shows, by manuscript memoranda upon it, that Mr. John Quincy Adams formerly owned it, and in 1805, at the age of thirty-eight, when he was a Senator of the United States, after having been minister at three European courts, he committed to memory the two thousand and more French verses, each containing a Greek root, at the rate of thirty a day, — beginning on the *4th of July*, and ending on the 13th of September.

"Perstat, et infixis alte *radicibus* haeret."

he took the next quarter, and so on through. When the grammar was thus learned, all these "Greek Primitives" were committed to memory with equal thoroughness; and only after this was he permitted to begin reading. The theory was, that the grammar gave him all the rules and forms, and if the roots were then acquired, all subsequent learning consisted in applying the rules of formation and syntax to the roots. Whether the theory was a sound one, I do not know. It would probably work better now that the true principles of Greek grammar are more accurately understood than they were then. But I thought the method a bad one then, because it was exceedingly wearisome; and I think so now, because I never saw any very good scholarship produced by it.

My father originated or promoted the publication of other books; and I remember particularly how much he was interested in the edition of Griesbach's New Testament, published by William Wells and William Hilliard, in 1809, and dedicated to the President and Fellows of the University, as having been undertaken "eorum hortatu et auxilio." It was reprinted from a copy which Luzac had sent my father, and which he furnished to the publishers for that purpose. I have at this time the presentation copy of Griesbach, bound in morocco, which the publishers sent to him, in return for the copy with which he supplied them. The senior member of the firm was the Mr. William Wells of whom I have already spoken in a previous chapter, as one of my father's intimate friends. He was my own earliest school-teacher; and now, after fifty years have passed away, he is living in Cambridge, my neighbor, honored by all who know him, and loved by all who are near him, and loved most by those who are nearest.

My father never sent any of his children to a public school, but was much interested in them, and was at times quite active in promoting their interests. I remember (but very imperfectly) hearing, when a boy, of a conference on the subject of the schools, at which my father uttered some sentiments that I have often thought of. About them I have no doubt; and so far as I can recall the attendant circumstances, they were these. There was a movement in the town of Boston (a town it then was) for the improvement of the schools, at a considerable increase of their cost. There was much opposition to it; and at a meeting of gentlemen, some of whom favored it and some did not, one wealthy person, of much influence, spoke almost angrily of what he deemed an attempt to make him pay his money for benefits which went to others exclusively. He sent his son to Mr. Clap's school, — and he said, in substance: "I pay a round bill there, and am willing to do so. I get my money's worth, and it is fair that I should pay for it; but the public schools are not such, and will not be such, as I should wish to put my own children in; and why should not they pay for them who profit by them?" As I have heard the story, my father answered: "You are mistaken. You will not probably want these schools for your children, and possibly they will not want them for theirs; but many generations that succeed them will be sure to need the schools for their own families, for they are in all probability to be poor. In this country, the wheel of fortune not only may, but must, revolve; faster in some instances than in others, but turn it must. The rich of any generation are the descendants, and generally the immediate descendants, of the poor. *Their* descendants will in almost every case take their place among the poor, in one or two generations more; and because there are many more of the poor than of the rich, each family must number many more of its generations among the poor than among the rich. If, therefore, you wish to provide for the greater number of your own descendants, provide now, permanently, for the poor."

I confess it seems to me that this principle should be remembered in reference to all the other establishments of this country for the general good, as well as its schools;

and will be so applicable while our laws and institutions remain unchanged; and that the almost inevitable hostility between the rich and the poor would be greatly modified, if not prevented, if this principle were distinctly and generally recognized by the rich in the disposition of their property.

While my father greatly preferred Greek to Latin, he had a complete collection of the Latin classics, — of some authors many editions, — and read and wrote the language with great ease.

The first I ever heard of my father's interest in scientific inquiries was in relation to an occurrence which took place in 1790, but was long remembered in the family. While living in Newburyport, he had imported what was called a Woulfe's Apparatus, but is now superseded by one of the same name, which is much simpler and better. By it water was saturated with a gas. It was then a new instrument; and he was using it one evening to saturate water with carbonic acid gas, (making what is now known as soda water), gently blowing from him the superfluous gas as it escaped from the top of the apparatus. My mother came up without his knowing it, to see what he was doing, and stood opposite him; and thus he blew the gas from himself to her. The first knowledge he had that she was there was by seeing her fall insensible. He knew at once what the cause was, and carried her into the fresh air, where she was soon restored. This became one of the family stories, which I often heard.

This apparatus, with many other chemical instruments, came into my possession after his death; but I never saw him make any use of them, and I believe he did not after his removal to Boston. Chemistry was a more burdensome and inconvenient study in those days than it is now. The instruments were bulky, and experiments were difficult and laborious. Dr. Wollaston had not begun to practise that "microscopical chemistry," as he called it, by which so much may be done and learned on a small table. My father, for these or other reasons, gave up experimenting, but continued to import and read chemical works, and in this way kept up with the progress of that beautiful science; and the new results, which in the beginning of this century were regarded with so much interest and hope, were often subjects of conversation in his parlor.

His most intimate friend among scientific persons was the Rev. Dr. John Prince of Salem. This gentleman found or made time to indulge himself in a most engrossing love not so much for science as for the instruments of science. He not only had tools and machinery for making them himself, but imported them for individuals and public bodies; and, for some years, nearly all the instruments received in this part of the country came through his agency.

With unsated and ever new delight I used to hear that Dr. Prince was coming, or had actually come. His visits were not unfrequent; but I was sure, whenever he made his appearance, that some new instrument would come out to be examined and tried, or some old ones would be taken, and new trials made. Of whatever was going on, I was heartily welcome to see all I could, if only *I touched nothing;* for this, from my earliest days, was a condition absolute.

Among these instruments I remember best a set of magnets, an electrical apparatus, his great telescope, and some small microscopes, with one very superb one, called Adams's Improved Lucernal Microscope. This is now in our family. The case is some two or three feet long and eight or ten inches square. Of course it cannot compare with the recent achromatic microscopes, which have revealed such wonders; but for the extent of its field, the large size of its objects, and the splendor of its exhibitions, it seems to me even now to have advantages over any that I have seen.

Another gentleman with whom my father lived in great intimacy was Mr. William Bond, the father of Professor William C. Bond of Cambridge. This gentleman was born in Plymouth, England, in 1754, and was a goldsmith in London; but, in 1784, transferred his property and his family to this country. He first established himself in Portland (then Falmouth) as a merchant and ship-owner, but in 1790 removed to Boston, where he resumed a part of his old occupation, and stood at the head of the business of dealing in watches and chronometers until he transferred it to his son and his grandsons. His shop in Boston, when my father moved there, was in Washington Street (then Cornhill), opposite the Province House, and but two or three doors from Milk Street. It was, of course, very near the house which was my father's home, in Bromfield's Lane; and an acquaintance, which began with his procuring for my father the best watch for astronomical purposes then to be obtained, soon ripened into personal intimacy and regard. My father was first interested in him as an ingenious and very skilful mechanic, and as of great use to him in that matter so important in practical astronomy, the obtaining of exact time. But he soon discovered in Mr. Bond the higher qualities of general intelligence, right feeling, and perfect integrity; and they were friends as long as he lived. Mr. Bond survived him more than thirty years, dying in 1844, at the age of ninety. I frequently met him; and there was no other person who was so sure always to remind me of my father, and speak of him in terms of affection and respect. I think I never knew him fail to do this in any one instance.

Mr. Bond suffered a little for the "Americanism" which induced him to migrate to this country as soon as we became a nation. While living in London, he quarrelled with a man who was abusing "America," and ended with knocking him down, and was duly arrested and fined for this breach of the peace. He was the only person, as far as I know, who can be said to have *fought* for us in England while we were fighting our own battles here.

The watch he obtained for my father has a long second-hand traversing the whole face of the watch. Professor Bond told me that this was quite as unusual in those days as chronometers are now. We have this watch still; and well do I remember my father's frequent use of it in his astronomical observations.*

No event of my childhood stands so distinctly in my memory as the great eclipse of the sun, in 1806. I was then nine years old; and my father delighted me by employing me in some of the very subordinate work attending his observations. The roof of our house was flat, and there he had his telescope, which was the best that Dr. Prince could get for him; three or four scientific friends were with him, and most careful observations were made. For a long time before, he had been endeavoring to regulate a tall clock which was screwed up in the corner of our sitting-room, and the watch he had from Mr. Bond, so as to secure accurate time. He had calculated this eclipse when a student in college; and then it seemed to be ages ahead. As it drew near, and he began to think he *might* live to see it, he grew very nervous about it, and would sometimes laugh at the fear which he could not shake off. When the event

* But a few months have passed since Professor William Cranch Bond related to me, with his pleasant smile, these anecdotes about his father. Upon my return home, I wrote them here. And now I have to add, that on Saturday, the 29th of January, 1859, he died of an attack of *angina pectoris*, from which disease he had suffered at times for many years. The ample and emphatic testimonies to his skill and accuracy as an observer, and his high rank as an astronomer, leave nothing to be said on this score. But we have lived very near to each other for many years, and for many more have been intimate, as our fathers were; and I had almost forgotten the eminent man of science in the neighbor and friend, whose purity of life and character, and constant, simple, and unassuming goodness, won the confidence and affection of all who knew him.

came, and passed by, I believe it lifted quite a burden off from him. As the eclipsing shadow retreated, and light broke forth to relieve the inexpressible sense of untimely night and gloom which weighed upon all on whom that shadow had fallen, — animals as well as men, — it seemed to brighten his face with more than his share of the universal gladness.

From some of his papers which I have preserved, it would seem that his observations of this eclipse were communicated widely in various directions, and made the foundation of important calculations.

The electrical apparatus, which I mentioned above, was very complete. Most of it I have now; nor could I now get anything better of its kind. The experiments with this apparatus were brilliant and startling, and therefore to be remembered by a boy; which may be the reason why it seems to me that this apparatus was in more frequent employment than any other which he had. Another reason was, that he made much use of it for his rheumatism, for which it was once thought — and he always thought it — to be almost a specific.

Among other things, Dr. Prince imported for him a collection of lenses and the like, for optical experiments. I do not recollect much about them; but I remember his telling a droll story of the effect of them, when he lived in Newburyport. In that town there were men of education and intelligence; but my father stood almost entirely alone in his love for physical science, and his strange experiments sometimes led to strange results. Dr. Prince had supplied him with lenses for some experiments on light, which, when placed in the shutter of a darkened room, threw upon the opposite wall an inverted image of whatever was before them. One day, a domestic was sent for by him for some purpose while using this apparatus, and at the moment she came in, persons were seen upon that wall walking with the head downwards. She retreated as soon as she could, and told the story; and he was obliged to change the room for one which looked, not into the street, but into his garden; for complaint was made to him that certain persons of the fair sex were afraid to walk by his house! This seems now not only absurd, but impossible; but it must be remembered that science was then as rare as it now is common.

My mother was fond of mentioning another anecdote, worth telling if only as a possible solution of some ghost stories. They were travelling together, and put up at an inn. Soon after going to sleep, my mother awoke, and saw distinctly, sitting close to the wall at the foot of the bed, but at some height above the floor, a woman, knitting; and observed her draw out her needle and put it in again. She awoke my father, who looked a moment, and noticed that he saw the wall of the chamber through the woman. He rose, and found that the bed was against closed shutters. Through a small, circular hole light appeared to stream; and, upon looking through this, he saw the woman, that is, the original woman, sitting in a chamber on the opposite side of the street, with a strong light close to her; and, by holding a paper near the hole, and then carrying it slowly towards the wall, he showed how the image was made. The next day, they ascertained that the woman was watching with a sick person.

Another time, a large mirror in "the best room," so called, which was in those days a drawing-room never entered but on company occasions, broke into pieces, with an explosion heard in the adjoining rooms, when no one was in the room with it. My father satisfied himself in some way that the glass was not perfectly level, and had been pressed level, and kept level by force, in the frame; and that, while in this state of tension, a shrinking of the frame, or some change of temperature, had broken it. But the superstition, then prevalent and not yet extinct, that the breaking of a large glass is an omen of woe, connected itself with the impression already existing about my father's strange doings, — the lenses and gas-making experiment, for example, — and it was with some difficulty that the domestics were kept in the house.

Botany was among the things he studied, especially structural botany, — such as it was in his day, — to which he applied his microscopes. He taught this to some young people, as I shall have to say in another chapter; but I have no reason to suppose that he knew much of this science. He discovered the *Magnolia glauca* in a swamp near Gloucester, on Cape Ann, about the year 1803. At that time this plant was not known to exist so far north, and that swamp remains its northernmost habitat. He did not himself know the name of this beautiful flower, until, having brought it home, he ascertained by his books what it was. He had in his library many botanical works, some of which were very costly.

So, too, I might add, that he had a collection of fossils and minerals, some of which were valuable. But they were given him by various friends, and I never knew him to spend much time about them. Some forty years ago, I gave them to Dr. Walter Channing for the Linnæan Society, of which he was then an active member, and which held its meetings and kept its collection in a large room over the Boylston Market. What became of them afterwards, I never knew.

Of all his studies, that of mathematics was, I suppose, his favorite. I infer this in part from the mass of manuscripts which he left on various mathematical topics, which seem to have been written, the earliest in his preparation for college, some in college, and others in every successive period of his life. They are the earliest, and they are the latest, which I have.

There is, outside of these, evidence that he had great

knowledge of mathematics. Mr. Bowditch, in the second edition of his Navigator, published in 1808, says, in the chapter on obtaining the longitude by lunar observations: "We shall now give a third method, ... being an improvement on Mitchell's method, which was published in the former edition of this work. This improvement was made in consequence of a suggestion from a gentleman eminently distinguished for his mathematical acquirements." In a foot-note to this passage, he names my father as the person from whom he derives this improvement.

In all computations, a frequent change from corrections which must be added, to those which are to be subtracted, is a source of much error. It is especially injurious, when these changes must be made by sailors unaccustomed to computation, and who have to ascertain their longitude by working out lunar observations (in which calculations are many such corrections), in utter ignorance of the reasons for the processes they use. In 1847, Mr. Airy, the Astronomer Royal of England, submitted a paper to the Royal Astronomical Society (Transactions, Vol. XV. p. 329), in which he says: "In consequence of this [frequent change of signs], the most incessant attention is necessary to secure correctness of signs in the products and in the sums of the products; and, in spite of every care, a greater number of errors is produced by this cause than by any other. It has long been with me a matter of earnest desire to put these corrections in a shape in which no change of signs should occur, except, of course, in the very last step, by which the final result is exhibited. The method which I now submit to the Society does completely attain this object." Now, it happens that this is what my father accomplished by his invention in 1807; not so completely as Mr. Airy did in 1847, but to a great extent, and in a very similar way. It would be out of place to give here these methods in full; but I will quote two or three lines from Mr. Bowditch's account of my father's improvement. He says: "*If either of these angles be less than ninety degrees, the corresponding correction will be additive; but if more than ninety degrees, subtractive.* This rule, being uniform for applying all the corrections, makes it more easy to be remembered." The Italics are Dr. Bowditch's own, and are intended, I suppose, to indicate what he considered the great advantage of the new method.

Chief Justice Parker, in a note to his Charge, states that Mr. Bowditch received communications of value from him on the subject of a comet which had then recently appeared.

Mr. Elisha Clap, the schoolmaster, loved mathematics as well as my father. I remember a mass of papers which they seemed to be working over together, about the great comet which appeared in the year 1807. Mr. Clap spoke of my father's discovering, and of his showing to him, new methods of investigating a comet's path; but what they were I know not.

Nicholas Pike, of Newburyport, published, in 1788, a system of arithmetic, which my older readers will be sure to remember as "Pike's Arithmetic." It superseded every other, and was for many years the only one in use in New England. An old friend of my father's, Henry Lunt, Esq., formerly of Newburyport (where both Mr. Pike and my father resided), and now living in honored old age, tells me that Mr. Pike said to him, that my father had given him his most useful rules and methods, but had forbidden any reference to him in the book.*

My own judgment of the extent and character of his mathematical knowledge is, that he certainly was not a mathematician of the same rank that Dr. Bowditch held, or that Professor Peirce now holds; nor do I suppose

* Again I have to speak of a friend to whom I am indebted for assistance in preparing this work, as having died while these sheets are passing through my hands. On the 4th of March, 1859, at Dorchester, Mr. Lunt closed, with a peaceful death, his useful and honorable life.

that this would have been possible, without a nearly exclusive, or at least a very especial, devotion to this study. I do not suppose that he had pushed his investigations of the calculus very far. That he had an acquaintance with fluxions I know, from his books and papers. But he decidedly preferred geometry, and gave much time and study to all its higher branches, and especially to their applications to spherical trigonometry and to practical astronomy. On each one of these topics I have a mass of his papers.

I suppose my father not only preferred geometry to the calculus, but regarded it as much the higher thing. I must confess it seems to me that he was right; that analysis is to geometry rather as means to an end; and that, however certain the results of analysis may be, they are results reached as it were by machinery, and are not clearly seen or clearly exhibited, until they can be made to assume a geometrical form. Of course I do not deny that every astronomer, and perhaps every student of applied mathematics, must use the calculus, and that many of the greatest discoveries of modern times were made by this instrument alone, and, in the present state of human knowledge, could not be made otherwise; and yet, I repeat, geometry seems to me the higher thing. And I know that, in saying this, I state the conclusion of other intellects, which are more capable than I am of bringing the whole subject within their contemplation.

Some of his papers have the appearance of having been nearly prepared for the press. Others are evidently attempts to find new solutions of old problems, or new and better methods of seeking the results which the astronomer must find. Considering that all this was a matter of mere amusement, that it occupied but a corner of a very busy life, and that he actually made some discoveries and inventions which have been generally adopted and found useful, I think I am warranted in the belief that he had a considerable degree of the mathematical faculty, and found very great enjoyment in the exercise of it. This enjoyment grew upon him with advancing age. The summer before he died, he was very busy with a paper on the theory of Parallel Lines. I insert this in the Appendix, because it is as nearly prepared for the press as any other mathematical paper which he left, and because it was his latest work, and also because I believe it has some merit in itself. I am told that the late Mr. Sears C. Walker, who was one of the greatest mathematicians of his day, published a theory of parallel lines quite similar to my father's. I never saw Mr. Walker's, and I am sure that he never saw my father's; for no eye but my own has fallen upon its pages for more than forty years.

Perhaps I am moved to publish it, also, by another circumstance. It was written — as I shall presently have to say — while I was beginning to share my mother's anxiety respecting my father's apparently breaking health. I perfectly remember his walking up and down our long sitting-room, studying this very paper; and when he went out of the room, my mother exclaimed, "O dear, dear! how I wish your father would forget those parallel lines, and everything of the kind!"

I add also, in the Appendix, a paper upon the extraction of the roots of Adfected Equations, which is one of the many which seem to have been prepared as if for the press, and, as I am told by those who should know, contains matter which might be useful now. I am also told, that the principles and method of the calculus are applied in this paper, although the name is not used.

With all his Greek, and Latin, and Physics, and Mathematics, he read much History, and was a great novel-reader; or, rather, he read a great many novels. Chief Justice Parker, in a note to his Charge, says that "Judge Tudor, who was the classmate of the Chief Justice in college, and, in the college phrase, his chum, has frequently told me that, after the usual exercises, Parsons was in the habit of taking his slate and amusing himself with some deep mathematical calculation, and that he would vary his recreation by reading some tale or novel, it seeming indifferent to him which of these amusements first fell in his way. I have, within the last seven years of his life, found him indulging the same propensity, finding him with his slate and pencil so deeply engaged that I would not disturb him for some minutes after my entrance; and not unfrequently as deeply engaged in some modern novel or other work of fancy." In the Charge itself, he speaks of this matter more accurately. He says: "When fatigued with the labor of deep legal research, or exhausted by a continued train of thought upon one subject, it was not uncommon for him to relax his mind with some abstruse arithmetical or geometrical demonstration, or to turn over the pages of some popular and interesting novel." This, I think, is the truth. My father did not take up a novel, or a work of philosophy or science, as one or the other happened to be within reach. But when he was fatigued, and especially in the evening, when what would otherwise have been amusement became a labor, he turned to that which was never a labor, — to history or to novels. I have now, for instance, a manuscript book of his, of thirty-six pages, containing an abstract of Robertson's History of Scotland, beside fragments of similar compositions. Some of his children inherited his love of reading, and as he put little restraint upon it, and there were circulating libraries within reach, (not to say that his own library contained a complete collection of the classical English novels of that day, imported by him,) there were always novels lying about the house; and none, I think, ever went out of the house without his trying them. Of some, a few pages sufficed; of others, he would read more or all, but always rapidly. And in the course of an evening many such volumes would be despatched.

Of poetry he did not, I believe, read much; but he was tolerably familiar with the older English poets. His favorite was Pope; by which I mean only that he quoted him more freely, and gave him more praise, than any other. One of my sisters, who is a few years older than I am, remembers his repeating the whole of Pope's Messiah, one evening, to his children. If present, I was too young to notice it sufficiently to remember the occurrence. It seems to me, indeed, that poetry, of every kind, stood rather low in his regard.

In speaking of him as a man of letters, I must not forget to say that he was one of those who originated the Boston Athenæum, in the year 1807. I look upon this institution with so much respect; it has manifested so much strength in overcoming the obstacles and perils which have beset it; it has approved itself so well adapted to the actual wants of the community, as is shown by the liberal support it has received; and at this moment has so firm a foundation, and rests its claims for continued support upon so much utility, that I deem it most honorable to my father that he was one among those who assisted it in its beginning. But he was only one among them, and was far from the foremost. There were others who were much more active than he was, if I do not mistake, in bringing it into being, and in nursing its infancy. He was the first President; but this office was given him, probably, because of his social and literary position, rather than because he was chief among its founders.

A letter of the late Governor Sullivan, written to a friend in 1785, says that my father had received an appointment as Professor of Law in Harvard University. I should have been glad to verify this. It would have interested me much to know that I have now held for ten years a place to which he was invited. But I can find not the slightest evidence of it on the College Records, and from what I am told of the usages of the Corporation at that time, I suppose that the appointment was offered to my father, but, not being accepted by him, it did not appear upon the records, as a formal vote.

In 1804, he received the degree of Doctor of Laws from Harvard College. The letter announcing this to him happens to be preserved; and I give it below, to show the curious mistake which good President Willard made in writing it. It was a mistake my father never profited by. He had great respect for the honor indicated by the letters D. D., but I am quite sure that he never availed himself of the President's permission to append them to his name.

Harvard College, August 31, 1804.

SIR:

It is with great pleasure that I officially acquaint you, that the Corporation and Overseers of Harvard College have conferred on you the degree of Doctor of Laws, which was publicly announced on Commencement day, the 29th instant.

I hope this degree will not be unacceptable to you, as I am sure it will be pleasing to the community at large, who have long known the high rank you have holden in the republic of literature and science, and your profound knowledge in everything respecting your profession.

This official communication will authorize you to take the title of D. D., should it be agreeable to you.

I am, Sir, in the name and behalf of the Corporation of Harvard College,

Your humble servant,

JOSEPH WILLARD, *President.*

THEOPHILUS PARSONS, ESQ., LL. D.

The degree of Doctor of Laws was conferred upon him also by Brown University, in 1809.

In 1806 he was chosen a Fellow of Harvard College. Our Alma Mater was incorporated in 1650; and was for so long a time almost the only corporation, excepting towns, &c., and for a considerable subsequent period the principal corporation of the State, that when I was a boy, and for many years afterwards, "the Corporation," in common conversation, always meant the College Corporation; and to be a

Fellow of the College was to be a member of "the Corporation." Indeed, this use of the word has not yet disappeared, although persons away from Cambridge, and young men when they speak of it even in Cambridge, generally now qualify it as the College Corporation.

He remained a Fellow until a short time before his death. During this period he took a very great interest in the College, and freely gave to it whatever time and whatever attention the duties of the office required. The most important thing he did was in helping to make Dr. Kirkland President. There were many candidates; and some of these were very prominent men. The high qualities of Dr. Kirkland, and his peculiar fitness for the office, would very probably have pointed him out to the Corporation and secured his election. But it was understood that my father was from the beginning most decided in his favor. I remember when some one came into the house and informed him that President Webber — who had held that office but four years — while stooping in his study to pick up a pin from the carpet, had fallen forward dead (from the rupture of a vessel in the head, as was afterwards ascertained). I think I remember also hearing Dr. Kirkland's name mentioned in our house, that day, as the man who must be the next President. I am not sure of this, because I do not remember how it was said; but I am certain that it was generally understood, almost at once, where my father's choice lay. It was a matter we were all interested in. Kirkland was our pastor; and, as I was preparing for college, I listened carefully to everything which indicated who was to be my President, and made up my mind about it very early. I suppose my father's influence in favor of Kirkland was the greater, because every one knew that he made in this a great personal sacrifice to the good of the College. Very few things did he ever appear to regret more than the loss of Kirkland's intimate and frequent companionship.

It has been said to me, that my father insisted upon Kirkland's appointment in the belief that he would give to the College new life; that is, not only more life, but a new kind of life. It had been separated from society, and was, in its seclusion at least, almost a monastic establishment. But Kirkland, although a clergyman, was — I use the phrase in its good sense, for it has such a sense — a thorough man of the world. He was not so much a member of society as a master of it; and he brought the College at once into the closest relations with men and institutions which could be useful to it. I have no doubt my father expected this, and promoted it, and was glad of it. But I have some doubts about something else which has also been imputed to him in connection with the College.

It has been said, for example, that this was the turning point in the *religious* history of the College; that it was trembling on the verge, and could with equal ease have been turned back to its original Orthodoxy, or confirmed in its new Unitarianism; and that he, being a Unitarian, determined upon this last result, and made use of Dr. Kirkland as a means for producing it; and that the Unitarianism of Cambridge, from that day to this, is due to the success of my father's efforts. If this be true at all, I think it is so only with much qualification. How far my father was a Unitarian, I shall say in a subsequent chapter, now remarking only, that, so far as Unitarianism means only non-Calvinism, he was most certainly a Unitarian; and I have no doubt whatever that he desired to prevent the College from being exclusively, and in a sectarian way, Calvinistic; and that Kirkland's sympathy with him on these points was one of the grounds of his preference. But I am sure that he did not wish to make the College Unitarian in a sectarian sense. I have not the slightest evidence or reason for believing that he was a bigot *for* or *against* any form of religious belief or worship. He had chosen one for himself which he thought the best, and might naturally and properly desire that it should have fair play, and a reasonable opportunity of presenting itself to those who might prefer it just as he did. But I am certain that he did not wish to give even to his own faith undue superiority or dominion, or anything in the nature of exclusive rights; and, if this were the place to speak of my Alma Mater, gladly would I offer my testimony to the entire impartiality, and absolute freedom from all regard to religious preference, with which all the affairs of the University and all its Schools are conducted, excepting only the Divinity School, which was a special creation, formed for a special purpose, by the contribution of certain individuals.

In a word, I am willing to admit so much of this last reproach upon my father as to say, that he desired to make old Harvard just what it is, in point of religious freedom; that being, as far as I can see, just what it should be; and, most certainly, I am not a Unitarian, in any common or technical sense of that word.

Kirkland and my father were bound together by the closest friendship; and Kirkland seemed to me almost as a second father. He was more often and more intimately in our house than in any other, scarcely excepting that which he called his home. When I entered College, in 1811, I went at once into his family, as a matter of course, and remained there during my four years. But however well I may have known him, I should have distrusted my own personal feeling too much to say of him what I think is true, if it had not happened that all my peculiar opportunities for judging of him only defined and deepened in me the same sentiments that he inspired in all others.

Dr. Kirkland was not a man of profound learning, nor of a great variety of acquirements. Although he was capable of considerable application for a time, his habits were not those of a student, and, indeed, his general indolence was obvious and undeniable. But he had a knowledge of character, a power of penetrating into motives and purposes, and a sagacity in his judgment of persons and of things, and in his adaptation of means to an end, which, within my own observation, have never been equalled. This vigorous and penetrative intellect, which gave him a great mastery over all who approached him, was never with him a servant of ambition, either in the form of love of fame or love of power. To these things he was indifferent. The characteristic which marked him out from other men, and made him one of the most conspicuous persons of his age, was the marvellous union of intellectual force and faculties surpassed by none, with the most simple and unassuming manners, and a kindness, a warm, affectionate, universal, and unfailing kindness, so far as I have observed equalled by none. He was thoroughly disinterested. He had no capacity for meanness, no sly look-out for self, no small contrivance to bring things round to his own profit. Unmarried, with a good income, and no habits of personal expense, he gave away more than he spent, and gave with a cordiality and unreserve that made the gift tenfold more welcome. Nor was it money only that he gave; for that kind of liberality comes sometimes from indifference, as much as from generosity. But, busy as he was, he gave his time; and, indolent as he was, he gave his labor; and, careless as he was of his own interests, he gave patient thought and anxious consideration, when by any of these things he could help them who needed help.

He was a great man, and impressed himself as one upon all with whom he came in contact. But in the truthfulness and tenderness of his affections he was a child. He did not marry until, at the age of fifty-six, a palsy had stricken down, not his health only, but his relations with life; and until that hour the students of the College were as his children. I doubt if any one ever left him without the conviction, that whatever President Kirkland could do for him was sure to be done.

He was a writer of great excellence, and published some papers, of which his Life of his intimate friend, Fisher Ames, was perhaps the best; but he could never be induced to undertake the labor necessary for an extensive work.

As President of the College, with all his various and abounding merit, he had one fault. He acted upon no definite system; or if he had one, it was a system known only to himself, and which only he could carry out. He had few rules; and no predetermined method of procedure for any case. Perhaps he needed none; for, so perfect was his sagacity in meeting every exigency as it came, that he might have been hampered and hindered by rules or a system. He certainly did suppress disorder, and carry on the affairs of the College with unexampled felicity. His carelessness about money was another fault. It was certainly extreme; and sometimes it exposed him to misconstruction from those who were unable to comprehend how a sensible man could be so ignorant of the value of this great regulator of human affairs, as to keep no accounts.

During Kirkland's presidency the College flourished as it had never done before. Gifts flowed in from every side; and much of this liberality was undoubtedly due to the President's power of persuasion, and to the affection and respect generally entertained for him. But my father was neither idle nor unsuccessful where anything could be done for its benefit; and I have always understood that the grant of the Legislature, by which, after a cessation of assistance from the State for twenty-eight years, $100,000 was given ($10,000 a year for ten years), although not consummated until after his death, was owing in a good degree to his exertions. But I have no especial evidence of this.

My father was active in another matter of some moment to the College. By the charter, or rather act of 1642, the Board of Overseers consisted of the Governor, the Deputy-Governor, the President of the College, and the teaching elders of Cambridge, Watertown, Charlestown, Boston, Roxbury, and Dorchester. In the Convention for forming the State Constitution, a sub-committee was appointed by the general committee to confer with the President and Fellows on the subject of the College. Articles I. and II. of Section I. Chapter V., establishing the Corporation, were reported as prepared by the President and Fellows. Of Article III., concerning the Overseers, John Adams prepared the first part, which constituted the Board much as it had been under the charter. Then Caleb Strong prepared a provision that the Legislature should always have the same power to make alterations in the government of the University, conducive to its advantage, that the Provincial Legislature had possessed. Strong added this provision because it was even then believed that it would soon become necessary to make some material alteration in the Board of Overseers. As soon as my father became a Fellow of the College, he prepared a bill for the purpose of making such an alteration, which passed through the Legislature at once. By this, the Board of Overseers was composed of the Governor and Lieutenant-Governor, the President of the Senate, the Speaker of the House, the President of the College, and fifteen ministers of Congregational churches within the State, and fifteen laymen, all of these thirty to be elective. There was a provision in the bill, that it should take effect when accepted by the Corporation, and also by the Overseers. The bill was passed March 6, 1810. The Corporation formally accepted it on the 16th of the same month, and the Overseers accepted it on the 12th of the following April.

Before this bill had been in operation quite two years, on the 29th of February, 1812, it was repealed, and the old Board restored. This was done, not only without any request or suggestion from the Corporation or Overseers, or any concurrence or approval on their part, but directly against their wishes, and what may be regarded as their protest. In 1811, when this proposed repeal was in agitation, the Corporation appointed "President Kirkland and Mr. Parsons" a committee to prepare a memorial, with an appropriate historical sketch of the College. This sketch and memorial were prepared by my father, and presented to the General Court, and by them utterly disregarded. But in 1814, the repealing act of 1812 was itself repealed, thus reviving the act of 1810; but with the proviso, that the Senate should be added to the thirty elective members provided by that act. So the Board remained, substantially, until the recent change. This act of 1814, it should be noticed, contained a provision making its validity dependent on the acceptance of the Corporation and Overseers.

The Memorial bears no individual name, but purports to be presented by the President and Fellows of the College, in behalf of themselves and of the Overseers. I reprint it in the Appendix, not only because it seems to have been drawn by my father with great care, but because it presents, as I think, just views in relation to its extremely important subject.

In 1805, my father was active, with others, in founding the Professorship of Natural History. One hundred and fifty persons subscribed something more than thirty thousand dollars, of which my father, and his brothers and nephew, (whom, I suppose, he induced to subscribe,) contributed eleven hundred. William Dandridge Peck was the first Professor.

Peck was one of the peculiar men of that day. Born in Boston in 1763, and graduating at Harvard College in 1782, he tried to become a merchant in Boston; but finding that he could not suppress his natural tastes and tendencies, he retired to a small farm in Kittery, Maine (which he had inherited from his father), and there lived for twenty years; and, with very limited resources either in books or in money, he became, and made himself recognized by the scientific world as, a most learned botanist and entomologist. He came to Boston occasionally, and was upon terms of intimate friendship with my father, who always sought eagerly the society of men who were eminent for any kind of learning. Peck was indisposed, at first, to accept the professorship, and was induced to do so, as I have been told, mainly by the urgent advice and request of my father; but of this I have no evidence.

My father became a Fellow of the American Academy of Arts and Sciences in 1781. I do not know that he was ever an active member, and I should suppose not, from his preference for solitary study and labor. In the first volume of the Memoirs of the Academy are two papers, and only two, which do not bear the name of their author. They are both on mathematical subjects; and one of them seems to connect law and insurance with mathematics. From certain turns of expression, and their agreement with some memoranda of his which I have, I suspect that both of them were written by him; but do not know it. In the second volume of the Memoirs, Part II. page 12, is an astronomical problem, (with a plate,) occupying nine pages, to which his name is attached. It is the only thing, of any description, which I have ever found in print under his name. Among his papers I find the following letters, which seem to be connected with his membership.

Ipswich, August 10th, 1782.

SIR:

The rare phenomenon of a conjunction of the planets Saturn and Jupiter is expected to take place about the 3d of November. But these large bodies, as you are sensible, act powerfully on each other in this situation; and while the centripetal force of the sun on Saturn is increased, it is diminished on Jupiter, by which means they are greatly disturbed in their motions. The precise time, therefore, of their conjunction cannot be ascertained by our best astronomical tables. I have been desired to make observations of their approach to each other, in order to determine the true time of their conjunction, but find myself unable to make the necessary observations without a sextant. If you should not attend to this matter, and have no present occasion for your sextant, and will be so kind as to favor me with the loan of it until this phenomenon has taken place, you will do me a very particular favor. You may depend on its being very carefully used and safely returned. Captain Wigglesworth will wait on you with this letter, and, should you favor me with the sextant, will convey it to me by a safe hand.

I am, Sir, with sentiments of great esteem,

Your very humble servant,

M. CUTLER.

THEOPHILUS PARSONS, ESQ.

Ipswich, February 13th, 1783.

SIR:

You have been, I suppose, officially informed by Mr. Gannett that you were elected a member of a committee which the American Academy appointed at the last meeting. The gentlemen then present who were chosen on this committee supposed that it would be necessary that there should be a meeting of all the members of this committee as soon as possible, and proposed to meet at Cambridge; but, as they were very desirous that you should be present, concluded not to appoint the time until it could be known when it would be agreeable to you to attend. They therefore desired me to write to you, requesting that you would appoint a time, and inform me of it, and, if you had opportunity, acquaint Mr. President Willard and Dr. Warren of Boston, that the other members might be notified. It was thought probable you would attend the court at Boston on the 18th instant, which might be a convenient opportunity for you to meet with the committee. If you go to Boston next week, pray be so kind as to call upon me, or otherwise let me hear from you by a line.

I am, Sir, with the greatest respect,

Your most humble servant,

M. CUTLER.

THEOPHILUS PARSONS, ESQ.

Ipswich, March 10th, 1783.

SIR:

I wrote to you, four or five weeks ago, by the desire of the committee lately appointed by the American Academy; but as I have received no answer, and you have since repeatedly passed by, I conclude you have not received my letter. I suppose Mr.

Gannett has officially informed you of your being chosen on that committee, and the purpose for which it was appointed. But, as it is possible you may not have received a letter from him, I would observe, that the Academy, at their last meeting, accepted a report from a former committee, arranging the business of the Academy under three general heads, viz.: 1st, Geography, Mathematics, and Astronomy; 2d, Natural Philosophy, Natural History, &c., &c.; 3d, Physic; — a committee of three to be appointed on each head. The gentlemen chosen were, on the 1st, President Willard, Professor Williams, and Mr. Gannett; on the 2d, Theophilus Parsons, Esq., General Lincoln, and M. Cutler; on the 3d, Doctors Holyoke, Warren, and Tufts; and that these committees united shall be a committee to examine the communications on file, and, if they find sufficient materials, prepare for publishing a volume as soon as may be. The gentlemen chosen, who were present, supposed it highly necessary that there should be a meeting of the whole committee as soon as possible, and that they should meet at Cambridge; but as they were very desirous that you should be present, and it might be uncertain when your business would admit of your attending, did not appoint a day, but desired me to write to you, requesting you would fix on a day as soon as it would be in your power to attend, and inform me, that I might inform Mr. Willard, who would notify the other gentlemen that way. I have just received a letter from Dr. Holyoke, informing me that he heard you was in Boston, and wrote to you on the subject, but thinks you left the town before his letter arrived. He wishes to know whether you have fixed on a day, or whether there is any probability that you will be able soon to meet with the committee. Please to favor me with a line as soon as you can have opportunity.

I am, Sir, your most obedient and very humble servant,

M. Cutler.

Theophilus Parsons, Esq.

Upon the whole, my father's acquisitions as a scholar and a man of science were great, and perhaps remarkable; and it is easy to see, first, why they gave to him the very high reputation he had during life as a man of vast and universal knowledge, and next, that this was exaggerated, and to some extent erroneous. That it was so is proved simply by the fact that an impossible amount of general knowledge was attributed to him by many persons. Some of the reasons for this exaggeration are obvious enough.

In the first place, science was not widely diffused at that day. Even its elements were known only to a few persons. They formed no part of common education, and seldom entered into common conversation. Then, books and instruments were comparatively rare and costly, and often it was difficult to procure them at any price. There were few public libraries or associations for literary or scientific purposes. This arose from the very small number of those who were interested in such pursuits ; and it tended to keep this number small. There are in Boston and Cambridge, probably, fifty men now for every one to whom my father could have any resort, or with whom he could have sympathy or companionship in any of these studies. "Omne ignotum pro magnifico" is an old and a true saying; and in my father's days, almost all the science known to him was unknown generally, and even to his friends and associates. Hence they made of him a "magnifico" of the first class, although one who had all his knowledge now would probably be regarded only as a well and widely instructed man. It may be said, that the very fact of his overcoming all hinderances, and learning so much of that of which so few around him learned anything, proves a thirst for knowledge, an intellectual capacity, and a force of character, which would have profited now by the immensely increased means of study, and would have given him the same proportional prominence.

I have certainly no disposition to deny that his extent of information was the proof and the effect of great ability and industry, exerted in directions which would now have led to much more knowledge. But there is something more than this to be said. In his day, there were, perhaps, those who surpassed him in every specific thing which he had made a subject of study, excepting his professional topics. But he was probably rather near the head in most of them. Now, however, there is so much more that may be learned in every department of human knowledge, that universal knowledge implies of necessity universal superficialness. I mean, that every science, and every subject of inquiry, is now pushed so far, that he who would advance the boundaries of human knowledge by starting from the vantage-ground of all that is known, finds that this first requisite demands half, or all, the labor of a life. All science is now so popularized, that it is easy to learn the elements of all, and most well-educated persons do learn them. But if one advances far beyond the mere elements, he must choose his path; for, by attempting to go forward equally in all directions, he would find that in every one of them he fell far short of knowing all that could be known, and all indeed that every one who would be proficient in them must know.

I have used the word "superficialness"; but this word is, I think, used in many senses, or at least applied to many cases. I have used it in the preceding paragraph, not to mean that such a student could not learn all, but that he must devote himself so assiduously to *acquiring* knowledge, as to leave himself no time for *digesting* his knowledge; and this, I think, was never true of my father. He who has learned all that now is knowable on some particular subject, is still only at its surface, and is entirely superficial in comparison with the successor who is to come a century hence; just as the eminent man of a century ago could only know, of some subject to which he devoted his life, what now the school-boy learns. Superficialness, then, should not be used in reference merely to the quantity that is known. Its test should be the thoroughness with which that is known which has been made a subject of study, and the clearness with which it is understood and applied to purposes of life, or used as food for wisdom. He whose knowledge does not, in any point, go beyond the limits of a good school-book, if he has an intelligent comprehension of all that is there, and can turn it to good account, ought not to be called superficial, while another would merit the name who had gone over far more ground, and could exhibit even a complete knowledge of names and systems, *if all his knowledge lay on the surface of his mind.*

It is one thing to know *widely*, and another thing to know *well.* There are those who, to some extent, do both. But most reading men choose between a general and imperfect knowledge of many things, and a thorough knowledge of a very few. From fear of the fact, or of the reproach, of superficialness, scholars seem now to be seeking perfection, rather than breadth of knowledge; and, to one disposed to speculate upon the influence of the habits and tendencies of the day upon that future which will soon be here, the effect of the present division of mental labor might be an interesting subject of inquiry. The fact itself exists to a degree of which most persons are ignorant, merely because it has not existed long enough to be distinctly and generally recognized. A few years ago, Addison and other literary men exercised their wit, and rather contemptuously, upon those who were boyish enough to gather butterflies. It is amusing to read in Pope's correspondence, how he went to gatherers of unconsidered trifles for the crystals and ores and colored stones with which he ornamented his "grotto," as he called the passage under the roadway which divided his five-acre lot. And he was a little ashamed of himself for gathering some of the very stones which great men now-a-days write chapters about. But now a man of world-wide reputation is thought to be worthily employed, and to advance his position among the leading minds of the world, if he selects some one family of insects, and devotes years to the preparation of a *monograph* upon it. The very word I have just used — of recent introduction, but already common — illustrates this minute division of labor. It has not yet gone so far that one can be esteemed a *very* great man whose studies have been limited to one only of the smaller topics into which every science ramifies; but things are tending in this direction. It is rather the fashion for the most eminent men to select some such topic, and prove the minuteness, accuracy, and completeness of their knowledge, and the sagacity of their conclusions, in respect to it. It may be barnacles, or tortoises, or beetles, or roses, or oxygen, or phosphorus, that is chosen for this exhibition of labor and genius; and whatever it is, it cannot be so small but that all the certainties which are discovered leave uncertainties behind them to invite the industry of the next monographer. Even in history the same thing is done; few books, for example, are better worth reading than the charming little volume which Neander calls a Monograph on the Emperor Julian, and which is at once the flower and the fruit of long industry, profound learning, and patient thought.

Science has now advanced so far in all directions, that, as I have said, every man must select his own walk. Those who have gathered the greatest variety of knowledge, not only leave many important topics untouched, but must be deficient in respect to some which they include within their grasp. There is not only no such man now as Leibnitz was, or, rather, was thought to be; but he who should attempt to become such a man, be his genius what it might if only it remained human, would be sure to be foremost nowhere. How far is this to go? In England there are, it is said, (but I doubt it,) men who, from childhood to the grave, do nothing but make the heads of pins; and they acquire in this particular a rapidity and precision of movement, and a power of production, that are almost incredible. Are there to be such men in science? Or, let us ask as a question which others have asked, Are there to be in fifty years from to-day *only* such men?

There are, at least, two answers to this. One is, that there must be some such men, if the various departments of knowledge absolutely require for their utmost cultivation such a division of labor. But this utmost cultivation may not be the highest cultivation; for there may be a class of minds whose practice it will be to use the materials which other men have gathered, and by force of study or genius, or both combined, give to the common mind of humanity a deeper insight into things already known, and a clearer perception of their relations and their consequences. And thus, while some men gather facts, and grope into the darkest corners and least crevices of nature for them, others will gather these facts into bundles, and yet others discover higher principles of classification and order; and some, the highest minds, will work with what may be called the principles of principles, and so discover and exhibit the living forms which embody the Divine ideas.

Another answer is, that in some distant century enough may be known of the unity of truth and the mutual dependence of all the parts of the universe and of all knowledge of these parts, to prevent the isolation and apparent meanness of any pursuit, and enable him who knows many things to know them all well. Some glimpses of this, too slight and evanescent to be much regarded, we already have. It has been often remarked, of late, that as all knowledge appears to converge towards any one topic that is thoroughly examined, so any one topic, if well understood, throws back illustration through many of the provinces of thought. If a man, to-day, picked up a snail, and determined to learn and teach all that could be known about this creeping thing, he must begin with zoölogy at large, and add to it chemistry and geology, and all that these imply, before he could lay a foundation for the work he intended to construct. But if he lived to complete that work, the chemist and geologist would have to thank him for additions to, or useful illustrations of, their own sciences.

Every one now knows how the sciences lead and blend into each other; for each of them refuses to live alone. So far as this goes, the unity of truth is now acknowledged. It is seen, however, only as an amorphous mass, or at best only as a circular chain, which ends nowhere, but which is a chain only because the links happen to hook into each other. It may be suspected that more than this is true; that the various classes and forms and modes of being have to each other such definite relations, such unity of origin and purpose, as to imply some analogy or correspondence between themselves in respect to form and function and nature, and in relation also to that organized truth concerning these things which constitutes their science. Let this be seen and understood, and all increase of knowledge will flash as lightning from boundary to boundary. He who labors and advances anywhere, will know that others go forward with every step he takes, and that all their progress facilitates his own. I may owe some apology to the "common-sense" reader for even portraying as a fancy picture an order and a unity of labor and of knowledge, in comparison with which what seems to be the established and recognized method of intellectual pursuit and acquisition now, is what Chaos is to Kosmos; but it is, I think, a Chaos over which organizing Life has begun to brood.

One of the new things of this age, and, as I cannot but think, of this country, especially, is the endeavor to make science generally and easily attainable; and another is the employment of the most consummate skill in preparing works for the most immature intellects. At first, all this was attempted by inferior minds. But the strongest and best taught intellects no longer deem it an unworthy occupation to prepare elementary and general works, and thus, on the one hand, address themselves to a vastly wider audience than the few proficients compose, who, in former times, lived and labored for each other; and, on the other hand, educate the growing mind, in the first years of its growth, into that accuracy of knowledge, and that precision of thought, which will best promote all future improvement.

Not only are our best men thus engaged, but some of their greatest exertions are put forth in the endeavor to make clearly and easily intelligible, profound and far-reaching principles. For example, my old friend and classmate, Dr. Thaddeus William Harris, who has been called by the highest authority one of the first entomologists of the age, in a work prepared by order of the Legislature of this State, "On Insects injurious to Vegetation," exhibited vast learning, and made a book of the very highest value to those who are only men of science. But he has also, as an eminent man said to me a short time since, brought, by a command of language almost as remarkable as the extent of his knowledge, the principles and results of his science within the clear and easy apprehension of every farmer and gardener. So, too, one of the first of living botanists has lately published a little book for children ten or twelve years of age, entitled, "How Plants Grow," in which he puts some of the latest discoveries and most profound truths of his science within the reach of these children. Nor did he throw off this little book in an hour of leisure; for it bears all the marks of careful and skilful construction which characterize his larger works.

In all this I see, or I imagine, the possibility that the actual worth of childhood may be at some future day understood and acknowledged. The earliest years of a man's life color, if they do not determine, his whole career and his eternal destiny. And the character and the fate of a nation depend upon the education of its children. We are so much nearer to a recognition of this truth, both in theory and in practice, than any other nation ever was or now is, that possibly some future generation may intrust the care of its children to its best and wisest men; and its most learned men may think they put on the crown of their scholarship when they give to childhood the choicest fruit of all their genius and all their labor.

I dwell on this, because it is precisely what my father

loved best. He made no books, or published none; for this, his invincible dislike of coming before the public prevented his doing. But he would pursue a study as far as the means and resources at that time existing permitted; and then it was a great enjoyment to him to teach others what he had learnt himself. I shall speak of this more fully in the next chapter, and it will be seen that sometimes his pupils were very young indeed.

May I not say, that there can be nothing better than this for science itself. The best proof that one has learned a thing is the ability to teach it, and there can be no more certain test of the soundness and productive power of a principle than its capability of coming down to the apprehension of all men as a simple and certain truth. Upon the common mind this new effort is the beginning of a work of intellectual regeneration; and it is not too much to hope that the process by which discovered truth becomes the property of the many, and not the few, will be greatly accelerated. This process has always been going on, nor could mankind advance if it were checked. The civilized world is now in complete possession of some truths, — as gravitation, and the revolution of the earth, for example, — which but a few generations ago were known to but few, and scarcely known to them. And now, the learning of the scholar becomes the common knowledge of the multitude far more rapidly than ever before, and therefore the intellectual advancement of our race is far more rapid.

In addition to this preparation of elementary works in special departments, a further step is taken. By a somewhat striking coincidence, the woman who has won the respect and admiration of the age for the extent of her knowledge and the force of her intellect, and the man who, by common consent, is regarded as the Nestor of science, have endeavored to give to the world a general view of the farthest discoveries of science, and of their interdependence. Mrs. Somerville, in her admirable work on the Connection of the Physical Sciences, and Humboldt, in his Kosmos, have inaugurated a new department of intellectual labor. The path is now opened, and others will find it. Hereafter it will be recognized as one of the things which every age demands, that some of the ablest and most learned among the devotees of knowledge should employ themselves in extending and illustrating that *whole* which every educated man may master. While the division of labor goes on, and the specialities of science become perhaps more and more minute, it will be one other effect of the same division of labor, that there shall be those who do not seek to extend the reach of discovery in any particular direction, but to enlarge and open for general cultivation that realm, already wide, of common knowledge, which all minds of liberal culture may enter upon and possess. The delight and charm of knowledge, and, yet more, of the love and pursuit of knowledge, will grow, and be a common good; and the heart will be opened and softened, and the tastes raised and purified, as the mind becomes liberalized by its widening scope and reach, and invigorated by wise employment.

If my father had lived in the present age, he would not have been a "superficial man," in the sense in which that term may well be used reproachfully. But as between the two classes of minds of which I have spoken, one of which pursues some one or two trains of inquiry to the utmost possible distance, while the other seeks to give illustration and co-ordination to as many as possible, he would, I am sure, have belonged to the latter. I think so, not merely because his desire for knowledge was a universal one, and led him, in point of fact, into a multitude of inquiries, but because I have some reason to believe that he saw already the unity in diversity of all truth. That he loved to bring the various branches of his knowledge into correlation, and that it was a favorite pursuit with him to make them illustrate and aid each other, and that their connection was a favorite subject of inquiry, I think I know. Many a conversation on topics of this kind did he have with his old friend, Dr. Prince, who, as I fancy, did not quite agree with him, and sometimes made that a matter of pleasant reproach, which I cannot but regard as not only growing directly out of the constitution of my father's mind, but as one proof that this constitution was vigorous and healthy. When the good Doctor said that "he never seemed to want to know anything for its own sake, but for the sake of something else," if this were meant by way of rebuke, I should be nevertheless willing to accept it as a trait of my father's character.

My father was a poor correspondent; and I have been able to get but few letters of his writing. My friend, Mr. George T. Davis of Greenfield, has sent me copies of two or three written to his parents, who were among my father's intimate and valued friends. Mr. Wendell Davis lived in Sandwich, and was sheriff of the county. He was indolent and unambitious, loving his comfort rather better than anything else, but very intelligent. Mrs. Caroline Davis was one of the most attractive women whom I remember to have known. She was not much older than my eldest sister, and was regarded by my father almost as one of his children. The letter I give below contains what seems to me an excellent criticism of "Tom Jones," a work now banished from our parlors, and almost from our libraries, for its grossness, but unsurpassed in English literature for its artistic excellence.

How tastes change! — and for the better. Walter Scott speaks, in a letter written about forty years ago, of Mrs. Behn's novels as in his day thought to be too vile for any one to mention, but says that they were the fashionable reading of the preceding generation, and that good Queen Charlotte, who piqued herself upon the exactest refinement, chose them for her ladies of honor to read aloud to her and her family. No one ever sees or hears of Mrs. Behn now. Scott does not seem to think Fielding and Smollett in any way objectionable; and, in 1808, my father makes a lady, for whom he felt the utmost respect and regard, a present of "Tom Jones," which no one would now think of recommending to any such reader.

My dear Mrs. Davis:

In our conversation at your house, it was remarked, that there were few books in the English language in which private characters and domestic manners are justly delineated. Of these books, it was observed that Boswell's Johnson and Fielding's Tom Jones were among the best. As you have never read the latter, permit me to request your acceptance of it. It stands in the first rank, for learning, wit, and humor, and will, I hope, amuse you in the long evenings of the approaching winter. It is a work descriptive of a great variety of characters, and poor human nature is very justly portrayed from the life. Indeed, the fidelity of the picture has furnished an objection against the work, because the author has introduced some vicious characters, and his good characters are not free from great faults. Objections of this kind appear to me to be unreasonable. A uniform course of exalted virtue, or of infernal wickedness, is too unnatural to operate as an example, either to excite imitation or abhorrence, as they do not come home to us as natural or possible. Vice, when decked in all the blandishments of pleasure, is also a picture which no good mind would choose to contemplate or exhibit to others. But the virtues and vices which are incident to human nature may be usefully described as they actually exist; for then we may be excited to imitate the former by their intrinsic excellence and beneficial effects, and to shun the latter, from their degrading influence and painful consequences.

The history of Tom Jones has but few local allusions, and is equally interesting to readers in all periods. The scene is laid in the year 1745, when a second rebellion, to dethrone the Hanoverian family, was raging in the heart of the kingdom; and the opposition by the Tories to the accession of that family, in 1714, is observed in the disputes between Western and his sister. The

Wharf or Norway *rat* was not known in England till about the accession, whence the friends of the reigning family were nicknamed *rats* by the rustic Tories. It is not known that the author copied from any real characters, if we except his Allworthy, whose original was Mr. Allen of Bath, the friend of Pope, and celebrated by the harmonious numbers of that immortal poet. The various characters introduced are all strongly discriminated. Of the three clergymen, we can never confound the orthodoxy of Thwackum with the loose principles of Square or the tame servility of Supple. The braggart cowardice of Partridge is drawn with great humor, and his censure of the author's friend Garrick is perhaps one of the most elegant compliments to theatrical excellence that can be found in any language. The Episode of the Gypsies must not be considered as a work of mere fancy, but as a correct history of that singular people, so far as it was known by the nations among whom they wandered. And the battle of Molly Seagrim, in the mock-heroic style, will recall to your recollection "*Arms and the Man*," sung by the prince of the Roman poets. But I will not fatigue you with any further observations. After you have read the work, if, in an hour of leisure, you would write me your opinion of its merits, you would very much gratify me. I am not apprehensive that we shall disagree but on one point. For I am persuaded that the *fictitious* Sophia of Fielding does not possess more worth and excellence than the *real* Caroline of

Your obliged and sincere friend,

THEOPH. PARSONS.

Boston, November 16, 1808.

NOTE. — To this chapter also I annex an anecdote told me since these pages were electrotyped; for it seems to me illustrative of the extent and variety of my father's studies, and of the way in which he gave himself up to them. Mrs. Robert Hallowell Gardiner distinctly remembers his coming to the house of her father, — his classmate and life-long friend, Judge Tudor, — when he was about sixty years old, and there studying Dante in the original (which he did not own), with an intensity of interest that caught her attention at the time, and fixed the circumstance indelibly in her memory. He had some Italian books, but I have not stated that he knew the language, not having a clear recollection in respect to it.

CHAPTER VII.

OF HIM IN HIS PERSONAL, SOCIAL, AND FAMILY RELATIONS; AND OF HIS DEATH.

Let me begin this chapter with speaking of my father as a religious man. I am certain that I have a right to do this. At some time, since his death, I think I have heard intimations suggestive of a doubt on this point; nor is it difficult to account for them. He did not agree with the religious views which prevailed in his day; and while he was as far as any man could be from expressing, or indeed permitting the expression of, anything like contempt or disrespect of what he deemed religion or a true attribute of religion, he would sometimes indulge himself in an anecdote or sarcasm, which spoke very plainly of his disregard for some things which others regarded as religious, and which he considered hostile to religion.

Another reason was, his general silence as to topics of this kind. He was usually free and fearless in his talk, and unrestrained both in his topics and his manner of treating them, loving, indeed, and enjoying conversation — *when it really was conversation* — so much that he always practised and invited the most perfect freedom; and it was a little remarkable that religious topics alone seemed to be almost carefully avoided. It is not strange that this was sometimes attributed to his want of interest in such topics; but the truth was the very opposite of this. Conversation was with him a thing of recreation and amusement. His studying was done in solitude, with books or pen. And he did not think that anything which had the character, or even bore the name or aspect of religion, was a fit thing for amusement.

There was, I suppose, yet another reason for his silence. I have good cause to believe, that, while his religious feelings and convictions were strong and never shaken, his religious opinions were somewhat undefined, and perhaps somewhat uncertain.

I have said that he was a religious man. He had many books of a religious cast, and read them; and he was a critical student of the Bible. He brought up his family in a somewhat strict observance of the ordinances and exercises of religion. Sunday was observed as a Sabbath, with, I think, more exactness or severity than in any other family that I knew; and any unnecessary absence from church, or any levity of conduct while there, or indeed anywhere on the Sabbath, was sure to bring down immediate rebuke.

An eminent merchant in Boston, now long since dead, told me that he once had a very important question, in which foreign correspondents were interested to a large amount, and upon which he needed immediate advice; and he determined to ride to Newburyport and see my father, whom he always consulted. He rode there on Sunday, changing horses at Ipswich that he might return at night, as he must act upon the advice he received on Monday. He found my father in his study, and began to state his case. "Stop there," said my father; "I will not hear another word *to-day*." "But I must be back in Boston to-night." "Very good, you can go, and get the advice of somebody else. I will not attend to business on Sunday." The merchant pressed and urged him, but to no purpose, until my father said: "Thus much I will say to you, without knowing your case or charging a fee. Do you want to know about the law of it, or the justice of it?" "About the law of it only; for the moral right and wrong are plain enough." "Then," said my father, "I will answer you thus: if you will take upon yourself the responsibility of deciding what course is morally just and right, I will take the responsibility of holding that course to be the legal one." The merchant retired, acted upon this counsel, and found himself in the right.

On Sunday, his own books were put away, and his table cleared; and this was always done on Saturday night; and although he passed all his home hours on Sunday, as on other days, in reading and writing, the books he chose were not those of his week days. He required and expected the same thing of his family. Not only must the light reading of the week be given up, but the books themselves must be put out of sight; not hidden, but fairly put away. And I have no recollection of his ever permitting any riding for pleasure on any part of Sunday, although he always kept horses, which were freely used by the family on other days.

The inference I draw from all this will seem to be less certain to others than to myself, because others cannot know as I do his entire freedom from hypocrisy or pretence of any kind. He was always regardless of opinion; and, as it seemed, and still seems, to me, consulted nothing but his own sense of duty, or his own inclination, because it hardly occurred to him that there was anything else — anything, I mean, in public opinion, or appearance before the public — which was worth regarding.

Dr. Kirkland used to speak of an answer my father once made, which, beside its evidence of his own interest in religious questions, touches I think upon the very key-note of nine tenths of what likes to be called liberality and toleration. He was in Salem, and some one was rallying him about certain religious controversies which were conducted with much heat, in Newburyport, where he then lived, and in which he had taken some part. "Why," said this gentleman, "do you make such a disturbance about these matters? Differ, if you like; but why quarrel? Why not keep things quiet and comfortable, as we do in Salem?" "Because," was the answer, "we in Newburyport look upon religion as having a real importance. We think it worth quarrelling about; you don't."

I do not suppose that all his sentiments and habits rested upon exact intellectual conviction. They were, doubtless, in good part, the effect of education, and of established custom. As he was brought up, so he lived, and so he desired that his children should live; but he desired this in the firm belief that it was right and good.

Towards the close of his life, he joined the church of which Dr. Kirkland was pastor. I have often heard the question asked, why he had not joined the church, or, to use the phrase often employed, why he had not professed religion, before. I have no doubt whatever that the reason he gave himself was the true one. He said that his uncertain health would always make his attendance upon church exercises irregular, and possibly infrequent; and any apparent neglect of these exercises would be a bad example, and might exert an injurious influence. I anticipate what properly belongs to a later part of this chapter to say that he suffered much from rheumatism, especially of the head; and he thought that any exposure to cold or damp generally brought on an attack. The churches in those days were not warmed and ventilated even as well as they are now; and unless the weather was so cold that he was sure no one would open a window near him, or so warm that he did not dread the air, he went to church with fear, and frequently found, or thought he found, that he suffered from it.

Dr. Kirkland, as I have understood, represented to him forcibly that his refusal to join the church, by the misinterpretation to which it gave rise, was more harmful than any enforced non-attendance upon the ordinances could be. And my father, influenced also by my mother's wishes and reasons, became convinced that the step was one which he ought to take, as a good thing in itself, and that he should therefore perform his duty in relation to it as well as he could, leaving the results entirely to Providence. With these views, he made a public profession of religion, and partook of the sacrament of the supper, some years before his death.

I would add, as a circumstance not without interest, to myself at least, and as one to which he sometimes alluded, that, from that time until his death, his participation in that sacrament was constant and regular, and that the hinderances he feared very seldom occurred.

There is further evidence on the subject of his religious opinions. I may refer to the statements of Mr. Thacher, in his sermon preached after my father's death; and insert here an extract published from that sermon, in the second volume of the Christian Disciple for 1814, together with the head-note, as originally printed.

ON THE RELIGIOUS CHARACTER OF THE LATE CHIEF JUSTICE PARSONS.

[The following is an extract from a sermon preached at the New South Church in Boston, on the occasion of the death of Chief Justice Parsons. The testimony of such a man as this to the truth of Christianity ought to be generally known, as it cannot but command attention. It may be necessary to premise, that the former part of the discourse had been occupied with an exhibition of the adequacy and adaptation of the Gospel, — 1. To the speculative wants of man; 2. To his wants as an active being; and 3. To his sorrows as a being placed in a state of trial and suffering.]

4. "The fourth point which we proposed to consider was the adequacy of the Christian religion to support man in the prospect of death. I wish to illustrate this by an appeal to fact. I shall bring before you the example of that great and venerable man whose recent loss our country is called to lament. The character of such a man is the property of the public; and though I am little conversant with the language of pulpit panegyric, I feel you have a right to have it exhibited to you. I am not, however, about to speak of the qualities which constituted his intellectual greatness; of the astonishing extent and variety of his knowledge; of his intuitive sagacity; of his all but miraculous mem-

ory; of the purity and loftiness of the great maxims which governed his life; of his disinterestedness; of his fidelity to his principles in all the various relations which he sustained, as a man, a citizen, a counsellor, a statesman, a judge; or of those kind and amiable affections which endeared him most where a man is best known, — in the bosom of his family and the circle of his most intimate friends. These qualities will hereafter be spoken of by one the most worthy to speak of them as they deserve.* I mean only to speak of what has fallen peculiarly within my own knowledge, — of his religious principles, and the support which they gave him in the hour of death.

"Chief Justice Parsons added one more to the long list of the greatest and most revered names which live on record, who have esteemed it the privilege of their nature to sit at the feet of Jesus, and be numbered among his disciples. 'I examined,' he was accustomed to say to his friends, 'the proofs and weighed the objections to Christianity many years ago, with the accuracy of a lawyer; and the result was so entire a conviction of its truth, that I have only to regret that my belief has not more completely influenced my conduct.' Now we are to recollect that this was the testimony of a perfectly disinterested witness, — not of a priest, who may be suspected of professional bias; that it was the testimony of a lawyer, all whose life had been passed in sifting evidence, balancing arguments, unravelling sophistry, and detecting imposture; that it was testimony not only given freely to his friends in private, but declared voluntarily and openly to the world by a public profession in this church. We are to remark, too, that his was a discriminating and rational belief. It was not tinged with the deep and melancholy enthusiasm of Pascal, or darkened by the superstition of Johnson. It was founded on a calm and free examination of all the parts of the Christian system, as well as the general evidence of the whole. It was the religion of Grotius and Newton and Locke, — kindred excellences! — whose names take no dishonor from the one which I have now presumed to associate with theirs. Nor was the religion of Christ a subject to which he was contented to give only a slight and superficial examination. He delighted to bring

---

* A discourse was delivered on the afternoon of the same day, by Rev. President Kirkland.

all the powers of his mighty mind to assist him in sounding it to its depths. He was a proficient even in the technics of theology, and was a Biblical critic of that eminence that he could always interest, and often astonish, by the accuracy and originality of his views, those whose profession makes these studies the occupation of their lives. His belief was not merely a speculative assent to the truth and doctrines of the Gospel. It produced in him a sentiment of habitual and practical piety, which accompanied him to the last moment of rational life. Its strength and its power to support him were most seen when he needed it most. He possessed a temperament so peculiarly and delicately organized, that a slight shock was often sufficient to discompose it; and it might have been feared that the approach of dissolution would have filled him with agitation and alarm. But, by the blessing of God, his faith sustained him without fainting in the hour of trial; and he was enabled to make all his preparations for death with more calmness than he could for several years before summon for the arrangements of an ordinary journey. I found him in his last hours uniformly tranquil and collected, steadfast in his faith and hope, though without any ostentation of triumphant confidence; not affecting indifference to a life so dear to his family, but convinced of the better wisdom, and rejoicing in the benignant providence of God; humbly trusting, not in a life exempt from infirmities as constituting a claim on the Divine justice, but in the pardoning mercy of God declared by his Son to penitent man. His constant prayer, which I believe he did not fail in a single instance to desire me to put up for him, was, that, whether living or dying, he might be submissive and resigned; and, except some affectionate recognitions of his family, the last coherent words which this good and venerable man uttered were a request to me to repeat this petition for him.

"My friends, such a scene as this speaks volumes on the adequacy of the Gospel to support us in the hour of death. I will not weaken its impression by dwelling on it. But I have one word to say on the testimony of such a man as this, at such an hour, to the truth of the Gospel. The belief of the evidences of Christianity, as far as regards an ability to answer all the minor objections which a perverted ingenuity may easily bring to them, must necessarily, with a great part of mankind, be a business of authority. I would ask, then, those who have entertained doubts on this subject to come with me to the dying chamber of this great man. Consider that there never was a human being more capable of forming a correct opinion on such a subject than he who lies before you; that he has given to it the fullest and most deliberate examination; that he is aware that he is about to enter the presence of a God who must view hypocrisy with abhorrence; and that it is impossible that he can have any wish or motive to deceive you. You would not hesitate to trust to the decision of his wisdom and integrity, from the bench of justice, your lives, your fortunes, your best earthly hopes. Why should not your respect extend to his judgment, formed while his faculties possessed all their vigor, and now pronounced from the bed of death, on a subject in which you and he are both equally and eternally interested? Hear, then, this man to whom all science is familiar, this profound sage, this master of human reason,—hear him declare, with all the solemnity which the thought of death can impart to his declaration, '*I could as soon doubt of the existence of God himself, as of the truth of the Christian religion.*' These were his words to me, two days before his death. Hear these words, my friends, and then turn and listen to the accents in which infidelity lifts her puny voice, and pronounces that to be little which such a mind as this felt to be great; and, as you listen, weep for the infatuation with which youth and vanity can be blinded! What lofty heights of wisdom and of science ought he to have reached, who is entitled to look down with contempt on the faith and hope of such a man as this! What weight of years, what character for consistency and judgment, what habits of patient investigation, ought he to possess, who ventures to pronounce such a man as this ignorant of his premises and mistaken in his conclusions! What more than human sagacity, what angelic knowledge, ought he be able to command, who dares to declare that to be a delusion and absurdity which this sublime Intelligence confessed to be 'the wisdom of God, and the power of God to salvation'!"

I will add to this, another of the letters to Mrs. Davis, (given me by her son,) of which the first paragraph suggests my father's view of the evidences of Christianity. Nor do I withhold the second paragraph, for it will illustrate that love for children, which was one of his most characteristic qualities.

My dear Mrs. Davis:

I have taken the liberty to send you Belsham's *Evidences*, which I mentioned at Sandwich. The arguments are simple, and so compressed that they remain on the memory; and, being deduced from unquestionable facts, they convince the understanding and furnish a reasonable ground for our Faith. As the inspiration of the authors of the sacred books is not admitted by infidels, an argument resting for its support on that ground could have no weight with unbelievers. But it is a fact supported by history, sacred and profane, that the Gospels, and the greater part of the Epistles, were written by the persons whose names they bear. From these writings the characters of the authors are clearly marked, and their intention in writing cannot be mistaken. They must have been honest men, writing with honest views, and relating facts, the truth of which they well knew. On this plain ground, admitted by every intelligent man who has examined the subject, the little treatise which I send you has erected a solid structure, unassailable by the ridicule of scoffers, the cavils of sceptics, or the sophistry of philosophists.

Master Wendell's commission I have executed in a manner which, I hope, will satisfy him. Little Samuel is also entitled to my best wishes. He is young, innocent, and beautiful. But what are all these blessings, in the opinion of a wise world, without wealth? And alas! he is not rich. May I begin his little store? And if you will deposit the offering at the bottom of his box, who knows but it may be the foundation of his future fortunes; and, if his other treasures should take wing, it may remain at bottom, like *hope* in the box of Pandora? But, jesting apart, do oblige me by being his trustee of the enclosed, as a keepsake, until you can dispose of it better for my sweet little pet. Indeed I owe him much, for he gladdened many of the hours I passed at Sandwich.

Theoph. Parsons.

I give here, also, a letter to Mr. Davis; and express my regret that I have been able to procure so few of those which he must have written to different persons.

Boston, February 20, 1807.

My dear Sir:

I received, last evening, your favor of the 17th instant, informing us of Mrs. Davis's extreme illness, and of the favorable crisis of her fever. While we sincerely sympathize with you on her danger, we most cordially congratulate you on the prospect of her recovery. When at Boston, I was more apprehensive about her than either you or she herself appeared to be. I feared the severity of the weather in which she travelled, combined with her sister's approaching fate, would very much injure her health. On leaving her, after giving her a little airing, I felt a strong presentiment that she would be quite ill; but my fear of exciting an unnecessary alarm induced me not to mention it. I think I never bade adieu to any friend with more reluctance; and I have been, ever since, anxious to hear from her. It is with very great pleasure that I now learn that she is out of danger; and I sincerely wish that you and your excellent lady may live, mutually blessing and blest, many, many years after your *old* friends are gone and forgotten.

I have had a very sick family since you left Boston. Mrs. Parsons has been confined to her chamber by a pulmonic fever. Eliza, Lucy, and Charlotte have been afflicted with the epidemic influenza. Little William has been laid up with the mumps; one of the maids has been severely attacked by the rheumatism, and the man quite unable to keep about. Indeed, the house has been a hospital, but not of incurables. I trust they are all growing convalescent.

But, alas! Death has been walking among us. Mrs. Phelps, on Tuesday evening last, was deprived of her little Edward, a sweet boy in his fourth year. Well in the morning, he was seized with convulsion fits, and in the evening he was dead. The violence of the tempest prostrated the bud, as it was expanding into blossom. I have just returned from the funeral; and the dead child is at rest, by the side of my Henry.

If our misfortunes can be alleviated by a comparison with the calamities of others, how greatly should we commiserate ——, who seems to have drained the cup of sorrow to the dregs. You have doubtless seen announced, in the public papers, his marriage with ——, on the evening of the Sunday before last, and her death on Tuesday last. She appeared happy at the approaching connection until a few weeks before it was formed. She then became dispirited and much dejected, and her friends discovered in her a mind not quite regular. He, on the Wednesday before the marriage, discovered it for the first time, and was greatly distressed. He had but one of two alternatives in his power; either to proceed to the marriage, trusting that in a little time she would recover her usual soundness of mind, or to propose a delay of the union. The latter measure was extremely delicate from its nature; and he also feared that it might increase her derangement. The former he concluded on, and they were married. After they were married, her spirits continued low, and she appeared to be much distressed, but no marks of increasing insanity were discovered. On the morning of the last Tuesday, he arose at the usual hour. While dressing, she asked him of what he had dreamed in the night. He said, "Of nothing"; and he returned her the same question. She replied that she had dreamed of his wife, and that it seemed as if she must be with her. He left her in bed, and retired to his study. After remaining there about an hour, he went down stairs to breakfast, expecting to find her below. Not seeing her, he went to her chamber, when he discovered her suspended to the bed-post, by a string she used to confine her hair. She had, while standing on the bed, passed the string, with a single knot, round her neck, and securing the end to the top of the post, she sank down, bearing her weight on the string. She was immediately taken down and placed in bed; but animation was fled, and she was a corpse. Who, after this, will complain of disappointment or disease?

But enough in this melancholy strain. I took my pen to thank you for writing, and to thank you for not writing sooner. Had I heard of the sickness and danger of Mrs. Davis, and heard no more, it would have occasioned an anxiety very painful to

Your ever friendly

THEOPH. PARSONS.

WENDELL DAVIS, ESQ., Sandwich.

While I have sufficient evidence for calling him a religious man, and a sincere believer in Christianity, it is of a kind to afford little help in determining the exact form of his belief, and on this point I am quite uncertain.

My grandfather was an Arminian, or, rather, had strong tendencies in that direction. I suspect, but do not certainly know, that my grandmother went still farther. Her position imposed upon her some restraint; and there was indeed nothing that called for any exhibition or public declaration of her opinion. But many reasons convince me that she was decidedly anti-Calvinistic; and it was probably her influence, which in her own family at least was irresistible, that caused the somewhat remarkable unanimity of her numerous children in the same opinion, or the same denial. All the seven were known as — to use the phrase of fifty years ago — "liberal Christians"; and all ranked themselves among the Unitarians when that form of belief was distinctly developed, and those who held it were recognized as a class.

But then, as now, this class was far from homogeneous. The word Unitarian had, and I suppose has, many senses. Indeed it seems to be applied to, or adopted by, those who stand on no other common ground than that they reject the doctrine of a trinity of divine persons, and nevertheless desire to be called Christians. As Protestantism means only a renunciation of Romanism, so Unitarianism appears sometimes to mean only a rejection of the doctrine of three divine persons in the Godhead. And therefore it appears to embrace every kind of opinion; from that of persons who worship Jesus Christ and believe him infinitely superhuman, and are profoundly penetrated with the need of a change of heart, and believe this can come only by the grace and work of God, — to those who regard Jesus only as a man, very good and wise indeed, but liable to the errors of his age, and who consider salvation either as a universal fact, or as an effect to be wrought out by every man by his own unaided strength.

Precisely where my father stood in this wide field, I cannot say. I hope, and I believe, much nearer the first class than the second; but the hope may be the father of the belief, although I am not without some evidence. About fifteen years after his death, there was a funeral at the house of my uncle, William Parsons. I happened to go there very early, and found Dr. Kirkland alone in the drawing-room. I was then quite interested in theological inquiries, and our conversation turned upon subjects of this kind; and presently I said to him: "I have long wished to know my father's belief, and I wish you, who were his pastor and most intimate friend, would tell me what it was." He answered: "I am perfectly ready to tell you as well as I know, and that, I think, is as well as he knew himself. He was a Unitarian, as I am. But there are two kinds of Unitarians, and they differ much from each other. There are those who are unable to comprehend the doctrine of the Trinity known as Orthodox, and are shocked by that of salvation by faith alone, and deny these doctrines without substituting for them distinct and precise dogmas. I am one of these; I suppose your father and Mr. Buckminster, and my successor, Mr. Thacher, were others. There are, however, Unitarians who go so much farther as to have a system of faith about all these things which satisfies them, and they think they are able to understand the whole. But I do not agree with them." I do not give these as the very words of Dr. Kirkland, but I am certain that they express accurately his sentiments and meaning. I do not know that I can add to this. I am only sure that my father entirely rejected the doctrines of vicarious punishment, of arbitrary election, and of salvation by faith without works. I have heard him speak of "atonement" as meaning only "at-one-ment," or reconciliation; and he believed that this reconciliation was necessary, and was to be effected in some way by the influence, and through the life and death, of Jesus Christ; but in what way he supposed this work was to be done, I do not know. Even now I think I remember his reserve upon these subjects. I can distinctly recall his rejection, more than once repeated, of the doctrines of Calvinism; but he never spoke of them with harshness, or, as it seems to me now, with the freedom and unreserve with which he presented his views on every other topic, particularly if he wished to express dislike or disapprobation.

I do not well remember any conversation on religious topics between my father and Mr. Thacher or Dr. Kirkland, both of whom were frequent visitors. But I remember one or two with the Rev. Horace Holley, — then pastor of the Hollis Street Church in Boston, and afterwards President of Transylvania University, — who visited him very seldom, and from whom he seemed to differ very much. Mr. Holley had been educated and settled in the ministry in Connecticut, as a Calvinist, but afterwards became a Unitarian, and was somewhat lax and uncertain in his belief. My father said to a friend, from whom I had it: "Mr. Holley is like a bird that has escaped from a cage, and is now afraid to alight upon the branch of a living tree, lest it should prove another cage."

I remember more of his conversations with Dr. Prince, who came much more often, and with whom he agreed much better than with Mr. Holley.

One evening they had been conversing on some of the tenets of Calvinism, and agreed in their disapproval; and Dr. Prince closed with saying: "Well, if I *do* get to heaven, about the first thing I shall do will be to ask St. Paul what he meant by some of his strange sayings."

As I write, a little circumstance occurs to me, not wholly without its significance in this connection. My father requested Mr. Clap to make prominent among our school studies the committing to memory of the Sermon on the Mount, and other select passages of the New Testament, in the original Greek; and this was most thoroughly done. Thus I grew up with a familiar knowledge of my Bible, and, like all his children, trained to the habitual observance of the Sabbath, and to other religious usages, but wholly without doctrinal instruction of any kind whatever.

Among my father's multifarious manuscripts, one at least was of a religious character. He had said to Mr. Thacher, that he once studied into the evidence of Christianity, and examined the authenticity of the Gospels, with the purpose of ascertaining how he should view and state the evidence as a judge. Mr. Thacher, and some others of his friends, pressed him very strongly to put his views of this subject on paper, and he did so at considerable length. He supposed a case presented to a jury, in which their verdict must be determined by their conviction of the truth of the Gospels, or the failure of the evidence to produce this conviction. Then he supposed that the evidence was all in and the points argued, and that he was presenting this evidence, with the points raised by it, and the arguments thereon, in a charge to a jury. The manuscript, which filled some sheets of his close writing, was, as I remember it, quite complete; but none of the family have seen it for many years. I believe it was lent soon after my father's death, and lost.

Dr. Kirkland was among the nearest and dearest of my father's friends. I well remember when the question was taken in his religious Society, upon his application for a dismissal, upon his appointment as President of Harvard College. It was a Sunday afternoon, and the parishioners were requested to remain after service. When the question was stated, my father arose, and in a very low tone, oppressed by emotion almost to indistinctness, said, in substance, that, as a member of the Corporation of the College, he had deemed it his duty to join in inviting to the Presidency one who was better fitted for that office than any other person whom he knew; and now, as one of his parishioners, he was ready to vote to let him go there. No one could feel more sensibly, and no one could have more reason to feel, the irreparable loss which the separation would inflict upon the Society. But the same remarkable qualities which made him invaluable here would find in this new office, not only a wider scope for their exercise, but, as he thought, a field even better adapted to their employment, and one in which he would be continually sowing seeds that would bear fruit in successive generations for many ages. He knew what the College was asking from the Society; but, in view of the many reasons for the request, he could not but hope that the pain which Dr. Kirkland himself felt at the dissolution of his connection with them, might be lessened as far as it could be by their unanimous approbation of the step which he thought it his duty to take.

I believe the vote of dismissal was unanimous, although so much regret was felt, that there had been some expectation of objection, and even opposition.

Among those to whom I have written for such assistance as they could render me in writing this Memoir, is the Rev. Dr. Benjamin Tappan of Augusta, Maine. In his kind and prompt reply, he says: "When my father died, (who, being then pastor of a church in West Newbury, preached at the funeral of your grandfather, Rev. Moses Parsons of Byfield, and kept up afterwards an acquaintance with his sons,) he left his family with very little property, and your father obtained donations to the amount of seven hundred dollars in our behalf. My oldest brother (not now living) and myself, by his kind invitation, often visited him and his family at his hospitable mansion in Pearl Street [Boston]. Whenever I was in his company he treated me very kindly, and gave me such advice as he thought adapted to my situation and circumstances. . . . . . Your father happened to be in this place [Augusta] in June, 1811, about the time that I had received a call to settle here. In an interview with him, he advised me to accept the invitation, and cautioned me somewhat against preaching the doctrines of Calvinism." In another part of the letter, Dr. Tappan says: "I have not felt myself at liberty to adopt his theological views, or to follow his advice with respect to the character of my preaching."

Dr. Tappan also relates some anecdotes of my father.

Among them is one which I have heard from others, and it bears somewhat perhaps upon the subject of this chapter. It is this. At a dinner party at which Dr. Tappan met my father, some conversation arose about Hopkinsianism, which was then attracting much attention, and of which one of the prominent tenets was that of "disinterested love" and "a willingness to be damned for the glory of God." One and another spoke of it as unintelligible, inconceivable, &c., and my father was appealed to about it. "I think," said he, "I can understand it. I have been told that the Rev. Mr. Hopkins was once in the way of buying lottery-tickets; but, as he drew no prizes, he desisted. When, however, a lottery was authorized for the benefit of a College in which he was interested, Mr. Hopkins bought quite largely, and said to the person who sold the tickets: "My friend, I want you to understand on what ground I buy these tickets. I have bought others, and hoped for a prize, but drew nothing. Now, however, I do not expect a prize, nor care about it, nor desire it, nor think about it in any way, because I buy the tickets without any selfish view, but merely and exclusively to give the price thereof to the College; *and now I think I shall draw a prize.*"

It should be remembered, in justice to Mr. Hopkins, that buying lottery-tickets was then quite as respectable a way of gambling as dealing in stocks is now. When a lottery was authorized for Harvard College, my father bought a hundred dollars' worth of tickets, and distributed them among his children. Some of them drew prizes, which were reinvested in tickets; and in this way they were not all entirely gone for three or four years. During this time the subject was often talked about and laughed about, my father taking his share in the jest; but I never heard any whisper of objection.

I have now to speak of him in his family and his social relations. I approach this subject with hesitation, — I might almost say with reluctance, — so great is my distrust of my ability to do justice to it. And yet it is here that my recollections are most numerous and most distinct; for they are so interwoven with my whole nature, that they can be clouded or effaced only by that which could suppress all thought and memory. For this very reason, however, I dare not trust to them. Whatever my father was abroad, he was infinitely more at home; for there was his heart and life, — there was the clearest manifestation and the fullest development of his character. To him the whole world seemed divided into that which was his home and that which was not; and wherever he was, he desired to return to his home, and to that fulness and expansion of life, and that indulgence of established habits and tastes, which were possible to him only at home. Neither for health nor for pleasure or recreation in any form, nor for any cause but duty, did he ever leave his home; nor did he remain away a day after his return was permitted. And while he was at home it seemed as if he pervaded and filled every part of it with a living and universal presence. Well do I remember — and on this point I cannot be mistaken — the general sadness of the whole household, when the hour came for him to leave us; it was as if night had come; and when he returned, sunshine returned with him.

Even as I write these words, the beautiful definition of home in the Roman Civil Law recurs to me; and if that were ever the description of any man's home, it was of my father's. "In eodem loco singulos habere domicilium, non ambigitur, ubi quis larem rerumque ac fortunarum summam constituit; unde rursus non sit discessurus, si nihil avocet; unde cum profectus est, peregrinari videtur; quod si rediit peregrinari jam destitit." "Men have their home where each one has placed his hearth and the sum of his possessions and his fortunes; whence he goeth not unless called away; and if he departs seems to be a wanderer; and only when he returns ceases to wander."

All this, and the details which make up this whole, I well remember. And there is nothing left for me but to treat of this topic as honestly as I can, leaving it to my readers to make what allowance they will, for my perhaps inevitable partialities on the one hand, or, on the other, for my more than sufficient endeavor to guard against their influence.

To begin with my father's personal appearance. He was rather tall, and in early life quite six feet high, and thin. About the age of fifty he grew more stout; and was not so much a fat man as one who gave an impression of full muscular development and strength, which I believe he possessed. His complexion was light; although his hair was quite dark, his eyes were of a light gray with a tinge of hazel. He became bald very early, and wore a wig of hair as dark as his own had been, until his death; and this wig was seldom nicely combed, but was usually in the disorder indicated by the portrait.

There was one peculiarity about his eyes which may seem to be common enough, but, though I have looked for it, I never noticed it in any other person but Chief Justice Marshall. It was the faculty, and perhaps the habit, of fastening them upon any person who addressed him, and looking, *without winking*, for a very long time. It is strange, that, while we never notice that a person winks when looking at us, unless he does this with a nervous and disagreeable frequency, or with especial significance, or in some way to indicate disorder of the eye, when one looks *without winking*, it is observed at once. Many persons have spoken to me of this habit of my father's; and some in a way which reminds me of the remark of Mr. Lowndes of South Carolina, when, in Washington, I spoke to him of the similar habit of Marshall. "Yes," said he, "the good old judge finds it of great utility. When a lawyer is talking against time, or annoying the court with a repetition of platitudes, that cold, wide-open, never-winking gray eye fastens upon him, and I have seen men almost writhe under it, and at last yield to it, though most reluctantly, and close their argument, or what was meant for argument." Coleridge makes his Ancient Mariner, when he keeps from the wedding the unfortunate guest he has seized, "hold him with his glittering eye." But as it seems to me, a glittering eye is not a powerful eye. At all events, there was no glitter about my father's. I have heard people say it was very bright; but it almost gave me the idea of a pale eye, and while it had a curious power from the fixedness of its look, it was never, as I remember it, bright, unless in moments of excitement; but it was an eye of which the earnest look was hard to bear.

His step was remarkably firm, and very slow. I have heard him remark, — and verified it by observation afterward, — that the soles of his shoes were worn out with perfect evenness. "Right and left" shoes were then unknown, or at least not introduced here; and it was a rule with careful persons to change their shoes every day to secure their even wearing; but my father never had occasion to observe it. I may as well finish this account of his appearance by saying that, when he walked, his feet were always parallel, and that he was perfectly upright. He looked steadily before him; noticing, generally at least, neither persons nor things, but giving one the impression that he was engrossed by the consideration of some subject. Persons who knew him only by sight have spoken to me of the exceeding gravity, and almost solemnity, of his appearance, with that firm, slow step and fixed look. I think that he must have seemed to one who met him perfectly incapable of laughter, and wholly unacquainted with fun. If he did give this impression, it was an erroneous one.

His slow step was the more remarkable, because he was not only a strong and well-built man, but of an exceedingly nervous temperament. I have thought that it was the effect of a deliberate purpose to prevent his nervous impulsiveness from getting the mastery. Perhaps I have no reason for this opinion; and certainly the habit, whatever its origin, was firmly fixed. When I was about ten years old, a number of boys were playing in the garden of Colonel T. H. Perkins, in Pearl Street, which was separated from our own by but one estate, and my younger brother pulled over and upon him a marble statue, which stood on a pedestal in the centre of the garden. We could not lift it off, and my brother was insensible, and I thought dead. I rushed home, over the fences, and proclaimed the fact to my father, who said nothing, but took his hat and stick and walked to Colonel Perkins's garden, just as deliberately as I had ever seen him walk. I shall never forget my amazement at what seemed to be his indifference in such an appalling moment. My father reached my brother long after I did, — at least it seemed very long to me, — but lifted the statue off at once, and bore my brother home in his arms. The boy soon revived, and was found to be badly bruised, but not seriously injured, and escaped with a few days' confinement to his bed. But during the whole scene, including the measures taken to revive him from insensibility, and the examination by Dr. Rand, who was for a long time uncertain as to the extent of the injury, my father spoke and moved, and appeared to think, with his usual calmness and deliberation.

He was inattentive to his dress, to the last degree, and scarcely seemed to know what he had on, or how it was put on; and was as much under the constant supervision of my mother as one of her younger children. She often went with him on his circuits, and gave as one of her reasons, that, if she did not, he would not be dressed fit to be seen; and when he went without her, her anxiety on the subject was often expressed in an amusing way. There were droll stories told about him in this respect. One was, that upon his return, after the absence of a week, my mother found in his trunk none of the seven shirts she had provided, charging him to use one a day. Upon inquiry, however, she found that he had brought them all back, having come home wearing the seven shirts upon him. I have seen this story repeatedly in print; and there is this foundation for it. My mother did not find the shirts where she expected to, and upon asking him where they were, he said: "I only know I have put a clean one on every day, as you ordered. Perhaps I have them all on now." The shirts, however, were in his trunk, although not put where they should be; and my mother was not alarmed at his answer, for she knew that his care of his health — which he never forgot — would make him exchange his day linen, every evening, for the long, loose, and warm garment he slept in. But the story got round as a good family joke, and so was perpetuated.

Chief Justice Parker, in his Charge to the grand jury, to which I have so often alluded, says: "Should any one ask, Had this great man no faults, no foibles? I answer, He had, for he was a man; but none which ought to enter into a candid estimation of his character. I leave them to those who are hardy enough to violate the sanctity of the tomb, for the purpose of magnifying and exposing them."

He alludes here to my father's habitual and extreme hypochondria, which often displayed itself as a strange and very troublesome weakness of mind or of body, or of both. As far as I know, from reading or observation, hypochondria is of three distinct kinds; or rather this word is used to designate three different states of mind. One of these is an extreme proneness to melancholy and depression of spirits, and a disposition to take dark and cheerless views of things. Another is a tendency to believe the most fantastic follies about one's self; as in the case of the English statesman, who would have periods when he believed himself a coffee-pot, and would sit by the hour with his arms bent into the position of the handle and of the spout, and point to them as proofs that he was that utensil. In another case, the man thought himself a living plant, which required to be placed in the sun and regularly watered. Such at least are the stories in the books; but I have always read them with much doubt as to their accuracy or truth. Still a third form of hypochondria is an undue and excessive care for health, or fear of sickness, and a distressing watching for symptoms, and dwelling upon and exaggeration of them.

From the first two of these forms, my father was as free as any man ever was. So far from being habitually gloomy or easily depressed, he was nearly always, when not actually suffering, cheerful, and ready to laugh and make others laugh; and the little misfortunes and accidents of daily life were cast aside by him as one would brush off flies. And as to hypochondriac vagaries, he never had anything tending that way. There was as little of mere fantasy about him as about any one. Some stories were told looking that way, but when examined they amount to nothing. I have heard, or seen, but two, which seemed to indicate a diseased imagination. One was, that a few years before he died, while holding court, he had a violent cough, and told a friend that he should soon die, because he was every day expectorating his lungs piecemeal, and had already lost a good part of them. I know nothing about this circumstance. But I have already said that, when a young man, he bled freely from the lungs, as was supposed, and appeared to be dying of consumption, and during his whole life he was subject to a violent cough if he took cold. It was not, therefore, — at least it does not seem to me to be, — a marvellous folly, if he sometimes believed that he had active tubercles in his lungs, which were gradually reducing the substance of them into a condition in which they were removed by expectoration; for this is the case in all phthisis. It was, however, entirely a mistake. He had no consumption in his last years, and I do not believe he ever had any.

Another thing which I have heard insisted upon is, that, having once cut his thigh slightly, he asserted that he had opened the femoral artery, and kept his bed for a fortnight.

About this I do happen to know something. He was whittling a stick for one of his children, by drawing it under a knife held firmly on his thigh, and, by some slipping of the knife or the stick, he cut quite a gash in the flesh. A common plaster was put on, but for some reason the wound did not heal kindly. It suppurated deeply and extensively, and he was afraid that it would reach the artery which was just below it. His physician, Dr. Sawyer of Newburyport, shared, if he did not suggest, this fear, or at least directed him to abstain from all motion of the leg. Here, too, his fear may have been, and I dare say was, excessive; but it certainly was not insane.

When, however, we come to the third form of hypochondria, it must be admitted that he was a hypochondriac, and suffered himself, and caused suffering to others, by this disease.

In point of fact, his health was never very good after it was prostrated in his early manhood. He was perfectly intemperate in his studies while a young man, turning night into day, and disregarding utterly the laws of health, so far as rest of mind and exercise of body were required by them. He then broke down entirely for a time, and was somewhat of an invalid always. His standing complaint was indigestion, — dyspepsia we now call it, — which assailed him in all its myriad forms; and I do not believe he was entirely free from its influence, during any long interval, for many years. It is to this I attribute his hypochondria.

It may have been, in some degree, a family trait or tendency; not strong, perhaps, but excited and developed in him by his way of life. His brothers and sisters were all active persons, busily employed, and not with the brain only; and none of them exhibited any disposition to extreme solicitude about their health, with one exception. My Uncle William, who was an invalid from childhood, and therefore less active than the rest, — excepting my father, — was, in one way, extremely hypochondriac. He never imagined himself ill when he was not, nor exaggerated his actual illness, nor feared, unduly, sickness or pain, or death itself. But it was the business of his life to take care of his health; and he devoted himself to this work with a wonderful assiduity. He rode just so far each day, when the weather was fair, and at such an hour. He had a great variety of clothing, which he regulated with precision, by the thermometer, sometimes changing his dress many times in a day; and selected for his over-clothes, when he rode out, the very garments which the mercury indicated. He had a weathercock put upon his stable, within fair view from his bedroom and sitting-room; and that and his thermometer, and all possible or impossible signs of the weather, he was watching constantly, and found in these occupations a very agreeable way of employing all his day and all his days.

How far my uncle's long life was to be attributed to this excessive care, I know not. But he was never well; my own recollections of him extend over thirty years, and I am sure I never knew a day when he might not have been considered an invalid. But he outlived every brother and sister, every brother's wife and every sister's husband, and his own wife, and died in 1837, at the age of eighty-one. None of them lived to be so old as he; some, however, went beyond seventy, and were healthy and vigorous to the end; but none came within sight of my Uncle William's eighty years.

My father manifested no tendency to this form of hypochondria until his health gave way. But afterwards he was seldom wholly free from it. His way of life was unfavorable, because he lived, as far as he could, as others lived then; and when I recollect what the common customs of that day were, it is a marvel to me that men lived so long as they did. They were stronger than we are, or else dreadfully reckless. I never heard a cautious and habitually abstinent diet suggested to anybody. My father, who would probably have found in it a cure for most of his ailments, certainly never thought of such a thing. He would live for a day, a week, or more, upon gruel, or broth, or hasty-pudding, as ordered, taking, perhaps, active medicines all the time; and when the symptoms which troubled him were thus removed, he returned to his hearty food with the better appetite and the freer indulgence. The dinner was early,—never later than three,—and a heavy meat supper was a common meal; and excellent wine was easily obtained and very freely used. I do not much wonder that my father, who studied about half of every twenty-four hours, and took no exercise, had his headaches and other ailments frequently, and lived in constant fear of them. He was very sensitive to cold, made so, it was thought, by "nursing" himself so carefully, but constitutionally so as I believe; at all events he suffered very much from any exposure to it. He was liable to a troublesome cough, and any damp or cold weather brought on rheumatic attacks, or what passed for such.

I do not think Chief Justice Parker's expression, that "he shrunk at an eastern breeze, and started at the slightest pain," too strong. But I do not believe that he ever had any serious illness until his last. After he was fifty years old, he became much troubled with palpitations of the heart, and supposed there was ossification, &c. But he was, a few years afterwards, fortunately persuaded to make some slight changes in his diet and habits, and during his last few years these symptoms of heart disease quite disappeared. He had also some renal troubles during his last two or three years, which brought on nervous states, and were aggravated by such states. When I remember him, he slept as well as most persons who are growing old; at least, I never heard of any special complaints of this kind, or, if I did, have forgotten them. But I have heard fearful stories of his suffering from insomnolence in earlier years. Thus, while living in Newburyport, he was retained, and paid very largely, for defending some persons charged with piracy. The trial, to accommodate the crowd, took place in a meeting-house in Ipswich, and the accused were brought into court heavily ironed. The trial lasted some days; there was a verdict of not guilty; but my father returned home so exhausted and so excited, that, as he always himself supposed, he passed fourteen days and nights wholly without sleep. Dr. Sawyer, his excellent physician, said he was laboring under a low, nervous fever, and probably did sleep very little, although he could hardly have lain awake, as he himself believed.

It would seem that I have thus described a sick and nervous man, whose time and thought must have been so much occupied with his ailments and his fear of disease, that he would have neither strength nor opportunity for intellectual or professional labor. How can this consist with the industry and the efforts and the success I have elsewhere described? I can only answer, that both pictures are true; as true, that is, as I am able to paint them; and both rest, as I think, on good authority and plenary evidence. Nor are they so inconsistent as they at first seem. He had great energy and self-control; and whatever he wished to do, that he would do. Moreover, these ailments, and this nervousness about his health, were outside matters after all. They were more talk than anything else. They seldom prevented him from taking and enjoying his book or his pen, although they sometimes plagued and harassed him, and others through him. And very seldom indeed did they prevent his going abroad where any *duty* called. I used to think, and indeed to see, how a part of the notion of his hypochondria grew up. When any public festivity was going on, — a dinner, or a procession, or a reception, or the like, — and he was wanted officially or otherwise, he *always* refused, and always on the score of health. He had some trouble, actual or apprehended, to call upon; and whatever it was, it answered his purpose, for go he would not. He hated "demonstration"; never would he have said, with Persius, "At pulchrum est digito monstrari, et dicier, 'Hic est.'" It was a common saying, when it was proposed to invite him: It will be of no use, — his head or his heart or his stomach will be in the way, and he won't come. I remember once he was strongly solicited to join in some public procession, and the committee brought his physician, Dr. Rand, with them, and it was proposed, that the Doctor should go with him in his carriage, and that he should be at liberty to turn aside and slip out of the ranks as soon as he felt any symptoms of the coming plague. But no, he would not go. Yet, be it remembered, if a court had been in session, and he were needed on the bench, he certainly would have gone. In all of the letters we have from my mother, written while on the circuits with him, she speaks of his health, and often as if it were feeble; but never of his failing to hold his court.

Let it not be supposed that, when he brought out his hypochondria to ward off intrusion, he was a hypocrite. I do not believe he was. He certainly did not care a straw about being thought a hypochondriac; but then he would just as soon have said no as yes to any request he had no mind to accede to. But I believe he verily thought he was sick, or should be sick, when he said so. If, however, duty had called him, *he would not have thought so.*

Of these letters from my mother, written while on the circuits with my father, we have preserved some ten or twelve. In all, she speaks of his health, and in various ways; but never intimates that he lost a day or hour of *work.* In the first we have she says: "Wednesday Morning, 10 o'clock. I wrote you a line yesterday, just as the mail was closing. I hope you have received it, to ease your anxious minds. Your father had a good night's sleep, and opened court at nine this morning. — Three o'clock. Your father has just left me, to attend court, with half a dozen gentlemen; and I think he enjoyed his dinner and a good glass of wine as well as any of them. I think his health is much better than it was; and, if he does not have another pull-back, he will soon recover his usual strength. — Thursday Morning, 8 o'clock. Your father has had a very good night, and eaten his breakfast, and gone to court." Few of these letters have the year or the place stated in which they were written. This was from Worcester.

In the next, without any date, but apparently written at Portland, she says: "The court is now sitting, and your father is well enough to attend, although he was afraid he should not be, yesterday. On Monday, he had a very bad pain in his head and ear, something like what he was troubled with last winter. Your Aunt Cross made him some good tea; and with that, and the help of a little paregoric, he slept pretty well. He expects to set off for Augusta on Saturday morning."

In another: "Sunday Eve. We arrived at Northampton a little fatigued; but your father had a good night's sleep, and has been to meeting all day. — Monday Morning. Your father is very well this morning, and had as good a night as the heat would let him have."

In another: "Your father has been very well ever since we have been here, until this morning. He awoke with a little of his palpitation, but has eaten a good breakfast, and gone into court, and thinks he shall get rid of it without further trouble. He has concluded not to return home until after Worcester court is over, if he holds well."

If he were understood to be ill, and the children saw him dieting, and were hushed that we might not disturb him, let Dr. Prince come up from Salem, and there was at once a cheerful and animated examination of some new instrument, or a discussion of some new fact or theory, and the hypochondria was scattered to the winds.

He had two habits which I suppose affected his health very injuriously. One of these was the inordinate use of tobacco. He loved it as sedentary and studious men are apt to love it. He took snuff occasionally, usually carrying a large box with him. He chewed tobacco frequently, always having a roll of what was called (and may be so now) "ladies' twist" in his pocket, and smoked cigars constantly, when he could; that is, he did not smoke at his meals, or in bed, or in the street, or in court, or in church; but almost everywhere else he did smoke, beginning before breakfast, and ending only when he was going to bed.

He was led to give up this practice about the year 1807. He had always been subject to occasional vertigo; and in that year, while riding in his carriage in the State of Maine, upon a circuit, be became suddenly incapable of motion, and nearly insensible. He was not alone in the carriage. The driver hastened to the nearest tavern, and a physician there administered an active emetic, which relieved him from an undigested breakfast. He recovered rapidly, and held court in a day or two. The attack was believed by his physician and himself to have been caused only by indigestion; that is, by a sympathy of his brain with an oppressed stomach; but it led to some change in his habits. He gave up entirely the use of tobacco, and never resumed it, unless by taking an occasional pinch of snuff. The way in which he renounced the luxury was characteristic. He took with him in his next circuit his usual supply of cigars (which he always carried in a tin box made for the purpose, that held five hundred of the common size), chewing-tobacco, and snuff, and kept them all at hand and within reach, on the ground "that he would not help good resolution by the difficulty of breaking it." He also lessened his use of coffee, and for the last year of his life gave up wine, and confined himself to old Jamaica rum, of which he drank but one teaspoonful at a time, using it, however, three or four times a day. If I remember right, his limit was, never to use more than one wine-glass full in a day.

He even went so far as to try to take exercise, which was a perfectly new thing. I have read of German professors who did nothing but read; and that they can live and retain their health seems surprising. It is to be remarked, however, that they lecture constantly, and this is itself one of the best and most salutary modes of exercise. I have read somewhere, but cannot remember where, that Cicero speaks, in one of his letters, of curing himself of troublesome and alarming weakness, by reading aloud for some hours every day.

My father had a good deal of arguing to do when at the bar, and much travelling and some speaking when on the bench; but he very seldom took exercise for exercise' sake. At the beginning of each year he bought a pair of shoes, and they were not wholly worn out when replaced by the new pair next year. Of boots he had but one pair — the old-fashioned, high, red-top boots — for some years; and at his death they were given away, almost unworn. Excepting an infrequent walk of some minutes in the long entry which ran through the middle of our house, I think he almost never walked for mere exercise, until the attack I have spoken of. After that, he sometimes, though rarely, took a walk about the streets, or on the Common.

Under these changes, his health improved very considerably. The palpitation of the heart nearly disappeared, vertigo was much lessened, and sleep grew more regular. But he was still and always hypochondriac, watching for any symptoms of illness, dreading their approach, and magnifying their importance.

While in Newburyport, and afterwards in Boston, his office was always in his dwelling-house, which then was, and is now, very unusual in Boston. There he sat all the day; but his evenings were invariably spent in the large common sitting-room, unless upon the rare occasions when the absence of the family would have left him alone there. He had his chair by the fireside, and a small table near it, upon which the evening's supply of books was placed. There he sat, always reading (seldom writing in the evening or out of his office), but never disturbed by any noise or frolic which might be going on. If anybody, young or old, appealed to him, he was always ready to answer; and sometimes, though not very often, would join in a game or play, and then return to his books.

I have absolutely no recollection of his ever going out to company, either at dinner or in the evening. He did so, I know, somewhat, although very little, at earlier periods of his life; but I doubt whether he ever went into company, out of his own house, for a dozen times in as many years before his death. Nor was our family a visiting family. It was quite large, and we had very many friends and relations who always made our house their home when in Boston, and some of the neighbors visited us intimately. It was rather a rare thing for us to be quite alone. It was quite the rule for some amusement or other to be going on in the evening; and it seemed a great refreshment to my father to witness, if he did not partake it.

A lady, who was a frequent and always a welcome guest, told me of a little thing which may serve to show how he mingled with us. One evening they had all been trying their hands at rebuses, or rhymed riddles, which were then the fashion. Presently, there was a laughter so uproarious at one very bad one, that it roused my father, who asked to hear it. "That is dreadful," said he; "I could make a better one about anything in the room." "O do, do!" was the answer from one and all; and he immediately wrote down these lines:

My first connects related words;
My second forms the sharpest swords;
My whole supports the forest's pride,
Dispensing heat on every side.

Thus indicating the andiron which had caught his eye.

Judge Story says of my father, that "he was no poet," and certainly he was not. But I think the Judge implies, or at least seems to imply, that my father thought he *was* a poet. In this, however, Judge Story was utterly mistaken.

The Judge himself, it is well known, thought at one time so well of his own poetical talent, as to publish a volume of poems. My father never made a mistake of that kind. He rhymed with great facility, and often sent home to his younger children, while he was away, letters written in burlesque rhymes; but he never made a line, or tried to, so far as I know or believe, except in fun. He often said of himself, that he had not a particle of poetry about him, and was lucky enough to know it. Of the rhymed letters he used to send his children for their amusement, I thought all were lost; but have just now found, among the papers of a relative, one, which I insert, because I think it illustrates his constant thought for his children, and his desire to amuse them. It was written when he was visiting Boston in attendance on the courts, to a daughter aged seven. The names are taken from Mrs. Trimmer's delightful story of "The Robins," which was first published some sixty years ago, and, after half a century of forgetfulness, has been recently given again to our children. When my brother and sisters first had the book, the names of the young Robins were appropriated by them, and so remained for some years; and my father alludes to them.

Boston, March 2, 1795.

Dear Mary, by these lines you'll find
That your papa has kept in mind,
The promise made at Newburyport,
To write you when at Boston court.
Since then I have increased in health,
But added little to my wealth.
Enough there still remained in store,
To purchase books, in number four,
For Robin, Flapsy, Dicksy, Hopsy,
With stories filled, to turn them topsy
Such as poor Gulliver, of old,
To make folks merry, often told, —
Of little men, six inches high,
Of larks not bigger than a fly,

Of sheep much less than common rats,
And horses not so big as cats;
He next of monstrous giants talked,
High as a steeple when they walked;
Whose beasts and birds, and even flies,
Were all proportioned to that size.
An hundred curious stories more,
Which will delight you to read o'er,
These wondrous books in truth contain,
All sprung from his creative brain.
Do not, my dear, impatient burn
To read these books; on my return
I'll bring them safe, each child to please,
While Pecksy dances on my knees,
And dear mamma exults with pleasure,
To see around her all her treasure.

THEOPHILUS PARSONS.

So much for his fun. Let me connect with this another letter, of a more serious cast, written from Worcester, to the same daughter, whom he had left in Boston. She was still a young girl, but somewhat older than the "Robins."

MY DEAR MARY:

I thank you for your favor of the 10th instant, which we received at Northampton. I rejoice that your tooth is extracted, and I think it was very right that you submitted to the operation. You will now be quite well and ready for a pleasant ride to Taunton. I was delighted to hear that the family affairs were conducted with cheerfulness and good humor. Good humor is certainly a virtue of a high order, for it contributes very much to soften the asperities of life, and to promote rational enjoyment. Temper and passion were given us for wise purposes; but they were made to be servants to reason, their lawful and sovereign mistress; and when they rebel and usurp the authority of master, — order and happiness disappear, and the mind is a turbulent democracy. But under the direction of reason we shall behave with propriety, and then felicity will make her abode with us.

The rest of the letter is torn off.

It may seem strange, that one who loved society so well should never go out to find it. But he loved his books still more. And the company he found at home, especially at his Saturday dinners, was enough for him. Every stranger of note who visited Boston was brought to him almost as a matter of course. He came generally in the evening. Immediately afterward, my father called on him, and invited him for the next Saturday's dinner ; or, if he took a fancy to him, for all the Saturdays he should be in Boston.

Our house in Pearl Street was a large one; but the first thing my father did after he bought it was to extend the dining-room, so that it accommodated, conveniently, thirty persons; and very often the table was carried out to its full extent, and filled. One who knew him long and well writes me: "He was very social, and would readily adapt his conversation to the professional knowledge and employment of those he happened to be in company with. If any guest was diffident, and could not readily bear a part in the conversation, he would in a very easy manner draw him out, by leading him to talk upon subjects which were perfectly familiar to him, and where he was at home. I have heard him say that he was hardly ever in company with any one from whom he could not get some information or remark which would come into use and be of some value at a future time."

His pastors, Kirkland, and afterwards Thacher, were usually there. Of Kirkland I have already spoken. Of Samuel Cooper Thacher, his successor, I would say a word, although I fear that he is so much forgotten that only to a few old persons will my faint portraiture call up the remembrance of him who was once so much beloved. Mr. Thacher was not remarkable for talent, or for cultivation; he held a thoroughly respectable position as a scholar and as a writer, and nothing more. But he was so wise, so affectionate and gentle and courteous, and so deeply penetrated with the consciousness of the high duties belonging to his office, and so earnestly and constantly desirous to discharge them all, that he stands in my mind as more nearly the perfect exemplar of a clergyman than any person I have ever known. Fitted for the highest society by his manners and his tastes, and enjoying it thoroughly, he was yet intimately conversant with all of all classes within his sphere; and the poor especially felt his devotion to them. In company and at table he was always cheerful, and entered with interest into all that was going on. Still he never forgot that he was a clergyman; and never permitted any one to forget it; but he was beloved all the more, for he presented this character free from all austerity and repulsiveness, and full of everything that could win and hold affection and respect.

He had a long consumption. His people sent him many voyages; one to Southern Africa; and afterwards to the South of France; and were anxious to do everything which offered any chance of preserving a life so dear to them. But he died at the early age of thirty-two, in a foreign land. I well remember the tolling of the bell of his church, when it announced the news of his death; and I remember as well how much I was struck by the signs of profound and universal grief manifested by his people at the meetings which took place in reference to it.

The Rev. Joseph Stevens Buckminster was another frequent guest, and no one was more welcome. He and Thacher were intimate and dear friends. Of nearly the same age; pursuing the same studies; holding similar opinions; visiting Europe together; and devoted, with their whole hearts, to similar duties; — they were yet different, and indeed contrasted in much that belongs to character and to the exhibition of character.

The expression of Thacher's face was true to his nature, and therefore it was very attractive. But the features of Buckminster were all beautiful, and the singular brilliancy of his eyes was thought to be connected with the nervous excitability that, in its intensity, became the cause of his death, at the age of twenty-eight. Perhaps this was true also of his high spirits. That they had their ebb and flow, we know from that part of his Diary which has been published, and might have known from the laws of human life; but I saw him often in company, and there they were unfailing. Full of anecdote and illustration, prompt with all the resources which his keen observation had gathered, abroad and at home, and which his imagination presented with the inexhaustible variety of a kaleidoscope, interested in all topics and equal to all, always ready and never obtrusive, without vanity or affectation or self-thought in any form, he stands before my mind at this moment as one of the most fascinating of companions. His cheerfulness, or rather his playfulness, was as unfettered, as easy, and apparently as thoughtless, as that of a boy let loose from school. But there was always the silent restraint of his good taste and perfect refinement. He seemed to be sure that his own instincts and habits of thought would build an invincible barrier against coarseness or extravagance and excess; and he gave himself up to the feeling of the moment, relying upon this barrier fully and safely. His brilliant and seductive gayety never pained and never wearied, but enveloped all others in its own sunshine, and made them glad with his own gladness by a gentle compulsion to which they willingly yielded.

He, too, was most conscientious, assiduous, and devoted in the discharge of his clerical functions. And he was eminent as a scholar and a writer. He superintended the editiön of Griesbach, which I have already mentioned; and his Phi Beta Oration is one of the most charming compositions in our literature.

There were others who were frequent guests; and my father's connection with the College brought to his table many gentlemen from Cambridge. A large proportion of his guests were generally young men.

As I remember his Saturday dinners, they do not seem to me characterized by the quiet which would now prevail at such gatherings. My father loved to eat, and to drink, and to talk, and, above all, to laugh; and all these things he loved to have those about him do. He piqued himself upon his Sherry and Madeira, — which he generally imported, and they were the only wines he ever bought, — and he liked to see others appreciate what he thought their excellence. The truth is, those were days of less elegance and refinement than now prevail; but of far more hilarity and frolic. It seems as if men worked harder then; and when they relaxed, crowded into a brief space all the recreation it would hold. An eminent physician has said to me, that he thinks there was more acute disease then than now; but less health now than then.

I should state that a large and well-lighted closet opened out from his office, and in this some of his philosophical instruments were kept, and two chests of carpenter's tools. These he used frequently and skilfully, as some things which I have now attest. He designed, and partly made, a large rocking-chair with projecting arms, across which a board lay, movable, but kept in its place by suitable contrivances. And here he did nearly all his work. A small table, about three feet square, stood on each side of him, and held the books, papers, or instruments he was using. Seated in this chair, wearing his very large and loose camlet gown, he spent all the hours of the day which he was not obliged to employ elsewhere.

It was another trait in his character, that he was very fond of horses; and always kept from two to four, as soon as he could afford this luxury. He interested himself in everything about them; and was very watchful that they should be well treated. Indeed, he had a general love for domestic animals. His cow was of the best kind; he was as much interested as I was in my large rabbit-room; and he had a great pigeon-house, with divers contrivances for separating the birds, and sundry other purposes, which the carpenters made from his drawings, and some of which he made himself. He procured for me a young goat of the Cashmere breed; it was one of the most beautiful animals I ever saw, and a great pet, and a dreadful plague; but it was long before my father yielded to the universal outcry, and gave it away.

My mention of animals reminds me that the cry came into the office, one day, that a monstrous bird had alighted on the palings of the garden. So out my father went, and at once recognized a young, but well-grown eagle. He put a coal into the bowl of a large pipe, filled it with tobacco, and, when it gave out smoke freely, slowly approached the bird, and gently blew the smoke into its face. At first the eagle seemed offended, and threatened with beak and wing, but soon appeared to like it, and then, in a little time, was stupefied. My father then directed our man-servant to come up and seize the bird round the body, while he at the same moment caught at the throat with one hand and at the legs with the other. In this way he was safely captured and retained for a day or two, until reclaimed by his owner, from whom he had escaped.

There was attached to his house in Pearl Street a large garden; but I do not remember that he paid any more attention to it than was necessary to see that it was properly cultivated, as we depended upon it for most of our vegetables. He had no love for *horticulture* that I know of, but had, or thought he had, a great taste for *agriculture*. All he did about it was to gather and read agricultural books and enjoy a talk with farmers, — "gentlemen farmers" or working farmers. But he wished to do more.

About the time he removed to Boston, he desired very much to buy a large farm, called "the Johnson farm," in Byfield, which was then for sale, and was one of the best in

Essex County, with the purpose of living there in summer; but he was deterred by the earnest opposition of his wife and brothers. At that time, this way of life, now so common, was very infrequent. None, I believe, adopted it, but a few gentlemen who had retired wholly from business. My mother and uncles knew my father's love of seclusion and study, and feared that, if he should once settle down there, he would gradually renounce profession, friends, and society, and deprive his family of proper opportunities for their education and companionship. This might have happened; and it is of no great use to speculate about it; but I have always thought that the exercise and recreation of farming, and the pure country air, would have been salutary to both body and mind, and might have prolonged his life, as well as increased its happiness.

He did love study and retirement, but not these alone; nor did he love them well enough to sacrifice to them all his other tastes. He would never have lived without some society; and it would have pained him quite as much as his children, if he had taken them away permanently and altogether from their educational means or their social relations. Their friends were his friends; their intimates were his intimates; and his enjoyment of their companions was as great as their own. For he had one love as great and as certain as his love of books; and it was his love of the young. They loved to be about him, and he loved to have them there.

My friend, Richard H. Dana, Jr., Esq., the grandson of Chief Justice Dana, who was, as the letters in the Appendix will show, an intimate friend of my father's, writes me: "My aunts tell me that your father was very fond of children, and attached them to him very strongly. They were in great delight when he came to the house. This was after he was on the bench." Let me interrupt my narrative long enough to express the hope that my friend will find, or make, even in the midst of his engrossing business, leisure to give to the community a memoir of his ancestor, who was not only distinguished as the head of our judiciary, but so active and useful in our Revolutionary struggles, and in the construction of our institutions, that the history of those times cannot be well understood without understanding his conduct and character.

I have mentioned before, as among my father's traits, the great enjoyment he had in teaching the young. I had, until a few months since, a cousin, Moses Parsons Gray, the son of my father's sister Susan, who proposed to go to sea and earn his living in that way, as the large shipping interests of my two uncles offered him favorable opportunities. For this purpose he wished to learn scientific and practical navigation, meaning thereby, not the management of a ship, but the art of ascertaining the ship's progress and place by astronomical observations and calculations. Mr. Gray wrote to me: "Uncle offered to instruct me, remarking that it would be an amusement to him, and that he should like to brush up some of his old studies. I used to study in what leisure time I had in the day, and go to him in the evening, recite my lessons, and state what difficulties I had met with; and he, without ever having occasion to look at a book, would explain everything that looked to me dark, and make everything clear. I continued the study until I made myself thoroughly master of it; and I never found him at any time the least at a loss, for he had at command, and could call up at will, not only the theory, but all the rules of the science, as completely and promptly as though he had been employed all his life in teaching navigation, and nothing else. At this time he was in his fullest practice, and his days were all employed in his office in examining and deciding intricate and abstruse questions of law."

He very frequently formed classes of his children, and some of their companions, and taught them various things. The two I best remember his teaching thus were elementary astronomy, with the use of the globes, of which he had the best to be procured in London, and botany. Of this last science I do not think he knew much. Of structural botany little was known in his day, and he did not take much interest in systematic botany. But he was familiar with its elements, on the Linnæan system, and had the best books; and he seemed to take great pleasure in teaching those elements, partly, as I remember, by his books, and partly by inspection of flowers. I have even now the remains of a botanical microscope which Dr. Prince imported for him.

Such was my father; and so lived he in his home. There alone he seemed to live in freedom; for there he gave himself up to the occupations which he loved best; and there he found the refreshment and happiness which strengthened him for the discharge of those duties, which alone drew him abroad. He not only loved his home, but may almost be said to have loved nothing else. It was only duty and necessity which carried him abroad, while his own wishes always brought him back. And how was he welcomed there! Of slavish fear I never knew, or saw, or can now remember, the slightest sign. But it is impossible to imagine a family more devoted to its head.

I know that I fail to give my readers a just idea of him in his social and his family relations; for it must be difficult for them to reconcile the apparent incongruities of his character. He was not, at any time or in any measure, a silent, sullen, solitary man. He was not, in any sense of the word, or in any of his tastes or habits, a misanthrope. Few enjoy society more than he did; but it was, almost exclusively, society that came to him and found him in his own home. The world outside had little charm for him. Indeed, so far as taste and enjoyment were concerned, he seemed to take no cognizance of it. He must have known that he was, to some extent, and if only from office, an eminent man. But if he ever thought of popular applause or popular recognition, the very least I can say is, that he had *no* love for it.

It has been already intimated, that this man, who was for many years conspicuous in a profession which, more than any other, forces its members before the public, and who for some years held an office which required him to go forth and periodically hold open court before all the citizens in turn; who was an earnest student of a great variety of subjects, and loved to write, and did actually write very largely and variously, and supplied others with many things for them to publish; and who spoke as easily as he thought; — this man never published a word under his own name or any name, as his own individual work, (unless one mathematical paper published in the Transactions of the American Academy be an exception,) and never in his life made an oration, or address, or a speech of any kind, unless professional or official duty required it. He belonged to none of the numerous clubs of his day. And if I do not assert, that he never in his later years, and seldom if ever at any period, joined in any procession or public dinner, or took part in any popular gathering, it is because I have no means of proving what all that I have ever learned from his family or his friends concurs with my own recollection in leading me to believe. "For more than thirty years," said Chief Justice Parker, in 1813, "he has been acknowledged as the great man of his time." If this were so, I am sure that he did not greatly desire it, or greatly enjoy it.

Such was my father; and so he lived among us, until the hour came which brought his summons to live elsewhere.

In 1813, he sat during the March term in Boston, but he did not go to the State (then the Province or District) of Maine, to hold the Spring and Summer terms there; but he went to Worcester in the Autumn.

Chief Justice Parker says: "Parsons died in the zenith of his reputation, in the full strength of his understanding." And yet I think there had been some failure for a year or more before his death. I am entirely unable to point to any specific fact in proof of this; and, out of my own family, I never heard a word suggesting it. For the newspapers of the day, and all persons whom I have ever heard speak of his death, have represented it as finding him in the full vigor of his powers. Still, although I was quite young, I remember some change in his habits and appearance for months before. There was not the usual vigor and cheerfulness. He would sometimes lay down his book as if it wearied him, and sit silent for some minutes; and if he were writing, he would pause, lay down the pen, and rest his head upon his hand as if overworked. Sometimes he would come from the office into the sitting-room, and walk up and down a few times, or sit for a moment in a chair, silent and unoccupied, and then return. All this struck me the more, because, until that period, I had never known him *wholly unoccupied* at any time whatsoever. He was always doing something, with book or pen or instrument, or engaged in conversation. But this necessity of perpetual activity seemed to have given way to a necessity for repose. Perhaps my attention was drawn to this the more, because I observed my mother and my elder brother noticing such things with sadness and fear. If I may trust to my recollections at all, I should say that his intellectual powers had not abated, but that a sluggishness was creeping over them, and they could only be roused to do what once was done with prompt and eager spontaneousness.

But all things went on as usual, with rather less complaint of ill health than common, until the summer of 1813. It was then that he wrote a letter to Chief Justice Parker, in which he says: "I thank you for your line from Westfield, and very much regret that I cannot oblige my Hampshire friends by meeting you to-morrow evening at Northampton, as was indeed my intention and expectation when you left me. Since that time I have been very unwell, not from any return of my specific disease, but from a general increasing debility of my whole frame. It has been owing either to the failure of my constitution, or to the effect of this season of the year. My physician attributes it to the latter cause, and I am willing to believe him. He proposes to give me active medicine to-morrow, and assures me that I shall be able to meet you at Worcester next week. So be it. I shall do the best I can, and trust that I shall see you at our old lodgings in Worcester. If I do not, I shall almost despair of ever again discharging the duties of our department."

This letter is dated September 15th, 1813. Later in the month, my father went to Worcester, as has been said, and held court as usual. But while there, he began to be troubled by an irritating humor. After his return, this increased until it spread round his whole body. This irritation was violent and constant, accompanied by some fever. It harassed him the more, because it was a new thing, as he never before had the slightest eruption. He could not eat nor sleep; and was wearied, and then ill, and kept his chamber. Dr. Rand, whose prescriptions thus far had given no relief, said, one day: "There is a remedy, if you like to try it, which is sometimes extremely efficacious." "What is it?" "Water, almost scalding. Take a bath of water, just as hot as you can possibly bear it, and lie there as long as you can. I have known it cure skin disease almost at once." My father was ready to try anything. My brother, who put him into the bath, has told me that it was so hot he himself could not bear his hand in it, and that he begged my father to have it made cooler. But no; he got in, although shrinking, and evidently suffering extremely. He stayed there an hour, and then returned to his bed. The humor appeared to dry up almost at once, and in a day or two was all gone; and in three weeks my father was dead.

Whether the bath caused the retrocession of the humor, and whether this caused his death, can never be known. Dr. Rand thought the hot water might have cured the humor, but could not have made him sick. My mother and my brother thought it killed him. But if it were so, it may well be that it killed him only because his strength and vitality were so nearly exhausted, that a slight cause was sufficient to destroy the little that was left.

After the humor was cured, my father came down stairs for a day or two, complaining, however, of a new but incessant uneasiness in his head. He said it was not pain, but "great discomfort; and it won't let me do anything." He soon returned to his chamber, and sat there, neither reading nor writing during the day. For some days there was but little change, except that he seemed to grow weaker, and sleepy, and the uneasiness of the brain continued. One evening, as he sat in his chair, in his chamber, with most of his children around him, he looked up to my brother-in-law, Mr. Watson, and said, "Mr. Tudor, I wish you would —" and suddenly stopping, said, "Now what could have made me call you Mr. Tudor; was it not strange?" I perfectly remember seeing Dr. Rand, who sat by, start at this, and he said, almost immediately, "Judge, I should like to have your head shaved and blistered; I think it would relieve that uneasiness." "Do it then at once," was the answer; "let me get rid of that if I can." The blister was put on immediately, but did no good. The next day my father kept his bed, and became fully aware of his danger, which I think he did not apprehend before. He sent for Judge Jackson (to whom he had previously spoken on the subject) to make his will; and conversed, as one who knew that he was dying, with his wife, his brother, and his children, and with his pastor and one or two friends who were admitted to see him. For a few days his senses remained unimpaired. Then his sleepiness deepened into lethargy, and when he spoke, it was as one in a dream. Then he was altogether silent for a day or two, and then he died.

During his last illness, Dr. Rand had called into consultation, Doctors Warren and Danforth. After his death they met again, and, as I understood, were not quite agreed as to the cause of it. They, however, finally said, I believe, that he died of hydrocephalic apoplexy; or of pressure of water upon the brain. There was no examination; but I have supposed, on the authority of skilful physicians whom I have heard speak in recent times of his death, that it was a rapid termination of a softening of the brain which had began a considerable time before. This disease was not, as I am told, nearly so well known at that time as it is now.

Two circumstances attended my father's death, neither of which is unusual; but they struck us forcibly, as we were listening and watching with our whole hearts.

One was, the evidence that his thoughts, when he could no longer control them, went back to his duties and his business, and responded unconsciously to his condition, as death drew near to close his earthly career. When he spoke, it was as a judge, giving answers, directions, &c. At last, after a suspense of all speech so long that we thought we should never hear his voice again, he suddenly revived, and, with perfect distinctness, spoke for the last time on earth that formula which he had used hundreds of times: "Gentlemen of the jury, the case is closed, and in your hands. You will please retire and agree upon your verdict." *

---

* Within a day or two after writing this paragraph, I read Campbell's Life of Lord Chief Justice Tenterden, and was struck with the similarity of his last words. "An excess of fever supervening, he was put to bed, from which he never rose. He became delirious, and talked incoherently. Afterwards, he seemed to recover his composure, and, raising his head from the pillow, was heard to say, in a slow and solemn tone, as when he used to conclude his summing up in cases of great importance, 'And now, Gentlemen of the jury, you will consider of your verdict.' These were his last words. When he had uttered them, his head sunk down, and in a few minutes he expired without a groan."

The other circumstance was the expression upon his face. It told us that one life had ended only because another had begun. Byron's beautiful lines,

> "He who hath bent him o'er the dead,
> Ere the first day of death have fled,
> . . . . .
> And marked the mild, angelic air,
> The rapture of repose that 's there,"

illustrate a fact which has always been noticed by observant persons, that the face of the recent dead often wears an aspect of happiness and peace. My father's expression was observed by all who saw him, and could not escape notice. It was indeed one of triumphant joy. Southey, in his Life of Cowper, says, quoting from a relation of the circumstances of his death, by Mr. Johnson: "From that moment until the coffin was closed, the expression with which his countenance had settled, was that of calmness and composure, mingled, as it were, with holy surprise." Such a circumstance could not but suggest to the friends of Cowper, that the worn and wearied sufferer had discovered, as soon as death's kind hand opened to him the door of life, that there was a sun which could scatter the dark clouds that had enwrapt him with utter desolation. But my father's expression was entirely different. There was no surprise; but there was, I repeat, triumph. It was the look of one who had prevailed in a great controversy. It was that which he might have worn when he exhibited to a jury indisputable evidence of some great fact which he had asserted, and others had denied. His face was always expressive, but never more distinctly and strongly expressive than at that time. I shall never forget it, for the whole scene is as distinctly before me now as if it were but of yesterday. I am well aware how easily imagination deludes at such a moment, and should not venture to state such an impression if it were my own only. But many saw him, and saw in his countenance the same meaning; and, for them as well as for myself, I would say, that if that expression could have found utterance, it would have been in words like these: "See there the proof. I have believed; and when I could not believe, I have hoped; and through all objection, uncertainty, and despondency, I have kept my belief and my hope. And now, THERE IS THE PROOF THAT I WAS RIGHT."

APPENDIX.

NOTE.

In the course of the preceding Memoir, I have said of several papers, that they would be inserted in the Appendix. I regret here to say that the space already occupied compels me to omit many of them. The principal of these are the letters of my uncle, Theodore Parsons, written while he was attached as surgeon to the army, and my father's Memorial to the Legislature concerning Harvard College.

APPENDIX.

No. I.

ESSEX RESULT.

Result of the Convention of Delegates holden at Ipswich in the County of Essex, who were Deputed to take into Consideration the Constitution and Form of Government proposed by the Convention of the State of Massachusetts-Bay. Newbury-Port: Printed and Sold by John Mycall. 1778.

In Convention of Delegates from the several towns of Lynn, Salem, Danvers, Wenham, Manchester, Gloucester, Ipswich, Newbury-Port, Salisbury, Methuen, Boxford, & Topsfield, holden by adjournment at Ipswich, on the twenty-ninth day of April, one thousand seven hundred & seventy-eight.

Peter Coffin Esq; in the Chair.

The Constitution and form of Government framed by the Convention of this State, was read paragraph by paragraph, and after debate, the following votes were passed.

1. That the present situation of this State renders it best, that the framing of a Constitution therefor, should be postponed 'till the public affairs are in a more peaceable and settled condition.

2. That a bill of rights, clearly ascertaining and defining the rights of conscience, and that security of person and property, which every member in the State hath a right to expect from the supreme power thereof, ought to be settled and established, previous to the ratification of any constitution for the State.

3. That the executive power in any State, ought not to have any share or voice in the legislative power in framing the laws,

and therefore, that the second article of the Constitution is liable to exception.

4. That any man who is chosen Governor, ought to be properly qualified in point of property — that the qualification therefor, mentioned in the third article of the Constitution, is not sufficient — nor is the same qualification directed to be ascertained on fixed principles, as it ought to be, on account of the fluctuation of the nominal value of money, and of property.

5. That in every free Republican Government, where the legislative power is rested in an house or houses of representatives, all the members of the State ought to be equally represented.

6. That the mode of representation proposed in the sixth article of the constitution, is not so equal a representation as can reasonably be devised.

7. That therefore the mode of representation in said sixth article is exceptionable.

8. That the representation proposed in said article is also exceptionable, as it will produce an unwieldy assembly.

9. That the mode of election of Senators pointed out in the Constitution is exceptionable.

10. That the rights of conscience, and the security of person and property each member of the State is entitled to, are not ascertained and defined in the Constitution, with a precision sufficient to limit the legislative power — and therefore, that the thirteenth article of the constitution is exceptionable.

11. That the fifteenth article is exceptionable, because the numbers that constitute a quorum in the House of Representatives and Senate, are too small.

12. That the seventeenth article of the constitution is exceptionable, because the supreme executive officer is not vested with proper authority — and because an independence between the executive and legislative body is not preserved.

13. That the nineteenth article is exceptionable, because a due independence is not kept up between the supreme legislative, judicial, and executive powers, nor between any two of them.

14. That the twentieth article is exceptionable, because the supreme executive officer hath a voice, and must be present in that Court, which alone hath authority to try impeachments.

15. That the twenty second article is exceptionable, because

the supreme executive power is not preserved distinct from, and independent of, the supreme legislative power.

16. That the twenty third article is exceptionable, because the power of granting pardons is not solely vested in the supreme executive power of the State.

17. That the twenty eighth article is exceptionable, because the delegates for the Continental Congress may be elected by the House of Representatives, when all the Senators may vote against the election of those who are delegated.

18. That the thirty fourth article is exceptionable, because the rights of conscience are not therein clearly defined and ascertained; and further, because the free exercise and enjoyment of religious worship is there said to be *allowed* to all the protestants in the State, when in fact, that free exercise and enjoyment is the natural and uncontroulable right of every member of the State.

A committee was then appointed to attempt the ascertaining of the true principles of government, applicable to the territory of the Massachusetts-Bay; to state the non-conformity of the constitution proposed by the Convention of this State to those principles, and to delineate the general outlines of a constitution conformable thereto; and to report the same to this Body.

This Convention was then adjourned to the twelfth day of May next, to be holden at Ipswich.

The Convention met pursuant to adjournment, and their committee presented the following report.

The committee appointed by this Convention at their last adjournment, have proceeded upon the service assigned them. With diffidence have they undertaken the several parts of their duty, and the manner in which they have executed them, they submit to the candor of this Body. When they considered of what vast consequence, the forming of a Constitution is to the members of this State, the length of time that is necessary to canvass and digest any proposed plan of government, before the establishment of it, and the consummate coolness, and solemn deliberation which should attend, not only those gentlemen who have, reposed in them, the important trust of delineating the several lines in which the various powers of government are to move, but also all those, who are to form an opinion of the execution of that trust, your committee must be excused when they express a surprise and regret, that so short a time is allowed the freemen inhabiting the territory of the Massachusetts-Bay, to revise and comprehend the form of government proposed to them by the convention of this State, to compare it with those principles on which every free government ought to be founded, and to ascertain it's conformity or non-conformity thereto. All this is necessary to be done, before a true opinion of it's merit or demerit can be formed. This opinion is to be certified within a time which, in our apprehension, is much too short for this purpose, and to be certified by a people who, during that time, have had and will have their minds perplexed and oppressed with a variety of public cares. The committee also beg leave to observe, that the constitution proposed for public approbation, was formed by gentlemen, who, at the same time, had a large share in conducting an important war, and who were employed in carrying into execution almost all the various powers of government.

The committee however proceeded in attempting the task assigned them, and the success of that attempt is now reported.

The reason and understanding of mankind, as well as the experience of all ages, confirm the truth of this proposition, that the benefits resulting to individuals from a free government, conduce much more to their happiness, than the retaining of all their natural rights in a state of nature. These benefits are greater or less, as the form of government, and the mode of exercising the supreme power of the State, are more or less conformable to those principles of equal impartial liberty, which is the property of all men from their birth as the gift of their Creator, compared with the manners and genius of the people, their occupations, customs, modes of thinking, situation, extent of country, and numbers. If the constitution and form of government are wholly repugnant to those principles, wretched are the subjects of that State. They have surrendered a portion of their natural rights, the enjoyment of which was in some degree a blessing, and the consequence is, they find themselves stripped of the remainder. As an anodyne to compose the spirits of these slaves, and to lull them into a passively obedient state, they are told, that tyranny is preferable to no government at all; a proposition which is to be doubted, unless considered under some limitation. Surely a state of nature is more excellent than that, in which men are meanly submissive to the haughty will of an imperious tyrant, whose savage passions are not bounded by the laws of reason, religion, honor, or a regard to his subjects, and the point to which all his movements center, is the gratification of a brutal appetite. As in a state of nature much happiness cannot be enjoyed by individuals, so it has been conformable to the inclinations of almost all men, to enter into a political society so constituted, as to remove the inconveniences they were obliged to submit to in their former state, and, at the same time, to retain all those natural rights, the enjoyment of which would be consistent with the nature of a free government, and the necessary subordination to the supreme power of the state.

To determine what form of government, in any given case, will produce the greatest possible happiness to the subject, is an arduous task, not to be compassed perhaps by any human powers. Some of the greatest geniuses and most learned philosophers of all ages, impelled by their sollicitude to promote the happiness of mankind, have nobly dared to attempt it: and their labours have crowned them with immortality. A Solon, a Lycurgus of Greece, a Numa of Rome are remembered with honor, when the wide extended empires of succeeding tyrants, are hardly important enough to be faintly sketched out on the map, while their superb thrones have long since crumbled into dust. The man who alone undertakes to form a constitution, ought to be an unimpassioned being; one enlightened mind; biassed neither by the lust of power, the allurements of pleasure, nor the glitter of wealth; perfectly acquainted with all the alienable and unalienable rights of mankind; possessed of this grand truth, that all men are born equally free, and that no man ought to surrender any part of his natural rights, without receiving the greatest possible equivalent; and influenced by the impartial principles of rectitude and justice, without partiality for, or prejudice against the interest or professions of any individuals or class of men. He ought also to be master of the histories of all the empires and states which are now existing, and all those which have figured in antiquity, and thereby able to collect and blend their respective excellencies, and avoid those defects which experience hath pointed out. Rousseau, a learned foreigner, a citizen of Geneva, sensible of the importance and difficulty of the subject, thought it impossible for any body of people, to form a free and equal constitution for themselves, in which, every individual should have equal justice done him, and be permitted to enjoy a share of power in the state, equal to what should be enjoyed by any other. Each individual, said he, will struggle, not only to retain all his own natural rights, but to acquire a controul over those of others. Fraud, circumvention, and an union of interest of some classes of people, combined with an inattention to the rights of posterity, will prevail over the principles of equity, justice, and good policy. The Genevans, perhaps the most virtuous republicans now existing, thought like Rousseau. They called the celebrated Calvin to their assistance. He came, and, by their gratitude, have they embalmed his memory.

The freemen inhabiting the territory of the Massachusetts-Bay are now forming a political society for themselves. Perhaps their situation is more favorable in some respects, for erecting a free government, than any other people were ever favored with. That attachment to old forms, which usually embarrasses, has not place amongst them. They have the history and experience of all States before them. Mankind have been toiling through ages for their information; and the philosophers and learned men of antiquity have trimmed their midnight lamps, to transmit to them instruction. We live also in an age, when the principles of political liberty, and the foundation of governments, have been freely canvassed, and fairly settled. Yet some difficulties we have to encounter. Not content with removing our attachment to the old government, perhaps we have contracted a prejudice against some part of it without foundation. The idea of liberty has been held up in so dazzling colours, that some of us may not be willing to submit to that subordination necessary in the freest States. Perhaps we may say further, that we do not consider ourselves united as brothers, with an united interest, but have fancied a clashing of interests amongst the various classes of men, and have acquired a thirst of power, and a wish of domination, over some of the community. We are contending for freedom —— Let us all be equally free — It is possible, and it is just. Our interests when candidly considered are one. Let us have a constitution founded, not upon party or prejudice — not one for to-day or to-morrow — but for posterity. Let *Esto perpetua* be it's motto. If it is founded in good policy; it will be founded in justice and honesty. Let all ambitious and interested views be discarded, and let regard be had only to the good of the whole, in which the situation and rights of posterity must be considered: and let equal justice be done to all the members of the community; and we thereby imitate our common father, who at our births, dispersed his favors, not only with a liberal, but with an equal hand.

Was it asked, what is the best form of government for the people of the Massachusetts-Bay? we confess it would be a question of infinite importance: and the man who could truly answer it, would merit a statue of gold to his memory, and his fame would be recorded in the annals of late posterity, with unrivalled lustre. The question, however, must be answered, and let it have the best answer we can possibly give it. Was a man to mention a despotic government, his life would be a just forfeit to the resentments of an affronted people. Was he to hint monarchy, he would deservedly be hissed off the stage, and consigned to infamy. A republican form is the only one consonant to the feelings of the generous and brave Americans. Let us now attend to those principles, upon which all republican governments, who boast any degree of political liberty, are founded, and which must enter into the spirit of a FREE republican constitution. For all republics are not FREE.

All men are born equally free. The rights they possess at their births are equal, and of the same kind. Some of those rights are alienable, and may be parted with for an equivalent. Others are unalienable and inherent, and of that importance, that no equivalent can be received in exchange. Sometimes we shall mention the surrendering of a power to controul our natural rights, which perhaps is speaking with more precision, than when we use the expression of parting with natural rights—but the same thing is intended. Those rights which are unalienable, and of that importance, are called the rights of conscience. We have duties, for the discharge of which we are accountable to our Creator and benefactor, which no human power can cancel. What those duties are, is determinable by right reason, which may be, and is called, a well informed conscience. What this conscience dictates as our duty, is so; and that power which assumes a controul over it, is an usurper; for no consent can be pleaded to justify the controul, as any consent in this case is void. The alienation of some rights, in themselves alienable, may be also void, if the bargain is of that nature, that no equivalent can be received. Thus, if a man surrender all his alienable rights, without reserving a controul over the supreme power, or a right to resume in certain cases, the surrender is void, for he becomes a slave; and a slave can receive no equivalent. Common equity would set aside this bargain.

When men form themselves into society, and erect a body politic or State, they are to be considered as one moral whole, which is in possession of the supreme power of the State. This supreme power is composed of the powers of each individual collected together, and VOLUNTARILY parted with by him. No individual, in this case, parts with his unalienable rights, the supreme power therefore cannot controul them. Each individual also surrenders the power of controuling his natural alienable rights, ONLY WHEN THE GOOD OF THE WHOLE REQUIRES it. The supreme power therefore can do nothing but what is for the good of the whole; and when it goes beyond this line, it is a power usurped. If the individual receives an equivalent for the right of controul he has parted with, the surrender of that right is valid; if he receives no equivalent, the surrender is void, and the supreme power as it respects him is an usurper. If the supreme power is so directed and executed that he does not enjoy political liberty, it is an illegal power, and he is not bound to obey. Political liberty is by some defined, a liberty of doing whatever is not prohibited by law. The definition is erroneous. A tyrant may govern by laws. The republics of Venice and Holland govern by laws, yet those republics have degenerated into insupportable tyrannies. Let it be thus defined; political liberty is the right every man in the state has, to do whatever is not prohibited by laws, TO WHICH HE HAS GIVEN HIS CONSENT. This definition is in unison with the feelings of a free people. But to return—If a fundamental principle on which each individual enters into society is, that he shall be bound by no laws but those to which he has consented, he cannot be considered as consenting to any law enacted by a minority: for he parts with the power of controuling his natural rights, only when the good of the whole requires it; and of this there can be but one absolute judge in the State. If the minority can assume the right of judging, there may then be two judges; for however large the minority may be, there must be another body still larger, who have the same claim, if not a better, to the right of absolute determination. If therefore the supreme power should be so modelled and exerted, that a law may be enacted by a minority, the inforcing of that law upon an individual who is opposed to it, is an act of tyranny. Further, as every individual, in entering into the society, parted with a power of controuling his natural rights equal to that parted with by any other, or in other words, as all the members of the society contributed an equal portion of their natural rights, towards the forming of the supreme power, so every member ought to receive equal benefit from, have equal influence in forming, and retain an equal controul over, the supreme power.

It has been observed, that each individual parts with the power of controuling his natural alienable rights, only when the good of the whole requires it; he therefore has remaining, after entering into political society, all his unalienable natural rights, and a part also of his alienable natural rights, provided the good of the whole does not require the sacrifice of them. Over the class of unalienable rights the supreme power hath no controul, and they ought to be clearly defined and ascertained in a BILL OF RIGHTS, previous to the ratification of any constitution. The bill of rights should also contain the equivalent every man receives, as a consideration for the rights he has surrendered. This equivalent consists principally in the security of his person and property, and is also unassailable by the supreme power: for if the equivalent is taken back, those natural rights which were parted with to purchase it, return to the original proprietor, as nothing is more true, than that ALLEGIANCE AND PROTECTION ARE RECIPROCAL.

The committee also proceeded to consider upon what principles, and in what manner, the supreme power of the state thus composed of the powers of the several individuals thereof, may be formed, modelled, and exerted in a republic, so that every member of the state may enjoy political liberty. This is called by some, *the ascertaining of the political law of the state.* Let it now be called *the forming of a constitution.*

The reason why the supreme governor of the world is a rightful and just governor, and entitled to the allegiance of the universe is, because he is infinitely good, wise, and powerful. His goodness prompts him to the best measures, his wisdom qualifies him to discern them, and his power to effect them. In a state likewise, the supreme power is best disposed of, when it is so modelled and balanced, and rested in such hands, that it has the greatest share of goodness, wisdom, and power, which is consistent with the lot of humanity.

That state, (other things being equal) which has reposed the supreme power in the hands of one or a small number of persons, is the most powerful state. An union, expedition, secrecy and dispatch are to be found only here. Where power is to be executed by a large number, there will not probably be either of the requisites just mentioned. Many men have various opinions: and each one will be tenacious of his own, as he thinks it preferable to any other; for when he thinks otherwise, it will cease to be his opinion. From this diversity of opinions results disunion; from disunion, a want of expedition and dispatch. And the larger the number to whom a secret is entrusted, the greater is the probability of it's disclosure. This inconvenience more fully strikes us when we consider that want of secrecy may prevent the successful execution of any measures, however excellently formed and digested.

But from a single person, or a very small number, we are not to expect that political honesty, and upright regard to the interest of the body of the people, and the civil rights of each individual, which are essential to a good and free constitution. For these qualities we are to go to the body of the people. The voice of the people is said to be the voice of God. No man will be so hardy and presumptuous, as to affirm the truth of that proposition in it's fullest extent. But if this is considered as the intent of it, that the people have always a disposition to promote their own happiness, and that when they have time to be informed, and the necessary means of information given them, they will be able to determine upon the necessary measures therefor, no man, of a tolerable acquaintance with mankind, will deny the truth of it. The inconvenience and difficulty in forming any free permanent constitution are, that such is the lot of humanity, the bulk of the people, whose happiness is principally to be consulted in forming a constitution, and in legislation, (as they include the majority) are so situated in life, and such are their laudable occupations, that they cannot have time for, nor the means of furnishing themselves with proper information, but must be indebted to some of their fellow subjects for the communication. Happy is the man, and blessings will attend his memory, who shall improve his leisure, and those abilities which heaven has indulged him with, in communicating that true information, and impartial knowledge, to his fellow subjects, which will insure their happiness. But the artful demagogue, who to gratify his ambition or avarice, shall, with the gloss of false patriotism, mislead his countrymen, and meanly snatch from them the golden glorious opportunity of forming a system of political and civil liberty, fraught with blessings for themselves, and remote posterity, what language can paint his demerit? The execrations of ages will be a punishment inadequate; and his name, though ever blackening as it rolls down the stream of time, will not catch its proper hue.

Yet, when we are forming a Constitution, by deductions that follow from established principles, (which is the only good method of forming one for futurity,) we are to look further than to the bulk of the people, for the greatest wisdom, firmness, consistency, and perseverance. These qualities will most probably be found amongst men of education and fortune. From such men we are to expect genius cultivated by reading, and all the various advantages and assistances, which art, and a liberal education aided by wealth, can furnish. From these result learning, a thorough knowledge of the interests of their country, when considered abstractedly, when compared with the neighbouring States, and when with those more remote, and an acquaintance with it's produce and manufacture, and it's exports and imports. All these are necessary to be known, in order to determine what is the true interest of any state; and without that interest is ascertained, impossible will it be to discover, whether a variety of certain laws may be beneficial or hurtful. From gentlemen whose private affairs compel them to take care of their own household, and deprive them of leisure, these qualifications are not to be generally expected, whatever class of men they are enrolled in.

Let all these respective excellencies be united. Let the supreme power be so disposed and ballanced, that the laws may have in view the interest of the whole; let them be wisely and consistently framed for that end, and firmly adhered to; and let them be executed with vigour and dispatch.

Before we proceed further, it must be again considered, and kept always in view, that we are not attempting to form a temporary constitution, one adjusted only to our present circumstances. We wish for one founded upon such principles as will secure to us freedom and happiness, however our circumstances may vary. One that will smile amidst the declensions of European and Asiatic empires, and survive the rude storms of time. It is not therefore to be understood, that all the men of fortune of the present day, are men of wisdom and learning, or that they are not. Nor that the bulk of the people, the farmers, the merchants, the tradesmen, and labourers, are all honest and upright, with single views to the public good, or that they are not. In each of the classes there are undoubtedly exceptions, as the rules laid down are general. The proposition is only this. That among gentlemen of education, fortune and leisure, we shall find the largest number of men, possessed of wisdom, learning, and a firmness and consistency of character. That among the bulk of the people, we shall find the greatest share of political honesty, probity, and a regard to the interest of the whole, of which they compose the majority. That wisdom and firmness are not sufficient without good intentions, nor the latter without the former. The conclusion is, let the legislative body unite them all. The former are called the excellencies that result from an aristocracy; the latter, those that result from a democracy.

The supreme power is considered as including the legislative, judicial, and executive powers. The nature and employment of these several powers deserve a distinct attention.

The legislative power is employed in making laws, or prescribing such rules of action to every individual in the state, as the good of the whole requires, to be conformed to by him in his conduct to the governors and governed, with respect both to their persons and property, according to the several relations he stands in. What rules of action the good of the whole requires, can be ascertained only by the majority, for a reason formerly mentioned. Therefore the legislative power must be so formed and exerted, that in prescribing any rule of action, or, in other words, enacting any law, the majority must consent. This may be more evident, when the fundamental condition on which every man enters into society, is considered. No man consented that his natural alienable rights should be wantonly controuled:

they were controulable, only when that controul should be subservient to the good of the whole; and that subserviency, from the very nature of government, can be determined but by one absolute judge. The minority cannot be that judge, because then there may be two judges opposed to each other, so that this subserviency remains undetermined. Now the enacting of a law, is only the exercise of this controul over the natural alienable rights of each member of the state; and therefore this law must have the consent of the majority, or be invalid, as being contrary to the fundamental condition of the original social contract. In a state of nature, every man had the sovereign controul over his own person. He might also have, in that state, a qualified property. Whatever lands or chattels he had acquired the peaceable possession of, were exclusively his, by right of occupancy or possession. For while they were unpossessed he had a right to them equally with any other man, and therefore could not be disturbed in his possession, without being injured; for no man could lawfully dispossess him, without having a better right, which no man had. Over this qualified property every man in a state of nature had also a sovereign controul. And in entering into political society, he surrendered this right of controul over his person and property, (with an exception to the rights of conscience) to the supreme legislative power, to be exercised by that power, *when the good of the whole demanded it.* This was all the right he could surrender, being all the alienable right of which he was possessed. The only objects of legislation therefore, are the person and property of the individuals which compose the state. If the law affects only the persons of the members, the consent of a majority of any members is sufficient. If the law affects the property only, the consent of those who hold a majority of the property is enough. If it affects, (as it will very frequently, if not always,) both the person and property, the consent of a majority of the members, and of those members also who hold a majority of the property, is necessary. If the consent of the latter is not obtained, their interest is taken from them against their consent, and their boasted security of property is vanished. Those who make the law, in this case give and grant what is not theirs. The law, in it's principles, becomes a second stamp act. Lord Chatham very finely ridiculed the British house of commons upon that principle.

"You can give and grant, said he, only your own. Here you give and grant, what? The property of the Americans." The people of the Massachusetts-Bay then thought his Lordship's ridicule well pointed. And would they be willing to merit the same? Certainly they will agree in the principle, should they mistake the application. The laws of the province of Massachusetts-Bay adopted the same principle, and very happily applied it. As the votes of proprietors of common and undivided lands in their meetings, can affect only their property, therefore it is enacted, that in ascertaining the majority, the votes shall be collected according to the respective interests of the proprietors. If each member, without regard to his property, has equal influence in legislation with any other, it follows, that some members enjoy greater benefits and powers in legislation than others, when these benefits and powers are compared with the rights parted with to purchase them. For the property-holder parts with the controul over his person, as well as he who hath no property, and the former also parts with the controul over his property, of which the latter is destitute. Therefore to constitute a perfect law in a free state, affecting the persons and property of the members, it is necessary that the law be for the good of the whole, which is to be determined by a majority of the members, and that majority should include those, who possess a major part of the property in the state.

The judicial power follows next after the legislative power; for it cannot act, until after laws are prescribed. Every wise legislator annexes a sanction to his laws, which is most commonly penal, (that is) a punishment either corporal or pecuniary, to be inflicted on the member who shall infringe them. It is the part of the judicial power (which in this territory has always been, and always ought to be, a court and jury) to ascertain the member who hath broken the law. Every man is to be presumed innocent, until the judicial power hath determined him guilty. When that decision is known, the law annexes the punishment, and the offender is turned over to the executive arm, by whom it is inflicted on him. The judicial power hath also to determine what legal contracts have been broken, and what member hath been injured by a violation of the law, to consider the damages that have been sustained, and to ascertain the recompense. The executive power takes care that this recompense is paid.

The executive power is sometimes divided into the external executive, and internal executive. The former comprehends war, peace, the sending and receiving ambassadors, and whatever concerns the transactions of the state with any other independent state. The confederation of the United States of America hath lopped off this branch of the executive, and placed it in Congress. We have therefore only to consider the internal executive power, which is employed in the peace, security and protection of the subject and his property, and in the defence of the state. The executive power is to marshal and command her militia and armies for her defence, to enforce the law, and to carry into execution all the orders of the legislative powers.

A little attention to the subject will convince us, that these three powers ought to be in different hands, and independent of one another, and so ballanced, and each having that check upon the other, that their independence shall be preserved — If the three powers are united, the government will be absolute, *whether these powers are in the hands of one or a large number.* The same party will be the legislator, accuser, judge and executioner; and what probability will an accused person have of an acquittal, however innocent he may be, when his judge will be also a party.

If the legislative and judicial powers are united, the maker of the law will also interpret it; and the law may then speak a language, dictated by the whims, the caprice, or the prejudice of the judge, with impunity to him — And what people are so unhappy as those, whose laws are uncertain. It will also be in the breast of the judge, when grasping after his prey, to make a retrospective law, which shall bring the unhappy offender within it; and this also he can do with impunity — The subject can have no peaceable remedy — The judge will try himself, and an acquittal is the certain consequence. He has it also in his power to enact any law, which may shelter him from deserved vengeance.

Should the executive and legislative powers be united, mischiefs the most terrible would follow. The executive would enact those laws it pleased to execute, and no others — The judicial power would be set aside as inconvenient and tardy — The security and protection of the subject would be a shadow — The executive power would make itself absolute, and the government end in a tyranny —— Lewis the eleventh of France, by cunning and treachery compleated the union of the executive and legislative powers of that kingdom, and upon that union established a system of tyranny. France was formerly under a free government.

The assembly or representatives of the united states of Holland, exercise the executive and legislative powers, and the government there is absolute.

Should the executive and judicial powers be united, the subject would then have no permanent security of his person and property. The executive power would interpret the laws and bend them to his will; and, as he is the judge, he may leap over them by artful constructions, and gratify, with impunity, the most rapacious passions. Perhaps no cause in any state has contributed more to promote internal convulsions, and to stain the scaffold with it's best blood, than this unhappy union. And it is an union which the executive power in all states, hath attempted to form: if that could not be compassed, to make the judicial power dependent upon it. Indeed the dependence of any of these powers upon either of the others, which in all states has always been attempted by one or the other of them, has so often been productive of such calamities, and of the shedding of such oceans of blood, that the page of history seems to be one continued tale of human wretchedness.

The following principles now seem to be established.

1. That the supreme power is limited, and cannot controul the unalienable rights of mankind, nor resume the equivalent (that is, the security of person and property) which each individual receives, as a consideration for the alienable rights he parted with in entering into political society.

2. That these unalienable rights, and this equivalent, are to be clearly defined and ascertained in a BILL OF RIGHTS, previous to the ratification of any constitution.

3. That the supreme power should be so formed and modelled, as to exert the greatest possible power, wisdom, and goodness.

4. That the legislative, judicial, and executive powers, are to be lodged in different hands, that each branch is to be independent, and further, to be so ballanced, and be able to exert such checks upon the others, as will preserve it from a dependence on, or an union with them.

5. That government can exert the greatest power when it's supreme authority is vested in the hands of one or a few.

6. That the laws will be made with the greatest wisdom, and best intentions, when men, of all the several classes in the state concur in the enacting of them.

7. That a government which is so constituted, that it cannot afford a degree of political liberty nearly equal to all it's members, is not founded upon principles of freedom and justice, and where any member enjoys no degree of political liberty, the government, so far as it respects him, is a tyranny, for he is controuled by laws to which he has never consented.

8. That the legislative power of a state hath no authority to controul the natural rights of any of it's members, unless the good of the whole requires it.

9. That a majority of the state is the only judge when the general good does require it.

10. That where the legislative power of the state is so formed, that a law may be enacted by the minority, each member of the state does not enjoy political liberty. And

11. That in a free government, a law affecting the person and property of it's members, is not valid, unless it has the consent of a majority of the members, which majority should include those, who hold a major part of the property in the state.

It may be necessary to proceed further, and notice some particular principles, which should be attended to in forming the three several powers in a free republican government.

The first important branch that comes under our consideration, is the legislative body. Was the number of the people so small, that the whole could meet together without inconvenience, the opinion of the majority would be more easily known. But, besides the inconvenience of assembling such numbers, no great advantages could follow. Sixty thousand people could not discuss with candor, and determine with deliberation. Tumults, riots, and murder would be the result. But the impracticability of forming such an assembly, renders it needless to make any further observations. The opinions and consent of the majority must be collected from persons, delegated by every freeman of the state for that purpose. Every freeman, who hath sufficient discretion, should have a voice in the election of his legislators. To speak with precision, in every free state where the power of legislation is lodged in the hands of one or more bodies of representatives elected for that purpose, the person of every member of the state, and all the property in it, ought to be represented, because they are objects of legislation. All the members of the state are qualified to make the election, unless they have not sufficient discretion, or are so situated as to have no wills of their own; persons not twenty one years old are deemed of the former class, from their want of years and experience. The municipal law of this country will not trust them with the disposition of their lands, and consigns them to the care of their parents or guardians. Women what age soever they are of, are also considered as not having a sufficient acquired discretion; not from a deficiency in their mental powers, but from the natural tenderness and delicacy of their minds, their retired mode of life, and various domestic duties. These concurring, prevent that promiscuous intercourse with the world, which is necessary to qualify them for electors. Slaves are of the latter class and have no wills. But are slaves members of a free government? We feel the absurdity, and would to God, the situation of America and the tempers of it's inhabitants were such, that the slave-holder could not be found in the land.

The rights of representation should be so equally and impartially distributed, that the representatives should have the same views, and interests with the people at large. They should think, feel, and act like them, and in fine, should be an exact miniature of their constituents. They should be (if we may use the expression) the whole body politic, with all it's property, rights, and priviledges, reduced to a smaller scale, every part being diminished in just proportion. To pursue the metaphor. If in adjusting the representation of freemen, any ten are reduced into one, all the other tens should be alike reduced: or if any hundred should be reduced to one, all the other hundreds should have just the same reduction. The representation ought also to be so adjusted, that it should be the interest of the representatives at all times, to do justice, therefore equal interest among the people, should have equal interest among the body of representatives. The majority of the representatives should also represent a majority of the people, and the legislative body should be so constructed, that every law affecting property, should have the consent of those who hold a majority of the property. The law would then be determined to be for the good of the whole by the proper judge, the majority, and the necessary consent thereto would be obtained: and all the members of the State would enjoy political liberty, and an equal degree of it. If the scale to which the body politic is to be reduced, is but a little smaller than the original, or, in other words, if a small number of freemen should be reduced to one, that is, send one representative, the number of representatives would be too large for the public good. The expences of government would be enormous. The body would be too unwieldy to deliberate with candor and coolness. The variety of opinions and oppositions would irritate the passions. Parties would be formed and factions engendered. The members would list under the banners of their respective leaders: address and intrigue would conduct the debates, and the result would tend only to promote the ambition or interest of a particular party. Such has always been in some degree, the course and event of debates instituted and managed by a large multitude.

For these reasons, some foreign politicians have laid it down as a rule, that no body of men larger than a hundred, would transact business well: and Lord Chesterfield called the British house of commons a mere mob, because of the number of men which composed it.

Elections ought also to be free. No bribery, corruption, or undue influence should have place. They stifle the free voice of the people, corrupt their morals, and introduce a degeneracy of manners, a supineness of temper, and an inattention to their liberties, which pave the road for the approach of tyranny, in all it's frightful forms.

The man who buys an elector by his bribes, will sell him again, and reap a profit from the bargain; and he thereby becomes a dangerous member of society. The legislative body will hold the purse strings, and men will struggle for a place in that body to acquire a share of the public wealth. It has always been the case. Bribery will be attempted, and the laws will not prevent it. All states have enacted severe laws against it, and they have been ineffectual. The defect was in their forms of government. They were not so contrived, as to prevent the practicability of it. If a small corporation can place a man in the legislative body, to bribe will be easy and cheap. To bribe a large corporation would be difficult and expensive, if practicable. In Great-Britain, the representatives of their counties and great cities are freely elected. To bribe the electors there, is impracticable: and their representatives are the most upright and able statesmen in parliament. The small boroughs are bought by the ministry and opulent men; and their representatives are the mere tools of administration or faction. Let us take warning.

A further check upon bribery is, when the corrupter of a people knows not the electors. If delegates were first appointed by a number of corporations, who at a short day were to elect their representatives, these blood-hounds in a state would be at fault. They would not scent their game. Besides, the representatives would probably be much better men — they would be double refined.

But it may be said, the virtuous American would blast with indignation the man, who should proffer him a bribe. Let it now be admitted as a fact. We ask, will that always be the case? The most virtuous states have become vicious. The morals of all people, in all ages, have been shockingly corrupted. The rigidly virtuous Spartans, who banished the use of gold and silver, who gloried in their poverty for centuries, at last fell a prey to luxury and corruption. The Romans, whose intense love to their country astonishes a modern patriot, who fought the battles of the republic for three hundred years without pay, and who, as volunteers, extended her empire over Italy, were at last dissolved in luxury, courted the hand of bribery, and finally sold themselves as slaves, and prostrated their country to tyrants the most ignominious and brutal. Shall we alone boast an exemption from the general fate of mankind? Are our private and political virtues to be transmitted untainted from generation to generation, through a course of ages? Have we not already degenerated from the pure morals and disinterested patriotism of our ancestors? And are not our manners becoming soft and luxurious, and have not our vices began to shoot? Would one venture to prophecy, that in a century from this period, we shall be a corrupt luxurious people, perhaps the close of that century would stamp this prophecy with the title of history.

The rights of representation should also be held sacred and

inviolable, and for this purpose, representation should be fixed upon known and easy principles; and the constitution should make provision, that recourse should constantly be had to those principles within a very small period of years, to rectify the errors that will creep in through lapse of time, or alteration of situations. The want of fixed principles of government, and a stated regular recourse to them, have produced the dissolution of all states, whose constitutions have been transmitted to us by history.

But the legislative power must not be trusted with one assembly. A single assembly is frequently influenced by the vices, follies, passions, and prejudices of an individual. It is liable to be avaricious, and to exempt itself from the burdens it lays upon it's constituents. It is subject to ambition, and after a series of years, will be prompted to vote itself perpetual. The long parliament in England voted itself perpetual, and thereby, for a time, destroyed the political liberty of the subject. Holland was governed by one representative assembly annually elected. They afterwards voted themselves from annual to septennial; then for life; and finally exerted the power of filling up all vacancies, without application to their constituents. The government of Holland is now a tyranny *though a republic.*

The result of a single assembly will be hasty and indigested, and their judgments frequently absurd and inconsistent. There must be a second body to revise with coolness and wisdom, and to controul with firmness, independent upon the first, either for their creation, or existence. Yet the first must retain a right to a similar revision and controul over the second.

Let us now ascertain some particular principles which should be attended to, in forming the executive power.

When we recollect the nature and employment of this power, we find that it ought to be conducted with vigour and dispatch. It should be able to execute the laws without opposition, and to controul all the turbulent spirits in the state, who should infringe them. If the laws are not obeyed, the legislative power is vain, and the judicial is mere pageantry. As these laws, with their several sanctions, are the only securities of person and property, the members of the state can confide in, if they lie dormant through failure of execution, violence and oppression will erect their heads, and stalk unmolested through the land. The judicial power ought to discriminate the offender, as soon after the commission of the offence, as an impartial trial will admit; and the executive arm to inflict the punishment immediately after the criminal is ascertained. This would have an happy tendency to prevent crimes, as the commission of them would awaken the attendant idea of punishment; and the hope of an escape, which is often an inducement, would be cut off. The executive power ought therefore in these cases, to be exerted with union, vigour, and dispatch. Another duty of that power is to arrest offenders, to bring them to trial. This cannot often be done, unless secrecy and expedition are used. The want of these two requisites, will be more especially inconvenient in repressing treasons, and those more enormous offences which strike at the happiness, if not existence of the whole. Offenders of these classes do not act alone. Some number is necessary to the compleating of the crime. Cabals are formed with art, and secrecy presides over their councils; while measures the most fatal are the result, to be executed by desperation. On these men the thunder of the state should be hurled with rapidity; for if they hear it roll at a distance, their danger is over. When they gain intelligence of the process, they abscond, and wait a more favourable opportunity. If that is attended with difficulty, they destroy all the evidence of their guilt, brave government, and deride the justice and power of the state.

It has been observed likewise, that the executive power is to act as Captain-General, to marshal the militia and armies of the state, and, for her defence, to lead them on to battle. These armies should always be composed of the militia or body of the people. Standing armies are a tremendous curse to a state. In all periods in which they have existed, they have been the scourge of mankind. In this department, union, vigour, secrecy, and dispatch are more peculiarly necessary. Was one to propose a body of militia, over which two Generals, with equal authority, should have the command, he would be laughed at. Should one pretend, that the General should have no controul over his subordinate officers, either to remove them or to supply their posts, he would be pitied for his ignorance of the subject he was discussing. It is obviously necessary, that the man who calls the militia to action, and assumes the military controul over them in the field, should previously know the number of his men, their equipments and residence, and the talents and tempers of the several ranks of officers, and their respective departments in the state, that he may wisely determine to whom the necessary orders are to be issued. Regular and particular returns of these requisites should be frequently made. Let it be enquired, are these returns to be made only to the legislative body, or a branch of it, which necessarily moves slow? — Is the General to go to them for information? intreat them to remove an improper officer, and give him another they shall chuse? and in fine is he to supplicate his orders from them, and constantly walk where their leading-strings shall direct his steps? If so, where are the power and force of the militia — where the union — where the dispatch and profound secrecy? Or shall these returns be made to him? — when he may see with his own eyes — be his own judge of the merit, or demerit of his officers — discern their various talents and qualifications, and employ them as the service and defence of his country demand. Besides, the legislative body or a branch of it is local — they cannot therefore personally inform themselves of these facts, but must judge upon trust. The General's opinion will be founded upon his own observations — the officers and privates of the militia will act under his eye: and, if he has it in his power immediately to promote or disgrace them, they will be induced to noble exertions. It may further be observed here, that if the subordinate civil or military executive officers are appointed by the legislative body or a branch of it, the former will become dependent upon the latter, and the necessary independence of either the legislative or executive powers upon the other is wanting. The legislative power will have that undue influence over the executive which will amount to a controul, for the latter will be their creatures, and will fear their creators.

One further observation may be pertinent. Such is the temper of mankind, that each man will be too liable to introduce his own friends and connexions into office, without regarding the public interest. If one man or a small number appoint, their connexions will probably be introduced. If a large number appoint, all their connexions will receive the same favour. The smaller the number appointing, the more contracted are their connexions, and for that reason, there will be a greater probability of better officers, as the connexions of one man or a very small number can fill but a very few of the offices. When a small number of men have the power of appointment, or the management in any particular department, their conduct is accurately noticed. On any miscarriage or imprudence the public resentment lies with weight. All the eyes of the people are converted to a point, and produce that attention to their censure, and that fear of misbehaviour, which are the greatest security the state can have, of the wisdom and prudence of its servants. This observation will strike us, when we recollect that many a man will zealously promote an affair in a public assembly, of which he is but one of a large number, yet, at the same time, he would blush to be thought the sole author of it. For all these reasons, the supreme executive power should be rested in the hands of one or of a small number, who should have the appointment of all subordinate executive officers. Should the supreme executive officer be elected by the legislative body, there would be a dependence of the executive power upon the legislative. Should he be elected by the judicial body, there also would be a dependence. The people at large must therefore designate the person, to whom they will delegate this power. And upon the people, there ought to be a dependence of all the powers in government, for all the officers in the state are but the servants of the people.

We have not noticed the navy-department. The conducting of that department is indisputably in the supreme executive power: and we suppose, that all the observations respecting the Captain-General, apply to the Admiral.

We are next to fix upon some general rules which should govern us in forming the judicial power. This power is to be independent upon the executive and legislative. The judicial power should be a court and jury, or as they are commonly called, the Judges and jury. The jury are the peers or equals of every man, and are to try all facts. The province of the Judges is to preside in and regulate all trials, and ascertain the law. We shall only consider the appointment of the Judges. The same power which appoints them, ought not to have the power of removing them, not even for misbehavior. That conduct only would then be deemed misbehavior which was opposed to the will of the power removing. A removal in this case for proper reasons, would not be often attainable: for to remove a man from an office, because he is not properly qualified to discharge the duties of it, is a severe censure upon that man or body of men who appointed him — and mankind do not love to censure themselves. Whoever appoints the judges, they ought not to be removable at pleasure, for they will then feel a dependence upon that man or body of men who hath the power of removal. Nor ought they to be dependent upon either the executive or legislative power for their salaries; for if they are, that power on whom they are thus dependent, can starve them into a compliance. One of these two powers should appoint, and the other remove. The legislative will not probably appoint so good men as the executive, for reasons formerly mentioned. The former are composed of a large body of men who have a numerous train of friends and connexions, and they do not hazard their reputations, which the executive will. It has often been mentioned that where a large body of men are responsible for any measures, a regard to their reputations, and to the public opinion, will not prompt them to use that care and precaution, which such regard will prompt one or a few to make use of. Let one more observation be now introduced to confirm it. Every man has some friends and dependents who will endeavor to snatch him from the public hatred. One man has but a few comparatively, they are not numerous enough to protect him, and he falls a victim to his own misconduct. When measures are conducted by a large number, their friends and connexions are numerous and noisy — they are dispersed through the State — their clamors stifle the execrations of the people, whose groans cannot even be heard. But to resume, neither will the executive body be the most proper judge when to remove. If this body is judge, it must also be the accuser, or the legislative body, or a branch of it, must be — If the executive body complains, it will be both accuser and judge — If the complaint is preferred by the legislative body, or a branch of it, when the judges are appointed by the legislative body, then a body of men who were concerned in the appointment, must in most cases complain of the impropriety of their own appointment. Let therefore the judges be appointed by the executive body — let their salaries be independent — and let them hold their places during good behaviour — Let their misbehaviour be determinable by the legislative body — Let one branch thereof impeach, and the other judge. Upon these principles the judicial body will be independent so long as they behave well and a proper court is appointed to ascertain their mal-conduct.

The Committee afterwards proceeded to consider the Constitution framed by the Convention of this State. They have examined that Constitution with all the care the shortness of the time would admit. And they are compelled, though reluctantly to say, that some of the principles upon which it is founded, appeared to them inconsonant, not only to the natural rights of mankind, but to the fundamental condition of the original social contract, and the principles of a free republican government. In that form of government the governor appears to be the supreme executive officer, and the legislative power is in an house of representatives and senate. It may be necessary to descend to a more particular consideration of the several articles of that constitution.

The second article thereof appears exceptionable upon the principles we have already attempted to establish, because the supreme executive officer hath a seat and voice in one branch of the legislative body, and is assisting in originating and framing the laws, the Governor being entitled to a seat and voice in the Senate, and to preside in it, and may thereby have that influence in the legislative body, which the supreme executive officer ought not to have.

The third article among other things, ascertains the qualifications of the Governor, Lieutenant Governor, Senators and Representatives respecting property — The estate sufficient to qualify a man for Governor is so small, it is hardly any qualification at all. Further, the method of ascertaining the value of the estates of the officers aforesaid is vague and uncertain as it depends upon the nature and quantity of the currency, and the encrease of property, and not upon any fixed principles. This article therefore appears to be exceptionable.

The sixth article regulates the election of representatives. So many objections present themselves to this article, we are at a loss which first to mention. The representation is grossly unequal, and it is flagrantly unjust. It violates the fundamental principle of the original social contract, and introduces an unwieldy and expensive house. Representation ought to be equal upon the principles formerly mentioned. By this article any corporation, however small, may send one representative, while no corporation can send more than one, unless it has three hundred freemen. Twenty corporations (of three hundred freemen in each) containing in the whole six thousand freemen, may send forty representatives, when one corporation, which shall contain six thousand two hundred and twenty, can send but nineteen. One third of the state may send a majority of the representatives, and all the laws may be enacted by a minority — Do all the members of the state then, enjoy political liberty? Will they not be controuled by laws enacted against their consent? When we go further and find, that sixty members make an house, and that the concurrence of thirty one (which is about one twelfth of what may be the present number of representatives) is sufficient to bind the persons and properties of the members of the State, we stand amazed, and are sorry that any well disposed Americans were so inattentive to the consequences of such an arrangement.

The number of representatives is too large to debate with coolness and deliberation, the public business will be protracted to an undue length and the pay of the house is enormous. As the number of freemen in the state encreases, these inconveniences will encrease; and in a century, the house of representatives will, from their numbers, be a mere mob. Observations upon this article croud upon us, but we will dismiss it, with wishing that the mode of representation there proposed, may be candidly compared with the principles which have been already mentioned in the course of our observations upon the legislative power, and upon representation in a free republic.

The ninth article regulates the election of Senators, which we think exceptionable. As the Senators for each district will be elected by all the freemen in the state properly qualified, a trust is reposed in the people which they are unequal to. The freemen in the late province of Main, are to give in their votes for senators in the western district, and so, on the contrary. Is it supposeable that the freemen in the county of Lincoln can judge of the political merits of a senator in Berkshire? Must not the several corporations in the state, in a great measure depend upon their representatives for information? And will not the house of representatives in fact chuse the senators? That independence of the senate upon the house, which the constitution seems to have intended, is visionary, and the benefits which were expected to result from a senate, as one distinct branch of the legislative body, will not be discoverable.

The tenth article prescribes the method in which the Governor is to be elected. This method is open to, and will introduce bribery and corruption, and also originate parties and factions in the state. The Governor of Rhode-Island was formerly elected in this manner, and we all know how long a late Governor there, procured his re-election by methods the most unjustifiable. Bribery was attempted in an open and flagrant manner.

The thirteenth article ascertains the authority of the general court, and by that article we find their power is limited only by the several articles of the constitution. We do not find that the rights of conscience are ascertained and defined, unless they may be thought to be in the thirty fourth article. That article we conceive to be expressed in very loose and uncertain terms. What is a *religious* profession and worship of God, has been disputed for sixteen hundred years, and the various sects of christians have not yet settled the dispute. What is a free exercise and enjoyment of religious worship has been, and still is, a subject of much altercation. And this free exercise and enjoyment is said to be *allowed* to the protestants of this state by the constitution, when we suppose it to be an unalienable right of all mankind, which no human power can wrest from them. We do not find any bill of rights either accompanying the constitution, or interwoven with it, and no attempt is made to define and secure that protection of the person and property of the members of the state, which the legislative and executive bodies cannot withhold, unless the general words *of confirming the right to trial by jury*, should be considered as such definition and security. We think a bill of rights ascertaining and clearly describing the rights of conscience, and that security of person and property, the supreme power of the state is bound to afford to all the members thereof, ought to be fully ratified, before, or at the same time with, the establishment of any constitution.

The fifteenth article fixes the number which shall constitute a quorum in the senate and house of representatives — We think these numbers much too small — This constitution will immediately introduce about three hundred and sixty members into the house. If sixty make a quorum, the house may totally change its members six different times; and it probably will very often in the course of a long session, be composed of such a variety of members, as will retard the public business, and introduce confusion in the debates, and inconsistency in the result. Besides the number of members, whose concurrence is necessary to enact a law, is so small, that the subjects of the state will have no security, that the laws which are to controul their natural rights, have the consent of a majority of the freemen. The same reasoning applies to the senate, though not so strikingly, as a quorum of that body must consist of nearly a third of the senators.

The eighteenth article describes the several powers of the Governor or the supreme executive officer. We find in comparing the several articles of the constitution, that the senate are the only court to try impeachments. We also conceive that every officer in the state ought to be amenable to such court. We think therefore that the members of that court ought never to be advisory to any officer in the state. If their advice is the result of inattention or corruption, they cannot be brought to punishment by impeachment, as they will be their own judges. Neither will the officer who pursues their advice be often, if ever, punishable, for a similar reason. To condemn this officer will be to reprobate their own advice — consequently a proper body is not formed to advise the Governor, when a sudden emergency may render advice expedient: for the senate advise, and are the court to try impeachments. We would now make one further observation, that we cannot discover in this article or in any part of the constitution that the executive power is entrusted with a check upon the legislative power, sufficient to prevent the encroachment of the latter upon the former — Without this check the legislative power will exercise the executive, and in a series of years the government will be as absolute as that of Holland.

The nineteenth article regulates the appointment of the several classes of officers. And we find that almost all the officers are appointed by the Governor and Senate. An objection formerly made occurs here. The Senate with the Governor are the court to remove these officers for misbehaviour. Those officers, in general, who are guilty of male-conduct in the execution of their office, were improper men to be appointed. Sufficient care was not taken in ascertaining their political military or moral qualifications. Will the senators therefore if they appoint, be a proper court to remove. Will not a regard to their own characters have an undue bias upon them. This objection will grow stronger, if we may suppose that the time will come when a man may procure his appointment to office by bribery. The members of that court therefore who alone can remove for misbehaviour, should not be concerned in the appointment. Besides, if one branch of the legislative body appoint the executive officers, and the same branch alone can remove them, the legislative power will acquire an undue influence over the executive.

The twenty second article describes the authority the Governor shall have in all business to be transacted by him and the Senate. The Governor by this article must be present in conducting an impeachment. He has it therefore in his power to rescue a favourite from impeachment, so long as he is Governor, by absenting himself from the Senate, whenever the impeachment is to be brought forwards.

We cannot conceive upon what principles the twenty third article ascertains the speaker of the house to be one of the three, the majority of whom have the power of granting pardons. The speaker is an officer of one branch of the legislative body, and hourly depends upon them for his existence in that character — he therefore would not probably be disposed to offend any leading party in the house, by consenting to, or denying a pardon. An undue influence might prevail and the power of pardoning be improperly exercised. — When the speaker is guilty of this improper exercise, he cannot be punished but by impeachment, and as he is commonly a favourite of a considerable party in the house, it will be difficult to procure the accusation; for his party will support him.

The judges by the twenty fourth article are to hold their places during good behaviour, but we do not find that their salaries are any where directed to be fixed. The house of representatives may therefore starve them into a state of dependence.

The twenty-eighth article determines the mode of electing and removing the delegates for Congress. It is by joint ballot of the house and Senate. These delegates should be some of the best men in the State. Their abilities and characters should be thoroughly investigated. This will be more effectually done, if they are elected by the legislative body, each branch having a right to originate or negative the choice, and removal. And we cannot conceive why they should not be elected in this manner, as well as all officers who are annually appointed with annual grants of their sallaries, as is directed in the nineteenth article. By the mode of election now excepted against, the house may choose their delegates, altho' every Senator should vote against their choice.

The thirty-fourth article respecting liberty of conscience, we think exceptionable, but the observations necessary to be made thereon, were introduced in animadverting upon the thirteenth article.

The Committee have purposely been as concise as possible in their observations upon the Constitution proposed by the Convention of this State — Where they thought it was non-conformable to the principles of a free republican government, they have ventured to point out the non-conformity — Where they thought it was repugnant to the original social contract, they have taken the liberty to suggest that repugnance — And where they were persuaded it was founded in political injustice, they have dared to assert it.

The Committee, in obedience to the direction of this body, afterwards proceeded to delineate the general outlines of a Constitution, conformable to what have been already reported by them, as the principles of a free republican government, and as the natural rights of mankind.

They first attempted to delineate the legislative body. It has already been premised, that the legislative power is to be lodged in two bodies, composed of the representatives of the people. That representation ought to be equal. And that no law affecting the person and property of the members of the state ought to be enacted, without the consent of a majority of the members, and of those also who hold a major part of the property.

In forming the first body of legislators, let regard be had only to the representation of persons, not of property. This body we call the house of representatives. Ascertain the number of representatives. It ought not to be so large as will induce an enormous expence to government, nor too unwieldy to deliberate with coolness and attention; nor so small as to be unacquainted with the situation and circumstances of the state. One hundred will be large enough, and perhaps it may be too large. We are persuaded that any number of men exceeding that, cannot do business with such expedition and propriety a smaller number could. However let that at present be considered as the number. Let us have the number of freemen in the several counties in the state; and let these representatives be apportioned among the respective counties, in proportion to their number of freemen. The representation yet remains equal. Let the representatives for the several counties be elected in this manner. Let the several towns in the respective counties, the first wednesday in May annually, choose delegates to meet in county convention on the thursday next after the second wednesday in May annually, and there elect the representatives for the county—Let the number of delegates each town shall send to the county convention be regulated in this manner. Ascertain that town which hath the smallest number of freemen; and let that town send one. Suppose the smallest town contains fifty. All the other towns shall then send as many members as they have fifties. If after the fifties are deducted, there remains an odd number, and that number is twenty five, or more, let them send another, if less, let no notice be taken of it. We have taken a certain for an uncertain number. Here the representation is as equal as the situation of a large political society will admit. No qualification should be necessary for a representative, except residence in the county the two years preceeding his election, and the payment of taxes those years. Any freeman may be an elector who hath resided in the county the year preceeding. The same qualification is requisite for a delegate, that is required of a representative. The representatives are designed to represent the persons of the members, and therefore we do not consider a qualification in point of property necessary for them.

These representatives shall be returned from the several parts of the county in this manner—Each county convention shall divide the county into as many districts as they send representatives, by the following rule—As we have the number of freemen in the county, and the number of county representatives, by dividing the greater by the less we have the number of freemen entitled to send one representative. Then add as many adjoining towns together as contain that number of freemen, or as near as may be, and let those towns form one district, and proceed in this manner through the county. Let a representative be chosen out of each district, and let all the representatives be elected out of the members who compose the county convention. In this house we find a proportionate representation of persons. If a law passes this house it hath the consent of a majority of the freemen; and here we may look for political honesty, probity and upright intentions to the good of the whole. Let this house therefore originate money-bills, as they will not have that inducement to extravagant liberality which an house composed of opulent men would, as the former would feel more sensibly the consequences. This county convention hath other business to do, which shall be mentioned hereafter. We shall now only observe, that this convention, upon a proper summons, is to meet again, to supply all vacancies in it's representation, by electing other representatives out of the district in which the vacancy falls. The formation of the second body of legislators next came under consideration, which may be called the senate. In electing the members for this body, let the representation of property be attended to. The senators may be chosen most easily in a county convention, which may be called the senatorial convention. Ascertain the number of senators. Perhaps thirty three will be neither too large nor too small. Let seven more be added to the thirty three which will make forty — these seven will be wanted for another purpose to be mentioned hereafter — Apportion the whole number upon the several counties, in proportion to the state-tax each county pays. Each freeman of the state, who is possessed of a certain quantity of property, may be an elector of the senators. To ascertain the value of a man's estate by a valuation is exceedingly difficult if possible, unless he voluntarily returns a valuation — To ascertain it by oath would be laying snares for a man's conscience, and would be a needless multiplication of oaths if another method could be devised — To fix his property at any certain sum, would be vague and uncertain, such is the fluctuation of even the best currency, and such the continual alteration of the nominal value of property — Let the state-tax assessed on each freeman's estate decide it — That tax will generally bear a very just proportion to the nominal value of a currency, and of property. Let every freeman whose estate pays such a proportion of the state-tax that had been last assessed previous to his electing, as three pounds is to an hundred thousand pounds, be an elector — The senatorial convention may be composed of delegates from the several towns elected in this manner. Ascertain the town which contains the smallest number of freemen whose estates pay such tax, and ascertain that number. Suppose it to be thirty. Let that town send one, and let all the other towns in the county send as many delegates as they have thirties. If after the thirties are deducted, there remains an odd number, and that number is fifteen, or more, let them send another, if it is less than fifteen let no notice be taken of it. Let the delegates for the senatorial convention be chosen at the same time with the county delegates, and meet in convention the second wednesday in May annually, which is the day before the county convention is to meet — and let no county delegate be a senatorial delegate the same year — We have here a senate (deducting seven in the manner and for the purpose hereafter to be mentioned) which more peculiarly represents the property of the state; and no act will pass both branches of the legislative body, without having the consent of those members who hold a major part of the property of the state. In electing the senate in this manner, the representation will be as equal as the fluctuation of property will admit of, and it is an equal representation of property so far as the number of senators is proportioned among the several counties. Such is the distribution of intestate estates in this country, the inequality between the estates of the bulk of the property holders is so inconsiderable, and the tax necessary to qualify a man to be an elector of a senator is so moderate, it may be demonstrated, that a law which passes both branches will have the consent of those persons who hold a majority of the property in the state. No freeman should be a delegate for the senatorial convention unless his estate pays the same tax which was necessary to qualify him to elect delegates for that convention; and no freeman shall be an elector of a delegate for that convention, nor a delegate therefor, unless he has been an inhabitant of the county for the two years next preceeding. No person shall be capable of an election into the senate unless he has been an inhabitant of the county for three years next preceeding his election — His qualification in point of estate is also to be considered. Let the state tax which was assessed upon his estate for the three years next preceeding his election be upon an average, at the rate of six pounds in an hundred thousand annually.

This will be all the duty of the senatorial convention unless there should be a vacancy in the senate when it will be again convened to fill up the vacancy. These two bodies will have the execution of the legislative power; and they are composed of the necessary members to make a just proportion of taxes among the several counties. This is all the discretionary power they will have in apportioning the taxes.

Once in five years at least, the legislative body shall make a valuation for the several counties in the State, and at the same time each county shall make a county valuation, by a county convention chosen for that purpose only, by the same rules which the legislative body observed in making the State valuation — and whenever a State valuation is made, let the several county valuations be also made. The legislative body after they have proportioned the State tax among the several counties, shall also proportion the tax among the several plantations and towns, agreeably to the county valuation, to be filed in the records of the General Court for that purpose. It may be observed that this county valuation will be taken and adjusted in county convention, in which persons only are to be equally represented: and it may also be objected that property ought also to be represented for this purpose. It is answered that each man in the county will pay at least a poll tax, and therefore ought to be represented in this convention — that it is impracticable in one convention to have persons and property both represented, with any degree of equality, without grèat intricacy — and that, where both cannot be represented without great intricacy, the representation of property should yield the preference to that of persons. The counties ought not to be compelled to pay their own representatives — if so, the counties remote from the seat of government would be at a greater charge than the other counties, which would be unjust — for they have only an equal influence in legislation with the other counties, yet they cannot use that influence but at a greater expence —— They therefore labor under greater disadvantages in the enjoyment of their political liberties, than the other counties. If the remote counties enjoyed a larger proportional influence in legislation than the other counties, it would be just they should pay their own members, for the enhanced expence would tend to check this inequality of representation.

All the representatives should attend the house, if possible, and all the senators the senate. A change of faces in the course of a session retards and perplexes the public business. No man should accept of a seat in the legislative body without he intends a constant attendance upon his duty. Unavoidable accidents, necessary private business, sickness and death may, and will prevent a general attendance: but the numbers requisite to constitute a quorum of the house and senate should be so large as to admit of the absence of members, only for the reasons aforesaid. If members declined to attend their duty they should be expelled, and others chosen who would do better. Let seventy five constitute a quorum of the house, and twenty four of the senate. However no law ought to be enacted at any time, unless it has the concurrence of fifty one representatives, and seventeen senators.

We have now the legislative body (deducting seven of the senators.) Each branch hath a negative upon the other — and either branch may originate any bill or propose any amendment, except a money bill, which should be concurred or nonconcurred by the senate in the whole. The legislative body is so formed and ballanced that the laws will be made with the greatest wisdom and the best intentions; and the proper consent thereto is obtained. Each man enjoys political liberty, and his civil rights will be taken care of. And all orders of men are interested in government, will put confidence in it, and struggle for it's support. As the county and senatorial delegates are chosen the same day throughout the State, as all the county conventions are held at the same time, and all the senatorial conventions on one day, and as these delegates are formed into conventions on a short day after their election, elections will be free, bribery will be impracticable, and party and factions will not be formed. As the senatorial conventions are held the day before the county conventions, the latter will have notice of the persons elected senators, and will not return them as representatives — The senatorial convention should after it's first election of senators be adjourned without day, but not dissolved, and to be occasionally called together by the supreme executive officer to keep the senate full, should a senator elected decline the office, or afterwards resign, be expelled, or die. The county convention in the same way are to keep the representation full, and also supply all vacancies in the offices they will be authorised to appoint to and elect as will be presently mentioned. By making provision in the constitution that recourse be had to these principles of representation every twenty years, by taking new lists of the freemen for that purpose, and by a new distribution of the number of representatives agreeably thereto, and of the senators in proportion to the State tax, representation will be always free and equal. These principles easily accommodate themselves to the erection of new counties and towns. Crude and hasty determinations of the house will be revised or controuled by the senate ; and those views of the senate which may arise from ambition or a disregard to civil liberty will be frustrated. Government will acquire a dignity and firmness, which is the greatest security of the subject : while the people look on, and observe the conduct of their servants, and continue or withdraw their favour annually, according to their merit or demerit.

The forming of the executive power came next in course. Every freeman in the State should have a voice in this formation ; for as the executive power hath no controul over property, but in pursuance of established laws, the consent of the property-holders need not be considered as necessary. Let the head of the executive power be a Governor (or in his absence, or on his death, a Lieutenant Governor) and let him be elected in the several county conventions by ballot, on the same day the representatives are chosen. Let a return be made by each man fixed upon by the several conventions, and the man who is returned by any county shall be considered as having as many votes, as that county sends representatives. Therefore the whole number of votes will be one hundred. He who hath fifty one or more votes is Governor. Let the Lieutenant-Governor be designated in the same way. This head of the supreme executive power should have a privy council, or a small select number (suppose seven) to advise with. Let him not chuse them himself — for he might then, if wickedly disposed, elect no persons who had integrity enough to controul him by their advice. Let the legislative body elect them in this manner. The house shall chuse by ballot seven out of the senate. These shall be a privy council, four of whom shall constitute a quorum. Let the Governor alone marshal the militia, and regulate the same, together with the navy, and appoint all their officers, and remove them at pleasure. The temper, use, and end of a militia and navy require it. He should likewise command the navy and militia, and have power to march the latter any where within the state. Was this territory so situated, that the militia could not be marched out of it, without entering an enemy's country, he should have no power to march them out of the state. But the late province of Main militia must march through New-Hampshire to enter Massachusetts, and so, on the contrary. The neighbouring states are all friends and allies, united by a perpetual confederacy. Should Providence or Portsmouth be attacked suddenly, a day's delay might be of most pernicious consequence. Was the consent of the legislative body, or a branch of it, necessary, a longer delay would be unavoidable. Still the Governor should be under a controul. Let him march the militia without the state with the advice of his privy council, and his authority be continued for ten days and no longer, unless the legislative body in the mean time prolong it. In these ten days he may convene the legislative body, and take their opinion. If his authority is not continued, the legislative body may controul him, and order the militia back. If his conduct is disapproved, his reputation, and that of his advisers is ruined. He will never venture on the measure, unless the general good requires it, and then he will be applauded. Remember the election of Governor and council is annual. But the legislative body must have a check upon the Captain General. He is best qualified to appoint his subordinate officers, but he may appoint improper ones — He has the sword, and may wish to form cabals amongst his officers to perpetuate his power — The legislative body should therefore have a power of removing any militia officer at pleasure — Each branch should have this power. The Captain General will then be effectually controuled. The Governor with his privy council may also appoint the following executive officers, viz The attorney General and the justices of the peace, who shall hold their places during good behaviour — This misbehaviour shall be determined by the senate on impeachment of the house. On this scheme a mutual check is thus far preserved in both the powers. The supreme executive officer as he is annually removeable by the people, will for that, and the other reasons formerly mentioned, probably appoint the best officers: and when he does otherwise the legislative power will remove them. The militia officers which are solely appointed, and removeable at pleasure, by the Governor, are removeable at pleasure by either branch of the legislative. Those executive officers which are removeable only for misbehaviour, the consent of the privy council, chosen by the legislative body, is first necessary to their appointment, and afterwards they are removeable by the senate, on impeachment of the house. We now want only to give the executive power a check upon the legislative, to prevent the latter from encroaching on the former, and stripping it of all it's rights. The legislative in all states hath attempted it where this check was wanting, and have prevailed, and the freedom of the state was thereby destroyed. This attempt hath resulted from that lust of domination, which in some degree influences all men, and all bodies of men. The Governor therefore with the consent of the privy council, may negative any law, proposed to be enacted by the legislative body. The advantages which will attend the due use of this negative are, that thereby the executive power will be preserved entire — the encroachments of the legislative will be repelled, and the powers of both be properly balanced. All the business of the legislative body will be brought into one point, and subject to an impartial consideration on a regular consistent plan. As the Governor will have it in charge to state the situation of the government to the legislative body at the opening of every session, as far as his information will qualify him therefor, he will now know officially, all that has been done, with what design the laws were enacted, how far they have answered the proposed end, and what still remains to compleat the intention of the legislative body. The reasons why he will not make an improper use of his negative are — his annual election — the annual election of the privy council, by and out of the legislative body — His political character and honour are at stake — If he makes a proper use of his negative by preserving the executive powers entire, by pointing out any mistake in the laws which may escape any body of men through inattention, he will have the smiles of the people. If on the contrary, he makes an improper use of his negative, and wantonly opposes a law that is for the public good, his reputation, and that of his privy council are forfeited, and they are disgracefully tumbled from their seats. This Governor is not appointed by a King, or his ministry, nor does he receive instructions from a party of men, who are pursuing an interest diametrically opposite to the good of the state. His interest is the same with that of every man in the state; and he knows he must soon return, and sink to a level with the rest of the community.

The danger is, he will be too cautious of using his negative for the interest of the state. His fear of offending may prompt him, if he is a timid man, to yield up some parts of the executive power. The Governor should be thus qualified for his office — He shall have been an inhabitant of the state for four years next preceeding his election, and paid public taxes those years — Let the state tax assessed upon his estate those years be, upon an average, at the rate of sixteen pounds in an hundred thousand annually.

The Lieutenant Governor should have the same qualifications that are required from the Governor. In the absence out of the state of the Governor and Lieutenant Governor, or on their deaths, or while an impeachment is pending against them, or in case neither should be chosen at the annual election, let the executive power devolve upon the privy council until the office is again filled. By ascertaining in this way the qualification required from the Governor in point of property, and from the other servants of the state of whom a qualification in point of property is required, that ambition which prompts a man to aspire to any of these offices or places will benefit the state as the public tax he pays will be one criterion of his qualification. By electing the Governor in this manner, he hath the major voice of the people, and bribery or undue influence is impracticable. The privy council have also the major voice of the people, as they are chosen by a majority of the representatives: they are also selected from the senate, which it is to be presumed, will be composed of some of the best men in the state. As a further security against any inconveniency resulting from the length of time a Governor may hold the chair, no man ought to be a Governor more than three years in any six. There ought also, as soon as the circumstances of the state will admit of it, to be a gradation of officers, to qualify men for their respective departments — a rotation also of the senators will prevent any undue influence a man may acquire, by the long possession of an important office. After a period of six years let the following rules be observed. Let no man be eligible as Governor, (or Lieutenant Governor) unless he has had a seat in the senate or privy council for two years, or hath formerly been Governor or Lieutenant Governor. Let no man be eligible as senator, unless he had a seat in the house, senate, or privy council, the preceeding year — And let one fourth of the senate (which for this purpose is to include the privy council) be annually made ineligible to that rank, for two years; and let this fourth part be ascertained by lot. This lot, together with the provisions just mentioned, will introduce a rotation in the chair, privy council, senate and house: and the state will have a sufficient number of it's members qualified for these important offices, by the gradation established. These servants of the state should have competent and honourable stipends; not so large, as will enable them to raise a fortune at the expence of the industrious classes of the people; nor so small, that a man must injure his estate by serving the public. An inadequate salary would exclude from service, all but the vainly ambitious; and the ambitious man will endeavour to repay himself by attempting measures which will hazard the constitution. These stipends should be paid out of the public treasury, and the Governor's should be made certain upon fixed principles, otherwise the legislative body could starve him into a state of dependence.

There still remain some other officers to be elected —— Let the legislative body choose the delegates for Congress, and the Receiver General and Commissary General, and let each branch have a right to originate or negative the choice.

Let the following officers, who may be considered as county officers, be thus elected — Let each county convention every three years choose the Sheriff, Coroners, and county Registers; and let that convention annually choose a county Treasurer, and a deputy Attorney General, to prosecute on behalf of the state at the court of sessions, in the absence of the Attorney General.

Let us also consider in whose hands the power of pardoning should be lodged. If the legislative body or a branch of it are entrusted with it, the same body which made or were concerned in making the law, will excuse the breach of it. This body is so numerous that most offenders will have some relation or connexion with some of it's members, undue influence for that reason may take place, and if a pardon should be issued improperly, the public blame will fall upon such members, it would not have the weight of a feather; and no conviction upon an impeachment could follow — The house would not impeach themselves, and the senators would not condemn the senate. If this power of pardoning is lodged with the Governor and privy council, the number is so small, that all can personally inform themselves of the facts, and misinformation will be detected. Their own reputation would guard them against undue influence, for the censure of the people will hang on their necks with the weight of a mill-stone — And impeachments will stare them in the face, and conviction strike them with terror. Let the power of pardoning be therefore lodged with the Governor and privy council.

The right of convening, adjourning, proroguing, and dissolving the legislative body deserves consideration. The constitution will make provision for their convention on the last wednesday in May annually. Let each branch of the legislative, have power to adjourn itself for two days — Let the legislative body have power to adjourn or prorogue itself to any time within the year. Let the Governor and privy council have authority to convene them at pleasure, when the public business calls for it, for the assembling of the legislative body may often be necessary, previous to the day to which that body had adjourned or prorogued itself, as the legislative body when dispersed cannot assemble itself. And to prevent any attempts of their voting a continuance of their political existence, let the constitution make provision, that some time in every year, on or before the wednesday preceeding the last wednesday in May, the Governor shall dissolve them. Before that day, he shall not have power to do it, without their consent.

As the principles which should govern in forming the judicial power have been already mentioned, a few observations only, are necessary to apply those principles.

Let the judges of the common law courts, of the admiralty, and probate, and the register of probate, be appointed by the

Governor and privy council; let the stipends of these judges be fixed; and let all those officers be removeable only for misbehaviour. Let the senate be the judge of that misbehaviour, on impeachment of the house.

The committee have now compleated the general out lines of a constitution, which they suppose may be conformable to the principles of a free republican government — They have not attempted the description of the less important parts of a constitution, as they naturally and obviously are determinable by attention to those principles — Neither do they exhibit these general out lines, as the only ones which can be consonant to the natural rights of mankind, to the fundamental terms of the original social contract, and to the principles of political justice; for they do not assume to themselves infallibility. To compleat the task assigned them by this body, this constitution is held up in a general view, to convince us of the practicability of enjoying a free republican government, in which our natural rights are attended to, in which the original social contract is observed, and in which political justice governs; and also to justify us in our objections to the constitution proposed by the convention of this state, which we have taken the liberty to say is, in our apprehension, in some degree deficient in those respects.

To balance a large society on republican or general laws, is a work of so great difficulty, that no human genius, however comprehensive, is perhaps able, by the mere dint of reason and reflection, to effect it. The penetrating and dispassionate judgments of many must unite in this work: experience must guide their labour: time must bring it to perfection: and the feeling of inconveniencies must correct the mistakes which they will probably fall into, in their first trials and experiments.

The plan which the preceeding observations were intended to exhibit in a general view, is now compleated. The principles of a free republican form of government have been attempted, some reasons in support of them have been mentioned, the out lines of a constitution have been delineated in conformity to them, and the objections to the form of government proposed by the general convention have been stated.

This was at least the task enjoined upon the committee, and whether it has been successfully executed, they presume not to determine. They aimed at modelling the three branches of the supreme power in such a manner, that the government might act with the greatest vigour and wisdom, and with the best intentions — They aimed that each of those branches should retain a check upon the others, sufficient to preserve it's independence — They aimed that no member of the state should be controuled by any law, or be deprived of his property, against his consent — They aimed that all the members of the state should enjoy political liberty, and that their civil liberties should have equal care taken of them — and in fine, that they should be a free and an happy people — The committee are sensible, that the spirit of a free republican constitution, or the moving power which should give it action, ought to be political virtue, patriotism, and a just regard to the natural rights of mankind. This spirit, if wanting, can be obtained only from that Being, who infused the breath of Life into our first parent.

The committee have only further to report, that the inhabitants of the several towns who deputed delegates for this convention, be seriously advised, and solemnly exhorted, as they value the political freedom and happiness of themselves and of their posterity, to convene all the freemen of their several towns in town meeting, for this purpose regularly notified, and that they do unanimously vote their disapprobation of the constitution and form of government, framed by the convention of this state; that a regular return of the same be made to the secretary's office, that it may there remain a grateful monument to our posterity of that consistent, impartial and persevering attachment to political, religious, and civil liberty, which actuated their fathers, and in defence of which, they bravely fought, chearfully bled, and gloriously died.

The above report being read was accepted.

Attest, PETER COFFIN, *Chairman.*

No. II.

JUDGE PARKER'S ADDRESS TO THE GRAND JURY.

A Sketch of the Character of the late Chief Justice Parsons, exhibited in an Address to the Grand Jury, delivered at the Opening of the Supreme Judicial Court at Boston, on the twenty-third day of November, 1813, after the usual Charge. Published at the unanimous Request of the Grand Jury and the Bar of Suffolk. By Isaac Parker, Esq., one of the Associate Justices of that Court.

INTRODUCTION.

Chief Justice Parsons was born in February, 1750, and received the rudiments of his education under the celebrated Master Moody, at Dummer Academy, in his native parish of Byfield, within the ancient town of Newbury. His father was minister of that parish. He received the ordinary honors of the University in Cambridge in 1769. He entered upon the study of the law under the late Judge Bradbury, in Falmouth, now Portland, and while there kept the Grammar School in that town. He practised law there a few years; but the conflagration of the town by the British obliged him to withdraw to his father's house, where he met Judge Trowbridge, as stated in the Address. He, in about a year from this time, opened his office in Newburyport. He has been honored with degrees of Doctor of Laws from the University of Cambridge and Dartmouth College, and from Brown University in Rhode Island. In 1801, he was presented by President Adams with a commission of Attorney-General of the United States, which he did not accept. He had been also, by the choice of our State Legislature, one of the commissioners to settle a controversy with the State of New York. He continued faithful to his chosen profession until he was appointed Chief Justice of the State, which was in the summer of 1806.

ADDRESS.

Gentlemen of the Grand Jury:

At the first assembling of this court in this place, after the death of that eminent man who has for some years been its head and ornament, our minds are naturally and forcibly led to a contemplation of those extraordinary qualities which had secured to him an uncommon share of the veneration of his fellow-citizens.

Eulogies upon the dead have become, in public estimation, but equivocal evidence of their virtues and talents; and indiscriminate panegyric conveys no honor to its subject, and no benefit to survivors.

But the *illustrious* dead, — those who have brought signal reputation to their country, who have aided in rearing and supporting the edifice of state, whose learning has been devoted to general use, whose private virtues have afforded an example to the young, whose strength of mind and character has added to the dignity of man, — these ought not to be forgotten.

The stores of human wisdom could never be increased did not such men speak, even though dead. Their lives and their actions, recorded with truth, are the voice of history speaking to successive generations, calling them to emulate what is great and noble, and showing the practicability of almost infinite improvement in the capacities of the human mind.

I shall not be accused of fulsome panegyric, in asserting that the subject of this Address has for more than thirty years been acknowledged the great man of his time. The friends who have accompanied him through life, and witnessed the progress of his mind, want no proof of this assertion; but to those who have heard his fame, without knowing the materials of which it is composed, it may be useful to give such a display of his character as will prove that the world is not always mistaken in awarding its honors.

From the companions of his early years I have learned, that he was comparatively great before he arrived at manhood; that his infancy was marked by mental labor and study, rather than by puerile amusements; that his youth was a season of persevering acquisition, instead of pleasure; and that when he became a man, he seemed to possess the wisdom and experience of those who had been men long before him. And, indeed, those of us who have seen him lay open his vast stores of knowledge in later life, unaided by recent acquirement, and relying more upon memory than research, can account for his greatness only by supposing a patience of labor in youth which almost exhausted the sources of information, and left him to *act* rather than *study*, at a period when others are but beginning to acquire.

His familiar and critical knowledge of the Greek and Latin tongues, so well known to the literati of this country, and to some of the most eminent abroad, was the fruit of his early labors, preserved and perhaps ripened in maturer years, but gathered in the spring-time of his life.* His philosophical and mathematical knowledge were of the same early harvest, as were also his logical and metaphysical powers.

Had he died at the age of twenty-one, I am persuaded he

---

* The following facts were communicated to me by the Hon. D. A. Tyng.

During the late visit of Fr. Ad. Vanderkemp, Esq., formerly of Leyden, but for many years past resident in the State of New York, I had the satisfaction of introducing him to our late excellent Chief Justice, and of witnessing a very interesting conversation between these two learned men on various topics of literature. After we left the Chief Justice's house, Mr. V. said to me, that he had been very much gratified with the interview, for which he had felt a strong desire, and particularly from a circumstance which he then related.

Some years since, Mr. V. received a letter from the late Mr. John Luzac, Professor of the Greek Language, &c. in the University of Leyden, who was the relative and intimate friend and correspondent of Mr. V., and confessedly the first Greek scholar of his day in Europe, in which letter Mr. Luzac inquired of Mr. Vanderkemp, whether he had made an acquaintance with a Mr. Parsons of Boston, of whom he had heard that he was called in America "the Giant of the Law." How well Mr. Parsons might be entitled to this appellation, Mr. Luzac said he could not judge; but he could of his own knowledge affirm that he was "a giant in Greek criticism."

Professor Luzac's opinion was founded on a correspondence he held with the Chief Justice, many years ago, occasioned by the latter sending to Amsterdam for some rare editions of Greek authors, which could not be obtained then either in this country or England.

At college, he was an excellent scholar in Greek and Latin. But he began the study of Greek again after he was forty years old, when his eldest son was fitting for college.

would have been held up to youth as an instance of astonishing and successful perseverance in the severest employments of the mind.

Heaven, which gave him this spirit of industry, endowed him also with a genius to give it effect.

There were united in him an imagination vivid, but not visionary, a most discriminating judgment, the attentiveness and precision of the mathematician, and a memory which, however enlarged and strengthened by exercise, must have been originally powerful and capacious.

With these wonderful faculties, which had, from the first dawnings of reason, been employed on subjects most interesting to the human mind, he came to the study of that science which claims a kindred with every other, — the science of the law.

This was a field worthy of his labors and congenial with his understanding. How successfully he explored, cultivated, and adorned it, need not be related by his contemporaries.

Never was fame more early or more just than that of Parsons as a lawyer. At an age when most of the profession are but *beginning* to exhibit their talents and to take a fixed rank at the bar, he was confessedly, in point of profound legal knowledge, among the first of its professors.

His professional services were everywhere sought for. In his native county, and in the neighboring State of New Hampshire, scarcely a cause of importance was litigated in which he was not an advocate. His fame had spread from the country to the capital, to which he was almost constantly called to take a share in trials of intricacy and interest.

At that early period of his life, his most formidable rival and most frequent competitor was the accomplished lawyer and scholar, the late Judge Lowell, whose memory is still cherished with affection by the wise and virtuous of our State. Judge Lowell was considerably his senior, but entertained the highest respect for the general talents and juridical skill of his able competitor. It was the highest intellectual treat to see these great men contending for victory in the judicial forum. Lowell, with all the ardor of the most impassioned eloquence, assaulting the hearts of his auditors, and seizing their understandings also, with the most cogent as well as the most plausible arguments. Parsons, cool, steady, and deliberate, occupying every post which was left uncovered, and throwing in his forces wherever the zeal of his adversary had left an opening. Notwithstanding this almost continual forensic warfare, they were warm personal friends, and freely acknowledged each other's merits.

The other eminent men of that day, with whom Parsons was brought to contend, did full justice to his great powers. I have myself heard the late Governor Sullivan declare, he was the greatest lawyer living.

So rapid and yet so sure was the growth of his reputation, that immediately upon his commencing the practice of the law, his office was considered, by some of the first men our State has produced, to be the most perfect school for legal instruction.

That distinguished lawyer and statesman, Rufus King, having finished his education at our University at an age when he was qualified to choose his own instructor, placed himself under the tuition of Parsons; and probably it was owing in some measure to the wise lessons of the master, as well as to the great talents of the scholar, that the latter acquired a celebrity, during the few years he remained at the bar, seldom attained in so short a professional career.

Many others of our principal lawyers and statesmen are indebted to the same preceptor for their fundamental acquisitions in the science of jurisprudence and civil polity.

I will not omit to mention, for I wish not to exaggerate his powers, that he enjoyed one advantage in his education beyond any of his contemporaries, except the learned, able, and upright Chief Justice Dana, whose long and useful administration in this court ought to be remembered with gratitude by his fellow-citizens. I refer to the society and conversation of Judge Trowbridge, perhaps the most profound common lawyer of New England before the Revolution. This venerable old man, like some of the ancient sages of the law in England, had pursued his legal disquisitions long after he had ceased to be actively engaged in the profession, from an ardent attachment to the law as a science, and had employed himself in writing essays and forming elaborate readings upon abstruse and difficult points of law.

Many of his works are now extant in manuscript, and some in print, and they abundantly prove the depth of his learning, and the diligence and patience of his research.

When Parsons had retired to the house of his father, a respectable minister of Newbury, in consequence of the destruction of Falmouth by the British, he there met Judge Trowbridge, who had sought shelter from the confusion of the times in the same hospitable mansion. How grateful must it have been to the learned sage, in the decline of life, fraught with the lore of more than half a century's incessant and laborious study, to meet in a peaceful village, secure from the alarms of war, a scholar panting for instruction, and capable of comprehending his profound and useful lessons; and how delightful to the scholar to find a teacher so fitted to pour instruction into his eager and grasping mind. He regarded it as an uncommon blessing, and has frequently observed that this early interruption to his business, which seemed to threaten poverty and misfortune, was one of the most useful and happy events of his life.

His habit of looking deeply into the ancient books of the common law, and tracing back settled principles to original decisions, probably acquired under this fortunate and accidental tuition, was the principal source of his early and continued celebrity.

He entered upon business, also, after this connection ceased, early in our Revolutionary war, when the courts of admiralty jurisdiction were open and crowded with causes, in the management of which he had a large share. This led him to study with diligence the civil law, law of nations, and the principles of belligerent and neutral rights, in all which he soon became as distinguished as he was for his knowledge of the common and statute law of the country. Twenty-six years ago, when I with others of my age were pupils in the profession of the law, we saw our masters call this man into their councils, and yield implicit confidence to his opinions. Among men eminent themselves, and by many years his seniors, we saw him by common consent take the lead in causes which required intricate investigation and deepness of research.

In the art of special pleading, which more than anything tests the learning of a lawyer in his peculiar pursuit, he had then no competitor.

In force of combination and power of reasoning he was unrivalled, and in the happy talent of penetrating through the mass of circumstances which sometimes surround and obscure a cause, I do not remember his equal.

His arguments were directed to the understandings of men,

seldom to their passions; and yet instances may be recollected, when, in causes which required it, he has assailed the hearts of his hearers with as powerful appeals as were ever exhibited in the cause of misfortune or humanity. I do not disparage others by placing him at their head. *They* were great men; *he* was a wonderful man. Like the great moralists of England, he might be surrounded by men of genius, literature, and science, and neither he nor they suffer by a comparison. Indeed, he seemed to form a class of intellect by himself, rather than a standard of comparison for others.

Even his enemies — for it is the lot of all extraordinary men to have them — paid voluntary homage to his greatness. They designated him by an appellation which, from its appropriateness, became a just compliment, — *the Giant of the Law.*

I have spoken now of his early life only, before he was thirty-five years of age; and yet it is known that common minds, and even great minds, do not arrive at maturity in this profession until a much later period.

From this time for near twenty years I lived in a remote part of the State, and had no opportunity personally to witness his powers; but his fame pursued me even there. He was regarded by those lawyers with whom I have been conversant, *as the living oracle of the law.* His transmitted opinions carried with them authority sufficient to settle controversies and terminate litigation.

On my accession to the bench, I had an opportunity to see him in practice at the bar, when he possessed the accumulated wisdom and learning of fifty-six years. Though laboring under a valetudinarian system, his mind was vigorous and majestic. His great talent was that of condensation. He presented his propositions in regular and lucid order, drew his inferences with justness and precision, and enforced his arguments with a simplicity, yet fulness, which left nothing obscure or misunderstood.

He seemed to have an intuitive perception of the cardinal points of a cause, upon which he poured out the whole treasures of his mind, while he rejected all minor facts and principles from his consideration.

He was concise, energetic, and resistless in his reasoning. The most complicated questions appeared in his hands the most easy of solution; and if there be such a thing as demonstration in argument, he, above all the men I know, had the power to produce it.

With this fulness of learning and reputation, having had thirty-five years of extensive practice in all branches of the law, and having, indeed, for the last ten years acted unofficially as judge in many of the most important mercantile disputes which occurred in this town, he was, on the resignation of Chief Justice Dana, selected by our present Governor to preside in this court.* This was the first, and I believe the only instance of a departure from the ordinary rule of succession; and, considering the character and talents of some who had been many years on the bench, perhaps no greater proof could be given of his pre-eminent legal endowments than that this elevation should have been universally approved. Perhaps there never was a period when the regular succession would have been more generally acquiesced in as fit and proper, and yet the departure from it in this instance was everywhere gratifying.

That the man who in England would, probably, by the mere force of his talents, without the aid of family interest, have arrived to the dignity of Lord Chancellor or Lord Chief Justice, should be placed at the head of so important a department, was considered a most favorable epoch in our juridical history.†

The imperfect system of judicature which had prevailed here until about that period, had rendered even great legal abilities inadequate to the establishment of a course of proceedings and uniformity of decisions, so necessary to the safe and satisfactory administration of justice. There had been no history of past

---

* So great was his reputation as a lawyer, that, upon his removal from Newburyport to Boston, it was customary for merchants of distinction, who had some unavoidable dispute, to make out a statement of the facts, and submit them to his decision; and in this way many important commercial questions have been settled, without incurring the expense or delay of a lawsuit.

† The assertion that Chief Justice Parsons would probably have been made Lord Chancellor or Lord Chief Justice in England, had he lived there, will probably be considered extravagant by those who are in the habit of magnifying objects in proportion to their distance. But from a comparison of him with Lords Mansfield, Kenyon, Ellenborough, Eldon, and Erskine, as they appear in books, and from the opinion of several gentlemen who have seen most of those dignitaries in the exercise of their high functions, I have little doubt that such would have been his destiny, and none that he would have merited it.

transactions preserved by a reporter, the sage opinions and learned counsels of departed judges had been lost even from the memory, and precedents were sought for only in the books of a foreign country. The most interesting points of law had been settled in the hurry and confusion of jury trials; and conflicting opinions of judges, arising from pressure of business and want of time to deliberate, were adjusted by that body which is supposed by the constitution and the laws to be competent to try the fact alone.

But a new era had arisen; our system had been wisely assimilated to that of England, imperfectly it is true, but with great improvements upon the old.

Its success depended much upon the character of those who were called to administer it. There were men upon the bench qualified to illustrate its advantages, (I need not say to a candid auditory that I speak altogether of others,) yet the appointment of Parsons was hailed by all, and especially by those who best understood our past difficulties, with the highest approbation. His profound learning, long and uninterrupted employment in the country and in the capital, and especially his accurate knowledge of forms and practice, peculiarly fitted him to take the lead in the new and improved order of things. How fully public expectation has been satisfied, I need not declare. The reformed state of the dockets throughout the Commonwealth, the promptness of decisions, the regularity of trials, attest the beneficial effects of a system which he has done so much to render popular and permanent.

If to some respectable and eminent men he at times appeared precipitate in his *nisi prius* opinions, I am sure they will admit that he of all men had the most right to decide promptly, and that the rectitude of his decisions generally justified their apparent haste.

On this subject I would also remark, that in the course of thirty-five years' practice almost every subject of legal inquiry had passed in review before his mind; that his memory, the most distinguished of all his great faculties, retained everything he had ever read, and almost everything he had ever heard; and that, thus supplied with principles and precedents, it is not astonishing that great minds should sometimes be surprised at the suddenness of his opinions, and should be inclined to impute to haste what was the effect of knowledge. He appeared to have an instantaneous perception of the legal merits of a controversy, and to see the beginning, middle, and end of a cause with one comprehensive glance. I acknowledge myself among those who have sometimes imputed to precipitancy what I have afterwards found to be the result of learning and memory.

To have had a depository for the preservation of the learned efforts of so eminent a judge, must be considered fortunate for us and for posterity. The six first volumes of the present series of Reports will long endure as a monument of the technical learning and deep juridical reasonings of the late Chief Justice. The principles of the common law relating to real estates are there clearly and familiarly explained, and most of our important legislative acts have there received constructions consonant to their real, but often obscure intent. In these books will also be found many important mercantile cases, in which the principles of commercial and marine contracts have been discussed with remarkable clearness, and the law merchant has been fully and satisfactorily explained. Had he been spared to us, as I had always hoped he would be, for a period of ten years of judicial life, the abundant stores of his knowledge would have been thus drawn out for public use, and his fellow-laborers who survive, and their successors, perhaps for centuries, would have enjoyed the fruits of his studies and experience. But more than two years ago it pleased Heaven to afflict him with a malady, which, though it left his mind unimpaired, rendered corporeal exercise, particularly that of writing, extremely irksome. In this respect only was his usefulness diminished; but the consequence has been a loss to the public of much of his learning and juridical wisdom.

But he possessed other qualities of a judge, not exposed to the public eye, but equally important with those which have been mentioned. He was a patient and diligent inquirer after truth, revolving and revising his own opinions until it was scarcely possible they should not be correct, communicating freely to his brethren his own reasonings, and candidly listening to theirs, suppressing all pride of opinion, and being ready to adopt another's instead of his own, if found more conformable to truth, and never being willing to give the sanction of the whole court to a principle, until it had been tested by every method which learning and ingenuity could devise.

The remarkable coincidence of opinion which appears in our Reports, is not more a testimony of his power of enforcing his own, than of his candid estimation of that of others. He was not an arrogant man; for, though he well knew his own powers, he also knew the fallibility of all human power, and that no man is so sufficient of himself as to want no assistance from others. The decisions of the court, with the reasons on which they were founded, when digested and committed to writing by him, were submitted to the consideration of his brethren, with a strong desire that they should be criticised and pruned, and he lent a willing ear to suggestions of alteration and improvement.

Though fraught with all the technical learning of the bar, and accustomed to strict adherence to rules in his own practice, he yet, like Lord Mansfield, was averse from suffering justice to be entangled in the net of forms; and he therefore exerted all his ingenuity to support by technical reasoning the principles of equity and right.

In the administration of criminal law, however, he was strict, and almost punctilious, in adhering to forms. He required of the public prosecutors the most scrupulous exactness, believing it to be the right, even of the guilty, to be tried according to known and practised rules; and that it was a less evil for a criminal to escape, than that the barriers established for the security of innocence should be overthrown. He was a humane judge, and adopted, in its fullest extent, the maxim of Lord Chief Justice Hale, that doubts should always be placed in the scale of mercy.

I have thus attempted a sketch of the professional and judicial character of Chief Justice Parsons; but he was always a man belonging to the public, and his political character requires some attention. I abstain from any observations upon the political doctrines he uniformly espoused, so far as they relate to the administrations of our government, for I wish not to offend the feelings of some who are obliged to hear, and who probably differ from him, and from me, upon that subject. I mean only to show what he has done, in order that you may not refuse to join me in ascribing to him the character of a statesman and a patriot. He was always tenaciously attached to home, and unwilling to engage in scenes which drew him from it; so that it was difficult to prevail upon him to take so great a share in public councils as his townsmen and the people of his county desired.

But on great and solemn occasions, when the Commonwealth was organizing, and when it was in jeopardy, he yielded to the impulse of patriotism and the solicitations of his neighbors, and gave his time and talents to the State. Accordingly, in 1779, he became a member of the Convention which deliberated upon and formed the frame of State government, which has so happily continued, in spite of the many rude shocks it has received, to the present day. At a time when the people had freed themselves from a government which had become tyrannical, when they were held together as a body politic by a sense of danger rather than by the restraints of law, and when an enthusiastic love of liberty was universally felt, so that the rigors of a bad government would naturally excite jealousy of any which should be proposed, it was no easy task to introduce into the compact vigor enough to prolong its existence beyond the time of peril, which seemed to supersede the necessity of all government.

There were great and amiable men in that Convention, so enraptured with the view of order, discipline, and regard to right, spontaneously existing without coercive power, that they in some measure lost sight of the lessons of history, and concluded that the people would always remain wise and virtuous, and that the most lax system of government for such a people was the best. There were others equally attached to true liberty, but less ardent in their feelings, who believed that man was, in all ages and in almost all places, the same, — a being of many virtues and many vices, thoughtful and moderate in adversity, rash and presumptuous in prosperity, and at all times requiring the strong arm of government and law to repress his passions and restrain his propensity to error.

In the latter class was Parsons; and he was indefatigable in his exertions to obtain as energetic a system as the people would bear, and to introduce into it those checks and balances which would insure its durability. I have the authority of contemporary statesmen for declaring, that, among these wise men and patriots, Parsons, at that time not thirty years old, discovered an intelligence, strength of mind, and force of reasoning, which gave him a decided influence in that venerable assembly. Many of the most important articles of the Constitution were of his draft, and those provisions which were most essential, though least palatable, such as dignity and power to the excutive, independence to the judiciary, and a separation of the branches of the legislative department, were supported by him with all the power of argument and eloquence which could be derived from deep historical information and wise reflections upon the nature and character of mankind. Wherever he was placed, his influence was immediately felt, and his assiduity and patience of investigation, added to his ability to enforce his opinions, put him in the front rank in all arduous and anxious conflicts.*

After this Constitution had been adopted by the people, and had gone into operation, he appeared but seldom in the political assemblies of the State. The ordinary business of legislation was not of importance enough in his mind to draw him from a profitable pursuit of his profession, which was necessary for the support and education of an increasing family. Yet, when the seeds of disorder sprang up in the community, and the most dangerous principles of disorganization had begun to spread, he was again prevailed upon to take a seat in the Legislature, where his great political knowledge and his peculiar address contributed largely to the preservation of that Constitution he had done so much to establish.

But another great national revolution occurred. The Constitu-

---

* It is not generally known, that, before this convention of the people by their delegates was called for the purpose of making a constitution, the existing government, which was exercised by a convention, in the year 1777, drew up the form of a constitution, and presented it to the people for their acceptance. This appeared to some gentlemen in the county of Essex so loose and inefficient in its texture, that they urged a representation of their towns in a county convention, which accordingly met in 1778 at Ipswich. Parsons was one of this convention. They agreed to advise the towns to reject the constitution which had been proposed. A committee of this county convention was appointed to take into consideration the proposed constitution, and report thereon. Parsons was upon this committee. The report is undoubtedly his, though he was probably aided by others, at least with their advice. This elaborate report is called the "Essex Result"; and it contains an able discussion of the principles of a free republic, and shows clearly the defects of the proffered form of government.

The people rejected the constitution. A convention was called for the express purpose of making another, which was finished and accepted by the people in 1780.

tion of the United States was presented to the people for their approbation, and a convention of delegates from the several towns in this Commonwealth was assembled to discuss its merits, and adopt or reject it. This was the crisis of life or death to the union of the States, and ruin or prosperity hung upon the decision. Parsons again appeared in the cause of order, law, and government, the cause indeed of the people, though they did not recognize it; for no doubt was entertained that, at the first meeting of that Convention, a great majority of its members were predetermined to reject the Constitution. I, then a young man, was an anxious spectator of these doings. I heard there the captivating eloquence of Ames, the polished erudition of King, the ardent and pathetic appeals of Dana, the sagacious and conciliating remarks of Strong, and the arguments of other eminent men of that body; but Parsons appeared to me the master-spirit of that assembly. Upon all sudden emergencies, and upon plausible and unexpected objections, he was the sentinel to guard the patriot camp, and to prevent confusion from unexpected assault. He labored there in season and out of season, the whole energies of his mind being bent upon the successful issue of a question which was, he believed, to determine the fate of his country. This finished his political engagements, except some few years in the Legislature at subsequent periods, when his influence was visible, but the subjects which occurred only of ordinary import.

But though he was only occasionally engaged as a member of the Legislature, he yet was an active observer of public measures, and without doubt contributed his counsels in many of the arrangements which took place. His political friends frequently sought his advice, and they always found him perfectly acquainted with passing events, and ready to communicate his opinions.

More has been imputed to him on the score of political influence than was true. By those who felt the weight of his character without enjoying his confidence, it was believed, or at least asserted, that he dictated most of the measures which his political friends adopted. From seven years' most intimate and confidential intercourse with him, I can testify that his influence has not been exerted during that period in *projecting* public measures; that it appeared only in giving advice when solicited for it; and that, if his opinions were adopted, it was not from any authority claimed by him or submitted to by others, but because they were deemed wise and beneficial.

He was undoubtedly a *bold* politician, and on any interesting crisis his system was to take the ground which he thought was right, and maintain it without regard to the difficulties to be encountered, and especially never to be deterred by fear of unpopularity. This sometimes led even his friends to think that his political courage partook of temerity, and that he overlooked expediency in pursuit of right. But it not unfrequently happened that the difference between them was owing to his greater share of political foresight, or to his instantaneous perception of what the times and circumstances required.

In his political as well as in his judicial character, there was an apparent suddenness of opinion, which at the moment seemed precipitancy, but which has in most instances been discovered to be the effect of a process of reasoning astonishingly rapid, or the immediate decision of judgment upon facts and principles stored in his memory, and always ready for use. Instances could be adduced in which his friends have rejected his opinions from a doubt of their correctness, and yet have been necessarily brought, by the course of events which he had the sagacity to foresee, to the very point from which they had prudently, as they thought, receded.

I add, that I most sincerely believe that he had no private or personal views to gratify, and that his sole object was the permanent interest and prosperity of his country.

You will spare me a few moments, while I briefly exhibit to you the private character of this distinguished man. He was just, regular, and punctual in all his transactions. Simplicity and order presided over his household. Hospitality, without ostentation or ceremony, reigned within his mansion. Domestic tranquillity and cheerfulness beamed from his countenance, and was reflected back upon him from his happy and delighted family. It has been the misfortune of many, if not most, of those who have been devoted to literature, and who have attained great celebrity, to have been so much absorbed in grave contemplations as to acquire a distaste to those charities of life which are the sources of its happiness, or to become insensible to the ordinary excitements to recreation and pleasure. It was not so with Parsons. He was great even in common affairs. His conversation could instruct or amuse, as times and seasons suited. Neither philosophers nor children could leave his society without being improvèd or entertained. Amid the multifarious occupations of his mind in business and scientific pursuits, he had still found room for all the lighter literature, and was ready with his critique even upon the ephemeral works of fancy and of taste. The more solid productions of polite literature had passed the ordeal of his judgment, so that his materials for social converse were abundant, and his power of using them unlimited. Indeed, his memory may be considered a capacious storehouse, separated into an infinite number of apartments, in which principles, facts, and anecdotes were laid up according to their classes, marked and numbered, so that he could draw them out and appropriate them whenever occasion offered, without confusion or misapplication. His conversation was illumined with flashes of wit and merriment, which captivated his hearers, and rendered him at the same time the most edifying and the most entertaining of companions. He was accessible, familiar, and communicative, never morose or ill-natured, a patron of literature and literary men, a warm friend to the clergy and to the institutions of religion and learning, and a most ardent admirer and promoter of merit among the young.* He was not an avaricious man; for, after a long life of labor in a lucrative profession, with as much opportunity as was ever enjoyed to amass riches, he has left no greater estate than is frequently accumulated by a prudent and respectable tradesman.

The man whom he most resembled in powers of mind could be brilliant and astonishing, when surrounded by kindred spirits, and spurred on to intellectual conflicts; but when the tournament was over, he retired with exhausted spirits and debilitated mind, and

---

* The zealous attention of the Chief Justice to the interests of the College, while he was a member of the Corporation, was generally known. But his care for the interests of literature was in other ways exemplified. He had been for three years one of the supervisory committee of a grammar school, kept by Mr. Clap of this town. I have attended the examinations of the scholars, at all of which the Chief Justice was present. He generally took the lead in the examination, and discovered such a critical knowledge of the Greek and Latin languages as surprised everybody. His presence was useful in other respects; for he so interested and amused the boys with anecdotes concerning the men and the times about which they were reading, as to render their examinations pleasant, instead of being formidable to them.

sunk into the gloom of superstition and the horrors of self-condemnation. But Parsons could leave the theological controversy, the mathematical problem, or the legal inquiry, and enter at once with spirit and interest into domestic conversation, and even into children's sports. When fatigued with the labor of deep legal research, or exhausted by a continued train of thought upon one subject, it was not uncommon for him to relax his mind with some abstruse arithmetical or geometrical demonstration, or to turn over the pages of some popular and interesting novel. And, strange as it may seem, it is true, that from his earliest years to the latter season of his life these two sources of amusement were constantly enjoyed by him.*

I know that I am in danger of being thought so infatuated with admiration, as to exaggerate his talents, or at least to give them too high a coloring. But death has destroyed all motives for flattery, if any could have existed, and a month's interval has given opportunity to reflect upon the folly of overstrained praise. I confess, the more I contemplate his character, the more I revere it. To some of its strongest points I consider myself a witness, and should disdain to pass beyond the limits of truth. In relation to his professional and public judicial character, I speak in the presence of men who are witnesses as well as myself. As to his classical and literary acquirements, I profess not to judge, except from the testimony of those best qualified to decide. I can appeal with confidence to the learned and reverend governors of our University, who for more than ten years have enjoyed the benefit of his counsels, and witnessed the depth of his learning. For his mathematical and philosophical eminence, I could summon the chosen professors of those branches, and I could add

* Judge Tudor, who was the classmate of the Chief Justice in college, and, in the college phrase, his chum, has frequently told me, that, after the usual exercises, Parsons was in the habit of taking his slate and amusing himself with some deep mathematical calculation, and that he would vary his recreation by reading some tale or novel; it seeming indifferent to him which of these amusements first fell in his way. I have, within the last seven years of his life, found him indulging the same propensity, finding him with his slate and pencil so deeply engaged that I would not disturb him for some minutes after my entrance, and not unfrequently as deeply engaged in some modern novel, or other work of fancy.

to them the modest and scientific Bowditch.* For his knowledge in astronomy, mechanics, chemistry, and electricity, I would venture to call the most distinguished masters we have in those several branches, and I believe the testimony from each witness would be, that Parsons was great in each particular department.

Should any one ask, Had this great man no faults, no foibles? I answer, he had, for he was a man; but none which ought to enter into a candid estimation of his character. I leave them to those who are hardy enough to violate the sanctity of the tomb for the purpose of magnifying and exposing them.

That such a man as this, whose mind had never been at rest, and whose body had seldom been in exercise, should have lived to the age of sixty-three, is rather a matter of astonishment, than that he should then have died.

At this distance from the period of his death, when the first painful sensations at so great a loss have subsided, it is not unsuitable to take consolation from the possible, if not probable, consequences of a prolonged life. Beyond the age at which he had arrived, I do not know that an instance exists of an improvement of the faculties of the mind, but many present themselves of deplorable decay and humiliating debility. An opposite example exists in the case of that venerable Judge Trowbridge, whom I have had occasion to mention before in this address. The last twenty years of his life passed in almost entire forgetfulness of and by the world. Should it not be considered a happy, rather than a lamentable event, to escape the infirmities, the disabilities, and perhaps the neglects of a protracted old age? Parsons died in the zenith of his reputation, in the strength of his understanding; and, so dying, has left a legacy to his children and to the public, in his character, more valuable than exhaustless riches.

The testimony he bore, too, to the truth of the Christian reve-

* Mr. Bowditch, in his Practical Navigator, on the subject of lunar observations, speaking of a method of correcting the apparent distance of the moon from the sun, says: "It is an improvement on Witchell's method, and was made in consequence of a suggestion from a gentleman eminently distinguished for his mathematical acquirements"; and by a note referred to in this passage, Chief Justice Parsons is the gentleman alluded to. Mr. Bowditch also received some communications from him, on the subject of the comet which last made its appearance in our hemisphere, which showed ingenuity and learning.

lation should furnish a consolation for his death. It was the testimony of a most exalted human intellect, unclouded by the apprehensions of death, and unobscured by superstition. It was declared repeatedly in the best state of his health, and confirmed in the serene contemplation of his expected change. It was the result of a *trial of witnesses*, in which professional acuteness was aided by native powers of discrimination. He has left written evidence of the conclusion his penetrating mind had formed upon this all-interesting inquiry. It may seem unbecoming in a Christian to place much reliance upon human authority for his hopes of immortality and happiness. But a great portion of the world is governed by authority, and when some few great men have published their scepticism, and thus given confidence to the infidel of inferior understanding, it is comforting to the sincere and humble believer to be able to add the name of Parsons to the long list of great and good men who have given their living and dying testimony to the religion they profess.*

* About three months before the Chief Justice died, I had a conversation with him upon the subject of the Christian religion, and particularly upon the proofs of the resurrection contained in the New Testament. He told me that he felt the most perfect satisfaction on that subject; that he had once taken it up with a view to ascertain the weight of the evidence by comparing the accounts given by the four Evangelists with each other; and that, from their agreement in all substantial and important facts, as well as their disagreement in minor circumstances, considering them all as separate and independent witnesses, giving their testimony at different periods, he believed that the evidence would be considered perfect, if the question was tried at any human tribunal. I then did not know that he had made a public profession of his belief by becoming a member of any church, and I asked him why he had not thus testified his belief. He told me that he had postponed it a great while, because, as the general state of his health and his fear of exposing himself to the cold and damp air would prevent him from attending public worship constantly, and from those causes he might be frequently absent on communion days, he was apprehensive he might be thought not to act up to his profession; but that, two or three years ago, he had made up his mind to do his duty in joining the church, and as much of his duty as he could in attending upon the ordinance; and he accordingly joined the church of which President Kirkland was then the pastor.

A similar conversation was held by him with the Rev. Mr. Thacher

May the life and celebrity of this great man stimulate the young to diligence and perseverance in their studies, so that, at some future time, one may rise up from among them fit to supply his place in public estimation.

May his pre-eminent qualifications for the judicial magistracy, which cannot be reached by his fellow-laborers, incite them to greater zeal, labor, and attention, so that the chasm made by his death may be the less observed. And may his departure impress us all with solemn and suitable reflections upon the vanity of all human attainments compared with that wisdom which cometh from above, whose ways are pleasantness, and whose end is everlasting life.

While this Address was passing through the press, the following letter was received, and the testimony it contains cannot fail to gratify the public.

"Cambridge, 1st December, 1813.

"My dear Sir:

"Since I handed you the note containing the testimonial of Professor Luzac to our venerated friend's rank as a proficient in Greek learning, I have received a letter from my respected friend Vanderkemp, from which I extract the following.

"'We have then lost that ornament of the bench, that brilliant gem of your country. The Giant of the Law, the polished Greek scholar, is gone. I knew him. I had learned to revere him through my friend Luzac. You introduced me to him, and he afterwards honored me by visiting me three times at my lodgings in Boston. For this I was indebted to my deceased Luzac, whom

---

during his late sickness, through the whole of which he evinced a patience and resignation which, considering his extreme nervous irritability and apprehensions of disease when in his best state of health, can be accounted for only by the enlightened and satisfactory hopes he entertained of a happy immortality. It ought to be highly consolatory to his friends to know, that he whom they had seen to shrink at an eastern breeze, and to start at the slightest pain, should, at the certain approach of the king of terrors, collect all the energies of his wonderful mind, and contemplate his approaching dissolution with as much steadiness and composure as he would many of the ordinary events of life.

he respected. I flattered myself that I should yet gather a rich harvest from his acquaintance; and he seemed inclined not to disappoint me. "Make my compliments to Mrs. V.," — these were his last words to me, — "and tell her she ought to command you to return soon to Boston." Such a delicate compliment from a Parsons was a treasure to an epicurean in regard of praise.'

"The good man then indulges his hopes, in a strain of enthusiasm, that the excellent properties of our deceased luminary may excite the emulation of professors of the law who survive him, and of those who may hereafter arise.

"I am, dear Sir, your most obliged servant,

"D. A. Tyng."

No. III.

OBITUARY NOTICE.

[From the Boston Gazette of November 4th, 1813.]

[The following brief sketch of the character of the Honorable Theophilus Parsons is copied from the last *Palladium*. It is a chaste and unadorned commentary on the life of a man who had lived only to be useful; who had practised all the liberal and social virtues; and who died in the full and confident belief, "*that there was another and a brighter world.*"]

The death of this great man will be universally felt, and ought to be universally lamented throughout our State. The station he has occupied for the last seven years has given opportunity to all classes of people, in all parts of the Commonwealth, to see and hear the man whose fame had before reached their ears, and whose eminent professional talents had acquired to him, from common suffrage, the reputation of being the greatest lawyer of his day. This reputation was not confined to our own State, but had spread into the adjoining States, and even to the most remote parts of the Union; at least to all those parts where the law is known as a science, and where its distinguished sages, of whatever country, are reverenced and admired. The celebrated jurists, who have occasionally visited this metropolis to administer the laws of the nation, Jay, Chase, Patterson, and others, have all passed their judgments upon his legal character, and have pronounced him "the Great Lawyer." And most strangers of distinction, who have travelled into this quarter for curiosity or information, have been led, by his fame, to visit and converse with him, and have uniformly sanctioned common report, by their testimony to his greatness. With this uncommon celebrity he entered upon the first judicial office in this State; and whatever admiration he had excited as a lawyer, was immediately transferred to him as a judge. Commencing his career soon after a new and improved system of judicature had been adopted, the effect of his administration was instantly perceived in the despatch of business, in the promptness and wisdom of his opinions, and in the universal confidence they inspired. The most eminent counsellors seldom hesitated to submit and to be convinced when he declared the law, the juries felt no uncertainty or doubt when he had addressed them, and the suitors saw with satisfaction their expenses diminished, their delay shortened, and the time of the public economized, by the exertion of his wonderful faculties in the discharge of his official functions.

When associated upon the bench with his brethren, to hear and determine questions of law of great import to the public and to individuals, his profound yet familiar acquaintance with the principles of the common law, his astonishing recollection of usages and precedents not to be found in print, and his precise and accurate knowledge of the forms of pleadings and of the course of proceedings in the courts of the country from whence all we have to boast of in this regard is derived, gave a stability and respect to decisions honorable to the judicial character of the State, and useful to posterity as well as to the present generation. His readings upon many of the old statutes, and learned construction of those of modern date, being recorded in our books of Reports, will long stand as monuments of his deep legal and technical knowledge, his enlarged and liberal views of the principles of government and laws, and his acute and penetrating powers of discrimination.

In the development of his character as a judge, we see that he drew to his aid almost all the literature and the science which the human mind can embrace. Metaphysics, mathe-ematics, natural philosophy, and even theology, opened their sources of information to his comprehensive mind, and in classic learning there were few, if any, who ought not to admit his superiority.

But it was not only in his judicial capacity that the community has been benefited by his powers. He has been at times, though always reluctantly, prevailed on to take a share in the political arrangements of the State. He was a member of the convention which formed our State Constitution, of that which adopted the National Compact, and in several instances of our House of Representatives; in all which situations his sagacity, political foresight, and historical information were discerned by the wisest men, and used for the public good.

He was a republican in principle, and his works show it, for he has given his powerful aid in all those establishments which are intended to secure the Republic. He never condescended to flatter the people or their rulers; but, while ready to set bounds to the power of the latter, he was desirous also to provide checks and remedies to the instability and caprice of the former. He well knew the temper and disposition of man in all civil societies, ancient as well as modern, and knew that the purpose of government was to correct and restrain his passions. In all his political labors, therefore, he applied the lessons of experience; and with a strength of argument and force of reasoning which never could be combated with success, and which not unfrequently confounded and defeated the arts of his opponents, he was in many important instances the happy instrument of the triumph of truth over passion, and discretion over zeal. Instead of yielding to the popular current in times of agitation and frenzy, his patriotism was shown in breasting the dangerous flood, and presenting himself as a mound to resist its force, until it should subside into safe channels, and until calmness and tranquillity should be restored. He was one of the few men who *fearlessly* told the people the truth where it was offensive to their ears, trusting to the return of reason for his vindication, or willing to hazard every sacrifice in its cause. He was inflexibly engaged in the support of sound principles, and despised the threats and reproaches of the numerous pretenders to patriotism, who have from time to time cajoled the people into measures disgraceful and ruinous. For thirty years past this class of men have feared him, and they ought to, for he was "a terror to evil-doers," but he was also "a praise and encouragement to such as do well," and he had therefore the esteem, veneration, and love of the sound part of the community.

Such a man could never, in the common understanding of the phrase, be a *popular man*. He knew not the arts of popularity, and never sought it. But the influence derived from a deep sense of superior worth, from profound reverence of his wisdom, and from unqualified reliance upon his integrity, was his; and it was used for the great purposes of giving supremacy to the laws, and durability to the government, the only means of establishing and maintaining public liberty. However obnoxious the stern tenor of his political life may have been to those whose purposes have been defeated by his persevering exposition of truth, yet even these will not deny him the credit of intrepidity, frankness, and incomparable ability in his contests with them.

The loss of such a man, at this time, ought to strike us with dismay, did we not trust in Divine Providence, which in former days has raised up new props and pillars of the State, in the room of those which it has seen fit to remove.

A newspaper's limits are too narrow to admit even a sketch of the various excellences of the deceased. It requires the deliberate labors of a biographer.

But what he has done in the cause of literature ought not even here to be omitted. For many years he was a member of the Corporation of Harvard College. He imparted wisdom and vigor to their councils, energy to their government, and efficacy to the studies they prescribed. His associates were men capable of discerning his greatness, and were great enough themselves to acknowledge it. He claimed no authority but that of reason and wisdom, to which they as well as he were always ready to submit. His regard for religion as well as literature was also shown by his attention to clergymen of every denomination, many of whom have lost in him a zealous patron and friend.

In private life he was not so much known, and therefore probably much misunderstood. So great a man abroad, would naturally be suspected of an uncomfortable greatness at home. But the reverse of this is true. His friends know that there never was a more amiable, kind, and affectionate head of a family. Wit, humor, facetiousness, combined in him to relieve the fatigue of moral lessons and grave discourse. His power of conversation was equal to his other powers. His facility of communicating knowledge has been equalled only by his diligence in obtaining it. All participated of his knowledge, for he lived not to himself, but was ready to give freely to others what had cost him severe labor to acquire. No man ever loved more, or was more loved by, his family.

We should speak of his charities, but they had better be left, as he would have left them, unspoken of, except by those worthy objects who, having been deprived of their earthly support, are now living in ease on the fruits of benevolence which he was the happy instrument of procuring.

In his last sickness he displayed the fortitude, resignation, and composure of a Christian philosopher. He died in the full faith of the Christian Revelation, having frequently declared to the writer, that he had examined its testimonies with a lawyer's accuracy, and that the examination had resulted in an entire conviction of its truth. This same sentiment he expressed to the reverend friend who comforted and consoled him on his death-bed, in some of the last conversations he was able to hold.

Thus has passed away a man in every respect valuable to the community. May his example, and the memory of his greatness, be the means of raising up others to adorn and support the important institutions of our country!

No. IV.

ESSAY ON PARALLEL LINES.

By Theophilus Parsons.

Remarks on the Twenty-ninth Theorem in the First Book of Euclid's Elements of Geometry.

Euclid, in the Twenty-ninth Theorem in the First Book of his Elements of Geometry, proposes to demonstrate, that a right line, intersecting two parallel right lines, makes the alternate angles equal, — the exterior angle equal to the interior opposite angle on the same side of the intersecting line, — and that the interior angles on the same side of the intersecting line, taken together, are equal to two right angles. To demonstrate this theorem, the author has assumed as an axiom in geometry self-evident, and not requiring any demonstration, the proposition, that, if a right line meets two right lines, making the two interior angles on the same side, taken together, less than two right angles, these two right lines, being continually produced, shall meet upon that side on which are the two angles which are less than two right angles. This proposition, not being self-evident, but admitting a demonstration, ought not to be received as an axiom; and, as Dr. Simpson observes, it has given ancient and modern geometers much to do. A demonstration of this twenty-ninth proposition has been attempted in several ways; — by demonstrating Euclid's axiom; by assuming some new axiom; by introducing new definitions; or by reasoning from the definitions already given, without the aid of any axiom. In looking into the subject, it appeared surprising to me, that there should exist any difficulty in demonstrating a theorem so manifestly true, if there were no defect in the definitions. To amuse a vacant hour, I have examined these definitions with some attention; and I have supposed that a new definition of parallel right lines, derived from Dr. Reid's definition of a right line, may be given, which will remove all difficulty from the subject.

Let us then examine some of the first elementary definitions of geometry.

Professor Playfair defines a point to be *that* which has position, but not magnitude. By having no magnitude, it has neither length, breadth, nor thickness. By having position, it is susceptible of change of place. And when two points meet, they have the same position. A line is length, without breadth or thickness. A point being moved, its path, whatever may be its direction, will have length, but will not have breadth or thickness, because a point has none. A line may therefore be conceived as produced by the motion of a point, and will have position.

A superficies is *that* which has length and breadth, but not thickness; and it may be conceived as produced by the motion of a line, and will have position.

Among these definitions, we have a line defined as a genus of magnitude. And it is self-evident, that, when a line has limits, those limits are points; and that the place of the intersection of two lines is a point.

But lines are of different species, the general division of which is into the right line, and the curve line; and an adequate definition of the right line is required. Euclid has defined a right line to be a line which lies equally between its extreme points. By this definition, it has been observed by geometers, that we have no direct knowledge of a right line. If it be asked, When does a line lie equally between its extreme points? Euclid will furnish no answer. The most obvious one is, When it is a right line. But this is defining in a circle. Euclid has given no general definition of a curve line, of which there are several species. And the only general definition seems to be, that a curve line is a line no part of which is a right line. But geometers, in defining any species of curve line, deduce the definition either by its mechanical construction, or by comparing it to some point or line not in the curve. Euclid has defined but one species of curve, — the circumference of a circle; and his definition results from comparing the curve to a point within the circle. Why then are we to suppose that a right line can be defined, without a reference to a point or line without it? Dr. Reid concludes from Euclid's demonstration of the first theorem in his Eleventh Book, that, in defining a right line, Euclid compares it with another line. But Euclid has nowhere given a definition, in any form, of a right line, by comparing it with another line; and for this definition we are indebted to Dr. Reid.

Dr. Reid's definition substantially is, "that two lines, which *must* wholly unite when any two points in one line unite with two points in the other, are right lines." The converse of this definition is also true, — "that two right lines *must* wholly unite, if any two points in one right line unite with two points in the other." As it is supposed by the definition, that two lines separately exist before their union, it may be illustrated by a diagram, Fig. I. Let A B and C D be two lines. Let *m* and *n* be any two points in the line A B. Let the line A B be so moved that the points *m* and *n* be united to *o* and *p*, two points in the line C D. Then if the line A B *must* wholly unite with the line C D, those two lines are right lines. And *e converso*, let *m* and *n* be any two points in the right line A B, and *o* and *p* be points so assumed in the right line C D, that when the point *m* is united to the point *o*, and the point *n* is united to the point *p*, then the right lines A B and C D *must* wholly unite. And the only restriction in the assuming of the point is, that the line *o p* must be equal to the line *m n*.

Fig. I.

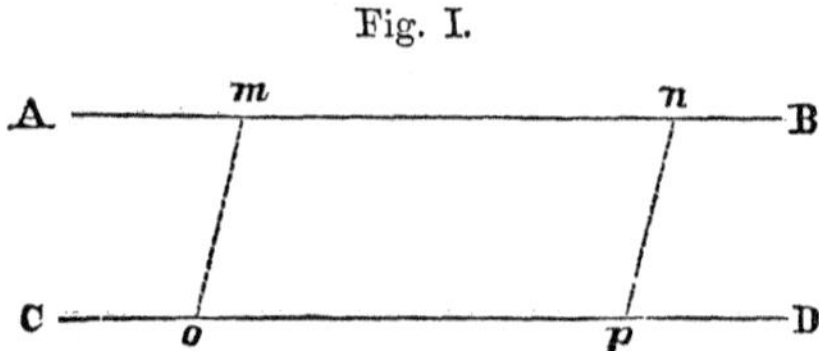

Similar parts of equal and similar curves *may* wholly unite, when united at two points; but it is not necessary that they should unite. In Fig. II., A B C may be the union of two arcs of the same circle, or of equal circles, the points *m* and *n* being

Fig. II.

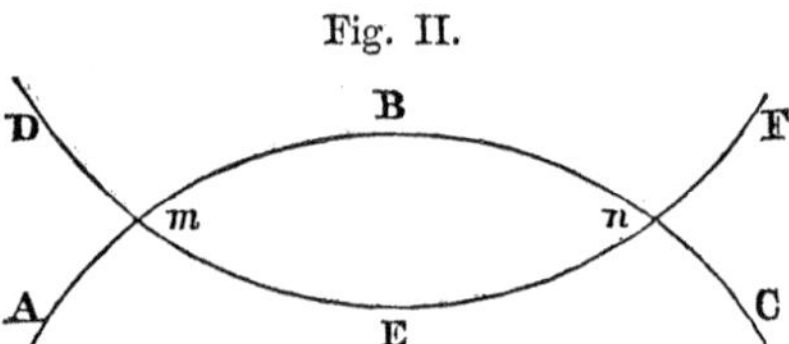

points in each arc. But while the points *m* and *n* remain fixed, the arcs that were united may be conceived to be separated, and one of them be turned on the fixed points m and n, when all the other points in it will change their position, and the arc may have the place of the curve D E F.

But a curve and a right line can never be united but in two points. In Fig. III., let A b B be a right line, and C D E a curve line meeting at the points m and n. The curve may be turned on the fixed points m and n, when all the other points in it will change their position, and the curve may lie on the other side of the right line, in the place of F G H, but no other point in it can be made to meet a point in the right line. But if the right line A b B be conceived to be turned on the same fixed points m and n, all the other points in it, or the whole line, will retain the same position.

Fig. III.

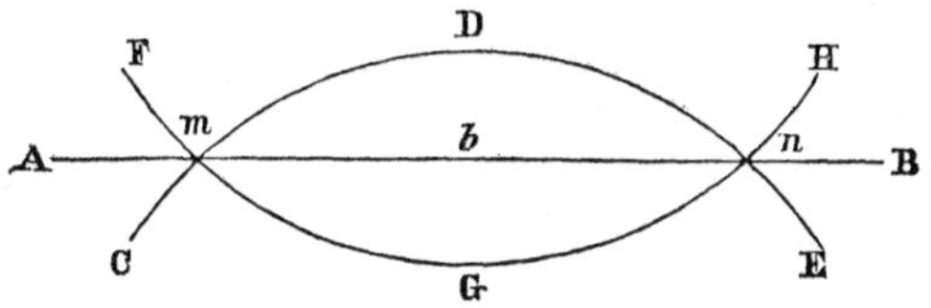

We have now, from Dr. Reid, a definition of a right line, complete and strictly geometrical. For a line may as well be conceived to be moved to another line to determine their species, as to be moved to generate a superficies, or as a superficies to be moved to produce and define a solid.

From this definition several useful corollaries result.

1. There can be but one right line drawn between any two points.
2. There is but one species of the right line.
3. The distance between any two points is the length of the right line drawn between them.
4. A right line being produced ever so far, from either extreme point, the whole line, including the part produced, is a right line.
5. Two right lines meeting at their extreme points wholly coincide, and are equal.
6. Two equal right lines, wholly coinciding, meet at their extreme points.

7. Two right lines, intersecting each other, cannot include a space. As a point in one right line is united with a point in the other at their point of intersection, then, to include a space, the right lines must again meet and unite in two other points, in which case they must wholly unite.

8. A part of one right line cannot be a part of another right line; or two right lines cannot have the same segment.

9. When the positions of any two points in a right line are determined, the positions of all the other points in the line, or of the whole line, are determined.

The fifth and sixth corollaries seem to be included in the eighth axiom in Euclid's First Book, which is derived from the principle of congruency. The seventh and eighth corollaries are mentioned by Professor Playfair; and, in his opinion, the ninth corollary is a good definition of a right line.

I proceed to consider the subject of parallel right lines, and to give a definition of the position of two finite right lines, which constitutes their parallelism. According to Euclid, parallel right lines are such as are in the same plane, and which, being produced ever so far, both ways, do not meet. This is not a definition of the position of two finite right lines, which constitutes their parallelism, but of an effect or consequence of such position; and we cease to consider them as finite right lines, when they are conceived to be produced without limitation. But finite right lines which approach nearer to each other as they are produced, are not parallel. And it must be presumed, that finite right lines which, if produced, never meet, do not approach nearer to each other. And Euclid has not defined any property of a right line, whence this presumption is self-evidently true. And in geometry, there are lines which, in a given position, may, when produced, continue to approach nearer to each other, and yet never can meet, when ever so far produced.

As Dr. Reid, in his definition of a right line, has determined that two right lines have the same position, when any two points in one right line are united to two points in the other, so have I attempted, by the position of any two points in one right line compared with the position of two points in the other, to determine the position of two right lines which constitutes their parallelism, in the following

Definition.

Parallel right lines are such as are in the same plane superficies, and from any two points, at any given distance in either line, equal right lines can be drawn, without intersecting each other, to any two equally distant points in the other right line.

The converse of this definition is: Right lines which are in the same plane superficies, and from any two points of which, at any given distance in either two, equal right lines can be drawn, without intersecting each other, to any two equally distant points in the other, are parallel. And if the right lines so drawn from two points in one right line to two points in the other, are unequal, those lines are not parallel.

To illustrate this definition, let A B and C D (Fig. IV.) be two right lines in the same plane. In the line A B assume any point, as *m*, and in the line C D any other point, as *o*, and draw the right line *m o*. In A B assume any other point, as *n*, and in B C take the point *p* on the same side of the line *m o*, so that *o p* may be equal to *m n*, and draw the right line *n p*. Now if the line *m o* is equal to the line *n p*, then A B and C D are parallel; but if *m o* and *n p* are unequal, then A B and C D are not parallel. If the point *p* had been taken on the other side of *m o*, as at *q*, and *n q* had been drawn, it must have intersected *m o*; and *m o* and *n q* would not have been drawn agreeably to the definition.

Fig. IV.

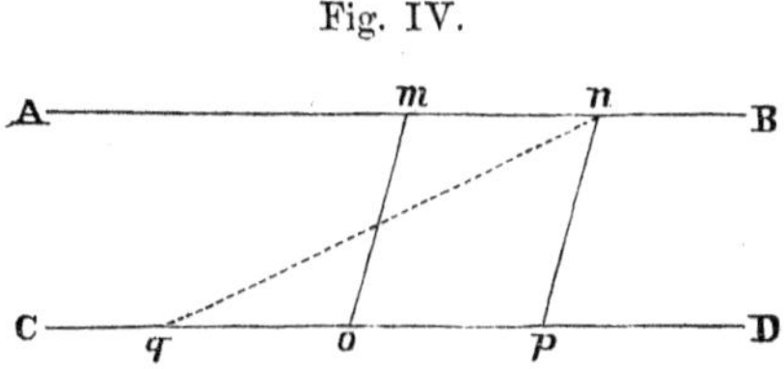

Several corollaries result from this definition, either self-evident or capable of a simple demonstration.

1. Parallel right lines, produced ever so far on either side, can never meet. For let A B and C D be produced ever so far, the points *n* and *p* may be assumed at any greater distance from the points *m* and *o*, and the right line *n p* will be equal to the right line *m o*.

2. Right lines not parallel, but in the same plane, may be produced on the one side or the other, until they meet, and then they are said to incline to each other. There are therefore but three different relations which two right lines in the same plane can be conceived to have to each other. They may be conceived as wholly united, or as parallel, or as inclined to each other.

3. Two equal right lines drawn between the extreme points of two equal parallel right lines, are also parallel. For *m* and *o* are the two extreme points of the right line *m o*, and *n* and *p* are the two equally distant extreme points of the right line *n p*; and the right lines *m n* and *o p* are equal and parallel. This corollary is included in the 33d proposition in the First Book of Euclid.

4. Let A B and C D (Fig. V.) be two parallel right lines, and let the right line *m o* be drawn from any point in A B to any point in C D, and let any number of points be assumed in A B, as *q r s n*, and an equal number of points, as *t v x p*, be so assumed in C D on the same side of *m o*, that *m q*, *m r*, *m s*, and *m n* may respectively be equal to *o t*, *o v*, *o x*, and *o p*; and let the right lines *q t*, *r v*, *s x*, and *n p* be drawn from the several points in one line to their corresponding points in the other line; then the right lines *q t*, *r v*, *s x*, and *n p* are all equal. For by the definition, as A B and C D are parallel, and *m q* is equal to *o t*, *q t* is equal to *m o*; and by the same reasoning, *r v*, *s x*, and *n p* are each equal to *m o*, therefore they are equal each to the other.

Fig. V.

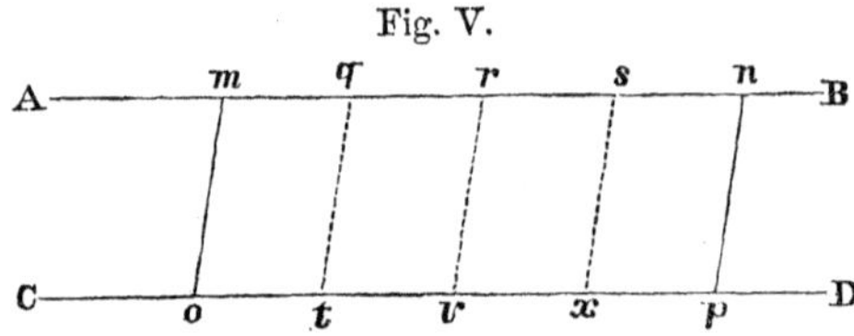

5. The right lines *m o*, *q t*, *r v*, *s x*, and *n p* are each parallel to the other. This is a consequence of the third corollary. For *m o* and *q t* are equal right lines, drawn between the extreme points of two equal parallel right lines, *m q* and *o t*; therefore *q t* is parallel to *m o*. Also *m o* and *r v* are two equal right lines, drawn between the extreme points of two equal parallel right

lines, *m r* and *o v*; therefore *r v* is parallel to *m o*. And *q t* and *r v* are two equal right lines, drawn between the extreme points of two equal parallel right lines, *q r* and *t v*; therefore *r v* and *q t* are parallel, and each is parallel to *m o*. The same reasoning may be applied to the other lines, *s x* and *n p*. This corollary is Euclid's 30th proposition of his First Book. As the converse of this,

6. Two right lines intersecting each other are not each parallel to the same right line.

In Fig. VI., let A B and C D be two parallel right lines; let E F be a right line intersecting C D in *m*, then E F cannot be parallel to A B. In C D and E F take two points on the same side of *m*, as *p q*, so that *m p* may be equal to *m q*, and through *p* and *q* draw the right line *p q o*, meeting A B in *o*. In A B take the point *n* on the same side of the line *o p* that *m* is on, so that the line *o n* may be equal to the lines *p m* and *q m*. Because A B and C D are parallel, *p o* is equal to *m n*; but *q o*, a part of *p o*, is less than *m n*; therefore E F is not parallel to A B.

Fig. VI.

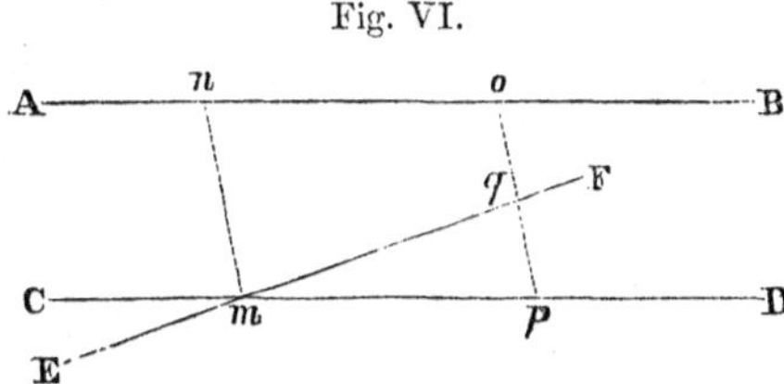

Professor Playfair's axiom, substituted for Euclid's, that two right lines cannot be drawn through the same point, parallel to the same right line, without coinciding together, is an obvious consequence of this proposition. For if they do not coincide, they must intersect each other, when they cannot both be parallel to the same right line.

But Professor Playfair's axiom will admit of a demonstration independent of the last corollary. In Fig. VII. let A B be a right line, and C *m* and *m* D two other right lines, meeting in *m*, and both parallel to A B, then C *m* D is a right line. From *m*, the point of meeting, draw a right line in any direction to A B, meeting it in *n*. In *m* D and *n* B take any two points, *p o*, so that $m p$ be equal to $n o$, and draw $p o$, which will be equal to $m n$; because m D is parallel to A B. In m C and n A take any two points, $r q$, so that $m r$ and $n q$ will be equal, and draw $r q$, which will be equal to $m n$, because m C and A B are parallel. Therefore the right lines $r q$, $m n$, and $p o$ are all equal, and C m D must be a right line, by the fourth corollary. (Prop. 7, Lib. I.)

Fig. VII.

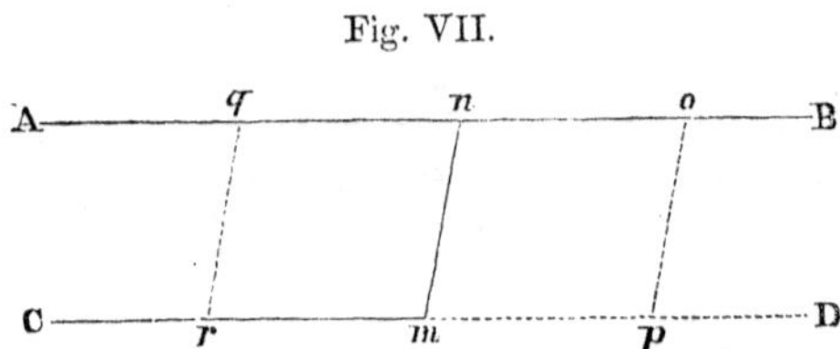

The definition of parallel right lines preferred by D'Alembert is, "that two right lines are parallel, when there are two points in the one, from which the perpendiculars drawn to the other, on the same side, are equal." This definition, as Professor Playfair admits, sufficiently determines the position of the two right lines; but he adds, that D'Alembert justly acknowledged that it was difficult to demonstrate that all the perpendiculars drawn from one of these lines to the other are equal. Perhaps the difficulty would vanish, by recurring to Dr. Reid's definition of a right line, and by altering the definition approved by D'Alembert, so that right lines should be parallel, when, from any two points in the one, equal perpendiculars could be drawn to the other.

The objection in this form does not lie against the definition I have given. Because, if this definition be admitted, it is shown in the fourth corollary that, if the right lines be parallel, the right lines drawn from any number of points in one line to their corresponding points in the other, as explained in the fourth corollary, must all be equal. The objection, if it have any weight, is against this definition. And it should be insisted, that it ought to have been proved, and not assumed as true, that, if two right lines are parallel, from *any* two points in one line there can be drawn to their corresponding points in the other line two equal right lines. This objection admits, that there may be two points in one of the right lines, from which may be drawn to their corresponding points in the other equal right lines. But as no reason can be assigned for limiting the definition to two particular points and their corresponding points, it may extend to any two points whatever. Now a similar objection may be made to Dr. Reid's definition of right lines. For it may be said, that although there may be two points in a right line, which, united with two points in another right line, must produce an entire union of the lines, yet Dr. Reid ought to have shown that this is true of *any* two points in a right line. But as all the points in one right line are united to their corresponding points in the other, it must be true of *any* two points. So, when all the points in a right line thus united are conceived to be separated from their corresponding points, and are so moved that all the points in one right line are equally distant from their corresponding points in the other, any two points in the one right line must be equally distant from their corresponding points in the other. And when all the points in one line are equally distant from their corresponding points in the other, the whole of that line is equally distant from, and parallel to, the other. This definition of two parallel lines, therefore, flows from Dr. Reid's definition of a right line.

On examining these definitions, there appears to be a great analogy between them. As the definition of a right line is obtained by comparing it with another right line; so the definition of the position of two right lines, which constitutes their parallelism, is obtained by comparing it with the position of two other parallel right lines.

Having obtained a definition of parallel finite right lines, there will be no occasion for any axiom in demonstrating the 27th, 28th, and 29th propositions in Euclid's First Book.

Euclid has demonstrated, in the 27th and 28th propositions, that, when two right lines are intersected by a right line, if the alternate angles are equal, the exterior angle and the interior opposite angle on the same side are equal, and that the sum of the two interior angles on the same side is equal to two right angles. I will now demonstrate that, when the two alternate angles are equal, the two right lines are parallel; and, *e converso*, when the two right lines are parallel, the alternate angles are equal.

Let A B and C D, Fig. VIII., be two right lines intersected by the right line E F in the points *m* and *n*, so that the alternate angles *m n o* and *n m p* are equal. From *m*, draw a line *m o* in any direction to C D, meeting it in the point *o*. On the opposite side of the intersecting line in A B, make *m p* equal to *n o*, and draw *n p*. There are two triangles, *m n o* and *m n p*, having by construction the two sides *m p*, *n o* equal, and the side *m n* common, and, by the hypothesis, the included angles *n m p* and *m n o*,

Fig. VIII.

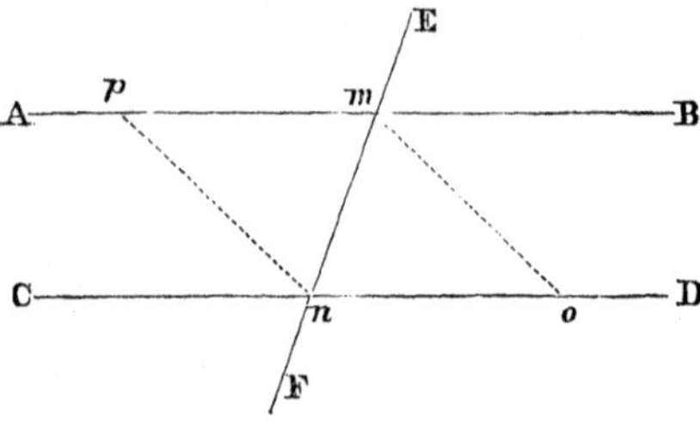

the alternate angles, equal. Therefore (Prop. 4, Lib. I.) the opposite sides *m o* and *n p* are equal, and, by the definition, the right lines A B and C D are parallel. If A B and C D are parallel, then the triangles *m n o* and *m n p* are equal. By the definition, the sides *m o* and *n p* are equal, because by construction the sides *m p* and *n o* are equal, and the side *m n* is common. Therefore (Prop. 8, Lib. I.) the angles *m n o*, *n m p*, the alternate angles, opposite to the equal sides, are equal.

No. V.

FORMULA.

FOR EXTRACTING THE ROOTS OF ADFECTED EQUATIONS.

LET there be proposed the general equation of this form,

$x^m + bx^{m-1} + cx^{m-2} + dx^{m-3} + ex^{m-4} + fx^{m-5} + gx^{m-6}$, &c. $= 0$, to find x.

Let r be assumed nearly equal to x, either a little greater or a little less, and make

$$\left.\begin{array}{l} 1 \times r^{m-0} \\ b \times r^{m-1} \\ c \times r^{m-2} \\ d \times r^{m-3} \\ e \times r^{m-4} \\ f \times r^{m-5} \\ \&c. \end{array}\right\} = a, \text{ and } \left.\begin{array}{l} 1 \times m\, r^{m-1} \\ b \times \overline{m-1}\, r^{m-2} \\ c \times \overline{m-2}\, r^{m-3} \\ d \times \overline{m-3}\, r^{m-4} \\ e \times \overline{m-4}\, r^{m-5} \\ \&c. \end{array}\right\} = s, \text{ and}$$

$$\left.\begin{array}{l} 1 \times m \times \frac{m-1}{2} r^{m-2} \\ b \times \overline{m-1} \times \frac{\overline{m-2}}{2} r^{m-3} \\ c \times \overline{m-2} \times \frac{\overline{m-3}}{2} r^{m-4} \\ d \times \overline{m-3} \times \frac{\overline{m-4}}{2} r^{m-5} \\ \&c. \end{array}\right\} = t.$$

Then the difference between r and x is $\pm \dfrac{\sqrt{\frac{1}{4}ss \pm at} \mp \frac{1}{2}s}{\pm t}$.

Call this difference e, that is to say $\pm e$, according as this difference is an affirmative or negative quantity. Then $r \pm e$, or $-r \mp e = x$. Now, to determine the signs of the several terms of the formula, attend to these two rules.

1. Whenever in the equation to be resolved a and t have like signs, then at in the formula is negative; but otherwise at is affirmative.

2. If in the equation to be resolved s is affirmative, then in the formula it is $+\frac{\sqrt{\frac{1}{4}ss \pm at}-\frac{1}{2}s}{t}$; but if s is negative, then it is $-\frac{\sqrt{\frac{1}{4}ss \pm at}+\frac{1}{2}s}{t}$.

3. The sign of t in the denominator is always the same as in the equation.

EXAMPLE 1.—Let $x^4 * -3x^2+75x-10000=0$, to find x.

Now, to compare this equation with the general equation, make $m=4$; then the general equation is transformed to

$$x^4+bx^3+cx^2+dx+e=0.$$

Hence, we have $b=0$, $c=-3$, $d=75$, and $e=-10000$. Assume $r=10$.

Then $\left.\begin{array}{r}10000\\-300\\750\\-10000\end{array}\right\}=450=a.$ And $\left.\begin{array}{r}4000\\-60\\75\end{array}\right\}=4015=s.$

And $\left.\begin{array}{r}600\\-3\end{array}\right\}=597=t.$

Now the formula is $+\frac{\sqrt{\frac{1}{4}ss-at}-\frac{1}{2}s}{t}$. And $\sqrt{\frac{1}{4}ss-at}=1939.4$, $-\frac{1}{2}s=-2007.5$. $1939.4-2007.5=-68.1$. And $\frac{-68.1}{597}=-0.114$. And $10-0.114=9.886=x$ nearly. If you want to find the value of x more accurately, then assume $r=9.886$.

EXAMPLE 2.—Let us take the same equation as in the last example, and let r be assumed $=9$.

Then $\left.\begin{array}{r}6561\\-243\\675\\-10000\end{array}\right\}=-3007=a.$ And $\left.\begin{array}{r}2916\\-54\\75\end{array}\right\}=2937=s.$

And $\left.\begin{array}{r}486\\-3\end{array}\right\}=483=t.$

Now the formula is $\frac{\sqrt{\frac{1}{4}ss+at}-\frac{1}{2}s}{t}=+0.8$, &c., and $x=9.8$, nearly. By assuming $r=9$, you will not have so many figures in the root true by the first operation as when you assume $r=10$; because 10 is much nearer the true root than 9.

EXAMPLE 3.—Let $x^3 - 17x^2 + 54x - 350 = 0$, to find x. Comparing this equation with the general one, by making $m = 3$, we have $b = -17$, $c = 54$, and $d = -350$.

Assume $r = 15$.

Then $\left.\begin{matrix} 3375 \\ -3825 \\ 810 \\ -350 \end{matrix}\right\} = 10 = a$; and $\left.\begin{matrix} 675 \\ -510 \\ 54 \end{matrix}\right\} = 219 = s$;

and $\left.\begin{matrix} 45 \\ -17 \end{matrix}\right\} = 28 = t$.

The formula is now the same as in the first example, viz.:

$$\frac{\sqrt{\frac{1}{4}ss - at} - \frac{1}{2}s}{t} = -0.04593,$$

and $$x = 15 - 0.04593 = 14.95407.$$

EXAMPLE 4.—Let $x^4 + 3x^3 - 28x^2 - 36x + 150 = 0$, to find x.

Here $m = 4$, $b = 3$, $c = -28$, $d = -36$, and $e = 150$. Assume $r = 2$.

Then $\left.\begin{matrix} 16 \\ 24 \\ -112 \\ -72 \\ 150 \end{matrix}\right\} = 6 = a$, and $\left.\begin{matrix} 32 \\ 36 \\ -112 \\ -36 \end{matrix}\right\} = -80 = s$,

and $\left.\begin{matrix} 24 \\ 18 \\ -28 \end{matrix}\right\} = 14 = t$.

Now, because s is negative, the formula is $-\frac{\sqrt{\frac{1}{4}ss - at} + \frac{1}{2}s}{t}$. And $\frac{1}{4}ss - at = 1516$; and $-\sqrt{1516} = -38.9357$; and $-38.9357 + (\frac{1}{2}s = 40)$ is $= +1.0643$; and $\frac{1.0643}{14 = t} = 0.076$. Then $x = 2.076$, nearly.

EXAMPLE 5.—Let $x^3 * + x - 9282 = 0$, to find x. And let $r = 20$. Here $b = 0$, $c = 1$, and $d = -9282$.

And $a = -1262$, $s = 1201$, and $t = 60$. Here the signs of a, s, and t, being the same as in the second example, the formula is the same; and $\frac{\sqrt{\frac{1}{4}ss + at} - \frac{1}{2}s}{t} = 1.005$. Then $x = 20 + 1 = 21$.

EXAMPLE 6. — Let $x^3 - x^2 + x - 46526760 = 0$.

Here $b = -1$, $c = +1$, and $d = -46526760$. Assume $r = 400$.

Then $a = 17313640$, $s = 479201$, and $t = 1199$.

And the formula is

$$\frac{\sqrt{\frac{1}{4} ss - at} - \frac{1}{2} s}{t} = 40, \quad \text{and} \quad x = 400 - 40 = 360.$$

Here 360 is accurately equal to x; but if I had pursued the formula further I should have -40.16, instead of -40; which would have made $x = 359.84$, too little.

EXAMPLE 7. — As the equation $x^4 * - 3x^2 + 75x - 10000 = 0$ has a negative root, let us resume that equation, and assume $r = -10$, and we have, as before, $b = 0$, $c = -3$, $d = 75$, and $e = -10000$.

$$\text{Then} \quad \left.\begin{array}{rl} r^m & = 10000 \\ b\,r^{m-1} & = 0 \\ c\,r^{m-2} & = -\ 300 \\ d\,r^{m-3} & = -\ 750 \\ e\,r^{m-4} & = -10000 \end{array}\right\} = -1050 = a.$$

$$\text{And} \quad \left.\begin{array}{rl} m\,r^{m-1} & = -4000 \\ b\,\overline{m-1}\,r^{m-2} & = 0 \\ c\,\overline{m-2}\,r^{m-3} & = -\ 60 \\ d\,\overline{m-3}\,r^{m-4} & = 75 \end{array}\right\} = -3865 = s.$$

$$\text{And} \quad \left.\begin{array}{rl} m \times \frac{m-1}{2}\,r^{m-2} & = 600 \\ b \times \overline{m-1} \times \frac{m-2}{2}\,r^{m-3} & = 0 \\ c \times \overline{m-2} \times \frac{m-3}{2}\,r^{m-4} & = -3 \end{array}\right\} = 597 = t.$$

Now, $-\frac{\sqrt{\frac{1}{4} ss + at} + \frac{1}{2} s}{t}$ is the formula for this equation. But $\frac{1}{4} ss + at = 4361406.25$ and $-\sqrt{4361406.25} = -2088.3$. And $-2088.3 + 1932.5 = -155.8$. And $\frac{-155.8}{597} = -0.26$.

Therefore $x = -10 - 0.2600 = -10.26$, r being in this example negative.

Roots of adfected equations may also be extracted by another formula, in which the extraction of the square root is avoided. After having found a, s, and t as before, and having assumed r nearly equal to the true root, then the difference between r and x is $\frac{a}{s \pm \frac{at}{s}}$, which is to be added to, or subtracted from r, as r is assumed less or greater than the true root.

EXAMPLE 8. — Let us take the equation in the first example, $x^4 * - 3x^2 + 75x - 10000 = 0$, where $r = 10$, $a = 450$, $s = 4015$, and $t = 597$. Then $\frac{a}{s - \frac{at}{s}} = 0.1139$, which, subtracted from 10, because r was assumed too great, leaves $9.8861 = x$.

This formula is called a rational formula, as the former one is called an irrational formula.

EXAMPLE 9. — To take another example, in which the irrational formula is used, let us take the last equation,

$$x^4 * - 3x^2 + 75x - 10000 = 0,$$

where x in example 7th was found nearly equal to -10.26. If r is made $= -10.26$, then $a = -4.236$, $s = -4183.622$, and $t = 628.6056$. The formula is $-\frac{\sqrt{\frac{1}{4}ss + at} + \frac{1}{2}s}{t}$. And $\frac{1}{4}ss + at = 4378336.032912$. $-\sqrt{4378336.032912} = -2092.399846$, to which add 2091.811, the sum is -0.588486; and this divided by $t = 628.6056$ is $= -0.009361767$, which added to -10.26 gives for x, -10.2609361767.

EXAMPLE 10. — Let $x^3 * - 19x + 32 = 0$, and assume r equal to -5. Then $a = 2$, $s = 56$, and $t = -15$.

$$\frac{1}{4}ss + at = 814.$$

$$\sqrt{\frac{1}{4}ss + at} = 28.5306.$$

$$-\frac{1}{2}s = -28.$$

$$\sqrt{\frac{1}{4}ss + at} - \frac{1}{2}s = + 0.5306.$$

$$t = -15.$$

$$\frac{\sqrt{\frac{1}{4}ss + at} : -\frac{1}{2}s}{t} = -0.03537.$$

And $$-5 - 0.03537 = -5.03537 = x.$$

These six figures are all true, as may be easily known by making $r = -5.03$, and repeating the operation.

Suppose I assumed $r = +2$. Then $a = 2$, $s = -7$, and $t = 6$. Then

$$-\frac{\sqrt{\frac{1}{4}ss - at} + \frac{1}{2}s}{t} = 0.5, \text{ and } x = 2.5.$$

Suppose, again, that $r = 2.5$. Then $a = +0.125$, $s = -0.25$, and $t = 7.5$.

$\frac{1}{4}ss = 0.015625$, $-at = -9375$, and $\frac{1}{4}ss - at = -0.921875$.

But $\sqrt{-0.921875}$ is an impossible quantity. Consequently this equation can have no affirmative root.

But for a further trial, suppose $r = +3$. Then $a = 2$, $s = 8$, and $t = 9$. $\frac{1}{4}ss - at = 16 - 18 = -2$, and $\sqrt{-2}$ is an impossible quantity. However, 2.5 very nearly answers to the definition of a root of the equation; for substituting 2.5 in the equation instead of x, we have 15.625 $*$ — 47.5 + 32 is nearly = 0. For, adding the terms together, their sum is 0.125 = 0.

To find the value of a, s, and t, it will be most convenient to make three columns of the powers of r, the head of the first column being r^m, making the second term r^{m-1}, the third term r^{m-2}, &c. And make the head of the second column r^{m-1}, and the second term r^{m-2}, &c. And make the head of the third column r^{m-2}, the second term r^{m-3}, &c. Thus supposing $r = 10$, and $m = 5$. Then the three columns will stand thus:

1st.	2d.	3d.
100000	10000	1000
10000	1000	100
1000	100	10
100	10	1
10	1	
1		

Then we shall have

$$\left.\begin{array}{r} 100000 \times 1 \\ 10000 \times b \\ 1000 \times c \\ 100 \times d \\ 10 \times e \\ 1 \times f \end{array}\right\} = a, \text{ and } \left.\begin{array}{r} 10000 \times m \\ 1000 \times b\,\overline{m-1} \\ 100 \times c\,\overline{m-2} \\ 10 \times d\,\overline{m-3} \\ 1 \times e\,\overline{m-4} \end{array}\right\} = s,$$

$$\text{and}\quad \left.\begin{array}{r} 1000 \times m \times \frac{m-1}{2} \\ 100 \times b \times \overline{m-1} \times \frac{m-2}{2} \\ 10 \times c \times \overline{m-2} \times \frac{m-3}{2} \\ 1 \times d \times \overline{m-3} \times \frac{m-4}{2} \end{array}\right\} = t.$$

Or it will be sufficient to make only the first column, and then all the terms of it multiplied respectively by 1, b, c, d e, &c., $= a$; all the terms but the first multiplied by

$$\left.\begin{array}{l} m \\ b\,\overline{m-1} \\ c\,\overline{m-2} \\ d\,\overline{m-3} \\ \quad\&c. \end{array}\right\} = s;$$

and all the terms but the two first multiplied by

$$\left.\begin{array}{l} m \times \frac{m-1}{2} \\ b \times \overline{m-1} \times \frac{m-2}{2} \\ c \times \overline{m-2} \times \frac{m-3}{2} \\ \quad\&c. \end{array}\right\} = t.$$

In a manner nearly like this may be investigated a general theorem for extracting the roots of pure powers; or rather this formula is equally applicable to the extraction of such roots.

Suppose I want the cube root of —7. The equation is now $x^3 * \cdot * - 7 = 0$. Make $r = 2$.

Then $\left.\begin{array}{r} 8 \\ -7 \end{array}\right\} = 1 = a, \quad 12 = s, \quad \text{and} \quad 6 = t.$

And $\dfrac{\sqrt{\frac{1}{4}ss - at} - \frac{1}{2}s}{t} = -0.089.$

And $x = 2 - 0.089 = 1.91$, &c.

But there is a general irrational formula more convenient than this, which I formerly investigated.

No. VI.

LETTER OF JUDGE WHITE.

[I received the following letter from the Hon. Daniel A. White, of Salem, after the text of this Memoir was electrotyped. But its contents are so interesting, to me at least, that I place here nearly the whole letter. It is the testimony of one who knew my father well, and was among his most valued friends during a great part of his life.]

Salem, September 15, 1858.

My dear Sir:

You must not impute to indifference my long delay in complying with your request to furnish you with my reminiscences of your late honored father. No man living entertains a sincerer veneration for his memory than I do, or would more gladly aid you in your contemplated Memoir of his life. I wish it was in my power to afford you valuable aid. My recollections of your father extend through many years, and have ever been cherished by me. I can, I am sure, recall most of my earlier interviews with him. There was always something in his manner and conversation to impress me with his kindness, in addition to the veneration I felt in common with others. You have doubtless read, in Mr. Morison's Life of Judge Smith, the passage relating to your father, in which Judge Smith expresses his "heart-felt acknowledgments of his kindness," adding: "He was ever ready to assist such as manifested a desire for instruction. This part of his character, I believe, has not had that justice done to it which, in an eminent degree, it deserved." This remark accords with my own experience and observation. I never left your father's presence with any other than a pleasing impression of his condescension and kindness.

To begin with my earliest reminiscence of your father, I must go back to my childhood, when I heard some men, who had come from court, talk about "Lawyer Parsons" in a way that made a strong impression upon me; but I remember only that he was so eloquent as to make *all the jury cry*, — and this became associated with him in my mind. Many years afterward, I was charged with a message and *a fee* to him from one of my elder brothers, when the Court of Common Pleas was in session at Newburyport. It so happened that I first saw your father in court earnestly contesting some point with Lawyer Bradbury, in a case which I afterwards understood was about a militia fine. I was quite disappointed in regard to his eloquence, — so different from what I had expected. I remember being much troubled to get access to him, following him repeatedly to his office while surrounded by others, and I was so embarrassed that I should hardly have persevered but for the fee I had for him. I waited a long time in his office for my turn to speak, not presuming to do so till I found him alone; but he received me so kindly, that I at once felt easy. After attending to my message, he talked about other matters, and made some pleasant allusions to the *ten-shilling* case, as he called it, in which he and Brother Bradbury had been engaged. The summary manner in which he appeared to dispose of matters, as now recollected, reminds me of what the late Mr. B. Gorham, who studied law with your father, once told me of his manner of dealing with verbose clients. He would listen patiently till he clearly understood the case, and then stop them short, saying: "I now understand your case perfectly; a single word more will only confuse what you have said." I remember another thing mentioned by Mr. Gorham, showing your father's exactness in business. It was his practice to put away the money collected for any person in a parcel by itself, properly labelled, to be delivered when called for just as it was received.

My only subsequent call at your father's office in Newburyport was some eight or ten years later, — I think in January, 1800, — which presented a striking contrast to the first. I found him absorbed over a book, surrounded by four or five studious pupils, like Plato with his disciples, or, rather, Pythagoras, for profound silence appeared to prevail among them. My purpose in calling was to see my college friend, Michael Hodge, who was a student in the office. We soon came out together; and in respect to your father, I had only the satisfaction of seeing him in a new position, and receiving an impression that was always interesting to me. Mr. Hodge afterwards told me that he was rebuked for not introducing me to him, when he learned that I was a Tutor at Cambridge. Among your father's pupils I observed Robert Treat

Paine, the poet, who had just delivered a eulogy on Washington in Newburyport, as I had done in Methuen, where I had been passing the college vacation, which makes me remember the time.

Not long after, your father must have removed to Boston. The next time that I recollect meeting him was in December, 1802, at the sale of Nathan Frazier's splendid library, which drew together a company of more eminent gentlemen than I ever saw on any similar occasion. Mr. Frazier was a graduate of Harvard College, 1784, and a distinguished merchant of Boston. His library, attractive as it was from the exterior elegance of the books, was still more remarkable for their classical and intrinsic value. The company was not very numerous, most of them being seated round a long table, at the head of which stood the auctioneer, who passed the books down the table. I had the good fortune to sit next to your father, opposite to whom was Fisher Ames; and they kept up a characteristic pleasantry in their remarks on books and authors, affording a delightful entertainment to all who sat near them. I have also an instance of your father's kindness to remember. He offered me a beautiful copy of Pliny's Letters, struck off to him, which I was very glad to take. In the afternoon or next morning, before the sale commenced, as he was examining the books, I asked him, on observing Cunningham's Law Dictionary near him, which was best, that or Jacob's. "None," he replied, "is best"; adding, presently, "Kinnicum's," (as he called it,) "I suppose, is as good as any." Having had the gift of Jacob's, I was looking for a commendation of that; but his pointed remark put me out of conceit with both.

I have no recollection of meeting your father again till about the time of my admission to the bar in Essex, which was in June, 1804. I well remember an interesting evening which I passed with some other young lawyers in his company at Mrs. Perkins's, in Ipswich, his usual lodging-place at court times. We were all impressed by his affability and kindness, and the richness of his conversation. His manner with younger members of the bar was peculiarly kind and condescending, as well as dignified, somewhat in the spirit of Juvenal's "Maxima debetur puero reverentia." His conversation turned chiefly upon classical learning, and the writings and character of Cicero. He expressed a high opinion of Middleton's Life of Cicero, — and upon some one's observing that he had never read it, he pleasantly said, "No man is fit to talk about Cicero who has not read Middleton's Life of him."

With the older lawyers your father was more familiar and jocose. Dexter and Otis, for instance, he would call Sam and Harry, and evidently to their gratification. All looked up to him at the bar, — even the court itself, — while he looked down upon nobody. He was not only pre-eminent, but singularly so, — like Johnson in his literary club. Since his death, I have often thought of what Burke, as stated by one of his biographers, said upon the death of Johnson: "Johnson is dead, and there is nothing left to remind you of him, or that has a tendency to remind you of him!"

[After speaking of two or three cases in which he had heard Mr. Dexter and my father, Judge White goes on : —]

Mr. Dexter's stately bearing and dignified style of speaking better accorded with my academic ideas of eloquence, than your father's more simple and natural manner. In this view they were most strikingly different. The former, in addressing the court or jury, seemed to be delivering a finished oration, while the latter, in doing the same thing, appeared only in earnest and animated conversation. Mr. Dexter never forgot his dignity as an orator; your father evidently thought nothing about it, even when producing the noblest effect of oratory. All that I subsequently learned of your father tended to raise my admiration of his powers and attainments, as well as of his character and public services. The very next time that I listened to him at the bar, which was in the same Crowninshield cause and opposed by the same eminent advocate, he made a deeper impression than I have ever received from any other lawyer, or from himself on any other occasion. . . . . .

It was at one of the terms at Salem, that I heard this great argument. It was made in reply to Mr. Dexter, on his motion to the court, — a motion which brought up the whole question of law in the Crowninshield case. Mr. Dexter had prepared himself for a powerful effort, and he succeeded in it to admiration. All who listened to him, I believe, felt that your father had a great effort to make in his reply; he certainly made one, and succeeded to still greater admiration. Instantly rising as Mr

Dexter closed, he followed him step by step with wonderful accuracy of memory and knowledge of the law, demolishing, as he proceeded, the whole fabric of the argument, which had been so ably constructed. Yet it was not the legal learning and the clear, cogent reasoning displayed by your father on this occasion, that most deeply affected his hearers, but the prodigious resources at his command on such an emergency, and his masterly use of them. . . . . .

Not long before your father's death I came from his house one evening in company with Judge Parker, whose conversation, in our walk, turned upon the wonderful attainments of the Chief Justice, one of which was the power of expressing himself on any subject in the fewest and best words.

Very soon after this April term of the court in Essex, your father was appointed Chief Justice, — to the satisfaction, I believe, of all parties and all persons in the Commonwealth, with the single exception of the senior Justice on the bench, — your father's senior too, — who, from the exalted stations he had held in the general government, as well as from his seniority, could not but feel entitled to the appointment. Yet such was the universally acknowledged pre-eminence among lawyers of the individual selected, that the disappointed Judge himself manifested no exception. I need not say how fully the public expectations from this memorable appointment were realized. The various volumes of Reports of Cases in the Supreme Judicial Court while your father presided over it, have established his fame for ever. You will remember the noble tribute paid to his memory by the late Judge Smith of Exeter. . . . . .

That the new Chief Justice, in the discharge of his office, with the mass of unfinished business which he found on the dockets of the court, and with his paramount sense of duty, should have met the approbation of all parties in all cases, was not possible in the nature of things. It is not at all remarkable that he should sometimes have been thought "arbitrary," and even "overbearing," especially by lawyers who were cut short in their meditated displays of eloquence, or embarrassed by suggestions which he might make to them. Time, in his view, was precious, and public duty more imperative than personal regard. The accumulated business of the court forbade any useless consumption of time. Of course, when an advocate appeared to forget all this in his ambitious or mistaken prolixities, the Chief Justice would interpose to set him right, and it mattered not how eminent he might be. If very eminent and anywise imperious towards the court, I can well imagine that he might receive a treatment which he would think "harsh." In arguments addressed to the court, if time were needlessly taken up on matters undisputed, or about which the court already agreed with the advocate, it might be expected that the Chief Justice would interpose, and perhaps direct his attention to points on which the court wished to hear him. How natural for any lawyer, — especially an eminent lawyer, — who thought more of his own fame than of the court's duty, to feel disturbed by such an unwelcome interruption, imposing silence where he had prepared himself to speak with effect, and directing attention to points on which he was not prepared to speak at all! How natural that this should be complained of as arbitrary, and taking the argument into the court's own hands, and that the Chief Justice, in thus presuming upon the faithful preparation of counsel, and thus earnestly faithful himself, should seem "despotic"!

From my own experience and observation, under the administration of Chief Justice Parsons, I have none but pleasing recollections of him. At the last term of the court which he held in Essex, — April, 1813, — I had the honor to argue a cause to the jury before him, which may afford some illustration of his manner of proceeding in jury trials. It was upon an appeal from the Court of Common Pleas, where I had obtained a verdict on a demand resisted chiefly upon the ground that it was barred by the Statute of Limitations. To prove acknowledgment within six years, my client brought the same witnesses (and there was quite a number of them) that had been examined in the court below. After going through with the first witness, I was proceeding to call another, when the court stopped me, saying, that the fact was already sufficiently proved if the witness were not impeached, and he should so instruct the jury. I recollect no other interruption in the course of the trial. This would seem conducive, not only to the saving of time, but to a clearer apprehension of the fact by the jury, than they might have had from a multitude of witnesses. Your father's repugnance, while on the bench, to superfluous words from others, was not more remarkable than it had been to the use of them himself when at the bar. Soon after the trial just mentioned, I had occasion to call on the Chief Justice in Boston, about some matter connected with it; and he then informed me that it was his practice, after every court, to revise the opinions he had given in any cases, and that in my case he had made a mistake in not directing the jury to allow interest on my demand as well as the principal. This avowal struck me as an instance of honest frankness, to be looked for only from a truly great mind. I remember hearing your father, when at the bar, say that it was a rule with him, after getting through with a cause, to dismiss it from his mind, — a rule seemingly opposite to the judicial practice stated to me, — yet both were founded in the same wisdom. The advocate, by withdrawing his thoughts entirely from a finished cause, is better prepared to enter upon a fresh one, as the judge, by a revision of former opinions, becomes better qualified for future cases. Your father, with all his superiority of intellect and learning, never felt above the ordinary means of knowledge, but assiduously improved them for public usefulness to the last days of his life. What a noble example for humbler minds, as well as for his peers!

About this time my acquaintance with your father had become somewhat more intimate. I had partaken of his hospitality, and been in a measure honored with his confidence. In the year 1812, while I was a member of the Senate, I had various interesting conversations with him on the subject of a bill which had been introduced in the Legislature by the dominant party, to repeal the Act, passed two years before, "to alter and amend the Constitution of the Board of Overseers of Harvard College." This important act originated with your father, who was, at the time, a member of the Corporation; and though so fatally assailed by the violence of party, — a violence that spares nothing in its way, — it will live in history as one of the durable monuments of his wisdom. From my intercourse and conversation with him at this period, I learned much respecting the Constitution of the Commonwealth, as well as that of Harvard College, illustrative of your father's public services in relation to both. . . . . .

Your father had ever been an earnest friend to the College. I remember hearing of his taking a lively interest in its welfare, long before he was a member of the Corporation, particularly in respect to raising the standard of education, and providing more permanent instructors than were the tutors of that day. The interest he felt in his Alma Mater did not spring from his personal attachment or love of learning, so much as from his profound appreciation of the means of enlightening and improving the people, the noblest of which was the University. He saw in the intelligence and virtue of the people the only solid foundation of their liberties and social well-being. . . . . .

I am here reminded of a very different exercise of your father's powers, at the close of a law term of the court, — I think, the last he held in Salem. It appeared to me the most astonishing exhibition of intellectual power that I had ever witnessed. In the morning of the last day of the term the Chief Justice delivered the opinion of the court in every case that had been argued, — some six or eight, — apparently without a word in writing before him. Taking up the parcel of papers pertaining to a case, he named and stated the case, and then gave at length the opinion of the court upon it, in the clearest manner and without the least hesitation, as much at his ease as in common conversation; and so he went through with the whole. The completeness and accuracy of his memory were more wonderful to me than his familiarity with the law, or his logical precision and perspicuity; all together inspired profound admiration, and afforded a rich intellectual treat, which has ever remained unique in my memory. Of all men I have ever known, I should apply to him the memorable lines of Shakespeare:

> " Turn him to any cause of policy,
> The Gordian knot of it he would unloose
> Familiar as his garter."

Of your father's early political and patriotic services I can of course know nothing except through others and from history. In these ways I have learned enough to be deeply impressed with their value. He never, I believe, desired any office or political station for his own benefit, and never held one in which he did not earnestly seek to promote the public welfare. His early patriotic services appear to me to have been of more importance to the country than all his juridical labors, great as these unquestionably were. To what one man are we more indebted for the excellence of our State Constitution as originally formed, or for the successful adoption in this Commonwealth of the Federal Constitution? The "Result" of the Delegates at Ipswich in the County of Essex, April 29th, 1778, to take into consideration the Constitution prepared by the Legislative Convention of the State, was from his pen. A printed copy of it in the Salem Athenæum bears the written attestation of the late John Pickering, LL. D., that it was drawn up by Theophilus Parsons. This famous "Essex Result" mainly conduced to the rejection by the people of the crude Constitution proposed by the State Convention, and thus led to the adoption of that which has proved so rich a blessing to Massachusetts, and which in its spirit and principles served as a model for the Federal Constitution. . . . . .

I have no doubt that your father was a master spirit in the Convention of 1779, for framing the State Constitution, as well as in that of 1789, for adopting the Federal Constitution. The "Essex Result" established his reputation as a civilian, and doubtless served to give him the conspicuous influence which he exerted on these occasions. Although the youngest of the delegates from Newburyport to the Convention of 1779, he was placed at the head of the three selected from the county of Essex as members of the general committee of thirty for preparing a Declaration of Rights and form of a Constitution, to be laid before the Convention. Of the proceedings and debates in this committee, little appears to be known; but I cannot doubt that the writer of the "Essex Result" exerted the same influence there which he did in the Convention itself. The Bill of Rights and Constitution of government, reported by the general committee, contained essentially the same principles that had been so ably stated in the "Result." When, after long debates upon the famous third article, the Convention decided that it should be taken into a new draft, your father was chosen one of the committee for the purpose. So also was he one of the committee for preparing the address to the people with which the Convention closed their labors, in June, 1780. . . . . .

We cannot but regret that he did not think enough of his fame to leave us the means of ascertaining more justly the extent of his meritorious public services. While absorbed in his devotion to the public good, he thought little of himself. But enough is known, or may be inferred from undoubted facts, to place him in the foremost rank of the great lawgivers of Massachusetts. The "Essex Result" contains, I believe, beyond any other political document of that day, a clear exposition of the principles upon which the organic laws of a free state should be founded, — the very principles essentially adopted in framing the Constitution of Massachusetts.

The same wise and patriotic exertions distinguished your father's whole course in relation to the adoption of the Federal Constitution. In the Convention of 1788 he was conspicuous among the eminent members, and as efficient as he was conspicuous. . . . . .

One curious instance of his success with individuals I learned from his own lips. A delegate who objected to the Constitution, that it had not the name of God in it from beginning to end, was told that the same objection might be brought against one of the canonical books of the Bible; which he could hardly believe, and promised, if it were so, he would give up his objection. He was desired to read the book of Esther, which he did, and voted for the Constitution. . . . . .

The noble spirit which actuated your father in his efforts for the adoption of the Federal Constitution, and for the establishment of that of Massachusetts, abode with him, as you know, through life. There was neither love of office nor thirst for popularity, to tempt him in the slightest degree to deviate from his steadfast political principles. The same sagacity and patriotism which had guided him in the institution of the State and Federal governments, continued to guide him in regard to the administration of them. With Governor Bowdoin in Massachusetts, and President Washington at the head of the nation, he supported all constitutional measures adopted with a single eye to the public good. If there were any true patriots on earth in those times, your father most assuredly was one of them; and it was, I believe, in consequence of his being such a patriot, that he was considered a chief among those denominated the "Essex Junto," a name by which, considering its origin, he had reason to feel honored. . . . . .

DANIEL A. WHITE.

No. VII.

LETTERS TO THEOPHILUS PARSONS, SENIOR,

FROM VARIOUS CORRESPONDENTS.

[These letters are selected from those which I have, and are arranged in the order of time.]

From Stephen Higginson.

Philadelphia, April, 1783.

Dear Sir:

I have given, in some of my letters to Lowell and Jackson, a partial view of the state of politics; those letters I suppose you have seen, as I desired them to be communicated to you and a few others. They will show you how far the opinions of our politicians in Massachusetts have been right, as to the views and conduct of the powers in alliance with us. There has been for a long time a party in Congress so thoroughly in the interest of France as to have preferred her interest to ours, whenever they came into competition. They carried through the memorable instructions to our ministers, which threw them entirely into the hands of Mons. Vergennes. Their views, however, by the inadvertence of Vergennes and the firmness of Jay and Adams, have been completely defeated. Their surprise and chagrin when the despatches were read, they could not conceal; and, finding that these instructions would no longer bind those ministers, and that if they remained in Europe commercial negotiations would next engage their attention, though not sufficiently commissioned to complete them, they have endeavored to remove such *dangerous persons*, by passing an unjust censure on their conduct during the negotiations for peace; — but in this also have they failed.

I expect, when the definitive treaty arrives, and we have a full view of the whole negotiations, that Congress will, in the strongest terms, approve of their conduct, though I am sure every possible means will be used to prevent it. Should this happen, their chagrin will be complete I think, for it will necessarily open the way for a commission to negotiate a commercial treaty with Britain.

France has been, and still is, exceedingly afraid of such a connection. She wishes, if possible, to prevent it, especially since she finds that Britain has wisely determined to give us every advantage in trade. But shall we neglect to avail ourselves of such an opening? It is our business to cultivate a friendly intercourse with every trading nation, and to secure to ourselves as great and extensive advantages, in the way of commerce, as possible. The extravagant ideas which Europeans have formed of the advantages that they will derive from a trade with us, we certainly ought by no means to root out, but rather to make the most we can of them all. To lose so lucky a moment, and to neglect the improving such impressions to our own benefit, would surely argue a great want of discernment, and show a great deficiency in our political character. The advices from Mr. Dana discover a knowledge of mankind and the interests of the powers in Europe, which does him honor; but the same leaven has leavened the whole lump. He is so restrained by the French Minister at Petersburg, that I am afraid he will derive no advantage to us from his mission. Being bound to consult him, he dares not make any direct and explicit overtures, though persuaded that everything in that court was ripe for negotiation. I wish he may follow the example of Jay and Adams, and show the world that no dishonorable bands can fetter Americans.

We are still hammering on a strange, though artful, plan of finance, in which are combined a heterogeneous mixture of imperceptible and visible, constitutional and unconstitutional taxes. It contains the impost, quotas, and cessions of Western lands, and no part of it is to be binding unless the whole is adopted by all the States. This connection and dependence of one part on another is designed to produce the adoption of the whole. The cessions are to serve as sweeteners to those who oppose the impost; the impost is intended to make the quotas more palatable to some States; and the receiving it in whole is made necessary to secure the adoption of the whole, by working on the fears of those States who wish to reject a part of it only. It may happen that a State, strongly impressed with the necessity of public taxes, may be thereby induced to receive it in whole, though opposed to some part of it, lest, through the failure of public funds, great evils may result; but I cannot imagine that such a plan will succeed, — the artifice is not complete. The States will see, I trust, that Virginia and New York mean only to give them what is of no value, and not their property to dispose of, in order to secure to themselves a valuable territory which they now have no good claim to, and oblige the continent hereafter to guarantee and defend it for them. Madison has clearly, I think, shown that such is their intention in this scheme; this he did in an unguarded moment.

Rhode Island has approved in the fullest and strongest terms of Mr. Howell's conduct. South Carolina and Massachusetts have repealed their impost acts, and yet these people will not only insist upon another trial, but make all provision for supplies depend on the success of the impost. Is not this hazarding the public peace and safety, and urging a measure against all hope of success? If the public creditors see no provision made to secure their debts, and not even a prospect of receiving the interest, they will grow very uneasy and clamorous. What then will they think of the present scheme, which will most certainly fail of success, and occasion the loss of two years' time in making the attempt? The truth is, they are so very desirous of carrying the impost, that they are willing to hazard much rather than give over the pursuit. Connecticut, New Hampshire, New Jersey, expect great relief from it, and will swallow it at all hazards. North Carolina and Virginia hope that it will be duly collected, if adopted, in many of the States, but have not the most distant expectation or intention of collecting it themselves. New York and Pennsylvania have other views in pushing for it. Pennsylvania has passed an act for paying the interest to their own subjects on Continental certificates, and to charge it to the requisition for the year. Massachusetts has the same right to take care of her subjects, and they will expect it; but will not this encourage the delinquents to make no proper provision for that part of the public debt, and has it not a direct tendency, if the principle be extended, to produce confusion and dissension? We may as well apply the whole, as a part, of the requisition; we may redeem the old money which our subjects have by them upon the same principle, but how then is the public treasury to be supplied? It may, perhaps, result in each State's sitting down with its present respective burden, and be an additional bar against a general settlement.

Congress have not yet tried the strength of the Confederation, nor have they had a good opportunity to do it. If quotas are assigned to the several States, equal to the interest of the public debt and the current expenses, and a majority of the States should make provision competent to the discharge of their quotas, will they not find means to coerce those that are delinquent? Will not two or three frigates in time of peace be sufficient for that purpose? Every State except Jersey depends much on its trade, and could not long bear the suppression of it; but should a majority of these prove delinquent, a vote for coercion could not obtain, though Congress were possessed of the means. There must be a thorough disposition in the States, or a large majority of them, to act honestly, to take their respective shares of the common burden, and to adhere strictly to the principles of the Confederation, or the Union will necessarily be dissolved.

I am sorry that Massachusetts has proposed a general impost through New England; it cannot succeed, and may excite jealousies. New Hampshire and Connecticut will imagine it to be against their interest. The same reasons that induce them to push for a general one, will lead them to reject your proposition. Let each State take its own course, and impose those duties at its own time and in its own way. Their necessities will oblige them to make use of such means, sooner or later; and when they have once adopted such taxes, and find all prospect of a general impost has vanished, then you may make such a proposition with advantage. In the mean time care must be taken that your own impost shall operate only on your consumption, to prevent your trade from being transferred to the other States.

I saw a letter from Mr. Dalton to Mr. Gorham that diverted me; he writes that our late impost operates very kindly, — that those evils which he apprehended do not result from it, and that our people have become so fond of that mode of taxing, and are so very desirous of extending it, as to be prepared for a general impost through the Continent. This was written at or about the time of their repealing their late law, and appeared to me extraordinary. But when I considered the person writing, and him to whom it was written, my surprise ceased. It must, I think, be a mistake. How agreeable it is to see a man open to conviction!

I shall send you by Mr. Osgood, in three weeks, your dividend of the bank interest. The power will not answer the purpose of letting me into the management of the bank stock. My respects to all friends in Newbury, &c.

I am, with due esteem, your most humble servant,

S. HIGGINSON.

P. S. I can't spend time to copy, — you must read as well as you can. Pray let me have a long letter, showing the state of politics with you.

FROM TIMOTHY PICKERING.

Philadelphia, June 3, 1786.

DEAR SIR:

I received your favor by Mr. Mycal. He has been trying to obtain subscriptions for Mr. Pike's book;* but it seems with small success. I shall endeavor to procure some among my acquaintances. It is a fact, that some gentlemen here cannot persuade themselves that any literary work of eminence can originate in New England. I believe you have heard repeated what Dr. Erving, Provost of the University of Pennsylvania, wrote to his friend in New York. It was in a letter of recommendation of a man who had taught the mathematics in the University, in a subordinate station, and who was going to direct the same branch of learning in the College at New York. The Doctor expressed himself to this effect, — that this person was well qualified to teach the mathematics, and that certainly he had no equal *eastward of the Hudson.*

The bank is alive, — and alive like to be. The *Constitutionalists*, having had a majority in the Assembly, have taken away its charter, which has done it an injury, by lessening the circulation of its notes; and the scarcity of money, and general embarrassments of commerce, have prevented such extensive discounts as were formerly made. Nevertheless, the discounts are readily given, where the drawers and indorsers of notes regularly supported their credit by punctual payment at the bank.

I have received two dividends on your stock, amounting, in the whole, to twenty-four dollars, which wait your orders.

I am, dear Sir, with respect and esteem,

Your very humble servant,

TIMOTHY PICKERING.

---

* See *ante*, page 280.

From Rufus King.

New York, 8 April, 1787.

Dear Sir:

I wish it was in my power to say that the affairs of the Union bore a more favorable appearance than when I saw you last; but the contrary is the fact. What the Convention may do at Philadelphia is very doubtful. There are many well-disposed men from the Southern States, who will attend the Convention; but the projects are so various, and all so short of the best, that my fears are by no means inferior to my hopes on this subject.

With the highest respect and most sincere esteem, I am, dear Sir,

Your obedient and very humble servant,

Rufus King.

From Nathaniel Gorham.

Philadelphia, June 18, 1787.

My dear Sir:

It was with singular pleasure I saw your name in the list of Representatives. I hope all the measures of your body will be dictated by the principles of honor and justice. Among the various subjects which will come before you, the requisition of Congress of the last year will undoubtedly be one. I hope you will excuse me for just suggesting to you, that I think it will be burdening the people to no essential purpose to comply with that requisition any further than applies to the cash part of it; — not that I have any doubt of the justice and duty of paying the domestic debt; but it is in vain for Massachusetts alone to expect to support the public credit; for six or seven States have absolutely refused to comply with the one of the year before the last, and, of those who have complied in appearance, very few will make any effectual payments; and I presume there will not be any that will comply with the one that is now to be considered by you, excepting the cash part of it, and with that numbers will comply. In short, the present Federal Government seems near its exit; and whether we shall in the Convention be able to agree upon mending it, or forming and recommending a new one, is not certain. All agree, however, that much greater powers are necessary to be given, under some form or other. But the large States think the representation ought to be more in proportion to the magnitude of the States, and consequently more like a national government, while the smaller ones are for adhering to the present mode. We have hitherto considered the subject with great calmness and temper; and there are numbers of very able men in this body who all appear thoroughly alarmed with the present prospect. I do not know that I am at liberty to write anything on this subject. I shall therefore only observe further, that all agree the legislative and executive ought to be separate, and that there should be a national judiciary.

I beg you not to mention having heard anything from me on the subject, except to your brother, to whom I should have written, but I am quite overcome with the heat of the weather. Please to make my compliments to him and to Mrs. Parsons, your brother William, &c. Please to remind your brother Ebenezer about my son John, and believe me to be

Yours, very respectfully,

N. Gorham.

From Fisher Ames.

Boston, January 8, 1788.

My dear Sir:

It seems to your friends that you, who are our Ajax, are deserting the common cause by your absence from the General Court. Surely, the last session did not inspire you with so much esteem for the present assembly as to induce you to think it safe to leave us alone. For two things we need you to extremity,— *the Lieutenant-Governor*, and a very extraordinary message from the Governor. He has come out, and tells us, that two very respectable States, Virginia and New York, propose a convention to consider amendments. But he is of opinion that a convention is improper. However, he declares openly for the amendments, and a great deal more of the same stuff. The judiciary system is in jeopardy.

Can you resist these reasons for coming here? Accept this letter as the effect of the combined wishes of the Federalists, who need your aid, and have long been in the habit of trusting to it. We conceive hopes of taking the ascendency in these transactions; but our hopes rest on *you*. If possible, be here on Tuesday.

I am, my dear Sir, with perfect esteem,

Your most obedient servant,

Fisher Ames.

P. S. You are desired to alarm the Cape Ann and Marblehead and other good folks, and bring them with you. We stand in extreme need of all our strength.

FROM GEORGE CABOT.

Beverly, February 28, 1788.

DEAR SIR:

I feel exceedingly disappointed in having you pass this way without stopping. I had so much relied on seeing you, that I could not believe you had left home, until yesterday I was informed that you had been very lately *seen* in Boston. I was about to inquire more particularly whether it was *you* or your *ghost;* but, recollecting that to determine this required more than common acuteness of sight and judgment, I waived a question which, by confounding my informant, might have placed him in a more humiliating point of view than a man is willing to be seen in. However, I am very glad to learn that you are still, *in any shape*, on this side the Styx; for I had begun very strongly to suspect that the old boatman had tumbled you into his scow, and paddled over the stream. As these apprehensions are of a nature that do not readily subside, I beg, before the old kidnapper takes advantage of you, that you would be doing whatever you have not already done toward rearing the *Conventional Edifice.* The impatience discovered by the few people I converse with, stimulated me to set about collecting such materials as were to be procured in this quarter. These I intended should pass your *sole* inspection, and only such of them as you should judge would be useful should be offered to the architects; but, having got into the depth of incertitude as to your *ubiety*, I forwarded all that I had collected in their rough state to Mr. Minot, with a request that such of them as are not suitable for any part of the building may be used for firewood, which I am sure is much wanted this cold weather. This last reflection is a very consolatory one to me, as I had felt much concern lest my lumber should not only fail of answering any good purpose, but might be prejudicial by encumbering the work-yard; whereas, if it arrives at the honor of warming the hands of my patriotic friends, and enables them more freely to execute the commands of their head, I shall be perfectly satisfied. With this sentiment operating in its full force on my mind, I proceed to make a little addition to what I had sent on before.

The objection to the fourth section of the first article is stated full as strongly in the paper I sent Mr. Minot as I remember to have heard or seen it made anywhere; and the argument that the people of one State have an interest in the elections of *every* State, may, if placed in the most striking light, be a satisfactory answer. But there is (in my mind) ground for an objection to that article, which, by going a little further back than the opponents have, may be taken and defended against anything I have ever thought of that could be brought against it. I mean that the objectors, instead of *conceding*, as they all do, by implication at least, that the powers of that article could not be fixed absolutely in the Constitution, and so reduce the question simply to what body it shall be lodged in, — if, instead of this, they should insist that it might and ought to have been fixed immovably in the Constitution, it will be difficult to answer them. For I cannot see why a rule might not have been made of a kind that should answer that description, and yet accommodate itself to the changes in population, &c. in all the different districts. The best answer to this which occurs to me is, "that, as the article now stands, the different States may each enjoy their own favorite mode," &c.; but this answer, if pursued, will very surely weaken the strongest argument we have ever used in favor of Congress having the right ultimately instead of the States. Pray think of the strongest objection possible to this article, and if you can answer it satisfactorily, it must be of infinite advantage.

I come now to the point for which I have thought it necessary to write to you at this time, and that is, to mention to you the two objections which, I am told, the people of the country find it the most difficult to get over. The first is that of the fourth section, mentioned above, and which I fear will never be entirely removed. The next is one which it seems to me may be pretty fully answered, — that of such a consolidation of the States as will dissolve their governments. Under the head of objections to the Senate, will it not be well to show how far the *injustice* of an equal representation in that body is balanced by the additional security it brings, that no measures will ever pass tending in the smallest degree to consolidation? — which must be always guarded against by small States: small States will outnumber great ones. This argument, well managed, in addition to the dependence of the Federal Government for the elections of all its branches, and the expressed and implied reference to the State governments in various parts of it, will show that the provisions for their existence are interwoven in the Constitution in such manner as not to be separated without rending it in pieces. I wish you would introduce among the preliminary observations of your address this idea, — that the General Government, being an institution that is to affect States as well as people, will be obliged to admit into one of its branches that equality which sovereigns independent of each other usually insist on. And there is *some fitness* in the principle which requires that, as the laws affect States as well as people, the consent of States as such, as well as individuals, should be first obtained, through their representatives or ambassadors; and as sovereign States cannot be expected to submit to an entire renunciation of claims which have been in a degree sanctified by the long usage of nations, it is a strong motive why the great States should concede something in this particular. *Verbum sapienti.*

I am your sincere friend,

GEO. CABOT.

FROM JOHN ADAMS.

Braintree, November 2, 1788.

DEAR SIR:

From the conversation that passed between you and me, when I had the pleasure to see you for a few moments at this place, I am apprehensive that you may think of me for a Senator, as I find that some other gentlemen have done and continue to do.

You know very well how ungracious and odious the non-acceptance of an appointment by election is; and therefore let me beg of you not to expose me to the necessity of incurring the censure of the public, and the obloquy of individuals, by so unpopular a measure.

I have long revolved in an anxious mind the duties of the man and the citizen; and, without entering into details at present, the result of all my reflections on the place of a Senator in the new government is an unchangeable determination to refuse it.

With much respect and sincere affection, I am, dear Sir,

Your most obedient and most humble servant,

JOHN ADAMS.

From John Adams.

New York, July 16, 1789.

Dear Sir:

I have received your favor of the 8th of this month, and am much obliged to you for the frank and manly representation it contains. I wish, however, you had written the same things to the President.

I doubt whether the President has prescribed to himself any rule so rigid as that you have heard of, to appoint all men who are in possession against whom there is no complaint. If superior merit and better qualifications are made to appear, I dare say they will have the preference. *Cæteris paribus*, the rule may be good, to make no change, but not otherwise. I have determined to lay your letter before the President this day, because it contains information that ought not to be concealed from him.

As you have begun, I hope you will continue to favor us with some of your sentiments on public affairs. We want all the speculations of the ingenious, as well as the prayers of the faithful; and, unless our countrymen are more highly favored than their prejudices, passions, follies, errors, and vices have deserved, all will not extricate them from the castigating rod.

Your testimony in favor of my John gives comfort to my inmost soul, and from my heart I wish you a double portion of the same consolation. Will you give him leave to visit us when it suits his and your convenience.

With great esteem, I am, dear Sir, yours,

John Adams.

From Fisher Ames.

New York, August 3, 1789.

Dear Sir:

I think it will not be unacceptable to you to peruse the bill reported in the Senate for the punishment of crimes; and therefore I enclose it. You will be gratified to hear that our excellent friend, General Lincoln, is nominated to the Collector's office in Boston. Every good man in Massachusetts will be gratified.

The Judiciary Bill has not been debated in the House. It is proposed to clear the table of some other business that is unfinished, in order to pay uninterrupted attention to that great subject. The District Judge should be a very respectable man. In order to make his office respectable, and to bring justice as much as possible to men's doors, would it not be proper to empower him to hold two of his four stated courts where he may think proper, and to extend his jurisdiction to all cases not capital, and to give the Circuit Court a concurrent original jurisdiction? Narrowing his jurisdiction will tend to degrade him. Haste will not allow me to enlarge; it is unnecessary to you, for I think your inquiring mind has long ago suggested every idea that I could present. It will be attempted to exclude the Federal courts from original jurisdiction, and to restrain them to the cognizance of appeals from the State courts. I think the attempt will fail.

I am, Sir, with sentiments of the truest esteem,

Your very humble servant,

FISHER AMES.

FROM THEODORE SEDGWICK.

Stockbridge, 16 January, 1792.

MY DEAR SIR:

When I left you in Boston I was of opinion that I should relinquish my seat in Congress; but, as the time of assembling approached, I found myself irresistibly impelled to avoid the reproach which would have attended a secession under my circumstances. I was the less reluctant, as since I saw you I had obtained considerable security. I have felt myself obliged to render to you an account of my conduct, from the debt I owe to your generosity.

By reason of a most distressing sickness in my family, I have been obliged to return home. When I shall again resume my seat, is uncertain. I shall not however consider myself authorized to absent myself longer than obliged by a regard to the first of all duties, that which I owe my family.

I fear, my friend, the national government has seen its best days. The distance at which it stands removed from the affections of the great bulk of the people; the opposition of so many great, proud, and jealous sovereignties; the undistinguished, perhaps indistinguishable, boundary between national and State jurisdictions; the disposition which both may possess to encroach; and above all, the rancorous jealousy that began with the infancy of the government, and grows with its growth, arising from an opposition, or supposed opposition, of interests, — produce in my mind serious doubts whether the machine will not soon have some of its wheels so disordered as to be incapable of regular progress. This disagreeable event, frequently contemplated by me as probable, and the consequences which are to result from it, have made an unpleasant impression on my mind. These are ideas I have never suggested but in confidence.

As I am induced to believe that epistolary addresses at least from me are disagreeable to you, from my never having been honored with an answer, I had it only in intention, when I assumed my pen, to have expressed to you the sense of gratitude I entertain for your generosity to me, and to have explained my motives for not relinquishing my seat in Congress.

By the way, Jenkins has commenced no new suit, and I have some reason to believe he is at a loss which course to pursue. After my return I again caused an offer to be made of a reference, which he neither refused nor complied with.

I really wish it was in your power, consistent with principle, to give countenance to Walker's petition for relief as Hyde's bondsman.

I am, dear Sir, with great regard and esteem,

Your affectionate friend and most obedient servant,

THEODORE SEDGWICK.

FROM GEORGE CABOT.

(Confidential.)

Beverly, October 3, 1792.

DEAR SIR:

It has been generally supposed that the increase of Representation in the National Government will be an increase of opposition, at least so far as relates to the Southern States. It must occasion some anxiety to the friends of the Union, that, although Connecticut and Rhode Island will send all good men, and Massachusetts likewise, yet a majority *may* be found in the new House whose principles will lead them to measures injurious, and perhaps ruinous, to the Federal Government. You need not be told that your friend Benson will decline the future service, — as will Mr. Lawrence, Mr. Wm. Smith, and Mr. Barnwell, — but perhaps you are not yet informed that in Pennsylvania and New York the opponents are well combined, and are incessantly active, while the friends discover a want of union and a want of energy.

I am informed in a manner that is satisfactory, that a very serious effort will be made to prevent the re-election of Mr. Adams; that in New York, where the Electors are to be appointed by the Legislature, every artifice will be practised to procure the appointment of such persons *only* as will agree to degrade Mr. Adams; that Governor Clinton is invited to stand a candidate for the Vice-Presidency, but if he refuses, the same party in Pennsylvania and New York are to fix on a new candidate of similar principles, and that he will be supported by the influence of all the Virginian and other malcontents. The ruin of Mr. Adams would be a triumph of the *Jacobins*, and would be an important step toward that general overthrow of our establishment, which is evidently intended. With these ideas upon his mind, a friend has written, by the last post, to know of me whether Massachusetts will send *all* men of right principles and good abilities, and especially whether she will send Mr. Parsons, whose assistance will be prodigiously important, and whose talents ought not to be withheld. I only answer, as you answered me, "that your family and subsistence could not be abandoned." It is, however, exceedingly to be lamented, that you cannot or will not come to our help.

You will recollect, among the late addresses of Governor Clinton, the name of our old friend Osgood; he is now, and has indeed long been, considered as deep in the principles of that party. Is it not probable that he may beat up for troops in this quarter to serve them the next campaign? My neighbor D. would probably aid his designs; some attention, therefore, will be necessary to secure the choice of good Electors as well as Representatives. I cannot with propriety take any part in these proceedings; but my concern for the public welfare leads me irresistibly to communicate to a few confidential friends such information as I have of the movements of the opposition, and as they may be supposed to desire. You have withdrawn yourself from the circle of politics, but you will often be in contact with those who are within it, and will impress those whom you touch; it cannot but happen, therefore, that you will do much good without great trouble to yourself.

I am, with very great respect,
Your friend and obedient servant,
GEORGE CABOT.

FROM GEORGE CABOT.

Philadelphia, January 8, 1794.

DEAR SIR:

A want of leisure has prevented me from making you the return I had promised for your obliging letter. You must, however, indulge me in the hope that my neglect will not discourage you from a repetition of the favor.

I sent you, by Mr. Amory, Genet's correspondence; but before it reaches you its contents will be less interesting, as you will have previously heard, what is incontestably true, that this fellow has been attempting to raise a large body of troops (to be embodied on the Indian Territory) for the purpose of attacking the Spaniards, as he pretends, but possibly to be employed in support of his faction and principles within the United States. These particulars may render his letters comparatively insipid. My respects to Mrs. Parsons.

Your assured friend,
GEORGE CABOT.

FROM GEORGE CABOT.

(Confidential.)

Brookline, August 12, 1794.

DEAR SIR:

At the close of the late session of Congress, I resolved to free myself from the torments of political anxiety, at least during the present recess. But to attain this desirable respite is no easy thing for any man who sincerely loves his country, who feels any sort of responsibility for its welfare, and who believes that anything remains to be done to secure or promote it.

The public good has always been the victim of private vices. We witness the ready sacrifice which personal ambition makes of equal rights; we see the facility with which a wicked faction has triumphed over public liberty by assuming popular names; we have seen the expression of the general will of a great society silenced, the legal representatives of the people butchered, and a band of relentless murderers ruling in their stead with rods of iron. Will not this or something like it be the wretched fate of our country, if the people can be excited to resist the laws of their own making, and to consider as tyrants those who are appointed to execute them? I know of no security individuals can have for the enjoyment of their equal rights, but the force of the laws, — these being so many declarations of the general will fairly and constitutionally made; but, if this general will is superseded by faction, and its supremacy can be no longer maintained, there is an end of that equality of rights which is the very essence of liberty.

All governments rest on opinion. Free governments, especially, depend on popular opinion for their existence, and on popular approbation for their force; if, therefore, just opinions and right sentiments do not prevail in the community, such systems must necessarily perish. Let me ask if such sentiments do prevail at this moment? On the contrary, are they not hostile or distrustful? and is not this hostility and distrust chiefly produced by the slanders and falsehoods which the *Anarchists* incessantly circulate? I think no honest, well-informed man will answer these questions in the negative.

It is the belief of many able statesmen, that no free government, however perfect its form and virtuous its administration, can withstand the continued assaults of unrefuted calumny. This is already verified in some degree in our country; and the fact is so alarming, that the real friends of liberty and order can no longer indulge themselves in that repose into which they are lulled by a confidence in the rectitude of their principles; for, while they slumber, the *Anarchists* are up and doing. These ideas, common to the minds of those with whom I generally converse, constrain me to solicit your exertion and co-operation with other good men, to counteract the mischievous attempts everywhere making to destroy the peace, order, and liberty of our country. Truth alone can be used by men of virtue in this contest; but truth will be a sufficient defence if extensively propagated. It is well known that you can give great aid in this honorable work, by timely explanations in conversation, by occasional paragraphs in the newspaper, by republishing from other papers such pieces as are calculated to inform and rectify the public mind, and, finally, by stimulating other patriots to join in these efforts. Conscious that I am actuated by those motives only which honest minds approve, no apology is necessary for this application to you on a subject so deeply interesting to all, and in relation to which I have always had the satisfaction to find your opinions and mine essentially agree.

With great esteem and respect,
I remain your friend and servant,
GEORGE CABOT.

FROM FRANCIS DANA.

Cambridge, January 20, 1796.

DEAR SIR:

Agreeably to my promise, I now enclose you my note of Holt's case, which you are at liberty to show, as you proposed, to our common friend, Judge Greenleaf. I shall, however, expect you to return it to me, at farthest, at our next Boston term.

I have this day read our Governor's Speech to the General Court, with much indignation against the foolishness, or, if you please, the wickedness of it. I confess I had supposed he had prudence sufficient to guard him against committing himself in so unequivocal a manner. But he has, in my opinion, proved either that he is the dupe of a faction, or a principal of it. Let him take his choice of the characters. I am not sure it will not be productive of good in the end. Their failure of carrying a concurrence with the Virginia Resolves in our Legislature augurs well. I think they will likewise fail in the other part of the *concerted* plan of censuring the Treaty. What think you of the answer of the New York Assembly to Governor Jay's Address? Does it not look as if plain common-sense would soon prevail, even in that mad, furious, democratic, Jacobinic quarter? I have read at last the vindication of R——; and he has left me more at a loss than before whether to mark him down as a fool or a knave. Indeed, Fauchet appears to me as much puzzled how to help R—— out of the mire, as he seems to be himself how to get out of it.

But I have one serious word to say to you; and I would not trouble you with it if I had your leisure, and, not to shock your modesty, your abilities. That is, I think it a duty you owe your country to come forth, as soon as the General Assembly have answered the Governor's Speech, with solid strictures upon it, and his character and connections, their views and designs, and the tendency of them. I repeat it, — I think this is your duty, being persuaded, that, if done in the manner you are capable of doing it, it will have a very happy effect upon the public mind.

But after desiring you to present our best regards to your lady, Judge Greenleaf, his lady and family, reserving a due portion to yourself, I must subscribe myself

Your friend and humble servant,
FRANCIS DANA.

FROM THEOPHILUS BRADBURY.

Philadelphia, 13 April, 1796.

DEAR SIR:

Ever since the resolutions respecting the President's Message refusing the papers were passed, which was about a week ago, we have been pressing to go into a committee of the whole upon the state of the Union, to take up the treaties, and to make the necessary appropriations to carry them into effect; but a majority of ten, last Monday, negatived the motion and brought forward other business; and we are told there will be a decided majority against making any provision respecting the British treaty. The business will come on when they please, and not before; I hope to-morrow, if not to-day. Should they form a majority, our situation will be disagreeable, and I think alarming. I wish every possible method may be taken as soon as may be to know the sense of the people; for to them must be the appeal. The Senate, we think, will consent to no appropriation act for the other treaties unconnected with the British, nor even to any for the military establishment. A disagreement between the Senate and House, if the latter is obstinate, may keep us in session till next March, and until the sense of the people is known. A bill for borrowing $ 5,000,000 of the Bank, payable in new-created stock at six per cent interest, irredeemable for fifteen or twenty years, for the purpose of paying anticipated loans due to the Bank, and paying the present year's instalment of our foreign debt, &c., is now before us. It is opposed by Gallatin *totis viribus*. If it fails, it will stop the wheels of government, for there is no

31

money in the treasury, and the Bank say they cannot advance any more by anticipation. The public papers will give you the debates on this question, which I have not time now to state. I fear this man will do much mischief. He is a man of considerable abilities and great art, and seems to take the lead of the Anti-Feds. Our situation is, I think, critical; but I do not yet despair of supporting our government against the secret machinations or open attacks of its pretended friends, but real enemies. I shall feel myself obliged by your sentiments respecting the parts the minority have hitherto taken, and upon the subject in general mentioned in this letter. With my regards to Mrs. Parsons and your family,

I am your friend and humble servant,

THEOPH. BRADBURY.

FROM JOHN JAY.

Albany, 1 July, 1800.

SIR:

On my return from New York, on Friday last, your obliging letter of the 5th of May, which arrived during my absence, was delivered to me. I am much gratified by the information it contains, and thank you for it.

Serious apprehensions were entertained that Anti-Federalism had gained considerable ground in Massachusetts; but I am happy to find, from the facts you state, that appearances do not warrant the conclusions which have been drawn from them.

The present aspect of our affairs is far from being agreeable. Although peculiarly blessed, and having abundant reason for content and gratitude, our nation is permitting their happiness to be put in jeopardy by the worst passions, inflamed and directed by the most reprehensible means. Whether the good sense of the people will avert the dangers which threaten them, is yet to be seen. If the sound and leading friends of their country could concur in opinions as to men and measures, their efforts would probably be successful. But, unfortunately, there is too little unanimity on many points, and the want of it exposes us to the hazard of many evils.

It really appears to me that the mission of our envoys to France has been treated with too much asperity. The President declared to the Congress, that he would never send another legation to Paris until he received assurances that it would be properly respected. As that declaration seemed to imply, that, when he should receive such assurances, he would again send envoys, it was not unnatural that he should conceive himself bound in honor to do so. His attachment to the dictates of honor and good faith, even supposing it to have been too scrupulous, was amiable and praiseworthy. Whether that declaration was advisable, and whether the nomination of the envoys was made exactly in season, are questions which, like others of the same kind, may receive different answers from different men. But having nominated the envoys and received the requisite assurances, I for my part consider the sending them as a matter of course; and do not concur in opinion with those gentlemen who think they should nevertheless have been detained.

I regret that my absence deprived me of the pleasure of seeing the Rev. Mr. Andrews; and the more so, as he would have answered my inquiries respecting many of my friends at Boston, and informed me of your health.

With the best wishes that you may now and long enjoy that valuable blessing,

I am, Sir, your most obedient servant,

John Jay.

From Timothy Pickering.

City of Washington, December 30, 1803.

Dear Sir:

I enclose Mr. Tracy's speech on the resolution for *altering* the Constitution, as to the mode of electing the President and Vice-President. I believe no one before has attempted fully to illustrate this part of the Constitution. Its distinguished excellence is not obvious; and hence the legislative propositions in time past, from several States, for changing it, — propositions founded evidently on a superficial view of the subject. If I were to say that even now its nature was not understood by half the members of the National Legislature, I believe I should do them no wrong. Many, however, who voted for the amendment, saw its evil tendency, and in their hearts reprobated it; "but they feared the people." In the Senate, if the vote could have been taken by *ballot*, unquestionably the resolution would have been rejected; perhaps even a simple majority would not have been obtained. Neither would it have been carried in the House of Representatives.

I can give you a curious dialogue between a Federalist and a Democrat. The proposed amendment of the Constitution was the subject.

"The amendment," said he, "now before Congress will bri ruin on the nation." "Well, you would not vote for it, then "Yes, by G—, I would." "On what principle?" "Why, t devil is in the people, and they will have it so. And the ne step may be, in imitation of France, to make Mr. Jefferson Pr ident for life." "And would you vote for that, too?" "Yes, I would, if the people wished it."

I am, dear Sir, with respectful esteem,

Your obedient servant,

TIMOTHY PICKERING.

P. S. I have taken the liberty to put two more copies of Mr. Tracy's speech under cover to you, to dispose of as may be thought best.

THE END.

www.ingramcontent.com/pod-product-compliance
Lightning Source LLC
LaVergne TN
LVHW020923110826
845150LV00004B/753

9781425553869